SORC

DOBL

EVENING COOKING

BRINGING YAM HARVEST HOME IN DOBU ISLAND
—THE COAST OF DUAN (NORTH NORMANBY
ISLAND) IN THE BACKGROUND

SORCERERS

OF

DOBU

THE SOCIAL ANTHROPOLOGY OF THE
DOBU ISLANDERS OF THE WESTERN PACIFIC

by

R. F. FORTUNE

Introduction by
BRONISLAW MALINOWSKI

A Dutton dep *Paperback*

NEW YORK
E. P. DUTTON & CO., INC.

To
MARGARET MEAD

PUBLISHERS' NOTE

The reader is advised that the author has made the following revisions in the original text (1932) of *Sorcerers of Dobu* for its republication in this Dutton Paperbacks edition: 1) an entirely new *Preface;* 2) additional text which appears on page 188; 3) additional text which appears on page 279; 4) a complete rewriting of Appendix I (DOBU AND BASIMA); and 5) a complete rewriting of Chapter VI, Section III (DOMINANT SEX ATTITUDES), which is printed as Appendix VIII starting on page 307.

CONTENTS

		PAGE
PREFACE		xi
INTRODUCTION BY PROFESSOR MALINOWSKI . . .		xv

CHAPTER

I. SOCIAL ORGANIZATION
Outline of Social Organization . . .	1
Marriage	21
Totemism	30
Terminology of Relationship . . .	36
Functioning of the System	43
Use of Personal Names	62
Custom and Magic	68
The Case of Yogalu	85
The Legend of Saido Sere and some general considerations	87

II. THE GARDEN
Sketch of the Concept of Ritual . . .	94
Social Organization in Gardening . . .	102
The Ritual of the Garden . . .	106

III. THE BLACK ART
Disease Infliction	133
Teacher and Pupil	147
Witchcraft and Sorcery . . .	150
Methods of Divination . . .	154
The Diviner at Work . . .	156
The Diviner refuses to work . . .	158
Considering the Diviner . . .	164
The Sorcerer in Action . . .	167
An Evaluation of Claims . . .	171
General Attitudes	175

IV. THE SPIRITS OF THE DEAD . . . . | 178

V. ECONOMICS
Marital Exchanges	189
Death and Mourning Exchanges . .	193
The Essentials of the Overseas Exchanges .	200
Overseas Expeditions . . .	210
The Ritual of the *Kula* . . .	214

CHAPTER | PAGE

VI. SEX
  Native Theory of Sex 235
  Native Theory of Procreation . . . 238
  Dominant Sex Attitudes 241

VII. DANCE AND SONG 250

VIII. LEGEND 262

IX. THE INDIVIDUAL IN THE SOCIAL PATTERN . 273

APPENDIX

I. DOBU AND BASIMA 280

II. VADA 284

III. ADMINISTRATION AND SORCERY . . . 288

IV. HEAT AND THE BLACK ART 295

V. FURTHER NOTES ON THE BLACK ART . . 298

VI. A BATCH OF DANCE SONGS 300

VII. CONCLUSION 306

VIII. REVISION OF CHAPTER VI, SECTION III . . 307

INDEX 315

LIST OF ILLUSTRATIONS

PLATE   PAGE

I. Evening Cooking.
Bringing Yam Harvest home in Dobu Island, the coast of Duan (north Normanby Island) in the background . . . . *Frontispiece*

II. Sister's children of the dead carrying funerary gifts of food to them from children of the dead. Funerary feast group, note widow with widow's neck-tie and long skirt . . . 18

III. Father and Children.
Woman digging for small shell-fish for soup 76

IV. Fish-net drying.
Fishing in shallows 120

V. In the early morning sun.
Dobuan House 168

VI. Old Sibor, Father of his village and resident in it.
Coming from the garden 208

VII. Girl with her young brother as chaperone.
Ceremonial Cooking 240

VIII. New house building.
Mourning over a corpse, the end of a house— the logs in front of it mark the close of its use 274

TEXT

FIG.

I. Village Plan 1

II. House Sites 2

III. Diagram of Marital Grouping 8

IV. Garden 110

V. Pottery making 203

Marks showing the signs of death . . . 281

Map 210

PREFACE

The Dobuan islanders discussed in this book are islanders of the Eastern Division of Papua, as are the Goodenough, the Fergusson, the Woodlark, the Rossel, the Sud-est, the Amphlett, and the Trobriand islanders. There is much that is unknown about their history, but they plant the yam and the taro, which have not grown in the wild type in north-east Africa or south-west Asia since the late Miocene. No evidence of blood antigens which are possible Mongoloid or possible Negro markers have been found in blood surveys in their wider area. They speak languages which D. MacDonald in his work *The Oceanic Languages* treats as proto-Semitic in family. There is some question about his classification, but there may, perhaps, be something in an opinion that they sailed from south-west to south-east Asia to the Pacific islands since the dates of the beginning of agriculture in south-west and in south-east Asia.

The domains of the Trobriand Island chiefs and of their home groups of about thirty men and their wives and children are not wide in area. They are areas of about a thousand acres, nine-tenths of which lie fallow in secondary growth in every season and which are cultivated by slash and burn agriculture. Such areas are not distinctive in acreage or in the method of agriculture used in them or in the number of persons who live on them from the areas of other social groups in the d'Entrecasteaux Islands and in the Trobriand Islands. In their social customs the Trobriand islanders differed from the Goodenough, the Fergusson, the Amphlett, the Rossel, and the Dobuan islanders, but not from the islanders of the Marshall Bennett group, in recognising distinctions of rank and in giving many of their daughters' hands in marriage to chiefs. They differed from the Samoans, the Fijians, the Tongans, the Hawaiians, Marquesans, and the Maori in the number of wives of chiefs. There is a suggestion in Malinowski that the Trobrianders were more nearly related to the Solomon islanders or the islanders of the New Hebrides than to other islanders of the Eastern Division of the Papua. It is unlikely, however, that such was the case. There are many

Dobuan and Trobriand islanders of the same clans. In neolithic society war refugees sometimes settled on land in the country of the next people, assuming their language in a generation or two. Their culture of stone tools was of polished stone and they also took care if they were Dobuan to curtsy or bend forward to their senior relatives by marriage as Trobriand or Fijian islanders did to chiefs and as Trobriand woman curtsied to their brothers. Malinowski assumed that the Trobriand Island way of working by the communal organization of agricultural labour to clear, burn, break, and plant the field of each member of the community in turn was not found in other islands in which slash and burn agriculture was practised. It was and is still, however, the general method which is used. War refugees who re-grouped on land in the country of the next people probably assumed the customs and manners of their country of adoption without difficulty.

In touching on the topic of neolithic society in the islands before 1883 when Papua was declared a British protectorate and united into a polity, Malinowski hazarded an opinion that the Trobriand islanders were united into a polity with one chief of limited powers, but of considerable influence, at its head. As a matter of fact, they were then disunited and Malinowski's estimates of the number of the wives, the extent of the area of influence, and the amount of the wealth of the eighteenth and nineteenth predecessors of the chief of the Tabalu lineage of the Malasi clan, who resided at Omorakana village in north Boyowa Island, are not supported by satisfactory evidence.

Clearly there is some impression about the history of the islanders. Malinowski was more impressed by the contrasts in the landscape and in the manners and languages of the islanders than he was by the continental derivation of their culture and its secondary association with the island landscapes. There was some adaptation of the islanders to the island environment and there was some mythology told about features in the landscape. For example, the volcanic ash soil of Dobu Island supported a density of population of 333 to the square mile in the year 1891, when the non-volcanic soil of north Boyowa Island supported less than half that density, 165 to the square mile. In south-west Normanby Island there is an extinct volcano called Mt. Bwebweso where there was once believed to be a home of the dead for those who were not killed in action, kept by Kekewage and by his consort, Woman Cleaner. On the other hand there is a mountain called Koyatabu, Holy Mountain, which rises from the coast of north-east Fergusson Island without a myth about it.

In this edition translations of some Dobuan works, published in the first edition, have been improved. Otherwise the book has not been revised extensively. Malinowski's introduction to the first edition is retained but is not all endorsed. Malinowski has written that his purpose was to state natural universal laws of behaviour, i.e., laws of culture independent of period, place, and circumstance, and to reduce the social sciences to terms of behaviourist psychology. Radcliffe-Brown, who supervised the work on which this book is based, wrote that the social sciences are natural sciences. It has been pointed out by many authors that the social sciences, which stem from Aristotle, ethics, and politics, do not, like medicine, rest upon a knowledge of the biological sciences, or upon any known natural laws. They are not any of the natural sciences. There is no doubt that, in so far as Malinowski and Radcliffe-Brown predicted the discovery of natural universal laws of behaviour and of society, they were, of course, wrong. It is therefore wrong to discuss mistaken detail in their work as if there were a correct solution within the terms of their presuppositions. Outside such terms there may be something to be said introductory to a discussion of late Oceanic neolithic society. A knowledge of the politics or of the ethics of a particular society is not necessary to an understanding of general works on such subjects, such as those written by Aristotle, John Locke, David Hume, John Dewey, and Bertrand Russell.

With reference then to the introduction to this book and to the folk-lore and mythology of the neolithic period, the lore about diseases thought then to be caused by imaginary small doubles of different species of the animal kingdom controlled by medicine men was confounded by Malinowski with a question as to whether the islander's enjoyed their sea voyages to one another's islands. The lore had nothing to do with the case, and it is probable that they enjoyed sea travel. Again, the myth that there was a pool of mobile yam tubers and the agricultural magic to win yam tubers from it were possibly not considered by him with sufficient detachment from unrelated matters. In the territory of Papua and New Guinea there was a widespread belief that there was a pool of mobile steel tools and other imported goods, and a cult aimed to win goods from it. It became known as the cargo cult and the administration aimed to discourage its adherents.

To read the political unity and the discouragement of some myths secured by the British colonial administration back into the period of neolithic society, or to read the mythology and magic of the neolithic period about pools of mobile yam tubers as a belief in magical theft of crops may be to misinterpret the period.

With reference to another myth as it is discussed in this book and in Malinowski's introduction, it may be noted that, when we went to south Boyowa Island with the Tewara islanders in 1928, we asked the Trobriand islanders to narrate their legend about human conception. The Trobriand islanders narrated the legend with pleasure, but the Tewara islanders did not like our request, and we surmised that it was an infringement of a taboo. Certainly Malinowski records that, when he met the Tewara islanders in south Boyowa Island and asked them to tell him the legend of Kasabwaibwaileta, an early sea voyager, they declined to do so, saying that they kept a taboo against doing so. The taboo probably applied to voyages outward bound, and in ports of call; for on the homeward-bound voyage someone narrated the legend of Kasabwaibwaileta spontaneously. In the first edition, p. 239, we did not connect these incidents, and we suggested that the topic of human conception was banned between the Dobuan and the Trobriand islanders as their view of its cause differed, and had been disputed between them in the past. It is also likely that all legends were taboo on voyages outward bound and in ports of call, and perhaps that breaches of this taboo were thought to be bad for business. At the early stage of their commerce in 1928, during which the Trobriand islanders assisted one of their trading visitors to break a taboo which they probably observed themselves, they were not yet prepared to disclose that they were willing to part with anything for any consideration whatsoever. When commenting in his introduction, Malinowski surmised incorrectly that we taunted the Trobriand Island narrators of a legend with unenlightenment for attributing human conception to reincarnation. He took it for granted that what the Tewara islanders had disliked about the incident was the point of his assumption about what happened, as well as the point of our assumption that the ban was due to a difference in viewpoint between the Trobriand islanders and the Dobuans. The text of p. 239 of the first edition is amended on this point in this edition, but Malinowski's text in his introduction on the same point is not amended, except by this note about it. The story of the origin of taboos is not given, as it is unknown. One of the south Trobriand islanders said that the myth that human conception was caused by reincarnation had diffused into the south Trobriands from northern Boyowa Island in the lifetime of his grandparents.

In this book there are some references to a neighbour in Basima who ran amok. His name was Wenoli. He was probably an epileptic. His skin was covered with ring-worm. He was worried that he was not married. Shortly after we went to live near him in north-east Fergusson Island, he and Kinosi said that a woman who was not his wife was his wife who had left him, as she was afraid of advanced civilization. Wenoli produced the young woman and her parents and purported to translate what we said, speaking Dobuan, in defence of advanced civilization into the Basima language. These people are not hard-hearted towards the afflicted, and their daughters marry those whom their parents and kindred select as their husbands. Wenoli won a wife in that way, and ran amok three times in his first month of marriage. Years later we heard that his wife had a lover who cut her throat and hanged himself. Kinosi's marriage to Kadibweara was arranged before we first landed in Tewara Island. One of the crew of the schooner that landed us possibly seduced Kadibweara in the absence of the Tewara men who were fishing for the palolo annelid on the reef that day. If so, we were never told the story. Kinosi worked for us, later married a woman of the Bwaioa Peninsular area of south-east Fergusson Island from which his father came, and subsequently served with an Australian magistrate charged with watching for the Japanese armed forces in 1942. Except that nearly all first marriages were arranged ones, there was nothing that was socially systematic in these human particulars which were not completely accounted for or surmised in the first edition. There were families, lineages and clans, and some modes of relationship behaviour, but owing to the variability in the human factor, some other human particulars which were tentatively attributed to the social system were not explained in those terms.

R. F. Fortune

Department of Archaeology and Anthropology
Cambridge University
November, 1962

ACKNOWLEDGMENTS

I OWE my best thanks, not only to all my teachers named in the preface, but also to my kind hosts and helpers in Papua. In a place so hospitable it is somewhat invidious to single out special names. Nevertheless, I am most deeply indebted to :—

His Excellency Sir Hubert Murray for his official encouragement.

The Rev. M. Gilmour and his associates in the Dobuan Mission for hospitality, and for their so kindly bringing up my stores and mails from Samarai with those of the Mission.

Mr. E. W. Harrison, of Sebulugoma, for his friendship, hospitality, and for his knowledge of the Dobuan native, as well as for his capacity for forgetting the native—a necessary form of detachment for continuous healthy living there.

The Rev. J. K. Arnold, of Bwaidogu, for his hospitality and for his good formal work, which he made accessible to me, on the Dobuan language.

For final criticism of this book I am deeply indebted to my wife, Dr. Margaret Mead.

INTRODUCTION

By Bronislaw Malinowski

DAY after day, looking over the glossy, dead waters of the lagoon, I used to gaze longingly southwards towards the islands of Dobu and of the Amphletts—imprisoned as I was in one or other of the coastal villages of the Trobriands between a mangrove swamp, the steep inhospitable coral ridge, and the muddy waters of the beach. My only pastime and exercise consisted in long rowing and punting excursions, when on calm days of the monsoon season I could see the clear southern horizon gradually unfolding with the distant outlines of Koyatabu and the other high peaks of the d'Entrecasteaux group.

There is no greater contrast anywhere round eastern New Guinea than that between the landscape and culture of the Trobriand Archipelago on the one hand, and of the d'Entrecasteaux group on the other. In the south, high mountains, volcanic cones, bronzed rocks framed in dense dark jungle, overlook bays and inlets of intensely blue clear water; where, near the shore, the coral bottom with its variety of colour and form, with its wonderful plant and fish life, presents an ever fascinating spectacle. In the north, a wide shallow lagoon, studded with flat coral islands, with reefs and sand-banks, spreads its opaque greenish waters, their natural monotony broken only here and there by the signs of native life: the fishing-canoes sailing along the passage; men and women wading for shell-fish; smoke curling up above the palm-groves of the coastal settlements.

This contrast between the two landscapes is intensified for the ethnographer by the entirely different character of the natives. In the prosaic open landscape of the Trobriands, on its fertile soil and around the rich waters of its lagoon, there lives a dense population, dwelling in large settlements, often not more than a stone's throw from each other; well organized into political districts, with chiefs, sub-chiefs, and headmen; united into a polity with one Paramount Chief as its head, whose power perhaps does not reach over the whole district, but whose prestige extends far beyond it. The Trobrianders represent the enlightened, light-hearted, easy-going civilized tribes of North-West Melanesia. Not so their neighbours, the inhabitants of the fascinating yet gloomy, beautiful yet treacherous, " mountain," the *koya*, as the Trobrianders call the southern district.

The Dobuans as well as their landscape are an object of superstitious awe and attraction. The *koya* has always been and still is an El Dorado, a land of promise and hope, to generation after generation of sailors and adventurers from the Northern islands. For the two districts are united by an interesting inter-tribal trade, the *kula*. In the past as now the Trobrianders sailed year after year to the southern district on *kula* expeditions. They regarded the Dobuans as their envied superiors in some ways, as despised barbarians in others—the Dobuans who ate man and dog, but could produce more deadly witchcraft than anyone else ; who were mean and jealous, but could fight and raid till they held in terror the whole *koya*. The Southerners were to the Trobrianders their partners and competitors, their foes and also their hosts—this latter in more than one sense, for at times a whole crew of Trobriand sailors were caught and eaten by their southern neighbours.

Living among the Trobrianders, sailing from one of their islands to another, around their archipelago and over their seas, I became susceptible to their legendary outlook on this landscape, on " the sea-arm of Pilolu ", that is, the waters which stretch from the mountains of the south to the coral atolls of the north. It was perhaps no wonder that all my romantic interest was attached to the southern *koya*, the land fraught with dread beauty and mythological associations.

When I heard therefore some time ago that this country was going to be explored anthropologically by a young but very competent worker, my interests became riveted on Dr. Fortune's field-work. It was a venture of no mean importance to the value of my own material. That land, veiled for me just as it was for my Trobriand friends, was at last to be explored. The home of cannibalism, head-hunting, of daring expeditions ; the country about which there circulated fabulous tales, partly native, partly European ; the country of the alleged high god, Yabwayna, the god of wars ; the country where Trobrianders believed sorcery had been born ; the country where, as I was assured by my native friends and also by some European residents, there existed mysterious forms of mother-right ; where as some said there were to be found crude sexual orgies ; while others affirmed that women lived in perfect chastity—this country was to be unveiled at last.

Dr. Fortune's book disperses some of the chimerical anticipations and discloses wonders far more interesting than those of the fairy tales which reached me. On one or two points Dr. Fortune has been able to correct some of the statements which I cautiously ventured to make about Dobu. On other points—I am glad to say, on most points—his information dovetails with that collected by myself, and supplies the most interesting and valuable framework to my picture of the Trobriand society, or rather develops this picture on the side on which it most needed development.

The results of Dr. Fortune's investigations laid down in the present volume have surpassed my most sanguine expectations. The book, though crammed with facts, is yet quick with the reality of native life. It is dramatic in its method of exposition, and instructive as one of the most penetrating sociological analyses in anthropological literature. I know, in fact, of no better account of field-work, nor one more informative. It is intensely interesting not only for myself and for those whose heart is in Melanesia, but it is also one of the most valuable introductions for the layman who wishes to become acquainted with what a really savage tribe really is.

Incidentally it is a triumph for anthropology, for here we have a study carried out over a relatively short time, six months, in which the specialist, unaided by any white resident, untrammelled by hearsay information received from Missionary and Government Official—information which so often confuses the field-worker more than it helps—was able to penetrate right into the heart of native society and of native culture, master their language, gain their confidence, and in many ways assimilate himself to the life. Comparing Dr. Fortune's book with my first account of field-work, which extended over the same length of time—I mean my monograph on the natives of Mailu—I cannot but feel envious, though this does not prevent me from expressing my satisfaction at the victory of my friend !

The only consolation which I can derive is that Dr. Fortune has adopted most of the methods to which I was driven in my own field-work, and which I so unreservedly recommended in my *Argonauts* (1922). It is with great satisfaction therefore that I noted in Dr. Fortune's book his complete reliance on himself, his ruthless avoidance of the Missionary's compound or of the Government station ; his determination to live right among the natives, and to get hold of the language as quickly as possible ; and, again, the even weighting of objective documentation, of linguistic analysis of texts and statements, and direct observation of native life. In this latter Dr. Fortune has the ethnographer's supreme gift : he can integrate the infinitely small imponderable facts of daily life into convincing sociological generalizations.

The present book may be regarded by the Functional Method as one of its triumphs in the field. Dr. Fortune's account presents the two qualities which good functional field-work claims as its own. On the one hand it is a precise sociological analysis of the tribal organization of the Dobuans. On the other hand, far from giving us merely the scaffolding of social structure, the book brings us right in touch with the living individual, it gives us the feeling of communal life, it allows us to re-live the fears, the passions, the deep traditional beliefs and superstitions of the natives.

The most spectacular chapter of the book, and the one which will attract not only the anthropologist but a wider public, is the account of sorcery, and Dr. Fortune has shown a shrewd appreciation of his book's appeal in choosing its telling title. The district of Dobu is, as it were, shrouded in a cloud of superstitious fear for all its neighbours. The very name of Sewatupa, the mythological centre of all sorcery, witchcraft, and evil things that befall man, strikes terror into the heart of Trobriander and Amphlett islander alike. Dr. Fortune was as impressed as I was by the difference in this respect between the Trobriand Islands and the *koya*, the mountainous southern archipelago. The Trobrianders, frightened enough by sorcery and witchcraft at home, become yet more panic-stricken as they sail south. The Dobuans, on the contrary, seem to breathe more freely in the healthy atmosphere of the Trobriands— healthy because deprived of really dangerous, pernicious, or aggressive magic.

The structure of belief in sorcery seems to be very different in either district. I have not yet published the full account of sorcery in the Trobriands, and am only now engaged in working it out. There seems to be the typical difference which runs through the two cultures : the Trobriand system is more elaborate, more methodical, containing more well-thought-out details and logical schemes. The main agent of the black art in the Trobriands is the male sorcerer, the *bwaga'u*. He proceeds by inflicting, at gradual intervals, increasingly strong doses of evil magic. While there are no professional diviners, a rival practitioner is invariably used to combat the sorcerer's attempts ; for every spell of black magic there is a counter-spell, and the contest of the two forces, evil and good, black and white, takes place almost openly.

The mechanism of magic in either district is also different. Evil magic is never carried on in the Trobriands by the Dobuan method of " personal leavings ", to use Dr. Fortune's term. The main method by which Northern sorcery is inflicted is by the smoke of medicated leaves burnt surreptitiously at a man's hearth. Hence in the whole area of Northern Massim nobody ever sleeps in houses raised above the ground. Even the Christian missionary teacher, who builds his imitation bungalow on piles, fills out the space beneath with a heap of coral stones. If it were left open the sorcerer might creep under the house at night and burn there the appropriate herbs impregnated with the evil spell, *silami*, so that the smoke would enter the interior of the dwelling and kill the occupants. The Trobrianders have also a culminating act of black magic, the boiling of a sharp bone in a magical cauldron, and the subsequent pointing of the bone at the victim.

In Dobu Dr. Fortune was told that the Trobrianders know no female witchcraft. This is a Dobuan legend. The Trobrianders themselves are very much afraid of the flying witches, whose methods are entirely akin to the Dobuan *werebana*. A comparative parallel of the whole attitude towards sorcery, witchcraft, and the terrors of night, as these affect the Trobriander and the Dobuan, would be very interesting. I never had a greater surprise in my field-work than on the first night which I spent in the island of Murua (Woodlark Island), inhabited by a tribe of the Northern Massim akin to the Trobrianders. Having come direct from Mailu, on the south coast, where the natives are very much like the Dobuans, paralysed with fear at night, never prepared to go out alone, I was dumbfounded to see that a small boy sent out at night quite happily went off alone on a distant errand. The same fearlessness I noticed again on my second expedition, when I went to the Trobriands. Men and women, boys and girls, walk alone at night from one village to another, venturing without fear into any distant place, however eerie it might appear even to an ethnographer. This would be quite impossible anywhere on the southern coast, and the Dobuans always struck me as being the most timorous of all the Melanesians I met. Even in the Trobriands my Dobuan servant boys would never be as bold as their native colleagues, although every Dobuan would tell me that there he felt absolutely secure.

Among the interesting details of the book I should like to point out the account about Vada sorcery, discussed by Dr. Fortune in his Appendix II. Remarkably enough, while working in the Amphletts, I found some extraordinary parallels to what I had discovered on the south coast, in the Sinaugolo district, as well as in Mailu, and I was also struck by the essential similarity between the beliefs of the Western Papuo-Melanesians from Port Moresby up to the Amphletts and by the profound difference between all these beliefs and those of the Trobrianders.

A small misconception of Dr. Fortune's I should like to correct : I did not obtain my account of the *Vada* in pidgin English, as I never worked through this misleading and unpleasant medium, all my work in Mailu and on the south coast being carried on in the native *lingua franca* of that region, in *Motu*, as I have said in my monograph on the Mailu (pp. 500 and 501).

But though sorcery is in a way the most sensational part of Dr. Fortune's book, it is not, in my opinion, the most valuable. His chapter on gardening is among the best accounts published of an economic pursuit and of the attached magical control. Those of us who know the Melanesians of New Guinea at first hand are well aware that their strongest passion is for their gardens. In his account Dr. Fortune has brought out this attitude clearly ; he has also shown the way in which magic interpenetrates practical activities, how it is an organizing and integrating force.

Here again in drawing a comparison between Dobu and the Trobriands, we shall find the difference as usual : Trobriand gardening is a bigger enterprise always organized on a communal scale ; with a garden magician as a public official, in a sense, representing the community. I am speaking in the future tense of the possible comparison, because though I have published here and there brief accounts of Trobriand gardening, the full material is only now being written up, and will appear, I hope, at not too distant a date. Some of the spells adduced by Dr. Fortune are almost identical with those which I obtained in the Trobriands.

The belief in magical thieving of crops is specifically Dobuan. I have found nothing like it in the Trobriands, where stealing of crops is attributed not to human beings but to wood spirits, *tokway*, who also play other pranks on human beings. This

difference is no doubt connected with the fact that the
Trobrianders are much richer in food, that they despise stealing
profoundly, and that even magical thieving would be scorned
by them—if I may reproduce from my own adopted Trobriand
mentality the attitude which they would show to the Dobuan
belief.

I was naturally most keenly interested in Dr. Fortune's
chapters on the *kula*, on Dobuan sexual and matrimonial
institutions, as well as their kinship system, since these aspects
of Trobriand ethnography I have already fully described. I
was specially gratified to see that his account of the southern
chain of the *kula* ring fits in extremely well with the data which
I obtained on the northern portion. Minor details of Dobuan
custom and belief which I gave from the Trobriand point of
view look different when correctly interpreted from the
Dobuan perspective. This is only natural, since accurate
knowledge of their neighbours is never characteristic of a
Melanesian native community, probably of no native community anywhere.

Incidentally, Dr. Fortune has throughout the book done a
most valuable piece of work in relating Dobuan custom and
institutions to those of my Trobrianders. I only wish he had
done the same in relation to the South Massim, so admirably
described by Professor Seligman in his standard work, *The
Melanesians of British New Guinea*. This book was a constant
inspiration to me in the field, and I was able to check its accuracy,
width, and penetration in my own field of work in the
Trobriands. Though this field of the North Massim is avowedly
one which Professor Seligman has merely surveyed, I have
found his survey perfectly correct. Professor Seligman's
material on the South Massim would have been found by
Dr. Fortune of the greatest use in every respect, but above all
in matters of folk-lore, sexual customs, social organization,
and totemism. The point on which he gives credit to
Professor Seligman in the text is in the discovery of *kula*.
Kula, however, is about the only institution in this region
which did escape Seligman's notice. He would be in fact
the last to claim the discovery. Mine was, I think, the first
description of this system of trading, and the word *kula* was
used in type for the first time by myself. I cannot, however,
claim the discovery of this institution, for I was told about it
in private conversation by the Rev. M. Gilmour, the
distinguished head of the Methodist Mission in New Guinea,

and by Dr. Bellamy, the Resident Magistrate of the District, then on his last few days' residence in the Trobriands.

In the very interesting account of sexual custom and ideas Dr. Fortune corrects an important point on which I was mistaken. The Dobuans had been represented to me by the Trobrianders as well as through their own accounts as very much chaster than they really are. As mentioned, I had a few Dobuan boys in my employment, and used to chat with them about the customs of the Trobrianders among whom we lived, and I always tried to lead them on to make anthropological comparisons. This fairy tale is, however, easily explained by the extraordinary jealousy of the Dobuans, which is one of the *Leitmotivs* of Dr. Fortune's account. The Dobuan boys would not even want to speak about the laxity of their women-folk ; while the Trobrianders, never obtaining any favours from Dobuan women, accused them of that unpleasant characteristic, chastity, in a wholesale manner.

Dr. Fortune draws a very interesting parallel between the Dobuan recognition of physiological paternity and the Trobriand disregard of it. I never found while in the Trobriands the interesting fact which Dr. Fortune tells us, that the subject is never brought up between Trobrianders and Dobuans, as it has been the cause of anger and quarrel too often in the past His experiment of taunting the Trobrianders once more ; the fury of the Dobuans against him for doing it, is another signal proof of the tenacity of the Trobrianders' ignorance of paternity. Whether this ignorance is essentially a lack of knowledge, or ignorance in the more active sense of culturally determined non-recognition, must remain for the present unanswered. But Dr. Fortune's endorsement of my discovery is of value to me because, though personally I have not the slightest doubt that my conclusions concerning this ignorance are correct, I find that this is one of the points in my field-work which seems to evoke a certain astonishment, if not incredulity, among many readers.

With all this, the most valuable part of Dr. Fortune's book will remain unquestionably his opening part on sociology. The precise, convincing, and well-documented manner in which he has described the functioning of the *susu*, the matrilineal group, consisting of brother and sister and her children on the one hand, and, on the other, the family, consisting of husband and wife and their children, provides us with an entirely new picture of a hitherto unknown sociological constellation. Some data concerning kinship terminology, above all, the custom of changing nomenclature on the death of a man, will supply the clue to a great many of the most discussed kinship puzzles.

The far-fetched theory propounded by Rivers, and accepted by many of Morgan's latter-day followers, that this terminology is brought about by anomalous marriages, has always seemed to me untenable. Dr. Fortune's discovery confirms my functional interpretation of cross-cousin marriage, and the terminology by which the paternal nephew is called by the same name as the father.[1] The Dobuan type of terminology for cross-cousins also obtains in the Trobriands. There, however, a man or a woman calls his or her father's sister's son by the term " father " from birth. This terminology expresses in the Trobriands merely the fact that the father's nephew is a substitute father or secondary father, or that he is the man who will, and to a certain extent already does, stand in *loco parentis*. The fact that in Dobu the verbal identification of the patrilineal cross-cousin with the father takes place only after the latter's death I regard as a crucial confirmation of my view. The same phenomenon of the change of terminology at death has recently been discovered in one or two places in Africa, notably among the Akan speaking people of the Gold Coast.

The enumeration of Dr. Fortune's discoveries in Dobu, each of them of the greatest importance for anthropological knowledge, could be indefinitely prolonged. The dual residence of a family, patrilocal and matrilocal, a year or so in the wife's village, and then another year in the husband's, is a rare and most interesting feature of social organization. It gives to the Dobuan family a unique constitution, and will throw new light on all our theories concerning kinship and descent. The distinction between villagers or citizens and " those-resulting-from-marriage ", or, as we call them in the Trobriands, " strangers ", *tomakawa*, is less startling, but also very important for the comparative sociology of primitive cultures. The prevalence of incestuous or semi-incestuous unions and even marriages found in Dobu parallels my observations in the Trobriands. There is also the same type of courtship by trial and error and gradually tightening unions. Dr. Fortune's analysis of love and romantic attitudes as well as the extent and importance of love magic, of which he incidentally gives some excellent spells, again show that Dobu does not differ from the Northern Massim in this respect.

[1] See chapter iv, section 4, of *The Sexual Life of Savages*.

The wealth of mythological data and the placing of myth within the context of culture which allows us to appreciate the function of myth, is one of the most valuable contributions of this book. Incidentally the data provided by Dr. Fortune bear out completely my preliminary evaluation of the function of myth among the Northern Massim, which I outlined in *Myth in Primitive Psychology* (1926).

A special merit of Dr. Fortune's monograph is the illustration by concrete examples, the " case method " in anthropological description, as it might be called. This method has been already handled brilliantly in her own writings by Dr. Margaret Mead, and I myself have always felt that in the presentation of my own data concrete illustrations are indispensable, that they and they only give life to general ethnographic descriptions.

All in all, *The Sorcerers of Dobu* is a pioneering piece of functional work, new in its way of approach, in its style of presentation, and in the construction of its sociological frame-work. Some of its outstanding qualities are beyond cavil and criticism. No anthropologist, however hostile to the functional method, can but acknowledge their value and importance. The tendency towards organic presentation, the broad full sweep over the totality of native culture, the placing of details within their proper context—all these qualities no one will contest.

But there are other points which will provoke criticisms, and in my humble capacity of godfather and standard-bearer of the functional method, I might be allowed to anticipate some of these. Many a fact-worshipping, theory-dreading, curio-hunting anthropologist will affirm that Dr. Fortune is con-stantly mixing abstract descriptions of a theoretical nature with the statement of solid fact ; that in his digressions on the nature of magic, on Melanesian communism, on the *susu* and the family, he is constantly making a case for this or that point of view. Dr. Fortune has almost run the risk of being convicted of following the bad example of *Crime and Custom, Sex and Repression*, and *Myth in Primitive Psychology* ! In defending him I am therefore putting in a plea *pro domo mea*, and I am doing it with a full moral conviction of being in the right in company with Dr. Fortune.

The first point concerns the definition of *fact*. As long as the anthropologist was supposed to do no more than report what was striking or sensational in a native community, he could move about just collecting observations of queer occurrences. Now that the functional method commands him to give a full picture of primitive culture, he has to analyse the forces of social cohesion, the sanctions of law, custom, and morality, the principles of primitive economic systems, and the structure of native ideas and beliefs. Nowadays, the anthropologist can no longer spread his nets far and wide to allow the queer fish of strange custom to float in, at his and their leisure. He has to investigate the relations between custom, institution, and type of behaviour. For we are now more and more interested in the connections between the component parts of an institution in the relations of institution to institution and of aspect to aspect. We are interested, that is, rather in meaning and function than in form and detail. Only an inductive generalization or a functional relation is to the modern anthropologist a real scientific fact.

The functional anthropologist has constantly to make inductive generalizations from what he sees, he has to construct theories, and draw up the charters of native institutions. In short, he has constantly to theorize in the field, theorize on what he sees, hears, and experiences.

Let him try to note down a native utterance. He will have to decide whether this is a fixed text, or whether it is a magical spell, or a prayer, or a song. He will have further to place and define the nature of the spell or song or prayer by its relation to ritual, to native beliefs, and to the whole organization of the magical or religious cult. Or let him again try to draw up the main outlines of a ceremony : he will have to eliminate the irrelevant details, and only retain what is essential. An act as trivial as the spitting of an old man may be completely irrelevant, due to the fact that the old man suffers from a cold or has swallowed a fly ; or else it may be an essential expression of belief and a most potent act of magic. Even in such obvious matters therefore as the collection of texts or the observation of ritual acts, the constructive mind must be ever at work. When it comes to the definition of a belief, to the establishment of a legal or customary rule, matters become even more difficult.

Thus Dr. Fortune is perfectly justified—he is doing nothing more nor less than his ethnographic duty—in analysing the function of Dobuan myth, in discussing the incidence of the sympathetic principle, as well as of the belief in supernatural agencies, in Dobuan magic. His description of the family and *susu* would be worthless had he not brought these two groups into relation with each other, because it is in their relation that the sociological reality of Dobuan kinship actually resides.

Dr. Fortune's book is therefore above any criticism from this point of view, for anthropological work of the functional school will have resolutely to go into this type of combined constructive and descriptive analysis of observations.

But though it is inevitable, this handling of theory and fact has to be done extremely carefully. For, however cautious an observer might be, he is always liable to confuse conjecture with induction. Thus, in building up his theoretical constructions, in drawing his inferences from detail to general rule, the anthropologist has to carry out all his operations in the open—within sight and control of his readers.

Dr. Fortune has, in my opinion, fully satisfied this requirement of method. The best proof of this is that the reader is enabled to disagree with the author's conclusions, and to disagree on the basis of the detailed information presented by the author himself. Thus, to digress on one of my own lapses, I arranged my evidence about Trobriand gifts in a distinctly theoretical and constructive manner (*Argonauts*, chapter vi, section vi, p. 179). On the basis of my own facts, however, my friend, M. Mauss, was able to show that my construction was theoretically inadequate.[1] I am glad to say that later on I was able to accept his criticism unreservedly (*Crime and Custom*, ch. viii).

Now in the present volume the concrete data are so clearly presented, that point after point I was able to scrutinize, and now agree and then again disagree with Dr. Fortune's conclusions. Thus, for instance, in his analysis of the relative social importance of the family and the *susu*, his synthesis embodied in the diagram on p. 19 is meant to show that the family is less important than the matrilineal group. But analysing his concrete data on pages 11 to 19, we can see that he has omitted two or three elements which obviously strengthen the family ; while he has registered as " gains " of the *susu* influences which obviously do not strengthen in any way the matrilineal group as against that of husband and wife.

Among the " gains " of the family I myself would emphatically list common work in the gardens ; permanent common residence, whether in the wife's or in the husband's village ; the strong emotional attitude of the father, documented by Dr. Fortune on pages 13 and 15 ; the solidarity between a man and his father's nephew ; the jealousies, which as we are

---

[1] " Essai sur le Don," in *L'Année Sociologique*, New Series, vol. i, pp. 171 sqq.

informed on page 9, rend the very core of *susu*, the group of blood brothers ; and finally the cases of incest between matrilineally related people. Thus, to the three points listed by Dr. Fortune, we must add at least six more, making the balance between the two groupings pretty even. We might also perhaps add the mortuary custom by which a widow or widower has to mourn a full year for the dead spouse, a custom which expresses the strength and importance of the matrimonial bond. Incidentally, I should like very definitely to contest the quite unnecessary introduction of a new term, viz. " marital groupings ", for the time-honoured and generally accepted term " family "— a term which perfectly well describes the members of the Dobuan household. Terminological neophily—to coin a new term for this love of new terms !—is a habit to which I have always been hostile.

The extremely interesting duality of paternal love and avuncular duty which makes a man tend to transmit as much as he can, but above all his magic, to his son, has been recently signalled in several more or less matrilineal communities. I found it in the Trobriands ; Mrs. Aitken (Miss Barbara Freire-Marreco) has reported it from the Tewa, a section of the Pueblo Indians of Arizona ; and Dr. Audrey Richards, who has recently returned from fifteen months' anthropological work among the Bemba tribe in Northern Rhodesia, tells me that the same strong tendency of surreptitious patrilineal transmission of property and influence obtains there also.

Without going into details, I should say that I could fully substantiate from his own material my disagreement with Dr. Fortune's conclusions about the importance of supernatural agencies in magic ; with his parallel between the Dobuan spells and religious prayers ; and with his interpretation of the present-day reality of mythological beings. Dr. Fortune presents his facts with such lucidity, precision, and detachment from his generalizations that a complete theoretical reinterpretation of his material is perfectly possible.

On the other hand, I am fully convinced by Dr. Fortune's theoretical interpretation of the function of *kula*. I am extremely glad that he has once more exploded the myth of Melanesian communism, put forward by no less an authority than Rivers, and that he once more shows the extremely small importance of that absurdly over-rated institution, the totemic clan.

Some of the more prosaic colleagues of Dr. Fortune and myself may grumble at the slight literary over-weighting of his material. Dr. Fortune sometimes might be accused of sacrificing clarity and sober presentation of fact to dramatic and narrative effects. The balance between dramatic presentation on the one hand, and scientific detachment, precision, and accuracy on the other, is a very fine one, and not everyone may be satisfied with the way in which Dr. Fortune has tipped it. However this may be, it must always be remembered that Dobuan culture is not as clear cut as that of the Trobriand Islands, and that there is a touch of the mysterious, one might almost feel tempted to say, of the really savage, in these people, their ideas, and their behaviour.

Dr. Fortune has done his first term of field-work in one of the most beautiful landscapes of New Guinea, he has done it among a people more difficult to explore, more elusive and attractive than any Melanesians I ever came across. He has done it in a region the knowledge of which supplies to us the key of many riddles of Pacific culture. He has given us a book of permanent value.

B. MALINOWSKI.

DEPARTMENT OF ANTHROPOLOGY,
   UNIVERSITY OF LONDON,
      LONDON SCHOOL OF ECONOMICS, W.C. 2.

12th September, 1931.

SORCERERS
OF
DOBU

CHAPTER I

SOCIAL ORGANIZATION

I

OUTLINE OF SOCIAL ORGANIZATION

The ideal village of Dobu is a circle of huts facing inward to a central, often elevated mound, which is the village graveyard.

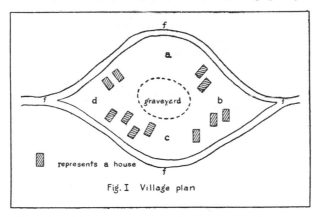

Fig. I Village plan

In point of fact there are usually gaps in the circle of huts as at a, b, c, and d. These gaps represent old house sites of extinct family lines. A path, f, goes around the village behind the backs of the houses. This is for the use of passers by, who are not allowed to enter the village unless they are closely related to its members, or unless they have legitimate business of moment to transact.

In the centre of the village a clear space lies open with only scattered brilliant leaved croton shrubs upon it. Here below the sod within their stone set circular enclosure lie the mothers, and mothers' brothers, the grandmothers on the distaff side and their brothers, and so, for many a generation back, the ancestors of the villagers on the distaff side. From the dead who lie in the central space individual ownership vested in soil and palm has come to the living. On the paternal side the ancestors of the village owners lie utterly dispersed in the villages of many stranger clans, the villages of their respective mothers and female ancestors.

In the following discussion I use the term villager in the restricted meaning of owner of village land and village trees. This use excludes those who have married into the village and who claim residence only through their spouses.

Each villager, male or female, owns a house site and a house. A woman inherits her house site from her mother, or from her mother's sister. The husband in every marriage must come from another village than that of his wife. His house site is in one village, his wife's house site is in another. A man's son cannot inherit the house site of his father in his father's village. After his father's death he must scrupulously avoid so much as entering his father's village. His father bequeaths his house site to his own sister's son. His own son inherits house site and village status from his mother's brother in his mother's village.

For the purpose of diagrammatic representation we may represent the village as one of its constituent units only.

We may represent the Dobuan situation graphically as below :—

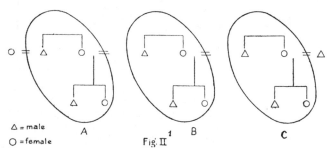

△ = male   A   B
○ = female   Fig. II[1]   C

[1] Where   ○   represents a female.

                   △   represents a male.

              ○ = △   represents female married to male.

              △ ○   represents brother-sister relationship.

              △ ○   represents a descending generation the children of a marriage.

The oval enclosing lines mark off villages A, B, and C. For brother and sister own house sites in the same village, and children inherit house sites in their mother's village, not possibly in their father's. Hence a man, his sister and his sister's children are the owners or potential owners of all village house site land.

Where a man's house land is inherited there is he buried in the central place adjoining the outer ring of house land. Thus no father is ever buried in the place of his children. A, B, and C represent a legal unit which keeps village land and the disposal of the corpses of its members strictly within itself.

The unit I have ringed about, of a man, his sister, and his sister's children, is called in Dobuan the *susu*. It extends down the generations so that it may include a man, his sister, his sister's children, and his sister's daughter's children, but not his sister's son's children, and so on. The children of any male member of the *susu* go out of it. In the above diagram I have represented each *susu* as a separate village in order to represent marriage out of the village. In reality, each village is a small number of *susu*, from four or five to ten or twelve, all claiming a common female ancestress and unbroken descent from her through females only. In practice only some of the number of *susu* can demonstrate this claim of common ancestry in their short known genealogies. But the claim is probably well founded, although not fully substantiated except by mythological validation in a mythical common ancestress.

All virtue in this system comes from descent through the mother. Every woman claims by right the inheritance of her brother for her male children. Hence this grouping is called *susu*, the term for mother's milk. A husband beating his wife falls out with her mother's brother, or with her brother whose inheritance she claims for her children. Her children are independent of her husband for legal endowment—they *must* by law be independent, and differently endowed. She is greatly independent of her husband, and only bound if he cares to indulge, as often happens, in suicidal self pity, and does not succeed in killing himself. Nevertheless, the suicidal resort is taken in a minority of cases ; divorce is possible in the majority. It has become popular now for offended men to embark for work in the white man's centres, rather than to attempt suicide, the more so since the old point of suicide, forcing one's kin to avenge one on one's cruel wife's kindred, is difficult now owing to the white man's laws against murder being fairly well enforced

Nevertheless, despite the new fashion, the old way still persists side by side with the new.

If we come upon the village in its everyday aspect, when all is quiet, all its marriages going smoothly, it gives little apparent evidence of the strength of the *susu*. The *susu* does not live in a house. A man lives with his wife and children, and the interior of their house is strictly forbidden to anyone else, except at night to a lover of the daughter of the house. The man's sister or the woman's brother, or any other visitor, cannot ascend into the house but must rest under its elevated floor on the sheltered ground beneath, or, in the case of two men who are friends meeting, they may sit together on the elevated platform in front of the house, a small roof-sheltered " verandah ".

The *susu* has no common house for its exclusive use. Its only exclusive communal resting place is the graveyard, the centre ring with its red croton plants upon it ; each hut of the many that surround the communal place of the *susu* shelters a biological family, the marital grouping as I shall term it throughout this account.

Normally the house interior is as rigidly restricted to man, wife, and their children, as the graveyard that the house fronts is rigidly restricted to the corpses of brothers, sisters, and sisters' children, it being understood that the house is restricted to the one unit, the biological family only, whereas the grave-yard is common to all the *susu* of the village. But in case of serious illness the patient is always removed on a litter to his or her own village, village of the mother, if residence at the time of sickness is otherwise. Then, and then only, entrance to the house is possible to the matrilineal kin of the patient despite the presence of the patient's spouse in the house. If serious illness turns to death the dead's spouse is immediately prohibited from the house and the village of death. Within the house the near matrilineal kin mourn their dead. The alignment of kin within the house is, for the first and only time, the same as the alignment of kin within the graveyard. The house has ceased to be a house in its normal function. It is deserted for a season then destroyed.

Each marital grouping possesses two house sites, each site with a house built upon it. The woman has her house in her village, the man has his house in his village. The couple with their children live alternately in the woman's house in the village of the woman's matrilineal kin, and in the man's house in the village of the man's matrilineal kin. The change in residence usually takes place each gardening year, so that the one spouse spends alternate years in the other's place and alternate years in own place ; but some couples move more frequently to and fro. It is thus required that every person spend at least every alternate year, he with his sister and mother, she with her brother and mother (and, of course, mother's brothers and sisters). Since every family grouping moves in this fashion, it follows that when a man is in his village his wife is also there, if his mother is in her village his father or his stepfather is also there, and if his sister is in her village his sister's husband is also there. His mother's brother may also be at home. Then his mother's brother's wife will be there. He and his sister, his mother with her sisters and brothers are all owners of the village land where they are resident, owners of the houses built upon it, and owners of the palms growing about the village.

They are the *susu*. His wife, his father, his sister's husband, his mother's brother's wife, on the other hand, own land, houses, and palms in their own different villages. They are representatives of the various *susu* of other places, and they are in the place of their affinal relatives temporarily for the year.

Now, although these incoming visitors, who are not local owners, have each a retiring place in the village exclusively to themselves with their respective husbands or wives—the interior of the house—they spend a great part of the day and the early evening outside their houses in sight of and in frequent communication with the local owners and the wives and husbands of others of the local owners. Certain rules and observances govern this communication.

The incomers are called Those-resulting-from-marriage, or strangers, as a collective class by the collective class which is called Owners of the Village. Owners of the village use personal names between themselves freely to persons of their own or a younger generation. To their elders they prefer to use relationship terms, though the personal name is not forbidden. But Those-resulting-from-marriage cannot use the personal name of any one of the owners down to the smallest child, except in the case of a father to his own child. They must use a term of relationship. Owners of an ascendant generation can and do use their names freely, however. Moreover, one of Those-resulting-from-marriage cannot use the personal name of any other person in the same class. Again, a relationship term must be used. Those-resulting-from-marriage, while they are yet newly married, must approach an owner's family sitting beneath the owner's house by a roundabout way, circling in unobtrusively and bending apologetically while they do so— their own spouse being the only owner excepted. By the time one or two children are born this behaviour is usually discarded towards the own mother-in-law's *susu*. But it remains even later towards other *susu* in the village (at least when an unusual mode of behaviour is set up, as when I might ask a man to come and introduce me to some of the more distant village relatives of his own mother-in-law's *susu*).

" Those-resulting-from-marriage " are not supposed to be themselves kinsmen. It happens sometimes that they are. But this develops from linked parallel marriages between the same two places which are strongly disapproved. " Those-resulting-from-marriage " are supposed to be on entirely formal terms with each other when they are resident in the owners' village, avoiding each other's personal names. It is not fitting that they should be kinsmen and of the one village ; and economic arrangements, as we shall see later, discriminate against such linked marriages. Moreover, in case two villages are linked by several marriages, as they are becoming nowadays in places where the population has receded seriously, a suicidal ending to one marriage might rend the others into two opposing groups bound to revenge and defence against revenge respectively. In the state of uneasy marriage found in Dobu it is fitting that one village should hesitate to involve itself over deeply with another, but prefer to spread its marriages widely. This is actually stated as the ideal.

" Those-resulting-from-marriage," if they are men, are always abnormally uneasy about their wives' fidelity. Now when a woman is in her own village, she has her kin next door and only too ready to eject her husband if he dares to lift a hand against her, or use foul language to her. She has no great dependence on her husband for care of her children, since a woman can nearly always get a new husband for future help, and her brother ultimately provides for them in any case. Consequently she behaves very much as she likes in secret. Suspicion and close watching are not relaxed by her jealous resultant-from-marriage. Sooner or later anger between man and wife flares up in public. Then the woman's kin tell the man to get out. He has no sympathy from the others-resulting-from-marriage. They are for the most part no kin of his, and they are not a united body as the collective class formed of the several *susu* Owners of the Village are. The result is that the unfortunate resultant-from-marriage gets out precipitately, usually being designated in uncomplimentary obscene terms by irate owners as he goes. Dobuan folklore is full of husbands pathetically packing up their goods and going home to their mothers and sisters after a child has informed them that their wife has been consorting secretly with a male member of a distantly related *susu* of her own village. All men of the village call all women of the village of their own generation sister, but some are not close parallel cousins in reality, their relationship being of a degree that cannot be determined from known genealogy.   Marriage within the village is strongly dis-countenanced, but casual sex affairs between distant " brothers " and " sisters " of other *susu* of the village occur often. The husband either gets out without insulting or striking his wife as in the folk-lore, or else both insults and strikes her and then gets out before he is injured, but under danger of injury, as I saw happen in real life. Conversely when a woman is in her husband's place she is jealous of him and watches for signs of his intrigues with village " sisters " of his. I do not know how much actual village " incest " of this order there is, but I do know that suspicion of it is frequently flaring up into as much trouble as if the suspicion were perfectly founded. The offended husband always believes his suspicion is true, the owners invariably repudiate it, and no conciliatory mechanism exists, apart from the husband sometimes pocketing his pride later, sometimes not, and sometimes resorting to a suicidal attempt on his life. In reality, as in the legends, children are enlisted as informers. Jealousy normally runs so high in Dobu that a man watches his wife closely, carefully timing her absences when she goes to the bush for natural functions. And when it is the time for women's work in the gardens here and there one sees a man with nothing to do but stand sentinel all day and play with the children if any want to play with him.

It will be apparent that the strength of the marital grouping is not improved by the solidarity of the *susu*, which is maintained by the rule of alternate residence. Incest prohibition is not too difficult to enforce within the small family. But when the children are grown adults, many with dead parents, belonging to different family lines that have only mythological validation of common ancestry, all thrust closely together by local residence and taught to regard their village mates as brothers and sisters, and people of other villages as dangerous sorcerers and witches, enemies all, then it is not unnatural that the strain of considering a woman of a friendly group as a sister sometimes breaks down. One's wife, after all, is a member of a group that may only modify its underlying hostility at best. Parents-in-law are frequently divined by the diviner as the sorcerer or witch that is making one ill. In the lower social forms the bee's division into three classes of queen, worker, and drone is a type that works with no strain. But sister-brother solidarity with an artificial extension of the sister-brother relationship does not work with the husband-wife solidarity very well under Dobuan conditions. One solidarity tends to gain predominance. Then friction tends to occur between the two groupings. This friction is expressed in sorcery and witchcraft terms as well as in terms of jealousy, quarrel, attempted suicide, and village " incest ".

The following diagram of marital grouping and *susu* respectively may be useful for a summary of the argument as far as it has gone :—

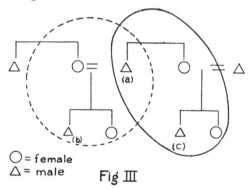

O = female
△ = male

Fig III

The circle enclosed group is the marital grouping, the oval enclosed group is the *susu*. It is evident that the man (a) is a member of both groupings. He has a loyalty to each group. The gain of one group from him will be at the expense of the other.

The *susu*, with the brother-sister solidarity at its base, has as its gains :—

(1) The inheritance and exclusive possession of a's corpse.

(2) The inheritance and exclusive possession of a's village land and palms.

(3) The right to exclude a's children from entering a's *susu's* village after a is dead.

(4) The right to enforce a to live in his sister's village every alternate year in despite of marriage ties, and reciprocally he is forced in alternate years to live in his wife's brother's village.

The marital grouping has as losses the inheritance of a's corpse, the inheritance of a's village land and palms, the right to enter a's village after a is dead (for widows as well as widows' children are excluded), and the right to live in one place in a settled manner, such as would probably be more in accord with marital congeniality. Related cultures, neighbours to Dobu, have fixed patrilocal marriage with *susu* right otherwise similar to Dobu. I studied one such culture fairly intensively. Divorce is not one-fifth as frequent as in Dobu. Moreover, " those-resulting-from-marriage " are all women come into their husband's place more or less permanently. The Dobuan custom makes " those-resulting-from-marriage " half men, half women of non-permanent residence, and non-permanent even in changing residence, because the chances of divorce are high. The oldest Dobuan in my main genealogy had had eight successive marriages, one of the youngest men in the genealogy had had four, one other youth, three, and this is fairly typical of an overwhelming majority of Dobuans. It is so in every separate sea-divided district that is Dobuan in culture. The result is that each Dobuan village shelters a heterogenous collection of men of different village allegiance who distrust one another thoroughly. Suspicion of sorcery and poisoning tactics *within* the village runs very high at times. In the patrilocal marriage of neighbouring cultures all the men of the village are " brothers ", owners of the village in every case. All resultants-from-marriage are women and suspicion of foul tactics *within* the village is not found. There can be no doubt that the rule of alternate residence, while it enjoins and expresses a solidarity between the owners, disrupts the relations between the owners and their separate spouses, " Those-resulting-from-marriage." We can quite fairly assign this custom as a gain to *susu* right and a loss to marital grouping right. Conversely a brother-sister tabu, if it were inaugurated and carried far enough, would prevent the alternate residence rule, or, at least, tend to prevent the extended " incest " that follows with alternate residence as it exists in Dobu. Such a brother-sister tabu would be a gain for the marital grouping over the *susu*. It would tend to put (a) with his wife and her

children more, and less with his sister and her children (see
Fig. III). It will be clear from the Dobuan situation how a brother-
sister *tabu* would strengthen the family by marriage.   There is
no hint of any such *tabu*, however, in Dobu, except that young
unmarried men do not sleep in the same house with their young
unmarried sisters. The young man is turned out of the parental
house, the daughter of the house remains in it.   The youths
go and sleep with the daughters of other houses, and the brothers
of other girls of other villages come to sleep with their sisters.
It is not a brother-sister *tabu*, for a youth with no sister is
excluded from his parents' house, but an active arrangement
whereby the young men seek out the sisters of other young
men who live afield.   The full estimation of the disruptive
possibilities in the Dobuan rule of alternate residence can only
be reached after a discussion of Dobuan sorcery. That I cannot
do within the limits of this chapter. Meanwhile, pending later
substantiation, it must be provisionally accepted from the results
that the rule is a gain of *susu* right, a loss for the marital grouping.

We may now consider in further detail these gains of the
susu, losses of the marital grouping. Firstly I shall deal with the
inheritance of the corpse.

When death has come there is first private mourning within
the house of the dead person by the members of the dead's
own *susu*. The spouse of such a mourner mourns kneeling on
the ground outside the house, away from the corpse, and not
looking upon it. The spouse of the dead has gone from the
village. Then after an hour or so has passed in this manner,
the corpse is carried from the interior of the house to the house
platform. Once the corpse is out on the house platform, it is
displayed and adorned. It is propped against or fastened to one
of the two huge logs which make a great inverted V in front of
the house platform of the house of death. Large yams are put
about the corpse if the deceased was a good gardener. Ornaments
of value are put on the corpse to indicate that the deceased was
rich. The eldest child of the eldest sister of the deceased takes
the personal possessions of the deceased, usually his or her
lime gourd and lime spatula, and sitting by the corpse uses
these much as the conductor of an orchestra uses his baton,
to beat the time to a slow dirge sung by the members of all the
susu who are owners of the village.   " Those-resulting-from-
marriage " either stay out of the village or remain closeted
within their spouses' houses. The dirge may go on through
 ᵃ night, or it may be terminated by burial before night. Others

of the sister's children of the dead take other belongings of the dead and enact a pantomime with them. One may take a fishing-net, if the deceased is a man, and go through all the pantomime of fishing. It is the only germ of public dramatics in Dobu. If the deceased is female, the conductors of the dirge and the mimes are female; if the deceased is a male they are male. Finally the sister's children, male and female, bear the corpse away and bury it. The burial party for a man is of his own *susu*, for a woman it is her sister's children of a parallel *susu*.

If the deceased is a man his wife and his children are not present, or in sight of any of these proceedings. It is most strictly prohibited. The *susu* takes exclusive right to mourning and burial. If the deceased is a woman her children are present, her husband is not.

The house of the dead is left empty with the great inverted V logs in front of it. A small enclosure walled in by plaited coco-nut frond mats is erected beneath it. Under the inspection of the owners of the village the spouse of the dead now enters the enclosure, sitting on a mat on the ground all day, walled off, speaking to no one and seeing no one. So begins the year's mourning incumbent upon any member of " Those-resulting-from-marriage " who survives an owner spouse.

Let us take the case where He-resulting-from-marriage is a man, a widower, and review his year of mourning as it approaches its close. To-morrow his year of mourning will be ended. To-night there is dancing in the village. The men stand in a circle beating the tympanums of their long drums with their hands, singing as they beat. Round the circle of men trip the women dressed in their finest grass skirts, some of the elder holding a girl child by the hand. The song is traditional, the widower's song :—

> Lie awake, lie awake and talk
>   at the midnight hour.
> First lie awake and talk
>   lie awake, lie awake and talk.
> Maiwortu, your charcoal body smear
>   by Mwaniwara below.
> Dawns breaks the black of night,
>   first lie awake and talk.

Maiwortu, it is understood, is the widower. He is to lie awake and talk with his children. Their mother is dead now a year gone by. For the year the father has remained in her village. When she died he could not see her corpse or mourn her intimately. He had to hide himself within a house. When afte

a long period of abstention dancing was allowed again in the
village he could take no part.   Again he had to hide himself when
at the breaking of the tabu on dancing the skull of the dead is
taken out by the sister's children of the dead.   Then the village
owners, the distaff kin of the dead, dance with the skull, singing
one of the finest of the dance songs of Dobu, the song that
begins :—

> I go hillwards to Bwebweso, Mountain of the Extinguished,
>   by Dokwabu's white pandanus flower,

so bodying forth the spirit on its path to Bwebweso, the hill
of the dead.

Just as the corpse may be seen by the owners of the village
only, so the skull in this rite may be seen by them only.   The
widower, the stranger, or resultant-from-marriage is debarred.
In the village of his dead wife the widower has not sung, he has
not smiled, he has not danced, he has not looked at another
woman.   The greater part of the time he has blackened his body
over with charcoal from the fires.   He has put away all his body
ornaments, all sweet scented herbs.   He has eaten the roughest
and worst food.   Bananas, pineapple, oranges, fish, pig, taro,
the better kinds of yams have been denied to him.   All the
coco-nuts he ate throughout the year were unripe.   He ate the
oldest yams of coarsest consistency.   Round his neck he wore
the many looped, black, rope-like *mwagura*, the badge of
mourning.   For the earlier month or two of mourning he
remained confined in the enclosure beneath the house of death
seated on the ground.   Later he emerged to do toilsome work
for his dead wife's mother or sister, work of no recompense
for him.

Harvest has come again since last harvest when his mourning
began.   At both harvests his village kin are obliged to bring
big gifts of yams and give them to the kinsfolk of his dead
wife, getting back smaller gifts, no great recompense, a few
days after each gift.   He has mourned all night before the day
of the final gift of yams.   After the gifts have been set up
ceremonially in a wood fenced square and then distributed
among the village kin of the dead, a sister's son of his deceased
wife will cut the loop, the *mwagura*, that was about his neck.
To-morrow comes this final rite—the time of his mourning
done.   The sister's sons and brothers of his wife will lead him
by the hand to Mwaniwara, the farthest eastern point of the
island.   There they will wash his body coat of charcoal from him
in the sea (for the year he has not bathed in sea or in stream).

They will cleanse him, anoint his body with oil, replace his body ornaments, and place fragrant herbs in his armlets. They will then lead him by the hand to his own village. *He will never enter their village again.*

In the song Maiwortu, the widower is dramatized, as talking night long with his children. They belong to the village of their dead mother. There they inherit village status and land, a girl from her mother's sister, a boy from his mother's brother. There they will stay. Their father is prohibited from entering their village once again. While the mother lived the father was " he who holds the infant in his arms ". He played with and carried the young children everywhere. But to-morrow a stranger goes to his own place.

So it came about that a widower informant gave me the widower's song with much feeling apparent in his attitude. The song depicts a high dramatic point in Dobuan life. Like most Dobuan songs it contains an overplay of meaning—dawn breaking from the black of night is at once a direct reference to the importance of the morrow and also a symbol of Maiwortu, the widower, emerging from his body covering of charcoal.

Widowers engaged in work for their deceased wife's mother or elder sister are usually in a vile temper. They are no use whatever to an inquiring anthropologist, and pardonably so. Their mourning is so arduous that they are glad to get out of it. Staying with their children has become associated with a year's misery. They leave their misery and their children's company together behind them.

A widow observes parallel custom in the village of her dead husband. Her children cook food frequently for the sister's children of their dead father or stepfather. The children can go as far as the outskirts of the village of their dead father, while the widow turns aside or back some distance away (as does the widower in his relation to the village of his dead wife also). Widow and children of the dead man cannot look on his corpse or on his skull when it is taken in the dance. The skull is kept by the sister's child of the dead—within the *susu*.

After a person's death his or her personal name and skull are inherited by the heir to the village house site. This former inheritance is made exclusive and is safeguarded by its being prohibited for any person not of the dead's own immediate *susu* to utter the name of the dead or the name of any common object which is also the name, or includes as a part, the name of the dead. Thus if a man dies his sister's son inherits his name.

The man's own son is prohibited from using the name of his dead father. Only the true sisters of the dead, their children, and their daughters' children are allowed to use the name in addressing the dead man's sister's son. Thus the name descends within the *susu*, the ringed groups in my various diagrams above. Every person has two personal names. One, the name of a dead person of the *susu*, is used within the *susu* alone to designate the heir of the dead. The other personal name is used by the other *susu* of the village, owners of the village outside own immediate *susu*, and by a father to his child. A relationship term only, as we have already seen, is used by Those-resulting-from-marriage to owners in the case of father to child. We have thus three grades of distance of relationship clearly demarcated in the use of terms of address. Not only does the sister's son inherit a dead mother's brother's name, but he also takes over his mother's brother's status in regard to terms of address used to the biological descendants of his mother's brother. Thus a man will call his dead mother's brother's son, my son. Reciprocally a man calls his dead father's sister's son, my father (if anyone wishes to refer back to Fig. III (b) calls (c) my father, after (a)'s death for (c) inherits (a)'s village land, (a)'s skull, (a)'s name, and (a)'s status ; (c) calls (b) my son ; see p. 8).

Previous to (a)'s death (c) called (b) *nibagu*, my cross-cousin, and (b) called (c) my cross-cousin also, i.e. a man calls his mother's brother's son cross-cousin until his mother's brother's death, the term being reciprocal. After his mother's brother's death a man succeeds to his mother's brother's property and status and calls his mother's brother's son, my son, instead of my cross-cousin. This change in terminology of address, as we shall see later, governs the entire mode of address, for all the near relatives of both the cross-cousins who change so, also change their terminology, the one party to the other accordingly.

The child of a dead father is called Boundary Man by the Owners of the Village of the deceased. The sister's son of the dead is Owner. Boundary Man is so called because he cannot enter his father's village boundary or eat a single nut or fruit of the trees of his father's village or any food grown on land that was his father's. His cross-cousin Owner can enter Boundary Man's village freely, however. While his father lives and the future Boundary Man is still unmarried and living with his father and mother, he goes every alternate year with his parents to the father's village. There with his mother he is one of Those-resulting-from-Marriage, a stranger, in relation to the Owners, careful never to utter an Owner's personal name. He is a member of the marital grouping as opposed to the *susu* grouping in that village. He has the one advantage that we have seen the marital grouping has over the *susu*—he is a member of the unit that lives in a common house. The marital grouping again goes gardening together—children with their mother and father. In the course of this everyday life in common it normally occurs that a great measure of affection springs up between father and child as well as between mother and child. The affection between mother and child is more stable than that between father and child because divorce is common. In case of divorce the mother-child association continues. The father-child association in such cases is cut short abruptly, for the father avoids his former wife, and since the children remain with her he can only see them infrequently when they are detached from their mother and come to visit him. If he acquires step-children by a new marriage he does not care for them sentimentally as if they were his own, if they are at all grown and independent. Nevertheless, in many cases a father remains with his wife and children until some, at least, of his children have won affection from him. There are many things that he cannot provide for his children. His village land, his personal name, his skull, his status, his village palms, and fruit trees he cannot by any possibility alienate from his sister's child in favour of his own child. In all these things his child is Boundary Man in reality as well as in name. But he can and he often does teach his child his magical formulæ. On the other hand, he is obliged by law and induced by his affection for his sister and her children to teach his sister's child his magical formulæ. In fact, he usually teaches both his child and his sister's child all the magic he knows and possesses.

This may seem natural enough and reasonable. But in reality it is a very horrifying and subversive action. It is not said to be either of these things by the Dobuan native, for he takes all established custom nonchalantly as the order according to which the universe was created. The subversive nature of this practice can only be realized when the Dobuan conception of magic is grasped. I cannot give this conception completely here ; but it will be shown later that magic is conceived as like a material thing. It gives power, status, and a small income, and it may be bought and sold. Or rather it is like a doctor's practice or a business place's goodwill, or a peer's title and lands. A doctor that alienated the one and the same practice by selling it or bequeathing it to two different persons who were not partners but business antagonists would hardly have his sale or will legally supported. The same is true of a business goodwill. A sovereign who gave two men the same peerage and lands in feudal days would have had rebellion at his gates. Yet in Dobu where Boundary Man and Owner Heir are not partners or close friends or sharers in common property, but are more apt to be antagonistic, a parallel practice is made legal enough. The one and the same goodwill is given to both men.

It cannot on the contrary be given to two men who are blood brothers. A father will never give his magic to two sons. If he has six sons, one will be chosen and five left magicless. A man will never give his magic to two of his sister's sons or sisters' sons. One will be chosen and the others left. Primogeniture is the great basis for selection, but it may be set aside as amongst ourselves, if sentimental considerations set against the eldest in a younger son's favour. The result is that blood brothers are usually very jealous of one another. After they come to youth and sexual maturity they never sleep side by side. It is not allowed, for were two brothers to sleep side by side their blood would change from one sleeper's body into the other's. This blood transfusion would result in quarrelling and maybe fratricide. Such is the superstition for the incompatibility. The real incompatibility springs from jealousy over inheritance and possibility of inheritance, and its origin is unmistakable. What is a rift between blood brothers of the one *susu* is also in part a rift between Boundary Man and his cross-cousin Owner. There is jealousy by Boundary Man of his cross-cousin succeeding to his father's status and village lands. So people watch Boundary Man and his cross-cousin Owner carefully to see how they get on together. If they walk together abroad the sight is said to be good. But blood brothers should not walk together. That is bad. Blood brothers, however, can trust one another not to employ sorcery one against the other, whereas Boundary Man and his cross-cousin Owner are the closest relatives who may yet fall out to the extreme of using sorcery against each other. So it is well that they should endeavour to cement this relationship rather than their relationships with their respective brothers ; at least it is more necessary.

So Boundary Man and cross-cousin Owner inherit the same

magic where blood brothers do not. It is this fact and the fact that magic is a unit like a title or a medical practice that makes the common inheritance of magic by a man's son and his sister's son appear subversive. The son is blocked out of village land and trees and the skull, for they are material and not so readily divisible. He is blocked out from inheritance of his father's personal name, although that is non-material. But, unless he has a stepfather who cares little for him—here again the mother-right system frequently provides this contingency and so blocks him—he is not blocked out from inheritance of magic. If, profiting by his closer intimacy, the son gets more of his father's magic than his father's sister's son gets from the same source, and his father dies, the son cannot legally retain his superior position over the man he now calls my father, his true father's sister's son. The latter may say to him : *Imu yawana 'u da ekara, igu yawana 'u da ekara ile nama*, " Your leaf you may carry, my leaf you carry returning hither to me." No more need be said. The son, Boundary Man, must then teach his father's sister's son his excess of magic immediately and without fee. But if the latter has an excess Boundary Man cannot obtain it from him. No reciprocal right exists.

It is otherwise between blood brothers. If elder brother A has all the magic, younger brother B has no hope of getting it ever. In one case I know of A taught some garden magic to B's wife—to save appearances he did not teach it to B, though B profited by his wife's gain, as garden crops of man and wife are pooled for their common use. B's wife gave A a tenth of her next year's crop as fee, " to make the magic pointed," i.e. to make it work well on the crops. Under a thin disguise this was really a transaction between the blood brothers, Alo and Kisi, of my own Green Parrot village.

This transaction was not typical of any general fact, however. Kisi's wife was a woman who had been adopted into the family as a girl. Adoption is never felt to be as binding a tie as blood kinship in Dobu. A foster parent will refer publicly and freely to an adopted child as " a bastard " or " an orphan " as the case may be. Even so, Kisi's marriage was somewhat subversive in that he had married a " sister " by adoption. Alo had more real affection for her than is usual between a man and his brother's wife. The more usual condition is that there is no transfer of magic between brothers whatever.

In this case of the inheritance of magic we see the first gain of the marital grouping besides its having a common house.

It is not a gain excluding all gain from the *susu* grouping but a division of gains.

Garden land lies afield from the villages. Here again a father gives some land to his son, some to his sister's son. (The eldest son usually inherits and allows usufruct of portions of the land to younger brothers.) This custom is as subversive of the general lean of the law in favour of the *susu* as is the custom governing the inheritance of magic. Its subversiveness becomes apparent when it is recalled that no child can eat of any fruit or any crop grown on land that was his or her father's. This applies as stringently to garden land as to village land. However, no one objects to eating crop or fruit grown on some-one else's dead father's land. So at harvest time the women dig a basketful or two of yams from their dead father's land, or the land of the dead fathers of their husbands, and then seek out someone else who is harvesting from land similarly inherited. They exchange baskets and gossip informally and then carry the yams home. Law is appeased.

A canoe must descend within the *susu* ; so must fishing nets, stone adzes, ornamental valuables, and all moveable personal property ; so must also the crop of the garden of the dead for the gardening season during which death took place. A great part of the harvest of the children of the dead man for that year passes over also to the sister's sons of the dead in gifts that must be made. All over Dobu as harvest time comes on the children of the dead men of the year are cooking and carrying gifts of the finest food to the sister's children of the dead, the former paying the latter for their funerary services— boundary men acknowledging the rights of their cross-cousin owners by adding even more to the latter's overplus of inheritance. It is strange to the European observer to see how harvest home, an occasion of rejoicing and church festival amongst ourselves, sets Dobu into concentration on the dead of the year, on ritual surrounding death. The secret of it is that the ritual involves inheritance as well as death ceremonial, and inheritance is of first importance to a people so poor. Dobu Island, a typical settlement, is 2 miles by 3, an infertile volcanic cone for the greater part of its area, and yet forty years ago it was inhabited by two thousand people. Now the population has shrunken to twelve hundred (although war has been abolished) and it looks to be shrinking further. But still the pressure of the population upon land is heavy.

We may summarize the respective gains of the marital

SISTER'S CHILDREN OF THE DEAD CARRYING FUNERARY GIFTS OF FOOD TO
THEM FROM CHILDREN OF THE DEAD

FUNERARY FEAST GROUP, NOTE WIDOW WITH
WIDOW'S NECK TIE AND LONG SKIRT

grouping versus the *susu*, father son right versus mother's brother sister's son right in the folllowing table :—

MARITAL GROUPING		SUSU	
Loss	Gain	Loss	Gain
(1) (2) (3) (4) } As shown to gain of *susu*.			Inheritance of— (1) Corpse and skull ; (2) Village land and trees ; (3) Canoes, fishing-gear, etc. (4) Personal name and status in re-lationship terms.
	(5) Magic with no right over any excess se-cured by *susu*. (6) Half of gar-den land with no right of eating its crop. (7) A house in common.	(5) Loss of mo-nopoly of magic. (6) Loss of mo-nopoly of gar-den land. (7) Loss of com-mon house.	(5) Magic with rights over excess secured by mari-tal grouping ; (6) Half of garden land with right to eat its crop.
(8) No common village (rule of village exo-gamy).			(8) Gain of com-mon village.
(9) Loss of solid-arity by rule of alternate resi-dence.			(9) Gain of solid-arity by rule of alternate resi-dence of marital grouping.
(10) No brother-sister taboo to prevent village incest.			(10) No brother-sister taboo to prevent village incest.
(11) Widower or widow cannot enter village of dead spouse ; child cannot enter village of dead father.			(11) *susu* relatives of the dead *can* enter villages of the dead's widower or widow or child-ren.

It will be readily apparent from this table that the social organization sets heavily towards *susu* predominance, or, as it is usually called, mother-right. There is some objection to this term. It might well be confined to the social organiza-tions where all important property is owned by women and handed down from mother to daughter. Then mother's brother's right, or some such differentiated term, might be used to distinguish social organizations where men own important property, but where a sister has legal claim over her brother's property for her children's interest. Logically the main possibilities for stress are :—

(1) Father to son.
(2) Mother to daughter.
(3) Father and mother bequeathing communal property to both son and daughter.
(4) Man to sister's child.
(5) Woman to brother's child.

In Dobu (4) is the strongest stress ; (2) is the second strongest ; (1) takes third importance ; (3) does not obtain as there is rigid separation of much wealth into man's property and woman's property. Stress (5) occurs very rarely.

Where (1) is the main stress the term father-right may be used suitably, where (2) is main stress mother-right. The third stress may be termed marital grouping right, the fourth mother's brother's right. The fifth we may term father's sister right. Then in these terms Dobu is dominantly mother's brother's right, secondarily mother-right, thirdly father-right, and very much less importantly has an element of father's sister right.

This last case is a rare and somewhat curious phenomenon in Dobu. When a man marries a woman of a far-away place he usually comes and settles permanently in his wife's place, affiliating himself with a local branch of his own clan in lieu of his own true village far away. Then if he dies away from his home, leaving a daughter by his wife this daughter may be required to leave her mother and her mother's place and go to her father's sister, far away. There she must stay until she bears a child in her father's place. She then has her choice of leaving her child to replace that place's loss of her father, and coming home to her mother, or of staying on in her father's place with her own child. In this way a curious rift is made in the *susu* line of mother, daughter, and daughter's daughter. Two of these three may remain together, but not three, and mother and young child are parted early. It is the one exception to the rule that a child may not enter a dead father's place. In this case a child must enter the dead father's place and the father's sister's house. If she stays there long in desertion of her mother after bearing her first child she becomes adopted as if she were a real daughter of her father's sister. Then she can stay with her own child. This course is not followed inevitably, or even frequently, in the rare cases where a man marries in a far-away place and dies there. But it may happen. I saw one such case. Its motivation I shall discuss later in discussing economic exchanges.

Although marriages between distant places are rare in Dobu, the existence of such a possible claim of the father's sister over her brother's daughter, as well as the claim of the son on the inheritance of the father in many more normal marriages, in a society where *susu* right is as strong as it is in Dobu, is convincing in proving the inadequacy of the old terminology of mother-right and father-right. The more exact terms are needed, for exactness in terminology may be always an aid to future observation. I began in Dobu with an outlook bound by the rigidity of the old mother-right conception, and loosened only in part by Dr. B.' Malinowski's evidence from the Trobriands ; in consequence I did not discover some of the exceptions until I was in my sixth and last month there.

I have as yet only shown the *susu* at work in death, mourning and inheritance, its most important aspect, with several pre liminary sketches of its working in marriage. The marriage picture requires now some further elaboration. We shall consider both the marital grouping in itself and in its relation to the *susu*.

II

MARRIAGE

We have already seen that convention compels a boy who has arrived at puberty to leave his parents' house for sleeping, while the daughter of the house of equivalent age is allowed to remain. The houseless boys usually sleep in the house of a divorced man who is temporarily without a wife, or, more frequently, roam in the night until they find a girl each who will grant them sex intercourse and houseroom for sleeping. No one builds a house except for marriage, the houses for food-storage excepted. The boys prefer to sleep with a different girl every night in order to avoid permanent entanglement. If a boy sleeps many times in succession with the same girl her parents will marry the pair out of hand by enforcing public recognition and public economic exchanges between the boy's kindred and themselves. Faithfulness between the pair is then considered necessary. If, however, a boy sleeps with very many different girls he avoids marriage, and his affairs he keeps private with no public recognition whatever. He must leave the girl's house before dawn to avoid being seen by the adult members of her village. If he oversleeps and is caught publicly in the place of his sleeping he has to marry the girl. The boys are careful to avoid entanglement usually until they are at least eighteen or more. Then one by one they become weary of the rigorous regime of late roving nights and early morning risings ; they fall into a deeper attachment with one preferred girl, and become afraid that a rival will marry her to their complete estrangement from her. So they deliberately over-sleep one morning. The mother of the girl gets up before the young pair and steps out on to the house platform. There she sits calmly blocking up the exit with her body. The young man rises. If even now he has an impulse to flee he cannot. He respects the girl's mother too much to ask her to stand aside. The village see an unusual event has occurred. They gather curious to see what youth will emerge. They send word to neighbouring villages and people from the environs gather. Everyone circles around and stares. Into this glare of curious publicity the youth and the girl descend at last from the house and sit side by side on a mat on the ground. The spectators remain and do nothing but stare for half a hour or so. This staring ceremony makes the engagement. It is aggressive publicity directed towards a relationship which was before as aggressively private. For no youth or maiden would speak of a mere sex relationship to any one whatever—except to perhaps one child confidant and helper. Before betrothal privacy is as aggressively sustained as at betrothal privacy is aggressively and staringly outraged. Finally, the starers disperse. The girl's mother, now formally the youth's mother-in-law, places a digging-stick into the youth's hand and says, " Go, make a garden," or if it is not yet the new garden season she gives him other seasonal work.

The youths do not sleep with the girls of their own village, terminologically their sisters. Their general relationship to the people of the villages where they do sleep with the girls, is peculiar. We have seen how Those-resulting-from-marriage are rifted apart from their spouses at their spouses' death, and how the *susu* steps in to deal with intimate mourning and the disposal of the corpse, to enforce an onerous and unpleasant kind of mourning upon the surviving widow or widower for a year (sometimes it is for two years), and finally how the *susu* lead the widow or widower away from their village never to be allowed to show face in it again at peril of death from the *susu* owners of the village. There is much more than ceremonial dictation in this matter. More often than not the rift will be reinforced by a wall of sullen suspicion on the one hand and resentment of suspicion on the other. The Owners of the Village suspect the village kin of the surviving spouse, widow, or widower as the case may be, of treacherous secret murder, by forces that leave no trace, done against their dead kinsman. Over this wall of private suspicion public gift exchanges between the rifted places will follow when next harvest home sets a wide round of mourning ceremonial in operation between all the villages. The observer of such exchanges will see no friendly intermingling of the parties concerned, but a distance set and strictly maintained, distance in sitting arrangements and reserve or even hostility in manner. It is unlike ceremonial hostility as commonly found. There are no social forms of hostility, only very real private feeling of the type that cannot be discussed in public. Moreover, the kin of the widow or widower pay to release their kinsman from mourning durance. They do not obtain a fair gift of equal value in exchange. But when later the survivor dies the balance in gift exchange will be redressed by the kin of the earlier dying party to the marriage reversing the arrangement. There will, however, be no one of their number to mourn the survivor at his (or her) death as he (or she) mourned his (or her) predecessor in death. The forces of murder that are suspected between the villages are sorcery and witchcraft.

One marries into a village of enemies, witches, and sorcerers, some of whom are known to have killed or to be the children of those known to have killed members of one's own village. The night divides the villages—apart from love-making, a hundred yards is as far as a thousand or ten thousand for all practical purposes. Even roaming for love-making should be done while the night is still young. In the dark spaces between the villages the agents of death roam—the death-dealing spirits of the women and men of all other villages, witches and sorcerers all. This village parochiality, cut off from all other villages by the great fear of the terrors of the night, a child grows up in. It is never forgotten. Later, in sentiment, the land of the village of birth and upbringing is felt as own land with a completeness of feeling probably deeper than that of our own landed families. In Dobu it is two villages by residence—but marriage with the father's village occurs very rarely. The feeling of strangeness in the village of marriage remains unaltered.

The boys who go out for love-making then, go out with great boldness into a night filled with terrors. They are usually supported by a good conscience in that they have not given offence to the adults of other villages, a fact not so true of their parents. Nevertheless, they go into dangerous territory, for it is well known that in matters of sorcery and witchcraft native vengeance may visit the sins of the fathers, mothers, and mother's brothers upon the children down the generations.

The terrors of the night are very real in Dobu. Blood-curdling shrieking breaks the silence of the night or the small hours of the morning fairly often in the villages, and more often than not the inmates of the terrified house are sick, listless, and stay at home next day.

In imagination, then, we can to some extent reconstruct the feelings of the youth caught definitely and finally in a strange village. Probably like Kinosi, my house boy, he remembers vividly a scare of his childhood when he went to stay a while with relatives afield. Iyem, Kinosi's younger brother, was better developed physically than Kinosi, despite his comparative youth. But Kinosi while yet a small child went to visit a strange place. The woman of the house he stayed in was a powerful witch. She swallowed Kinosi whole and passed him out whole through her anus. Kinosi's growth suffered thereafter, and his younger brother grew better than he. Strange places are places where nightmare is reality.

Accordingly the youth feels respect and fear for the powerful old witch, his mother-in-law, as she sits blocking the exit of her house where he has lain with her daughter. Under the staring ordeal of the strangers, many of them sorcerers and witches far feared, he feels respect and no little awe. They are Owners here and he a stranger, one of Those-resulting-from-marriage, hereafter in this place. When his mother-in-law gives him the digging-stick he goes off most obediently to dig a garden. So the economic system lays firmer hold of a boy than ever it did before. Now he is responsible to his relatives-in-law as well as to his own kin and his work is doubled at a stroke.

He begins at once to avoid the personal names of the owners

in the girl's village. He cannot eat or drink in the sight of any one of the owners until he is finally married. Before this takes place he must satisfy his future mother-in-law and father-in-law that he has a good garden, and he must work with them in their gardens. He continues to sleep with his betrothed regularly at night, but during the day he avoids her village unless he is specifically asked to enter it with gifts for his betrothed's kin.

Early in the morning he goes from her village with her father and mother to garden. The three work ; then about ten o'clock her mother cooks a little food in the garden and the elders, husband and wife, eat together. The unfortunate future son-in-law cannot eat or drink in the presence of his future parents-in-law. He goes on working, hungry and tired. Let the anthropologist speak to a parent-in-law while the affair is still at this stage, and the old man guffaws most merrily at the miserable predicament of his future son-in-law. He is so very hungry—guffaw—but he cannot eat—guffaw—he digs and digs and digs most earnestly and strongly—guffaw. To the Dobuan father-in-law it is a most humorous and highly appreciated situation. But the young man gets away about noon, hungry, hot, and weary, and escapes to his own village to satisfy his needs.

When he is not working for his parents-in-law to be, the youth is working with his own kin to accumulate the food and gifts that must be exchanged between the villages against the marriage. Then when, after a year's betrothal or longer all is prepared, the marriage takes place. The groom's relatives take a gift of ornamental valuables, arm rings of white shell and necklaces of red shell, to the bride's relatives. The bride's mother receives the gift and distributes it to her kin. She and her female relatives then go to the groom's village and formally sweep it throughout. At the same time they take a big gift of uncooked food, and after they have swept the village and given away most of this uncooked food, they cook some of the food which they retained for the purpose in the groom's village, give it to the groom's kin and receive a smaller gift of cooked food from the groom's kin.

Next day the groom's kin carry a big gift of uncooked food to the bride's village, give it to the bride's kin, cook a small part of it in the bride's village and give it to the bride's kin, and receive a smaller gift of cooked food from the bride's kin.

The bride's mother formally puts some food of her cooking

into the groom's mouth. Bride and bridegroom sleep in the house of the groom's parents for the first time. Next day the groom's mother prepares food and formally puts some of it in the bride's mouth. The pair are now married. Marriage is merely economic exchanges between groom's kin and bride's kin, and the groom eating food in the presence of his mother-in-law in her village for the first time, and the bride eating food in the presence of her mother-in-law in her mother-in-law's village for the first time.

During the betrothal period the youth often gave gifts of betel nut to his parents-in-law to be, but nothing further except gardening service.

The interesting point about the marriage validation is that the exchanges are made between villages organized in *susu* formation. The initial gift of armshells and shell necklace is presented by the youth, his mother and her sisters and brothers, and his own sisters and brothers. It is received by the bride's mother and distributed to her brothers and sisters, and sister's children. So also are the gifts of food exchanged. At one of these exchanges the owners of the village sit at the far end of their village. The distaff kin of the groom or bride who are the visitors bringing gifts sit at the end of the village nearest their own village. A wide space in between separates the two parties. There is no casual intermingling between the parties. Every woman present is with her brother. Every man present is with his sister and sister's children. No group of man, wife, and child is to be seen in either of the exchanging parties. Fathers-in-law are out of it, as are all of Those-resulting-from-marriage in either village. It is strange to a European to look on a marriage ceremonial which is celebrated with an entire absence of anyone in a family-by-marriage group. All marriage ceremonial, at its inception and later, however, is marked by a complete disappearance of the marital grouping. After dusk, when the day's ceremonial is ended, husbands come back to their wives and children. All day they were with their sisters and sisters' children, if they belonged to either of the contracting villages. If they did not belong to the contracting villages they either visited their sisters afield, or else formed male parties with other purely masculine business in view.

Each marriage is cemented by periodic exchanges of food between the owners of the contracting villages, one or two big inter-village feasting exchanges in the name of each marriage every season, and many smaller exchanges confined more to the true *susu* of the married parties rather than to all the *susu* of the villages concerned.

" Those-resulting-from-marriage " when they rejoin their spouses in the evening after the latter have been engaged all day in an inter-village feasting exchange in conjunction with brother or sister and sister's child, find plenty of food left over in the house. Officially they have no right to take part in the ceremony, but quite unofficially if plenty of the finest food is found ready cooked about the hut in the evening they are allowed to eat of it.

Marriage is forbidden—

(1) Between owners of the village.
(2) Between cross-cousins.

Marriage between owners of the village leads to severe coughing spasms in the offending pair, and much indignation, scorn, and ridicule heaped upon the offenders by their kin. It occurs very rarely. A few rare spirits have done it, however, warding off the danger of coughing spasms by strong magic, enduring the initial indignation and scorn of their kin, and bribing their kin back into a state of goodwill or at least toleration with heavy bribes. The few marriages of this type that I saw seemed to be the most enduring in Dobu. The spouse is not a resultant-of-marriage in an inferior position to protest against adulterous incest. Besides the joy in adulterous incest is considerably gone when marriage is incestuous, itself a greater adventure. Bickering did occur in one or two of these marriages. One man left his wife four times. But four times he came back to her and to her alone. She was in his village. How could he escape from her ? There is none of the *élan* in escape as in escape from marriage afield.

> "Now God be thanked that roads are long and wide
> And four far havens in the scattered sky."

Nothing of that—only

" It would be hard to meet you and pass by "—and even harder than meeting and passing by in a Dobuan village would be to introduce a new wife into a village where one had been married to an owner, and to have the new wife meet the old and pass by. It could not be done without bloodshed.

Accordingly the rare marriages between owners endure. But very few men can win their kin round to tolerating and licensing such incestuous marriage. Again, many persons may not fall in love with those with whom they commit village " incest ".

In all cross-cousin marriage a Boundary Man, male or female, would marry into a father's village, boundary man marrying cross-cousin owner. But since boundary man is not allowed in a dead father's village, he or she must not marry there while his or her father is still living for fear of future trouble with the rule of alternate village residence. Moreover, cross-cousin owner inherits food and food resources which boundary man cannot eat. Thus cross-cousin marriage would lead to boundary man violating the tabu on his entering his dead father's village. The tabus restricting inheritance within the *susu* operate against boundary man, the disinherited, marrying into the *susu*. The disinherited is given no back stairs entrance into the inheritance.

Marriage of two or three matrilineal kindred into the same village is discouraged. The sight of it is said to be ugly by those who are not involved in it. We may take the case of a woman X and her brother Y (an actual case) in illustration. Let (a) be their village and (c) be the village into which the woman X has married. A girl of (c) village wishes to marry Y. Y consults with X. He is drawn to the girl and rather wishes to marry her—she unswervingly and directly wishes to marry him. (A man or woman must always consult his or her matrilineal kin before marrying—neglect to do so provokes long-standing hostility.) X is thoroughly and completely opposed to it. She points out that if her husband's mother's brother kills a pig in (c) village and sends it to (a) for her relatives to eat, their (X's and Y's) mother's brother must distribute it. If Y is to get his share a part of the pig must be sent back to (c), the village whose present it is. This will be offensive to the people of (c), the owners of the village where she and her brother will be resident strangers. Her husband's mother's brother cannot cut off Y's share and give it to him in village (c), for the gift has to go from mother's brother of one spouse to mother's brother of the other spouse—and the latter alone decides whether it is to be eaten (in which case a return gift will be given later) or whether it is to be sent on to another village (d), where another of his maternal nephews or nieces has married, in which case the return gift will come from the resources of (d), through (c) to (a). So, also, of all the numerous gifts between affinal relatives. Y sees that these conditions would not conduce to the best relations between him and his proposed affinal relatives and he abandons the prospect of marrying the girl of the village of his sister's relatives in law. All brothers, in such a case, are not so dutiful, however. It is quite true that the economic exchanges may be hampered by such parallel marriages of matrilineal kindred as that proposed by X's brother. Sentiment is opposed to *ai epwepwopwo* as such marriage is termed. It may be that the root of the matter is that no one wishes to recommend his or her set of affinal relatives to a kinsman. One marriage only tends to make enough trouble between two villages in case of estrangement.

Marriage with other villages of the same totem is feebly discouraged, or at least it is deprecated by a majority who are not at the moment involved in it. A considerable minority are so married. Such marriage is called by the same term as that used for marriage within the circle of the owners of the village, *ai lokubuna*, " incestuous marriage." But it is only *ai lokubuna* within the same village that meets with serious hostility. If it is with another village of the same totem it is passed over.

Apart from these restrictions and impediments marriage is free for inclination in most cases. The youths try sex relationships with a wide circle of girls and finally settle on a choice of their own desire. Equality in age of youth and maiden is held to be desirable. In a small minority of cases parents betroth their children while they are still young, sometimes before puberty, for economic reasons. A family of outstanding gardeners may betroth its child to the child of a similarly rich family. In these cases the children are supposed to be faithful to each other after puberty when the wide circle of free love opens to most children. But the great majority of families strike such a dead level of riches or poverty that there would be no point in child betrothal except fear of entanglement with the few wastrel families. This fear is not strongly enough felt to limit the freedom of most of the youths and girls in practice.

The term free love is not altogether accurate. There is not necessarily love in it as we understand love. The youths sleep with the girls in the first place because it is the custom to deny them houseroom at home. They play jews' harps outside the houses of other villages until in one house a girl asks who the seranader is. She tells him to go away or else to come in, as she wishes. Sometimes a boy does not know anything of the girl who so admits him. Kinosi, my personal " boy ", once

told me how he found himself in a strange house. Luckily
he had matches. He struck one to have a look at the girl. Her
skin was covered with the scales of ringworm. He immediately
fled from the house. When a boy and a girl make stronger
preferences later, it is of their own inclination, however, and
in some cases their preferences are so contrary to their parents'
wishes or to the restrictions on marriage that I have mentioned
above, that they actually do make mesalliances in the teeth of
public opinion. These cases show that there is much real love
in Dobuan courtship, even if there is little or no romanticism.

III

TOTEMISM

The first reliable records of Dobuan population show that
there was an average of twenty-five persons, men, women, and
children, in each village. A group of neighbouring villages
forms a local unit with a local name. This local unit I propose
to call the locality. The locality numbers from four to twenty
villages. It is on terms of permanent hostility with other
localities. It is a unit that is for the most part endogamous.
In case a member of a locality is ill or dead the diviner or sorcerer
or witch does not divine a member of another locality as the
sorcerer or witch responsible for the trouble. The black art,
like marriage, keeps within the locality borders. War, on the
other hand, as opposed to more private black art feuds, was
carried on against other localities. Fighting to avenge sorcery
or witchcraft I class as private feud within the locality.

Dobuan population has now, after forty years of white
influence, missionary, trading, and government, dwindled to
where approximately twelve persons replace twenty-five.
(This is for Dobu Island ; in Tewara the case is worse ; other
places I do not know.) During this time there has been no war,
and open murder in private feuds has been detected and
punished. But still the localities keep their old barriers—
without war. The locality is still endogamous. Divination of
sorcery and witchcraft still keeps within the locality borders.

The village consists of several *susu*, several women with
their children and their brothers. Many cannot show a
genealogical relationship, for a *susu* only knows its own

genealogy back for four generations at the most. Back of the fourth generation there is an ancestress common to all the *susu* of the village. This common ancestress is not a human being, but a bird. It is possible that the genealogies of the different *susu* of the village might meet if they were carried back far enough, but the fourth generation back is not enough.

My best account of such ancestry was derived from Alo of the Green Parrot village.

" Green parrot became pregnant. She laid an egg and brooded over it. It hatched forth—it appeared, not a bird, a human being. The child, a female, grew. The nest collapsed. It fell to the ground.

"The husband, child of the White Pigeon, was at sea fishing with nets. The woman, child of the Brown Eagle, his wife, walked the shore looking for shell fish. She heard the child wailing. She took it to her village and suckled it. There it grew up. It became a very beautiful woman. The woman child of Green Parrot married. She bore four children, two male, two female. Her children grew to adult stature. The two brothers married women of the White Pigeon village. The two sisters married men of the Brown Eagle village. These children said ' we are the children of Green Parrot '. They founded our Green Parrot village.

"The woman hatched from the egg of Green Parrot was named Bolapas. Bolapas bore the daughters, Negigimoia and Daloyos. Daloyos bore Dosi. Dosi bore my mother."

This legend uses the idea of the pre-existence of the White Pigeon's line and the Brown Eagle's line to account for the nurture of the Green Parrot line. The former two lines, of course, presuppose the pre-existence of others for their nurture. Thus the combined legends of all the Dobuan totemic lines make a most illogical system. No Dobuan bothers to institute comparisons, however. So no one ever finds out that the system as a whole is self-contradictory. Each totem knows its own legend and each *susu* knows its own ancestry. But no one knows the legends of other totems or the ancestry beyond a generation or two of other *susu*. If the dead of other *susu* are known their names must never be pronounced. Personal names are often names of common usage ; thus in Dobu Island and elsewhere a mat is called *sita*. In Tewara it was *kebana* because Sita was dead. In Dobu Island first fruits is *mweia*; in Tewara it is *bwanawe* because Mweia, the mother of my informant of the Green Parrot legend, was dead. In Dobu Island perspiration is *kamweai* ; in Tewara it was *kasitana* until I was given the name of the dead Kamweai whose hut site I built upon, when it became both *kasitana* and *kamweai* again.

There are from two to four names for almost everything ; and by reason of this words do not have to be coined. Some have to be avoided carefully. I used *mweia* once carelessly to the son of Mweia, referring to harvest first fruits, and he winced as if I had struck him. If it is done by a native, the descendant of the dead will rate the offender violently, *kokoa gote* " a corpse that ", and bitter and angry reproach followed (as I heard done but twice only, so careful are they). It will be remembered how all this precaution ensures that the name of the dead is inherited in use exclusively within the own *susu* of the dead. Each *susu* in the village of the Green Parrot has the same legendary account without the same personal names as those in the account given.

The native term for totem is the term for bird. Thus one stranger may ask another " what is your bird ? " I once asked a strange old lady this question and she went off into a voluble declaration to the effect that there were no birds for sale in the village. The fowls had not had chickens for a long time now, and so on. But she was the only person of the hundreds I met who so misunderstood me. She took me for a tyro in native custom, as white men in general are.

The legend of the bird does not cover Dobuan totemism completely. But the bird is most important and is referred to alone in naming a totemic affiliation. It, alone of the totems, is believed to be an ancestor.

The locality in Dobu Island is made up of villages arranged in order of approach as in the following examples :—

	Locality : Edugaura
Asatupe	White Pigeon
Weita	White Pigeon
Doiluia	White Pigeon with an adopted Sulphur-crested White Cockatoo infusion
Tutuwana	White Pigeon
Nimnim	Green Parrot
Losina	*Coriphilus fringillaceus*, a Parroquet
Ubunebune	White Pigeon
Sowarat	White Pigeon
Warauia	White Pigeon
Memweara	Green Parrot
Lowana	Green Parrot
Mulusi'ia	Green Parrot
'Asanedu	Green Parrot
Gaura	White Pigeon

Next to Edugaura comes a locality with the following village affiliations in order of approach :—

Locality : Wabuna
Coriphilus fringillaceus
Green Parrot
Brown Eagle
Coriphilus fringillaceus
Green Parrot
Crow
Crow
Brown Eagle
Crow
Crow
Coriphilus fringillaceus
Crow
Crow
Coriphilus fringillaceus
Coriphilus fringillaceus
Green Parrot
Brown Eagle
Coriphilus fringillaceus
Green Parrot
Crow

The next locality shows the following order :—

Locality : Omuri
Crow
Brown Eagle
Crow
Crow
Coriphilus fringillaceus
Crow
Crow
Coriphilus fringillaceus

Going from Edugaura on the side of the island opposite to that of Wabuna and Omuri localities we find in order :—

Coriphilus fringillaceus
Coriphilus fringillaceus
Brown Eagle
Crow
Crow
Brown Eagle

making the first locality.

The next locality, Enai'a, shows :—

Coriphilus fringillaceus
Brown Eagle
Brown Eagle
Brown Eagle
Brown Eagle
Brown Eagle
Crow
Green Parrot
Crow
Coriphilus fringillaceus

The next locality, Adanatu, gives :—

Kilakila (bird unidentified)
Crow
Crow
Crow
Crow
Crow
White Pigeon
White Pigeon
Crow
White Pigeon

These localities, six of the twelve in all that are on Dobu Island, are thus made up of the following totems :—

Edugaura		Wabuna		Omuri	
White Pigeon	8	Coriphilus fringil-		Crow	5
Green Parrot	6	laceus	6	Brown Eagle	1
Coriphilus fringil-		Green Parrot	4	Coriphilus fringil-	
laceus	1	Brown Eagle	3	laceus	2
		Crow	4		

and going away from Edugaura on the coastline opposite to Wabuna and Omuri :—

?		Enai'a		Adanatu	
Coriphilus fringil-		Coriphilus fringil-		Crow	6
laceus	2	laceus	2	White Pigeon	3
Brown Eagle	2	Brown Eagle	5	Kilakila	1
Crow	2	Crow	2		
		Green Parrot	1		

We see that Omuri on the south coast is a Crow stronghold, and Adanatu on the north coast separated from Omuri by the entire width of the Island, and by four hostile localities, is also a Crow stronghold. The locality is not a totemic unit. Several villages of the one totem tend to aggregate in any one locality. There is by no means the maximum of totemic differentiation in one locality. Thus Edugaura is strong in White Pigeon and in Green Parrot to the complete exclusion of Brown Eagle, Crow, Kilakila, Sulphur-crested Cockatoo. Omuri is strong in Crow to the exclusion of White Pigeon, Green Parrot, Kilakila, Sulphur-crested Cockatoo. But despite a tendency towards an aggregation of two or three totems in a locality, these same totems are usually represented in adjoining localities. Thus Edugaura was at war with its neighbour Wabuna, although Edugaura numbers five Green Parrot villages and Wabuna four Green Parrot villages. Green Parrot fought against Green Parrot. The boundary of Wabuna is beyond a Crow village which opposes a Crow village, the first village in Omuri as one leaves Wabuna. Here the locality boundary, the war boundary, passes between two Crow villages. The same thing occurs elsewhere. It is evident that the co-operating unit, the locality, is but partially totemically united. The totemic affiliation is not one of co-operation in war, except where several villages of the one totem are neighbours in a locality. In any case allies in war are other totems than one's own, enemies include some of one's own totem. The principle of alliance is geographical boundaries, not claim to common descent from the same bird ancestor.

Within the locality villages of the one totem may tend to aggregate near together as close neighbours but not absolutely. Edugaura is a good instance. In Wabuna on the other hand, villages of the one totem are as separated as in Edugaura they are aggregated. Enai'a shows an aggregation of Brown Eagle villages, Adanatu of Crow. This may be seen by a glance at the tables where the villages are in order of approach.

Since the locality is endogamous for the most part (a small minority of marriages go outside the locality nowadays), since some totems tend to concentrate in one locality, since the villages are small and divorce and remarriage frequent, it will be seen that it is reasonable that marriage with another village of the same totem should occur in a considerable number of cases, as it actually does.

Different villages of the same totem, whether they are in the same locality or not, all claim descent from the same bird ancestor, all possess the same validating legend, and all their members of the same generation use the terms brother and sister to one another. This terminology is one of courtesy, however, and occasions of courtesy between village members of different localities occur so rarely that they do not matter. Within the one locality the terminology is one of courtesy to members of other villages of the same totem. But members of one's own village are usually married into other villages of the same totem. Then one drops the brother-sister terminology and adopts the terms for affinal relatives used by one's kinsman married into those villages. The trend everywhere is to restrict the brother-sister, common descent terminology to *susu* of one's own village, and to adopt the affinal terminology of others who are members of one's own village to all other villages in the locality, or else to use the term *gosiagu*, my friend, freely within the locality, rather than the terms for brother and sister in the case of other villages of the same totem within the locality. This is the natural expression of the fact that the village is a co-operative unit, and Green Parrot village A of Edugaura locality co-operates no more with Green Parrot village B of the same locality, than it does with White Pigeon village C or Parroquet village D also of Edugaura. The village group is the unit, the extended limit of co-operation except in war. Green Parrot village A of Edugaura does not trust Green Parrot village B of Edugaura not to employ sorcery or witchcraft against it. It is the enemy with whom one marries whereas Green Parrot village Y of another locality is the enemy against whom one makes war. These enemies are different. The enemies with whom one makes war one does not trust far enough to marry among. One marries into one's allies in war, but suspicion of sorcery and witchcraft in practice goes where marriage goes. In theory the enemies with whom one makes war are also redoubtable sorcerers and witches, but one has nothing to do with them apart from war. Sorcery and witchcraft are believed to be innocuous at a distance. One does not put oneself in the power of those dreaded persons afar. But one is closeted with nearer strangers by marriage ties outside the village, within the locality. Here one is in strangers' power. Here in practice evil work in the black art is suspected.

Each village has a set of linked totems, a bird ancestor, a fish, and a tree. Every person may make free with his or her own totemic objects, provided spouse or father is not also of the same totem. No person may eat the bird, eat the fish, or use the tree for firewood of the spouse's village ; no person may eat bird or fish or use the tree for firewood of the father's village. Deference is paid to the linked totems of a spouse even where they are also own totems, and deference is paid to the linked totems of the father, even where they are also own totems (i.e. mother's totems before one).

IV

TERMINOLOGY OF RELATIONSHIP

It has become one of the best known facts in anthropology that the use of terms in reckoning relationship normally mirrors social custom. This fact is very aptly demonstrated in Dobu. Two sets of terms are used from the point of view of the children and children's children, one when the formers' fathers are still living, one when the formers' fathers are dead. Thus Dobuan terminology depends largely on the life or death of that long-suffering outcast, the Dobuan father.

DOBUAN KINSHIP TERMS

Terms expressing blood relationships (without distortion due to inheritance)

II (as.)   *tubuna*, all members of the II generation ascendant and the II generation descendant, both sexes, either sex speaking.

I (as.)   *sinana*, all females of the I generation ascendant of one's own village.

wana, all males of the I generation ascendant of one's own village.

tamana, all males of the first generation ascendant of father's village.

kedeana or *yaiana*, all females of the first generation ascendant of father's village.

(ego)   *tasina*, own brothers (m.s.), and own sisters (w.s.), and parallel cousins of the same sex as the speaker.

nuuna, own sister (m.s.) and own brother (w.s.) and parallel cousins of opposite sex from the speaker.

nibana, cross cousins (m.s. and w.s.).

I (des.)   *natuna*, own children, children of parallel cousins and of cross-cousins of same sex as speaker (m.s. and w.s.).

wana, children of own sister, female parallel cousin and female cross cousin (m.s.).

kedeana, children of own brother, male parallel cousins, and male cross cousins (w.s.).

Affinal Terms

sinana, wives of all men of father's village first generation ascendant.

tamana, husbands of all the women, first ascendant generation of own village.

wana, husbands of all women, first ascendant generation of father's village.

kedana or *yaiyana*, wives of all men, first ascendant generation of own village.

tasina, wives of brothers and male parallel cousins and male cross cousin (m.s.), husbands of sisters, female parallel cousins, and female cross cousins (w.s.).

manena, wife or husband, spouse.

wana, children of wife's brothers, male parallel and male cross cousins (m.s.).

kedeana, children of husband's sisters, female parallel and female cross cousins (w.s.).

bwosiana, man ascendant generation in the village of wife, or in the village of the spouse of own brother or sister (m.s.).

lawana, female, ascendant generation in the village of wife, or of the spouse of own brother or sister (m.s.).

    Male or female ascendant generation in village of husband, or of spouse of own brother or sister (w.s.).

eiana, husband's sister, wife's brother, spouse of brothers and sisters and of cross and parallel cousins, such spouses being of the same sex as that of the speaker (m.s. and w.s.).

mono, male child in the village of spouse or in the village of spouse of own brother or sister, not called *wana* or *kedeana* (m.s. and w.s.).

neno, female child, as above.

After a man's death there is a change in the terminology used between his children and his heir and his heir's children. By the children, after the father's death, the heir of the father, the latter's sister's son, or sister's daughter's son, is called father, *tamana*, the heir's sister is called *kedeana*, father's sister, and their descendants are called by terms flowing from this distortion.

The children of a man called *tamana* in this fashion by his cross cousins are called *tasina* and *nuuna*. Since all the children of the men of a village are all Boundary Men to the same village this terminology may be cast into the Dobuan phrase " all who are Boundary Men to the same village are brother and sister of one another" (quite regardless of generation).

The children of a woman called *kedeana* or *yaiyana* in this fashion by her cross cousins may in exceptional cases be the direct heirs of their mother's mother's brother; this is provided they are of age to manage property and provided that their mother has no brother to keep the inheritance from them until his death. In such case they are *tamana* or *kedeana* according to sex to their mother's cross cousins. If this exceptional case does not occur, however, their mother's cross cousins usually term them *nibana*. Here usage is neither uniform nor consistent, however. Even Boundary Men cross cousins who call their female Owner cross cousins' children *nibana* teach their own children to call these *nibana*, their children's age mates, *tubuna*. This teaching would be consistent with the parents calling the same persons *tamana* and *kedeana*. This is actually done seldom.

Those who call their female Owner cross cousins' children *nibana* defend it on the grounds that it is reasonable to call their cross cousin who has inherited their father's personal name, father, and his sister, father's sister; that just as the children of such a *tamana* are *nuuna* and *tasina* so the children of such a *kedeana* should be *nibana* (as in the undistorted terminology before the father's death such a terminology follows); and finally that when the male cross cousin Owner dies and his personal name (originally their father's personal name), goes to the former's sister's son, then it is the correct time to call that heir father, and his sister father's sister. As for teaching their children to call their mother's mother's brother's daughter's children, grandparent, that is done because when children will be of age the necessary deaths to validate the terminology will have occurred.

The boundary man cross cousin usually allows his owner cross cousin's children the terms *yaiyana* (♀) and *tamana* (♂) if they were old enough to participate in the funerary feasts that immediately followed the death of his father—feasts given to an extended group of heirs, the chief heirs getting the best shares in this (*bwobwore* feast).

It is clearly felt by the Dobuan that the terms *tamana* and *sinana* primarily express ascendant generation, despite the fact that an age mate or a member of a descendant generation is called *tamana* and his wife *sinana* in case of the death of the true father. *Tama* and *sina* are common Oceanic terms for father and mother, and that is also the most deeply rooted meaning in Dobu ; similarly *tubu* for grandparent and grandchild reciprocally. This feeling of expression of generation difference in the terms is apparently so strong in Dobu that the kinship terminology reluctantly assumes a similar form to that found in the Crow Indians of the North American Plains, the Tshi of the West Coast of Africa and the Manus of the Admiralty Islands. A person referring to the village of his or her father's or mother's father will always say " village of my grandparents " and call everyone belonging to it, regardless of generation, *tubuna*.

Whereas age mates of the biological and true social father who are members of his village are all termed *tamana* by classificatory usage, age mates of the Owner cross cousin *tamana* who are members of his village are not called *tamana*. The range of the term is only extended as far as brothers who are descendants from a common grandmother, no further. Other cross cousins of the father's village are still called *nibana*. Only in the next generation the usage becomes classificatory with full village range. *Tubudi* (plural of *tubuna*) is a sign for an entire village regardless of generation of its members. Persons in this relationship have little to do with one another. Only the biological descent line of Boundary Men avoid the village of the Owners. The generation that first uses classificatory usage here is also the generation in which little notice is taken of the relationship and in which it drops from importance.

It will be clear, I think, from the custom of waiting for the death of the father, from the non-classificatory usage of the elevated terms in the first generation after the death of the father, from the way in which classificatory terminology is taught to the second generation possibly for the sake of simplicity, certainly not as marking any development of social interrelations, from the common Indonesian and common Oceanic use of the terms involved, and from frequent Dobuan statement, that in Dobu for certain the usage is distinctly one which expresses elevation of the inheriting group ; and that it cannot possibly be urged here that this system of terminology is one of neglecting generation differences in order to emphasize clan (or in this case village) solidarity. A man's sister's son in taking his mother's brother's name, is elevated in his *susu*. This is recognized not only by his *susu*, but also by his cross cousins.[1]

In Manus of the Admiralties, which is patrilineal and patrilocal, unit terminology for the female line is coupled with a belief that the female line has superior supernatural power gained from the family ghosts. The members of this group have no ceremonial or formal meeting. They live separately scattered. There is little evidence of anything but an ideal solidarity, in the Platonic usage of that term. Accordingly, if elevation is not the point in Manus, but expression of group solidarity, it is a blood kin that does not function as a group ever that has secured such recognition. On the other hand, there is no such evidence for elevation as in Dobu. It would appear to be possible that just as personal names, skulls of the dead, land, and other property and magic may be inherited in favour of one line of descent rather than another, as in Dobu, supernatural power in Manus and physiological theory may be divided so as to favour now one line, now the other, as in the Trobriands as has been ably shown by Dr. B. Malinowski (a discovery that I can confirm by my independent investigation) ; so elevation in relationship terminology may be cast into the scales for recognition. I do not wish to urge that this is true for other parts of the world, but only that such a degree of integrated development has occurred in Dobu.

In Dobu a different disregard of generation occurs in a terminology used within the circle of village owners. This is a purely optional usage, however, and differs in being such from the obligatory disregard between cross cousins after the death of the father of the one, mother's brother of the other. A lad sometimes calls his mother's mother's brother *tasina* brother, a girl sometimes calls her mother's mother *tasina* sister. In one case I knew the optional usage was clearly shown. When the mother's mother's brother began teaching

---

[1] An heir does not have to marry his predecessor's widow in order to secure ascendant generation kinship terminology from the widow's children. Inheritence of a name may be closer identification than inheritance of a mere resultant-from-marriage.

the boy magic the term changed from *tubuna* to *tasina*. Formality with a second ascendant generation person who is a village Owner is expressed by *tubuna*—all three grand-parents and their brothers and sisters who are not village Owners are nothing else than *tubuna* possibly. Here it is possible and necessary to infer an expression of solidarity within the clan, but only between grandparents and grand-children who are bonded also by common village allegiance.

Looking at these terms from another point of view we see that the terms used for younger generations flow from the terms used for the first ascending generation (before the death of the father).

FIRST ASCENDING GENERATION

Tamana	. .	Man, owner in father's village.
		Man, marrying into mother's village.
Sinana .	. .	Woman, owner in mother's village.
		Woman, marrying into father's village.
Wana	. .	Man, owner in mother's village.
		Man, marrying into father's village.
Yaiana (kedeana)	.	Woman, owner in father's village.
		Woman, marrying into mother's village.

These terms specify ascendant generation and sex of person spoken of or to. They do not distinguish between owners in one parents' village and those-resulting-from-marriage in the other parent's village. These two classes are " lumped ".

In ego's generation—

Tasina .	• .	Sibling of same sex as the speaker being a child of *tamana* and *sinana*.
		Person of opposite sex who has married a child of *tamana* or *sinana*.
Nuuna	. .	Sibling of opposite sex from the speaker being child of *tamana* and *sinana*.
Nibana .	. .	Children of *wana* and *kedeana*.

These terms specify ego's generation. The sex of both person speaking and person spoken to is obscure from the terminology as such, i.e. since the terms flow from the ascendant generation primarily they do not retain further specific indication of sex in their own right. They distinguish children of *tamana* and *sinana* from children of *wana* and *kedeana*. They do not, it may be observed, distinguish children of the *susu* from children outside the *susu*. *Nuuna* may be the child of true father's brother, i.e. of a male owner of father's generation in father's village, possibly of a remotely related *susu* to the *susu* of the father. Or *nuuna* may be the child of the opposite sex from one's own mother's womb. Similarly in the first ascendant generation *sinana* may be one's own mother, or a woman of another village altogether, married to a male owner of father's generation in father's village possibly of a *susu* remotely related to the *susu* of the father.

In the first descending generation we find—

Natuna	.	.	Child of *tasina* (m.s. and w.s.).
			Child of male *nibana* (m.s.).
			Child of female *nibana* (w.s.).
Yaiyana (Kedeana)	.		Child of *nuuna* (w.s.).
			Child of male *nibana* (w.s.).
Wana	.	.	Child of *nuuna* (m.s.).
			Child of female *nibana* (m.s.).

The latter two terms are reciprocal. The reciprocal of *natuna* is *sinana* to a woman, *tamana* to a man. Here the children of *nibana* are treated as are the children of *tasina* and *nuuna*—exactly. The sex of the person spoken to is again obscure. Only in the first ascendant generation is it clear. Some of the children called *natuna* and *wana* are in the speaker's *susu*, some are of other *susu* of the speaker's village, some are of the speaker's father's village, some again are of the villages the speaker's father's sons have married into.

The first ascending and first descending generation are reciprocally *tubuna* to each other.

It will be apparent that we have here a simple bilateral system of reckoning relationship. There are not special terms to demarcate the line of *susu* descent from other lines outside the *susu*. Persons marrying into the father's village acquire the terminology proper to owners in mother's village, and vice-versa, and the terms applied to later generations flow from this terminology used for the first ascendant generation. The child of a brother and child of a sister use a special term to each other, where children of brothers do not, and children of sisters do not. But the child of a man drops this distinction in speaking to the child of the child of his father's sister provided his father is not dead.

After the death of the father the terminology is applied to express the distinction between the non-inheriting line of descent and the inheriting line by an especial warping. The terms used specify generation more clearly than they specify anything else as used before the death of the father. The terms used in the warping bear the same relationship to one another as they do in the unwarped system, *kedeana's* husband is still *wana*, her child still *nibana* and so throughout. Here in this warping is an effective adaptation of a bilateral terminology to the unilateral stress, the casting of a system not suited to unilateral stress into the form of that stress.

In the following sections I continue to discuss kinship in terms of its functioning. This treatment demands more space than a purely formal statement. Consequently certain terms that imply distant relationship and that mark off degrees of distance within the system are not raised until Sections VI and VII.

V

Functioning of the System

We have already seen that Dobuan relationship hinges upon a conflict between the *susu* and the marital grouping in regard to inheritance and in their clash of incompatible solidarities. Husband and wife belong to different villages. The village makes its own solidarity by sharing in a common inheritance and by all its constituent *susu* pooling their wealth to help the economic affairs of any one *susu*. Marriage is created and sustained by economic exchanges between two contracting villages. Hence if a member of any one village is to marry any member of another village, if a man *x* is to marry a woman *y*, *x* is dependent on all the *susu* of his village for help in providing the heavy economic burden he must bear, and *y* is dependent on all the *susu* of her village for help in providing the heavy exchange burden that she must bear. By virtue of the village having paid for a marriage the village exercises a controlling interest in the marriage. People who are outside a marriage do not consider that it is not their business to interfere. On the contrary they have a right to interfere. Did they not pay for the marriage ? Hence a marriage must keep the approval of two villages to endure. Village solidarity further is expressed in the belief that disease and death amongst its constituent *susu* are not caused by its various *susu* members but by persons of other village allegiance, particularly persons with whom the village is connected by marriage—strangers introduced into the village or their kin in other villages. Village members are friends. Other villages are not to be trusted, although they must be married into.

In all the elements that make up village solidarity there is a disruptive element for marital solidarity ; a father can leave little to his children, a man is partly dependent on his village's toleration of his wife, a wife is partly dependent on her village's

toleration of her husband, and trust of village mates is the
obverse of distrust of mates from other villages (the former
" mates " being brother-sister or *tasina* and *nuuna*, the latter
mates being husband and wife).

This last fact comes into relief when a man speaks of a
divorced wife as Alo did to me of his divorced wife Bobo.
" Every morning I awakened weak in body, sometimes ill.
She had been engaging in witchcraft while I lay asleep. Her
witch double had crossed over my body as I lay asleep, going
out the doorway and away through the air on its witch errands.
Did I believe that she lay within my hut beside me ? But there
was only the empty skin of her beside me. She, the essential
she, was off and far away. So it came, my weakness, my
infirmity. I divorced her. Emu (one of Alo's village ' sisters ',
descendant from a common great-grandmother) came and sat
by my side while I was yet married to Bobo. She said : ' In
a little while let us marry, we two.' I thought of the witchcraft
of Bobo, of my morning infirmities. I said : ' In a little while
let it be as you have said.' "

Alo came to live with Emu. It was against the Dobuan
code—marriage within the village. Alo's brothers and kin
not only refused to sanction it, but two of his blood brothers,
both younger than he, deserted the village in anger. They
lived away for a few months. Alo ultimately bribed them into
coming back and not protesting further. The marriage was
accorded no economic validation as Alo's kin could not be asked
for help, and anyway Emu had no true kin surviving.

Bobo several times sounded a challenge on a shell trumpet
from her village a quarter of a mile away. Each time Emu and
a village " sister " or two answered the insulting summons.
They set out for Bobo's village. There a duel with throwing
of big stones and close quarter attack with large knives ensued
between the principals, Bobo and Emu. The men did not
interfere until blood was drawn. Then they stopped the fight,
aided by the fact that the formidable principals were feeling
more satisfied. Wounds comparable to those of a severe
German students' duel were inflicted first. I was lured in
another direction before I realised the situation. Another
time I was away overseas getting my stores and mails. The
feud began before I came to the area.

In this series of events we see a further dramatization of
the frequent refrain in the folk-lore. A man commits incest
with his village " sister ", and makes trouble between himself

and his wife, or trouble between her and her husband, and that with impunity, since he enlists all the forces of village solidarity against marriage solidarity. In this case village solidarity was itself somewhat shaken since the affair deepened into incestuous marriage. But for an incestuous episode merely, the injured husband or injured wife can look for no breach in village solidarity if he or she objects publicly. Such objection often means divorce.

Some two weeks after one of the Bobo-Emu duels, Bobo had recovered from her wound. It had healed cleanly. But she fell ill of a wasting disease, until she was mere bone with skin folded loosely over it, unable to eat or even to speak. The island expected her death any minute. I dosed her with chlorodyne when I discovered her condition, and she pulled up and recovered on a rice and jam diet. Meanwhile I said to my personal boys within my own house : " But who has bewitched Bobo ? Recently she fought with Emu." Immediately my boys were viciously corrective of me with the heaviest disapproval they ever showed me. " What if Alo (Emu's husband) were to hear this ? He would never speak to you again. Do you want to lose your main helper ? That is the thing that is never done—to *kawawerebana*, talk specifically of witchcraft and infer the witch. Haven't you any sense ? "

In point of fact a diviner was called in from sixteen miles away. He divined the name of the witch who was responsible for Bobo's serious condition, and left the island immediately for his overseas home, without making the result of the divining public. Privately he gave the result to Bobo's own mother. The diviner, supported by his prestige, himself acted most cautiously. My personal boys knew that I, like a fool, was rushing in without any power of divination by magic where a diviner himself feared to tread.

It is a most serious insult to refer to a woman's witchcraft so that her husband will hear of it. Of women of other villages with whom and with whose husbands one is not involved in personal relationships, statements of their witchcraft run freely. But no nearer home than that.

Even in cases where the diviner acts more bravely than in the Bobo case, divines his witch and beards her, charging her with it, it is gross insult for any person to refer to the event afterwards so that the woman's husband will hear of the reference.

The insult is only the more serious because it refers to a

matter the husband does not believe to be untrue. It touches him on a nervous spot as is seen in Alo's account of his married life with Bobo. Persons of other villages are freely whispered to be witches in confidences between the owners of the village, until one owner marries into the family of such notorious witch-women. Then the confidences must cease. The whole affective feeling connected with such facts remain. But to stir it up is deep insult.

Togo was the greatest wastrel in the island of Tewara. He had been brought there from Kelologea of northern Normanby Island, an orphan, and in Tewara fifty miles overseas he was adopted. He was taken into the local village of the White Pigeon clan.

In Tewara he proved to be an unfortunate acquisition. I knew him as a beetle-browed small man, inordinately lazy and quarrelsome, of lower than average intelligence, and without enough pride to hide his flinching at bodily pain when I doctored a leg-sore with bluestone. He must have been over thirty years of age. Four wives had left him. His fifth wife, Ile, was a handsome woman, younger than he, of fine light skin colour. Her mother's brother was Alo, head man of Kubwagai village and easily the most outstanding man of the four villages of Tewara.

The couple, Togo and Ile, lived alternate years in the White Pigeon village of Togo's adopted *susu* kin, and in Kubwagai, the Green Parrot village of Ile's *susu* kin.

When I knew the pair they were living in Kubwagai village of the Green Parrot folk. (This was also my village. There I had been given the land and the personal name of a Green Parrot man of an earlier generation who had died without any sister's children as heirs. One of the children, a woman, lived in another village, her mother's. She could not come into the Green Parrot village of her dead father. When I met her afield she called me " my father ", I called her " my child ", as I had succeeded to her father's estate. In this I behaved to her and she to me as is the custom between the child of the dead and the heir of the dead, although I was not the ordinary heir, the dead sister's son.)

At the time of my residence in Kubwagai, Ile was tired of her marriage to Togo. Togo became aware of this and resorted to desperate tactics to try to keep her. In private he threatened that if Ile left him he would kill her blood brother, Kinosi, by sorcery. Ile immediately told her mother's brother, Alo, of the threat. Her brother, Kinosi, was away at the time. Adjoining Alo's house was the house of Magile, an owner of village land and trees, where she lived with her husband Yogalu and her six children. Her eldest child was named Kinosi. He was not Ile's blood brother, only a lad of the same name. He cooked my food, cleaned my hut, and did my errands. Associated with Kinosi in this work was 'Inosi, Alo's cross-cousin, who had come from his far removed village to work for me in Kubwagai.

Magile overheard Ile's alarm. Village huts are close together and sound travels as easily as between close packed tables in a public restaurant. Kinosi and 'Inosi, my personal "boys", came to me pale with fear. Magile had not heard aright and the rumour had travelled falsely. They informed me that Togo was plotting to kill them by sorcery. I had a very difficult situation to meet. 'Inosi was determined to flee to Sanaroa, an island twelve miles away, immediately, and threatened, intermittently with his expression of panic, to put an end to Togo by his own sorcery. Kinosi was too terrified for constructive planning. 'Inosi stated that Togo was responsible for the deaths of his brother's wife's brothers. Everyone believed that Togo by sorcery or by poisoning them had killed them in quick succession. It was fully two hours before an unnatural whiteness of the two dark-skinned faces passed, they crouching within my hut the while. Finally they were relieved by learning that it was another Kinosi that was being threatened.

That evening Alo with Ile beside him lectured Togo in a sharp harangue of the short half spitting sentences with a good pause in between them that is usual on such occasions. The village kin sat in a circle about Alo without speaking. Yogalu, who was also of the White Pigeon village, and Togo's kinsman, stayed apart looking respectful and almost demonstratively unobtrusive. Togo listened without speaking, and without being seen or heard left the village in fear that the well considered biting lecture on his laziness, his unfair treatment of Ile, his lack of co-operation in village work, his bad gardening, and his inimical attitude towards the clan he had married into might turn suddenly into violence. Alo felt violent for the clear reason that bringing a man to book in a society where sorcery flourishes is playing with the most dangerous fire. But Alo as headman and most accomplished sorcerer in the place was more above fear than anyone, and his biting lecturing of delinquents took place several times during my stay in his village. A few days later Togo was back again from the White Pigeon village to Ile. But Ile was often to be seen with her mother's brother, Alo, with complaint against her husband Togo. Finally Togo struck her within their hut. Instantly she was with Alo and her village kin, and before any words could pass Togo was off in full flight to the White Pigeon village.

The next phase was some three weeks later. Togo was back in Ile's house in Kubwagai. Ile was out talking quietly with her kin. 'Inosi heard rattling noises in the night in Ile's house and cut Togo down before he had had time to kill himself by hanging. Ile lived with him thereafter, but deceiving him, for Alo had ruled that when the canoes went north shortly Ile was to be taken away to stay with relatives in the Amphlett Islands overseas. Togo was not informed of this plan.

Sago making for the canoes to carry on an extended northern trip went on apace, every man, woman, and child, except the oldest and infirm people, working from dawn to dusk and sleeping beside their work under rough improvised shelters by the foul sago swamp. Togo, however, did no work. The sago was brought home with two nights of dancing. Some of it was used in a feast in which Green Parrot and White Pigeon exchanged gifts of cooked food to celebrate the growth of a child of a White Pigeon woman by a Green Parrot father, Alo's brother. Togo took part in the feasting.

Then the canoes were filled with sago and the party of men set out for the north. Alo embarked Ile in his canoe. Togo alone of the men of the island was left at home with the women, a wastrel without his supply of sago for the trip. Suddenly realizing that Ile was missing he rushed to the shore as the canoes were about a hundred yards out to sea. There he set up the wail for the dead. Alo, unable to stand the spectacle, and a little afraid that Togo might be more of a nuisance as a suicide than he was living, contemptuously told Ile to swim back to shore. She swam.

The relationship of Alo to Ile and of Ile to Togo is one that throws into relief the major forces in Dobuan social organization. The mother's brother rules and directs, his nephew or his niece obeys. A husband seriously angry with his wife will insult or threaten her relatives. She will inform her relatives, her mother's brother or her brother immediately. Her kin as a united body will then intimidate her husband. The husband's claim on his wife then is lost unless he asserts it by attempted suicide, when he awakens pity and contempt in her kin. They tell her to stand by him lest he kill himself. She, on her part, does what her elders and kinsmen tell her to do, even although she does not care greatly if her husband kills himself or no, and in fact might prefer it did he succeed in his suicide. Her kinsfolk are motivated by the consideration of preserving good relations with the kin and the village of the would-be suicide, who will not blame the suicide, but the suicide's relatives-in-law.

A woman in Ile's case often commits adulterous incest with a village brother of more removed relationship. The reaction of the husband to such action by his wife is always predictable. He packs up his belongings and leaves. It is the only final way of getting rid of him. He cannot by native ideas of morality, live with his wife any longer. In the old days he might try to spear his wife's incestuous seducer. If he succeeded he began a feud between himself and his kin on the one hand and the kin of his former wife and the kin of his wife's village seducer on the other. More often the husband just left without violence. He had his wife's banded village to contend against ; for the entire village of his wife support both her and her " brother " in incest—as long as it is incest between fairly well removed relatives, and not marriage. I did not see Ile's marriage proceed to this stage. There is a regular thrust and parry procedure, however. The person wishing to maintain the marriage against the person wishing to dissolve it usually attempts suicide, usually fails to make it fatal, usually awakens pity and a contemptuous maintenance of the marriage. The person wishing to dissolve it may rely on village " incest " to break it up finally.

I saw more of the process in the case of Sina and Toni. Toni, the man, was informed by his kin of secret advances made to Sina by a village " brother " of hers. No more was proved than that the " brother " was soliciting " incest ". There was no proof that Sina had courted it. She did not tell Toni of the advances, however. No Dobuan woman will tell her husband of such a matter. In consequence, if the husband discovers anything, he always blames his wife for it, and he always suspects that the affair has gone to the limit. Toni cast the slur upon Sina which cannot be cast without carrying definite intention of desire for divorce with it. He said in fury : " Go, slut ; go copulate with the bush boars." Sina reacted as every proud Dobuan woman must under such insult. She took the strongest vegetable poison known to the Dobuans, the root of a species of derris, which is used to stun fish. It does not kill in the great majority of cases, although in some cases it does. Toni had followed Sina to the bush where she had fled. The village came hue and cry after Toni, caught him just as he was in the act of swallowing derris root also, dashed it from his hands, overpowered him, and watched him all that night.

I gave an emetic to Sina and got the poison out of her. The native emetics had been tried previously and had failed miserably. As she lay groaning in her hut that night I was summoned out again at about two a.m. Toni, despite his watchers, had succeeded in swallowing some root or other, not derris root but another. It did him no harm actually, probably being one of the many roots which are currently believed to be poisonous in Dobu, but which are really not so. I had given my last supply of emetics to Sina, so Toni got nothing but strong tea.

Two days after, the pair were together again. Their relatives stressed the need of it, lest one or the other attempt suicide again. Sina's father had died by self-inflicted derris poisoning before her.

A third case of serious marital disagreement that I saw was between Nela and Kopu. This happened in Kubwagai as did also the case of Togo and Ile. Nela was Magile's eldest daughter by her first husband, whom Yogalu, her present husband, had killed. One day when Kopu was away fishing, Nela had her hair cut in the village by 'Inosi, Alo's cross-cousin and my " boy " (my sister's son by native terminology inasmuch as he worked in my service as a native lad does for his mother's brother, the only relative who has him to command). Now the care of the hair is a reciprocal service between husband and wife. It is closely connected with intercourse. An adulterer will louse or cut the hair of the woman he has committed adultery with if he wishes to make the matter public and defy the woman's husband. Nela evidently wished to make trouble for Kopu. Kopu came home, went into a rage, but hardly earlier than Yogalu, Nela's foster father. The first indication I had of trouble was a raging yell from Yogalu at the top of his voice, a shout of " penis dripping with semen you ". Kopu retorted with " I'm done with all of you ". Yogalu replied with " We're done with you ".

Kopu flung out of the village in a rage and home to his own village of the Brown Eagle folk. An hour or two later his sister appeared in Kubwagai, claimed and took away Kopu's property. After dark Kopu came into my hut and sulked in a corner for hours while I wrote. Finally he expressed a wish that a white man's schooner would drop anchor. He would go to work for the white man far away. He went home to his Brown Eagle village. The two brothers of Nela who had been watching for Kopu's departure then came in, and expressed a wish to go away to work for the white man immediately. Their sister had lost her man. They would now have to work in her garden, and already they were weary from too much gardening. Had I been a recruiter of native labour here were offers worth pounds to me. Naturally I declined to have anything to do with making money from the situation, as they thought I might do. Later on Kopu came back to Nela.

Sati was a strong, aggressive widow of Dilikaiai, the White Pigeon village. During my stay in Kubwagai, Kisi, Alo's younger brother, made advances to Sati. Children observed, and reported that he had been seen going to Sati's garden. That meant adultery necessarily. Kisi's wife ran away from him. Alo took her side strongly, as he had a great dislike of Sati. Indeed, there could be little doubt that Kisi's wife was the better stamp of woman. Alo gave a sharp public harangue against Kisi. Sati shortly after appeared in Kubwagai in a state of offended majesty and aggressive purity. But she was worsted. Kisi treated his wife like a dog in his initial attitude of contempt when she came back. But she stayed.

To give a fair idea of the state of marriage in Dobu I may review in brief survey the entire personnel of one village, the owners of the Green Parrot village. During my stay of five months there—

Alo was newly wedded to Emu, his grandmother's grand-daughter, in defiance of the custom of village exogamy, and Emu's fights with Bobo were still continuing.

Kadi, Alo's daughter by Bobo, was living away from Bobo and her rightful village, in Alo's place.

Kadi's former husband, Kinosi, was a village owner. The two avoided each other meticulously and Kinosi was on the most formal terms with Alo.

Alo's cross cousin, 'Inosi, although not an owner of the village, was there, working for me in conjunction with Kinosi. 'Inosi was the child of the sister of Alo's father and had village entrance accordingly. 'Inosi was the seducer of Kadi, cause of the divorce of Kadi by Kinosi. This divorce was recent.

Ile, Alo's sister's daughter, nearly disrupted her marriage with Togo.

Nela, half sister of Kinosi, nearly disrupted her marriage with Kopu.

Kisi, Alo's younger brother, was committing adultery with Sati, to the outrage of his wife, who had been a girl adopted into his family before he married her.

Iyem, Kinosi's younger brother, was recently divorced from his wife of Sanaroa island, grounds adultery.

Over against this group of recently troubled marriages were those of Yogalu and Magile. Magile had borne nine children to Yogalu, one to a former husband.

Wonoloi, sister of Alo and her husband Pogudu.

Tawa, brother of Alo and his wife, Mwedi.

Various young children, among them a bastard, adopted by Alo, of no named parentage.

Of the marriages in the village that of Yogalu and Magile had stood for many years, Yogalu having speared Magile's first husband to obtain her. Kopu had committed adultery with Emu long before, when she was someone else's wife. A child had detected him and informed Emu's husband. The husband went after Kopu with a spear. Kopu invited the avenger to spear him, thrusting his chest against the spear point without flinching. He was spared and left the island to work a long term of years for the white man, returning after Emu's husband's death. He married Nela, but had been married to three other women in intermittent spells between leaving Nela and returning to her.

Kisi and Togo were in trouble during my stay, as well as Kopu. It will be apparent from the condition of Kubwagai, how troubled Dobuan marriage is. I found the same type of record in other villages that I did not come to know as well, but well enough to be sure of my ground of comparison.

The firmer marriages were between Yogalu and Magile, Tawa and Mwedi, Pogudu and Wonoloi. Yogalu and Mwedi were both without true kin in the island, having married in, and having left their homes nearly fifty miles away. They alone had no blood kin to interfere in their marriages. Pogudu was a low grade moron and Wonoloi, his wife, undesirable and covered with ringworm.

We have now reviewed the conflict of marital and kin

ties. We have seen how marriage itself is validated by villages in *susu* formation. We have seen how little totemic affiliation counts and how strongly the village operates as the unit. We have seen how the relationship terminology is recast from a simple bilateral system to express the conflict between *susu* and marital grouping. In this section we have seen a little more of the mechanisms by which kin solidarity trenches upon marital solidarity. In all we have dealt with the greater trends in Dobuan social organization. We may now move to an examination of the rarer and exceptional subversions of the system, and also to further concrete material which will document the general system as well as its occasional subversions.

It must be realized that the system as a whole has little organization for the prevention or punishment of offences against it. Boundary man, for example, does not eat of the fruits of his dead father's village because his father's sister's son who inherits protects his exclusive rights to his inheritance jealously. " The heir will arise and kill boundary man by sorcery if boundary man offends " say the natives. The heir will be supported by his village kin. In fact, boundary man does not attempt to usurp his cross-cousin owner's inheritance. Feeling about property runs too strongly. Similarly a man does not beat his wife when he is living in her village unless he wants to be drummed out of the village.

Where feeling does not run as strongly, however, offenders can offend and " get away with it " If the offence is not serious enough for the offended person or the offended village to take up sorcery with intent to kill the offender, or to drum the offender out of the village with threat and insult, the only means left to the offended is to talk scornfully in public of the offender. This is enough to restrain most individuals. But some desperate and hard-skinned persons prefer public scorn and ridicule to putting up with inconvenient .rks of the system. They bear scorn and ridicule, and finally the scorners become weary of scorning and the wicked have rest rest in established non-conformity. Again there are neat evasions of the spirit of the system which preserve the letter of the law without too great discomfort.

Towards insane persons and delinquents public opinion is most lenient. Or at least there is no machinery for dealing with such persons, and they are well treated. I knew one mildly insane man who often patted women on the back or head playfully—women whom he would not have laid a finger on in public had he been normal. It is scandalous conduct for a man to touch his wife or his sister in public or any other woman except only his father's sister, whom he is allowed to treat playfully. Women treated so dealt with the man under discussion kindly and well, humouring him and talking his attention otherwhere with good neighbourliness. The most abnormal symptom he showed was a pathological love of work for its own sake. He would work for anyone who commanded him to do it quite irrespective of whether they recompensed him or not, and without refusal to do anything, however difficult. It did not matter whether those wanting him to do work for them were his relatives or non-related persons. This characteristic of his was well known to everyone. Yet hardly anyone took advantage of it. When I wanted an errand done my personal boy would sometimes select the mad worker to do it and command peremptorily in tones he would never use elsewhere ; but he knew that I paid well, the mad worker as well as anyone else, and felt justified. Little advantage was taken of the mad worker. Everyone agreed that he was a good fellow—his form of madness made him a very good fellow. But it was felt that he had enough to bear, since of his own volition he would paddle a canoe for hours going right before a strong wind which, had he hoisted sail, would have carried him faster even than his strong unwearied paddling. Always he preferred to paddle for miles, whether the wind was with him or not. Then often he would fish all night long, unwearied, persistent, long after all the others had gone to sleep. He had no fear of the supernaturals of the night. The desire to work had him in its clutches. Nothing else mattered.

Men that run amuck and often nearly kill victims are not killed as in Malaya. Shouts go ahead of the runner and every one hides in the bush. The man amuck recovers from his frenzy later, but since he is not killed when he is out to kill he remains a potential danger at all times. Everyone shouted to me to drop a shot gun I took up once when yells and running showed me that a danger of some character, I did not know what, was upon the village. I dropped it because there was no time to load, more than because I was convinced there was no need of it. And the man amuck was right upon me with a spear before I had more time than to drop the shot-gun, get a cane, and emerge from my hut to see what was the matter. There just outside was my man foaming at the mouth, with con-torted features, body glistening with perspiration, and spear brandished above his shoulder. All the rest of the village, themselves scattered deep in the bush, had shouted to me " drop the gun, drop the gun. He'll be all right again to-morrow ". It is typical of their good treatment of abnormals that they should extend it even to dangerous abnormals. In this case the village did not consider me in their mad scurry. But after all there was no reason why they should. I was a stranger amongst them. And as it turned out I emerged unscathed. The man amuck was my own interpreter and he did not strike, though he stuffed earth into his mouth in horrid pantomine of eating me, still foaming, writhing, and threatening me as I trussed him up with rope after he was disarmed. He was not Dobuan, but my interpreter from Dobuan into a related language. The attitude towards his abnormality, properly speaking, belonged to his own people. Nevertheless I had Dobuans with me ; they amongst the others shouted back to me, and they told me afterwards that all Dobuans behave as I had seen for myself. My interpreter's sister, an old woman, alone had not fled, was not over-intimidated by her brother, and came to help me to disarm him boldly as soon as she perceived my situation *tête à tête* with him, I looking him in the eyes and wondering what would happen next. She came up from behind unnoticed by him and gripped the end of the spear poised behind him. Next day he was at work interpreting, quite oblivious of where he'd been the day before or what had happened except that he had felt strange on coming to from something, he could not remember what. No one told him anything that would have made him uncomfortable.

Negwadi was also an abnormal. She only made a pretence at gardening, making a garden about ten feet square, the size a child of seven or eight years makes when its parents help it, show it how to plant and encourage it to work a toy-sized plot. She never had any stored-up food, although she was a heavy eater. She lived from day to day, from hand to mouth —by stealing. " Is there a fine bunch of bananas ready ripe that we have planned to cut down to-morrow morning ? We go to cut. Negwadi has been there before us. We come back empty handed. Is there a paw-paw ripening on our land ? We go to get it. The tree stands stripped. Negwadi has been there. Is there a nest where our hens lay ? If we arise at dawn and wait for the day's egg or two we get it sooner or later. But if we go about our gardening has Negwadi any gardening of her own ? Is there a tree of our owning with oranges coming or a shrub with pineapples? We look to pluck the fruit shortly. But Negwadi knows our trees as well as we know them."

All this was said with a twinkle in the eye of my informant. What was the use of threatening Negwadi? What was the use of pouring scorn upon her for a thief? She would not care. She could not be controlled by those who controlled the elemental forces — thunder, rain, wind, plant growth, disease and death. No magic of control controlled Negwadi. She was positively more out of hand than anything known to a Dobuan. She was cursed continually, but people had given up cursing her to her face. It was useless. So a sense of humour, thoroughly exiled from great departments of life by the grand notions of humans being in control of the natural elemental forces, flourished at the spectacle of Negwadi with whom no one could do anything.

This tolerant attitude towards pathological delinquents is important. It must be remembered when we deal with subversions of the social organization. The Dobuans are either remarkably acidulous and intolerant, or else they are remarkably tolerant. They never have engaged in fighting except with spears. European sports such as boxing and wrestling they will not accept. So also they will use sorcery against an offender, or drum him out of the village, or pour scorn and ridicule upon him. But they are not good at scorning and ridiculing. They prefer to be infernally nasty or else not nasty at all. Even when they are engaged in a plot to kill a person by sorcery they studiously cultivate the person; by a show of friendship they better their opportunity, and help to remove later suspicion. When friendliness (apparently) often covers treachery it is ill to be too offensively unfriendly, unless one intends defiance to the utmost. It is apt to be interpreted that way, even if one does not intend it. So although scornful remarks are passed they are not passed over freely. They are inhibited considerably by fear of anger flaring up to the heat which kindles sorcery. Offenders against the social code provoke scorn and ridicule but they live it down aided by the offended persons' fear of going too far over an affair that may not be worth too much danger. We have seen that a sorcery duel is welcomed if necessary in cases of disputed inheritance of wealth or the break up of marriages. Here the issues are felt strongly and men act outside their ordinary restraints.

Occasionally a widower refuses to submit to mourning in his dead wife's village. He refuses to don the blackened mourning neck cord of pandanus fibre, blacken his body, eat poor food, refrain from dancing, smiling and possible intrigues with other women, and toil the while in his dead wife's kin's gardens, under a cloud in his dead wife's village. It is a hard ordeal. Nearly all men undergo it. But now and then it happens that a man is engaged in an intrigue with another woman when his wife dies. Then the ordeal appears in its worst aspect—a year's misery and drudgery. So some non-conformists go home to their own village and their freedom immediately. The village kin of the dead say : " There goes the man who did not mourn his wife " whenever they chance to meet him. It is felt as a stinging insult, but there are thick-skinned individuals. Such a man may have difficulty in getting another wife, but probably not much difficulty. Unfortunately I did not see the development of a case of a *wadai*, as this class of non-conformists are called. There is an equivalent class of women who elope with another man before their mourning for their dead husband is over.

If his children are young the widower invariably goes home to his own place after mourning, leaving them in the care of their mother's sisters and brothers, not often seeing them again. But if a child is full grown he or she may elect to desert his or her village and own dead mother's kin and follow the living father to his place. When the father dies such a child becomes boundary man and must go home to the mother's kin. In the interval between mother's death and father's death the grown child may stay most of the time in the father's place, cultivating his or her own kin by frequent visits back. In fact, I know of no case where a youth did this. But I found two cases where a grown unmarried girl was living with her father in his place after the death of the mother or her desertion by the husband. Public opinion was quite lenient to these cases, not caring whether the attachment was in part incestuous or whether it was not. If a man was a *wadai*, however, such a course could hardly occur. I never saw any relevant case.

Again I found one old widower permanently domiciled in his dead wife's place. He had left it after the death of his wife, and had stayed away from it duly. But when he became old the village of his dead wife now sheltered his prolific descendants for three generations below his own.

His children, grandchildren and great grandchildren were
a solid majority of the village. In consequence Sibor, now
very old, was almost father of the village. The village had
him back, a fair reward for his unusually prolific marriage
and his hale old age.

Further there are cases where a youth or a girl contracts
a union with a girl or a youth of his or her father's village.
It is a prohibited marriage. But sometimes the young people
defy public disapproval, build their house and live together
as married persons although their villages may refuse to sanction
or validate the marriage by the usual economic exchanges.
The young people do not care a rap for the economic validation.
It is a toll laid on their shoulders that they are only too willing
to escape. Other people say scornfully: " He has married
into his dead father's village " or " She has married into her
dead father's village ", but the young people live down the
ridicule. In such cases the rule of alternate residence is
observed. But since one person is boundary man in one
of the resident villages, the hut of the pair must be built on
the edge of the village boundary on land belonging to the
susu of the person whose mother's place it is, not by any chance
on land belonging to the dead father of the other party to
the marriage. Then when the couple spend the year on
boundary man's dead father's village margin, boundary man,
male or female, must keep to the margin and never enter
the village he or she spends the year (and every alternate year)
in—or more correctly half in. Again boundary man must
not eat of food and fruit which is the other spouse's rightful
inheritance. He or she must have a separate store. Yams
are earmarked as they go into the cooking pot, yams edible
by owner of the village being distinguished from the separate
store of boundary man. Or else the owner tries to barter
all his or her store for others' food. All persons, whether
in such case or not, refrain from food of their dead father's
place or his owning most rigidly—not only as far as true dead
father is concerned, but observing also the restraints incurred
by their blood kin for every one of their several fathers.
I bought the fruit crops of several orange trees from several
places, took as many as I needed and made a communal free
cache of the rest for my visitors and personal boys. The
result was that I saw the tabu on fruit of the father's place
and the fathers' places of blood kin respected rigidly by all
the owners of the village. Trees from different places were

not ripe at the same time, except once when my personal boys insisted on keeping the fruit from the two different sources separate.

Cases of cross-cousin marriage between boundary man and owner are rare, however. They are uncomfortable, and no rule is relaxed to make them otherwise. They trench on the serious matter of inheritance within the *susu*, an inheritance defended with sorcery in case of need. In a range of approximately forty-five married couples, whose affairs I knew, I found six cross-cousin marriages. It was within the same range that I had one non-conforming *wadai*, non-mourner of his wife, pointed out to me, that I found two cases of grown daughters living in their fathers' places (in one case in her father's house the two alone together) after the mother's death (in one case), after desertion of her mother in the other case and where I found one old man, Sibor, living in his dead wife's place. Within the same range also were found the mad worker, and Negwadi, the pathological thief. The man who ran amuck was outside this range and in another place. I lived with forty of the people known well for five months, and with the other hundred and sixty whose social organization I got to know for one month subsequent to my first experience with the forty. Apart from the man amuck all my cases are derived from within this range. It may be assumed in future that except where I explicitly state otherwise, I am discussing what I found in my six months amongst this same range of persons.

The six cross-cousin marriages were not significantly unevenly distributed, four boundary men being male, the two other boundary men being female. Of the six, two male boundary men married their true fathers' sisters' daughters. Two male boundary men married their fathers' village sisters' (of other *susu*) daughters. One female boundary man married her father's village sister's (of other *susu*) son, one female boundary man married her stepfather's village sister's son. This distribution shows no rule, as is fitting for heterodox and lawless behaviour.

One of these marriages was new during my stay. Obedaia's marriage to his female cross-cousin, Lisi, of his father's place was not opposed by Obedaia's village mothers on the grounds that he was marrying his cross-cousin, but on the grounds that Lisi was a bad gardener and *e'ai 'alena*, the very root of eating, a woman who ate too much and reserved too little

seed for planting in consequence. As they expected, they
found Obedaia hungry more than once and had to feed him
themselves—a serious insult against a marriage since all
reputable marriages are supposed to be self-supporting.
Obedaia and Lisi had no children as yet moreover. In this
manner feeling in Dobu runs upon more practical lines than
mere formalism and legality.

Within the same range there were three pairs of children
betrothed before puberty by their respective parents in order
to ensure good economic alliances. One of the three betrothals
was between children who were cross-cousins. Such betrothal
is aberrant, but this one case was doubly aberrant in this regard.
If two cross-cousins make a good economic match legality
is not much questioned, although boundary man must live
alternate years on the margin of a village that he or she
cannot enter. This consideration is not as powerful as
economic considerations in an area where population presses
heavily on very poor and scanty land. If Obedaia and Lisi
had a child there might occur a tragedy such as one hears
of from here and there in the Dobuan district ; here a man
in anger puts the baby on the blazing fire to burn to death ;
there a baby is found deserted in a solitary hut with its wrists
gnawed to the bone where it had torn at its own flesh in hunger
and pain. Obedaia and Lisi could not support themselves
without hunger. What of children ?

Marriage within the village occurred in three cases within
my range of observation. In such cases the village normally
splits, some *susu* associating with the one of the contracting
susu with whom they are the closer related, others with the
other contracting *susu*. Distance of village house sites from
one another marks off fairly clearly the distance of genealogical
relationship of the owners of the sites. Accordingly such
division is easy except when " a man stands up and marries
into the house next door " i.e. marries a woman very closely
related to him genealogically, as Alo did. In one village
where marriage within the village had occurred a row of logs
across the centre of the village divided it into halves. These
halves acted to each other with all the forms used between
separate villages connected by marriage. But in validating the
marriage of another of their village members who had married
normally outside the village both halves sank their division
and worked together, the one for the other's business and
reciprocally co-operating and pooling their wealth, instead of

halving it and exchanging their half's respective pools, as they did when validating the marriage within the village.

I heard of one case of son-mother incest outside my range of true knowledge. It is regarded as contamination, as father-daughter incest, or child and father's sister incest is not so seriously regarded. But greatest of all crimes, outrage of all outrages against the social system, is adultery between a man and his mother's brother's wife or a man and his sister's son's wife. Son-mother incest, after the father's death, is not interfered with actively. It is a private sin, not a public attack on the social system. Blood brother interfering with blood brother's wife, or blood brother blood sister incest I did not hear of. But I heard of two cases of trouble between sister's son and mother's brother over their wives. Here the *susu*, bulwark of Dobuan life, is rent, with difference in generation to make the matter worse. The mother's brother is guardian of the sister's son, his heir and ward. I heard of one such trouble in each group I was in—one historical case in Tewara Island, one more recent case in my Eduagaura locality of Dobu Island.

In Tewara a man committed adultery with his own sister's son's wife. His sister's son heard of it. He sought out his own mother's brother and drove a spear through his body killing him on the spot. The killer's mother sought out her village brothers and committed her own son to their vengeance urging them to take his blood for their and her brother's blood. His mother's village brothers so encouraged by their sister, his mother, pursued him through the island and into the sea at the straits of Gadimotu. There they hurled spears at the young man as he fled seawards until a spear thrown underwater caught him near the ankle. He collapsed and was killed. His mother went into mourning for her brother and her son. Then months after when the canoes were beached on the small island of Gabuwana many miles from home, the young true brothers of the hounded and slain young man slew the slayer who had thrown the spear which found its mark in their brother's ankle. They roasted the corpse and ate it. Other members of the party which pursued the boy trying to kill him took no vengeance on the boy's brothers for killing their brother's killer.

So the *susu* itself may be rent turning mother against son, and the village may be rent turning the young of one *susu* against the old of other village *susu* who did no more than perform a mother's will against her son, the mother being their village sister. So, at least, runs the history vividly remembered by eyewitnesses, vividly and unmistakably told.

In Dobu Island a similar affair occurred less tragically, and under the eye of white government. A man committed adultery with his mother's brother's wife while his mother's brother was away at indentured labour. The mother's brother came back and heard of it, but not before his sister's son had left for a long term of indentured labour immediately he knew of his mother's brother's impending return. The elder man threw his wife out with scorn and passion. Several years after when the young man came back the elder was long remarried to another woman, and no word passed between them. Only one boy will say to another quietly and with much significance " I know of a man who slept with his own mother's brother's wife ", with some awe and even horror in the tone. It is still a matter unforgotten. White government and indentured labour sanctuary for native crimes has taken much of the sting out of native sanctions. The culture tends to bend and weaken in action, but it still holds fast to its own ideas of right and wrong.

In the Tewara case we see exposed the strength of the brother-sister bond. A Dobuan tends to think of his sister first of all his ties when the question of breaking ties arises. Dobu practices the avunculate, inheritance from mother's brother to sister's son, but this is from no great sentiment between a man and his sister's son. Rather the sister enlists the brother in the interests of her children. Strength of sentiment obtains between brother and sister ; and if a man punishes his sister's children over-severely it is his sister that expresses a sense as of a personal outrage upon her. In a village where a man has beaten his wards, their attitude is comparatively stoical. They may cry a little, but long after their crying has ceased one hears their mother wailing the the lament that is otherwise only wailed over the dead.

VI

Use of Personal Names

The general relationship term used between all the members of two villages, one member of which is betrothed or married to one member of the other, is *eyena*. As soon as betrothal is announced the people of one village begin to collect gifts to give to their *eyenao*,[1] the people of the other village. At the same time all use of personal names between those now *eyenao* is discontinued. Not only does the engaged youth avoid the personal names of the persons of his future wife's village, but all his village enter into the same restriction, which is reciprocated towards them except that the youth himself alone may be named by the elder generations of the village of his fiancee, and the girl herself alone may be named by the elder generation of her groom's village.

The mother-in-law not only names her son-in-law freely, where she and all her village kin name none of his village kin, and where he cannot name her, but she has parallel privileges over him. For example, she may bleed him in a case of limb swelling. The wife and her brother hold the man firmly. The mother-in-law takes obsidian, and cuts a deep gash down the swollen limb. She then inserts the obsidian into the same now bleeding gash and cuts into it deeper again, the son-in-law usually writhing convulsively by this time, but firmly held. Sons-in-law are not allowed to hold or bleed their mothers-in-law in this fashion. Similarly the mother-in-law usually supervises the son-in-law's toils if he becomes a widower. Throughout the marriage she exerts a real if tempered dominance over him.

We have seen that in the spouse's village One-resulting-from-marriage can use no personal names except to his or her own children. Those-resulting-from-marriage cannot use one another's names. The relationship term signifying " married into the same place as I have married into " is *lamusiana*. That term may be used in such cases, or alternatively *gosiana*, friend.

One spouse does not use the personal name of the other. The term for spouse is *mwanena*.

Although a mother-in-law names a child-in-law, a brother-in-law does not name a brother or sister-in-law. Within the same generation the restriction on personal names is reciprocal.

A child may name its father, but it is not done frequently. A child objects also to naming its mother's brother. The child often describes its father as " bad ", or " harsh ". The mother's brother is " harsh in the extreme ". Both father

[1] Plural form of *eyena*.

and mother's brother enforce discipline on children, but the mother's brother particularly. If children offend it is customary to beat them and take no notice of their crying. If a mother beats a child of nine or ten years old, however, it usually imitates its father in a passion and smashes its mother's fragile cooking pots. The father does not beat a child arrived at this age although he may throw things at one to its hurt. The mother does not beat it, as she would lose her cooking pots, and the child would run away. If the child does get harsh treatment from father or mother however it runs to its mother's sister and her husband. Children call the husbands of their mothers' sisters " our navels ". Their " navels " are never harsh to children. The children can use the personal names of their " navels " freely, whereas the " navels " cannot reciprocate. In strictly parallel usage the children may eat of their " navels' " food, using also their property. Those-resulting-from-marriage are necessarily on more or less subservient terms to owners and owners' children. The children can also run away to their fathers' sisters and fathers' sisters' husbands. This class of relatives they name freely. The free usage in this case is reciprocal. A child is on free, even joking terms with its father's sister. Later in life the only woman a man can body-handle in public fun is his father's sister. It is not done often. Only at big feasts, or when a pig-hunting expedition comes in with a good bag and great excitement prevails a man may often be seen clapping a woman on the back, ruffling her hair or embracing her. The woman is his father's sister. A man may also refer to his father's sister's daughter to her face as a " grass skirt ". But I never saw any further liberty in this relationship.

The child usually runs to its " navels " to escape from its father. The mother's brother may beat children long after its parents have ceased to do so. I saw one case where a mother's brother removed from his village to his wife's village for his alternate year there. His sister with her two fifteen or sixteen year old girls and her husband stayed behind in her village. The sister's grown children climbed their mother's brother's coconut palms for coconuts without going afield to his wife's village to ask his permission. He discovered this and beat them for it severely, as he was saving the nuts to trade for tobacco. His sister, the girls' mother, wailed as for the dead for hours after the incident. Here we see how the rule of alternate residence may interfere with the affairs of one *susu*, although it is a way of consolidating two *susu*, each in turn. Again, I knew of a mother's brother who beat a grown married girl, his sister's daughter, beat her with a club, because she had chewed a root intended to procure sterility, whereas her mother's brother wanted a male heir of her issue. How serious such beating is in the native view can hardly be conveyed. A school has been established in Dobu Island by the missionaries. When I was in Dobu the native schoolmaster was away serving a year in gaol in Samarai. He had caned a schoolboy. The schoolboy's father had come after him with spears. The father threw two spears and missed. He then closed in with a knife. The schoolmaster clubbed his pupil's would-be avenger with the butt of a musket, felling him. He then clubbed him again as he lay, killing him. It was for this precautionary second stroke that the schoolmaster was doing his year's gaol. But the incident is typical of the native horror of corporal punishment.

Just as the " navel " is a refuge from the father, the father's sister and her husband are a child's refuge from its mother's brother. It will be noted that as the mother-in-law has freedom with her son-in-law and uses his personal name, so also the child uses the personal names of its " navels " and father's sister's husbands, where it has freedom, rather than the names of those more severe elders, father and mother's brother. It is in later life only that the child appreciates its father and its mother's brother more. This is more true of the mother's brother. Very often the fathers are indulgent from the beginning.

A man does not name his mother's brother's wife. If she survives his mother's brother, he inherits the property, but he usually gives the widow a little of it back, as much as he feels disposed to give. His mother's brother's widow cannot return to his village where her late husband lies buried. She cannot touch any of her late husband's village property, but some garden land afield from the village, and a few palms in the bush, not in the village, may be given her by the heir. The heir can enter her village where she remains a widow, her mourning done, if he wishes to do so. When he enters, however, he ignores her presence and she ignores his. No word or look passes between them.

In all of these cases of personal name avoidance we may notice an expression of distance. The use of the personal name means a wholly pleasant relationship for the user. Just so we have seen that the *susu* uses its own personal names within itself, names of its *susu* dead applied to living heirs, and forbidden in the mouths of other *susu* of the village, and of Those-resulting-from-marriage including the father. Here again we have an expression of nearness of relationship in the use of the personal name. The mother's brother is entitled to use a more intimate name to his sister's child, than the personal name used by the father to the same child, used by the father in common with members of the other *susu* of the village.

Parents-in-law can name children-in-law and invite their children-in-law to eat side by side with them. A child can eat with its elder sister and her husband. When the child is adult, however, it cannot go freely at inclination to eat with its sister and brother-in-law. It will be recalled that brothers-in-law's names, and sisters-in-law's names suffer a reciprocal restriction in disuse.

In the previous section on marriage we have already seen much of the relationship that develops between two villages connected by marriage. The disuse of personal names between members of the villages, respectively *eyena* to each other, falls correctly under the explanation of a feeling of distance.

In Dobu, however, social trends do not fall into clearcut exclusive categories. Just as we have seen that *susu* right is beset with opposing exceptions, marriage regulations sometimes set aside, and, as we shall see later, magic includes elements that smack of what is usually termed religious feeling, so the disuse of personal names is not invariably an expression of distance. It is primarily just this as I have shown ; but the idea of foregoing the use of the personal name has run riot in Dobu and become incorporated into the expression of other social feelings than its primary one.

Owners of the village, when they are old and the grey has come into their hair, avoid each others' personal names. They refer to each other as the father of *x* (naming the child), or the mother of *y*.

Again any two persons who have privately shared food together, or have given each other magical ritual, or have lain the two in close succession with a woman they have been co-operating in seducing, or have shared a journey on their common errand, avoid each other's personal names as a token of their friendship. It must be a private matter between two persons only. In an essentially similar way a youth never uses the name of a girl he has lain with in his nightly excursions, or she his. I have no evidence that the avoidance of names between two persons of the same sex who have shared in a private *tête à tête* affair is homosexual however. It is obviously wider than sex. For instance, I had to avoid the personal name of the man with whom I went for many days deep into the bush to learn magical ritual. We always called each other *igu esoi*, my partner of a day's private journey. Similarly, two men who share cooked sago privately call each other my sago sharer, or cooked fish, my fish sharer, or a joint seduction of a woman, my sharer in seduction. Persons who contract these privately chosen partnerships give each other private gifts often. The whole relationship is non-public, non-ceremonial, privately contracted friendship. Here the disuse of personal names connotes the opposite of distance in feeling. This category of disuse disposes of a very large number of relationships where personal names are not otherwise prohibited.

In general personal names remain only to be used firstly to persons one has a strategic advantage over, as a mother-in-law to a son-in-law, a child to his " navel ", or a child to his father's sister over whom he holds a joking relationship, and to her husband by extension—and secondly by father to child, mother's brother to sister's child, mother to child, and brother to sister where there is a strategic advantage in the first three cases (and naming of the elders by the children is not done usually) but not in the last case, the brother-sister relationship, which is one of reciprocal friendship and exchange of services, as is also the father's sister, brother's child relationship where naming is also reciprocal.

Linguistically there are three classes of possessive affixes which are attached to three classes of nouns according to nearness or distance of possession. The suffix *gu* is used for a part of the speaker's body, a state of his mind, a trait of his character, a legitimate relative of his. The prefix *agu* is used for an illegitimate relative of the speaker's, such as his bastard child, his name, his magical knowledge, his pubic leaf, and food intended for his eating. The prefix *igu* is used for the speaker's food which he intends to give to others to eat, his house, his canoe, his trees, his fishing and hunting gear, and in the case of a woman, for her grass skirt. We see the graduation of distance noticeably in the border line cases, legitimate and bastard child being on different sides of the first border, food for eating and food for giving away being on different sides of the second border. Again, a man's pubic leaf is on one side of the second border, whereas a woman's grass skirt is on the other side. In fact, a man can never remove his single pubic leaf without exposure, whereas the women wear many grass skirts one on top of another, and are constantly removing an upper skirt or two in order to work more freely. Skirts are often to be seen hanging up in the house or laid aside on the ground, their owner retaining an underskirt or two. Hence suffix *gu*, prefix *agu*, and prefix *igu* express the three grades of nearness and distance of the object possessed. The personal name is in the second class. Like food for one's own eating, it is not shared freely with others. When others use it, this fact is associated with more important liberties, as we have seen. The name is classed with food for eating, a man's magic, and a man's pubic leaf.

VII

CUSTOM AND MAGIC

We have seen how the village graveyard contains the dead ancestors of the various *susu* who are village owners. In some rare cases a corpse is buried in a strange village. Now it is strong native sentiment that a person's loyalty is to the village in the centre place of which sleep his mothers, mothers' mother, and the generations of the mothers of the village before them. The sentiment is native, and I have cast it into native terms, even our own euphemism " sleep " being also the Dobuan idiom. A Dobuan speaks of all the older generation female owners of the village as " our mothers ". In practice when a native's true mother was buried in a strange village—I knew of one case only—the native left his own village and lived in the place where his mother was buried. His mother's sisters, true and classificatory, and brothers, true and classificatory, were buried in his own village. But he followed a sentimental course and that led him to live where his mother was laid. He was given land there and adopted into that village, retaining only a secondary loyalty to his own village.

Inheritance keeps within the one small *susu* line, sentiment in the case cited above was within the one *susu* only, and in general the *susu*, a small unit, is the limit of strong loyalty. Terminologically all the elder women of the village are

" mothers ", but the term does not mean a great deal. Terminologically all the women of the village of one's own generation are " sisters ", but it is only within the *susu* that incest is great crime. Affairs, as opposed to marriages, with village " sisters " are not greatly condemned, and are often practised. The terminology, village wide, is correlated with a functional economic unity. In economic exchanges the village acts as a unit. But even here the *susu* directly implicated in an economic exchange for a marriage of one of its members, contributes more heavily than the other *susu* of the village who help it. Condemnation of marriage with a village " sister " is partly based on the fact that marriage should, and does normally, set up large economic exchanges between two villages, in which each village acts as a solid unit. Marriage within the village splits it up as if it were two villages, each part having its own economic pooling arrangement opposed to the other with which it must now exchange, instead of co-operating to make an exchange with an outside village. Such a marriage within a village cannot make for exchange on the grand scale that is possible with the exogamous arrangement. It is a " poor " marriage, as well as supernaturally dangerous.

In gardening each person owns his or her own seed yams. Husband and wife do not own seed yams in common ; there is always seed of the male, and seed of the female. Seed of the male is seed saved yearly from a line of seed handed down to a man by inheritance within his *susu*. Seed of the female is seed saved yearly from a line of seed handed down to a woman by inheritance within her *susu*. The same line of seed descends within the *susu*, never is it held in common by the marital grouping or bequeathed within the family by marriage. Man and wife have their distinct and separate annual garden plots with distinct and separate seed of separate strain. Yams then planted by anyone are of a strain that was planted before one by those ancestors of one's *susu* who lie in the central graveyard of one's village. They are not only of this strain—*but, they can be of no other*. A woman who eats up all her yam crop, saving none for seed, will not plant a garden in the ensuing years. The pressure of population upon the food supply is such that a person who has not kept his or her seed yams expects no relief, no seed yams from elsewhere, and does not get any. I knew of several women in this position. They were thieves, or fishers, sago workers and beggars. Fish and sago are not plentiful enough to support anyone. They are poor resources that must be eked out by thieving or begging. Negwadi, the woman I mentioned above, was one of those in this position. Fishers, who trade fish for yams, are heartily despised. They are the native beach-combers of Dobu. They have at one period lost their seed through privation and urgent hunger. Seed does not, like garden land, descend from father to child as well as from a man to his sister's child. It descends in the latter line only. The natives go through an annual season of privation when the yam supply is running low, when they live mainly on roots and wild leaves of certain trees with small remnants of yams or early yams taken from the new gardens before they are grown—and with the usual rare pigs taken hunting or small fish that are caught with much trouble and scant reward in the poorly stocked seas. Fishing methods are primitive, as well as the sea about Dobu being a poor fishing ground. Pigs are not caught often in the hunt.

A person eating into a personal stock of seed may get subsequent help from a blood brother or a blood sister in an unusually good year, if the brother or sister is willing to risk breaking up his or her marriage by giving away seed ; for although man and wife do not own seed in common they share the crop as their common household food. It is a marital right. Nevertheless there do exist the class of native beach-combers without seed, and without help in seed gifts from others. The theory is that a person who has eaten what should have been seed once will do so again. Hence it is not right that a brother should sacrifice himself for such a sister or vice-versa.

The Dobuans do not talk of pressure of population upon land in this regard. They say that only the seed descended within the *susu* will grow. If seed could ever be obtained as a gift from other *susu*, as it cannot, it would not grow anyway, far less seed from other villages.

Different villages of different totems have different garden magic. Yam seed, we have seen, is only handed down in the *susu* line, from a man to his sister's son. The dogma current in Dobu is that only the magic handed down from a man to his sister's son will grow the seed. This dogma is stoutly maintained as true by everyone. It is a social dogma the voicing of which is essential to salvation. Never can the dogma be questioned. My doing so only made everyone angry.

My questioning it, however, was well based. In practice men do teach their own children garden magic. My own teacher was teaching his daughter garden magic ; and I uncovered other such instances. My teacher's daughter belonged to the Brown Eagle totem and the local village of it, he to the Green Parrot. At my teacher's death his garden crop of the year of his death will be placed in his deserted house with religious care. It will be inherited by his sister's children of his own totem, the Green Parrot ; and before the time of its distribution the daughter of the Brown Eagle will be prohibited absolutely from so much as entering her dead father's village. She will inherit seed from her mother or from her mother's brother of the Brown Eagle totem. The garden magic she was being taught was her father's, an other-totem magic from the totem of her seed inheritance.

Practice here is in circumvention of the dogma, in direct contradiction to it. It is bad taste however to quote instances of contrary practice in dispute of dogma. The dogma that only magic descended in the distaff line can grow seed similarly descended would, if acted upon, preserve the inheritance of garden magic exclusively within the *susu*, as in the case of most inheritance. It is a dead letter in practice. But the letter lives in every native's mouth nevertheless. It is a matter of belief to which everyone must subscribe, but on which no one need act. No one does act on it. But the dogma that only magic bequeathed parallel with the bequest of seed will grow the seed, although it does not prevent a father teaching a child garden magic, does prevent a seed-dispossessed person from acquiring seed from anywhere outside the *susu*. My offer of seed from another island plus five pounds (ten months indentured labour equivalent in wages) in replacement of anyones' seed went untaken in Tewara. The dogma also is stated as the reason why charity to a seed-dispossessed person would be useless, and why such a person cannot buy seed in exchange for any native valuable, however precious. Seed so got would not grow, and everyone would laugh to shame a rash attempt at growing it, was the reply to my offer of money. Where traditional economic considerations support the dogma it lives in practice as well as in theory ; otherwise not in practice.

Behind the dogma stands the fact that the *susu*, the single own true *susu*, is the unit of loyalty. Even within the one *susu*, help with seed is difficult to give in cases one living member encroaches on his or her seed. Other members of the *susu* are bound by marriage ties and pressure upon the family food supply. By inheritance at the death of a member of the *susu*, seed may be gained by another member or members.

The *susu* stands out as a close and important unit. The marital grouping is another important unit. The village as a unit composed of several *susu* is less important. The locality is less important again. Next comes the totem, the least important and the largest grouping of all. The totem has its bird name. The locality, a geographical unit, has a geographical name. The village has a geographical name and, by virtue of its being a subdivision of a totem, it has a bird name that is rarely used, the geographical name having unambiguous reference. Within the village one's own *susu* is so much more important to one than other *susu* are that there are terms of unambiguous reference. All the women of elder generation are termed *sinana* mothers, but a mother of another *susu* may be specified as *sina-yaiabara-na* or *sina-yaeyumne*. A " sister " of another *susu* will be *nuu-yaiebara-na* or *nuu-yaiyumne*. *Yaiabara* means " across ". Hence my village mother or sister is my mother-across, or my sister-across as distinguished from my mother who bore me, or my sister from my own mother's womb. Similarly of all the terms, the classificatory relatives may be demarked by the root term being used with a qualifying adjective between root and pronominal suffix, or root term with qualifying adjective and loss of the pronominal suffix. *Yaiebara* or *yaeyumne* suffixed to the stem of a term signifies classificatory relative. This distinction is not made in ordinary term of address, but it is made often in explanation of a relationship. With the use of this terminology all the members of other *susu* than own *susu* are cut off apart.

All persons who are boundary men to the one place are brother and sister to one another by term of address, irrespective of generation. But the fact that they are not *tasina* or *nuuna* of own *susu*, or *tasi-yaiobara-na* or *nuu-yaiobara-na* of other *susu* of the same village as the speaker may be explained by saying *ina elaba tasina*, his boundary man brother or *ina elaba nuuna* his boundary man sister. Similarly a boundary man may designate the people who are owners in the village of the dead father as " my owner of the village relative " specifying the relationship. A member of the village in return may specify a boundary man, as " my boundary man relative " specifying the relationship. The term "boundary man" in this last case is *labalaba* for boundary man. The term is reduplicated, so distinguishing it from the unreduplicated form *elaba* that is used of relationship between persons who are all alike boundary men to the one place. It will be evident that, despite classificatory terms and a double use of them dependent on the life or the death of the father, and despite their use in unmodified form as terms of address, they may all be differentiated terminologically in the explanation of any particular relationship.

It may be noted of the terminology of relationship that it is very convenient for children who run away from elder oppression in the manner described in the previous section. A child running away from its mother's brother, it's *wana*, runs to its father's sister where her husband, the male head of the family is also a *wana* to the child. A child running away from its father, its *tamana*, goes to its mother's sister where the male head of the family, the child's "navel", is also by term of address *tamana*. So a child goes from a possessive ruling *wana* to an indulgent non-possessive *wana* and from a possessive ruling *tamana* to an indulgent non-possessive *tamana*. The social relationships of the child to its true *wana* and *tamana* are very different from its relationships to its father's sister's husband, *wana*, and its "navel", *tamana*. The former pair are possessive lords of the child's life. The latter pair are non-possessive strangers on good behaviour. The former pair leave property to the child ultimately, the latter pair leave nothing.

The way in which relationship terminology is used between boundary man and the owners of his dead father's place reflects social practice accurately enough. But the equivalence in terminology of *wana*, and *tamana*, etc., does not express equivalence of social function. Elder generation individuals married into the mother's place are given the terms of the owners of the father's place. Similarly individuals married into the father's place are given the terms of the owners of the mother's place. This terminology is one well adapted to reflect the social practice of the dual organisation ; but, in point of fact, Dobu with its ban upon cross-cousin marriage and its ban upon boundary man entering his or her dead father's place, presents a vicious denial of any trend in the direction of the dual organisation.

Reverting to the point of the husband owning " seed of

the male " and the wife owning " seed of the female " we
can easily see how important it is for a marriage to be made
between two good lines of yam seed. A man with a good
stock of seed should have a wife with a good stock also, if
their respective villages are to keep their pride in the economic
aspect of the marriage. Hence sometimes child betrothals
are made by the parents of two families. A beach-comber
woman who has eaten into her stock of seed seriously, will
hardly find a husband. Negwadi never did and never would.
Lisi, as we have seen, married her cross-cousin. Another
such woman lived with a white man. Despite Lisi's success
in finding a man, such success is rare in these cases. Hence,
when a stock of yam seed is lost, the line tends to be broken.
The woman usually finds no mate, and rears no children to
succeed to her poor inheritance, and to her despised poverty.

I have referred to the mother-in-law's strong hand over
her son-in-law, enforced by custom of social organisation,
and by the son-in-law's fear of her as a witch. The
Trobrianders are accustomed to comment on this grass skirt
domination over the Dobuan men and to make merry at it.
The women of Dobu do actually possess incantations for
malignant witchcraft, incantations which they believe enable
them to fly by night to make mischief, to kill, to dance upon
the graves of their former victims, to disinter their victims
and in spirit hold ghoulish feasting on them. Meanwhile,
the woman as " an empty skin " stays asleep in her house.
The Trobriand women do not possess these magical incantations and powers. Women's possession of such spells in
Dobu and non-possession in the Trobriands appears to be
an actual fact. For this stated reason Dobuan men feel themselves safer in the Trobriands, a strange place, than at home
in direct contradiction of their usual greater fear abroad in
strange places other than the Trobriands. Conversely the
Trobrianders are nervous in Dobu. A few Dobuan women
who have married into the Trobriands and settled there,
are greatly feared by the Dobuan visitors. Dobuan fear of the
night actually is discarded by Dobuan visitors in the Trobriands.

Eating in Dobu is a private affair. Restriction upon
eating in the village of the betrothed, and public eating from
the hand of the mother-in-law constituting formal marriage,
is consonant with the normal feeling. Eating is a single family
affair. Visitors are never invited to share a meal. They
may be given food, but if so they eat it apart with their backs

turned to the givers. Apart from ceremonial events each family follows its separate pursuits during the day, eats its separate meal at night, settles down to its separate conversation after it and sleeps each family in its separate house. When two families form an evening group for eating and conversation they are parents-in-law and children-in-law respectively. Otherwise families keep apart. Brothers from the one mother keep to the ground beneath their separate huts, each with his wife apart.

The family not only has the house. It also has the garden as its private resort. I have mentioned that visitors never enter the house. They sit underneath the house or on its projecting front " verandah ". Visitors also never enter another person's garden. It is said that the gardens are often the place for conjugal intimacy. My early visiting of gardens was always resented. Later I learned that it was not done. Early in betrothal and first year or two of marriage the child-in-law must garden in co-operation with the parents-in-law. Later in the marriage the garden plots of the pair become their own inviolable place. This rule applies even at harvest time. There is no inspection of other persons' harvests, as in the Trobriands, once a parent-in-law has had two or three years' right of inspection of a potential or new child-in-law's gardening.

The family by marriage has thus its stressed independence just as it has also its stressed dependences on kin groupings. It moves in and out of the village to take up residence in the alternative village of residence on its own initiative. The rule of alternate seasons is observed by nearly everyone, but one family may move at first fruits, another at full harvest, another a month or two after harvest, and so scatteredly.

It is only rarely that a wife stays apart in her own village and a husband apart in his own village. I saw only one such case. Their respective villages were engaged in preparing food and wealth to interchange in validation of the marriage of Nathaniel and his wife. Nathaniel escorted his wife and baby home every night to her village, and then returned alone to his own. He worked in the mornings with his kin, she with her kin. They met in public in the non-working afternoon and parted for sleeping at night. It was said that such separation was good since she helped her kin and he his, each waking up in the morning in the company of working mates, ready for work.

Such separation is very rare, however. Actually, in all such marriage validating exchanges, husband and wife are engaged separately, each co-operating with his and her kinsmen respectively. But they do not sleep apart as a rule in order to facilitate the work. When I pointed this out to my informants they capitulated from their lofty position of complete economic explanation, and said significantly " their bodies are weary ". The family had not moved from Nathaniel's to his wife's village for eighteen months. Now that the marriage was to be celebrated economically the wife's kin insisted on her staying in their village. Nathaniel's kin wanted his help, and the pair parted amicably for the time. It was a case in strong contrast to the usual rule of no parting for any consideration, except with a brawl occasioned by jealous suspicion, obscenity, recriminations and often attempts at suicide. In this case a family forfeited its privacy of house and garden mildly for the time being while its separate *susu* and village *susu* groups were at an economic high point. But the case was abnormal. The usual teaching of a Dobuan mother to her daughter is that the only way to keep her man faithful to her is to keep him as weary sexually as lies in her power.

When the family changes its village residence for the year it practically cuts off all else than ceremonial relations with the other village. In general there is little casual inter-village visiting.

Punctilio is observed, and a too friendly going to and fro would be regarded as unwarranted trespassing. In the native view a village of another place is not merely a village of actual or possible marriage ties knitting it to some member of the kin, but it is also in one aspect a village of sorcerers and witches who are suspected of having caused disease and death within the kin, and in another aspect it is a village with which ceremonial relations are kept up in occasional, but regular, ceremonial meetings—and once on a ceremonial footing always on a ceremonial footing is native sentiment. A man who went out of his way into another village would be immediately suspected of a will to adultery. In traversing a long path a traveller will circuit the outside of a village unless it is the village of his or her own living father or own spouse in which case he or she will be invited to enter. This condition of affairs in the state of the small sized village which obtains restricts the field worker's circle of informants

FATHER AND CHILDREN

WOMAN DIGGING FOR SMALL SHELL-FISH FOR SOUP

seriously, and he can do nothing to change it. There are occasional goings to and fro for healing incantations in cases of illness—different villages possessing specialists in causing and curing different diseases in many cases, and exchanging their services in healing in time of trouble ; and there are individual early evening excursions by the bachelors to the houses of the unmarried girls in other villages. Apart from these recognised practices the rule is that no person intrudes upon another village. Those-resulting-from-marriage when they are in Rome do as Rome does to a great extent. The family, once it has moved, stays apart from the place it has moved from, and a brother does not resort to his sister's and mother's place too often when he is resident in his wife's place. He must conciliate his wife's kindred by not seeming to run away from them too much. Moreover, he needs to watch his wife fairly closely for fear of infidelity. The reverse applies when the wife is in her husband's place. Jealousy and suspicion of adultery are sentiments of great and abnormal growth in Dobuan married life. Pathological cases are reported here and there where a husband does not leave his wife even when she wishes to perform the natural functions. He goes with her to the bush. These cases arouse merriment and disapprobation, because prudery in public is strongly insisted upon. Nevertheless, they are natural enough extensions of the normal feeling which is not so very far removed from such extreme cases. Every Dobuan man will say that a woman met alone apart is naturally an object to be picked up and carried into cover. They do not in the great majority of cases cry out or tell their husbands afterwards. They rarely have to be raped. Women rarely go alone, except when they evade their husband's notice by some chance. Theoretically a person alone is in danger of witchcraft. Hence there must always be an escort, if only a child escort, for men as well as for women.

In the marriage exchanges that inaugurate marriage it will be recalled that after the groom's kin take a gift of ornamental valuables to the bride's kin, the latter go to the village of the groom and formally sweep it throughout. This symbolic sweeping of a village is similar to two other customs. When the men returned victorious from war bringing home corpses for a cannibal feast, the women formally swept the villages throughout. It is the response of the woman's group to good behaviour by the man's group, for when the men returned defeated and empty-handed the sweeping was not done. The women tied their grass skirts under their loins in imitation of the man's pubic leaf instead—a woman's strike as the response to bad behaviour by the man's group.

The second related custom occurs when a widow runs away from the village of her dead husband before her mourning there is done, eloping with another man. In such a case the owners of the village of the dead go to the village of the man who has absconded with their widow. They litter the village with torn off leaves and branches, and plunder anything in the house of the man who has taken their widow that they can lay hands on. This littering of the village and plundering is done by the men. I did not hear of any case where a man refusing to mourn, *wadai*, married immediately, or of any littering of the place of an interloping woman who had captured a mourning widower. A widow to escape mourning must elope. A widower who refuses to mourn does not elope necessarily. He may merely go back in surly aloofness to his own village. He need not marry again until fear of reprisals has become old history ; but a woman to escape mourning must flee to a man who is willing to pay for it, and who has made secret advances in that direction.

It will be apparent that the machinery for punishing crime in Dobu does exist to a certain extent. Theft and adultery are spoken of as admired virtues if one can evade detection and accomplish them successfully. Incantations to aid in theft and in adultery are highly prized. There is very little public sentiment against such activity and a great deal of private sentiment directed towards being an accomplished thief and adulterer. One of the most respected men in the community once gave me an incantation for making the spell-binder invisible with the recommendation " now you can go into the shops in Sydney, steal what you like, and get away with it unseen. I have many times taken other persons' cooked pig. I joined their group unseen. I left with my joint of pig unseen ". Outwardly there is great respect for personality springing directly from the fear of hostile sorcery or witchcraft. But secretly there is a covert desire to do the worst by neighbours, springing also from the fear of their sorcery and witchcraft. Thus outward respect goes with as much as can be done in ill turns without detection. Sorcery and witchcraft are by no means criminal, because everyone indulges in one or the other according to sex, and everyone knows it, although it is covered up to a certain extent by the convention of avoiding unpleasant subjects.

Nevertheless, there are certain social self-protective sentiments and customs. One such is the littering and plundering of the village of the abductor of a widow in mourning. Adverse social comment is usually heartily disliked and prevents too many subversions of custom. It is used against persons who marry within the village, or who marry a native beach-comber without seed yams, or somewhat less severely against persons who marry their cross-cousins. Withholding of the public economic validations of marriage in such cases is customary and wounds the pride of the persons concerned in the marriage. Comment on the conduct of a widower who is a *wadai*[1] is felt severely. Obscenity used on a husband who has quarrelled with his wife by her kin is keenly resented by the husband. In Dobu obscenity is known as *bake*. It is used rarely and produces deep hurt. I have seen persons on whom *bake* has been used sulk silent and apart for a whole day afterward. If used between husband and wife themselves it is the traditional prelude to an immediate attempt at suicide by the injured party. " Go copulate with the wild boars of the bush " said by a husband to a wife leads to the wife attempting her life, as I saw for myself in one case. It is always deep insult. Togo who did not work the sago, yet took part in the subsequent feasting; when I asked why this was allowed I was told, "he would use *bake* on us if we gave him offence."

To call a man a successful thief or a successful adulterer is, however, to praise him. Such social comment does not wound a man's feelings, but exalts him in his own esteem. It is not to be classed with saying " he did not mourn his dead wife correctly " which is insulting, or saying " copulate with a pig " which is most deeply insulting. In consequence the only safeguard of fidelity in marriage is constant private vigilance by all concerned, and otherwise good treatment of a wife by her husband.

Private ownership in betel-nut and coconut palms is ensured in two ways.

On coconut and betel (nut) palms away from the village, there is to be seen the customary dried coconut palm leaf tied round the trunk. This leaf stays there always. The first missionary in Dobu, the Rev. W. E. Bromilow, D.D.,

[1] Non-mourner.

on enquiring what this heraldic device betokened, was told
that it made the tree " sacred from woman's touch " ; and
this ingenuous reply he has duly recorded in the *Reports
of the Australasian Association for the Advancement of
Science*.[1]

Actually the leaf is a warning that a spell for causing
elephantiasis, gangosa, tertiary yaws or the like, has been placed
upon the tree trunk. A thief will touch it at his peril. The
question naturally arises, how then can the rightful owner
of the tree gather the fruit of it ? The answer to this legitimate
question lies in a local census of the ownership of spells for
causing disease. It will then be found that different *susu*
of the same locality own the spells for different diseases. This
ownership is hereditary within a *susu* line of descent, and
one *susu* will never sell its peculiar different powers to another.
Magibweli, the old rain-making once cannibalistic woman,
of the next door village owns elephantiasis of the scrotum
and pubes, Sati, the unmarried widow with the two children
who has recently been involved in a scandal with Kisi,
someone else's husband, owns incontinence of urine and
incontinence of semen. Togo, the village wastrel of the
village next door, owns cerebral malaria and meningitis.
Yogalu, the most honest old character in the village, and appreciated for it by none, but rather depreciated, owns intestinal
mortification. The most influential family in the village
owns gangosa, limb paralysis and tertiary yaws. So the list
goes over a wide gamut of different diseases. By a dogma
of magic only he or she who knows the spell which will inflict
the disease, knows also the exorcism which will banish it.
Hence Magibweli puts elephantiasis of the scrotum and pubes
on her private property in trees. When she goes to pluck
the fruit she exorcises the disease. Sati does the same with
her spells for incontinences for her private property in trees,
and so on. Magibweli is afraid to go near Sati's trees, and
Sati near Magibweli's ; so for the locality. Persons belonging
to other localities do not trespass, and if perchance they do,
they will not be well informed of the situation regarding
property in trees and in spells in a strange locality.

If anyone in the locality contracts elephantiasis of the
scrotum, the kin of the patient repair to old Magibweli, bearing
water vessels. Magibweli breathes the spell of the exorcism

[1] Vols. xii and xiii, together with a great deal of other misinformation and
a little fact.

into a water vessel containing water, stops up the vessel to keep the spell within it, and takes a fee. The kin of the patient hurry with the charmed water to the patient and bathe the affected organ carefully with it. Then, if the patient has thieved from Magibweli's private trees, she at best has had her revenge, and received a fee for exerting her art of exorcism. Naturally, in such a case there will be general certainty either that the afflicted person has been thieving, or else that he had offended Magibweli in a more personal matter, and that she had succeeded in breathing the spell on to a bush creeper twined across the patient's path. No one knows which case is true, whether the disease is a legal sanction or the less legal sanction incurred in a more personal feud. Only the patient will know. He may tell himself that he once walked too near Magibweli's trees, even if he is not guilty of theft. I have known such an acceptance of the situation. Or he may secretly vow revenge on Magibweli if he has not thieved and if he does not recover. In any event, a complete avoidance is certain to spring up between himself and that old woman. She was liable to die at any time from the enfeeblement due to ageing years, when I knew her. But death from old age is not accepted as such by the natives. If someone in the locality contracted elephantiasis not more than several years before the old woman died there would be natural suspicion of foul play leading to her death. If not, there are other witchcraft scrapes into which the old woman had inevitably been plunged. Everyone is in, or only half out of, such troubles continuously.

Magibweli bears the weight of responsibility for all elephantiasis in the locality on her shoulders, in addition to protecting her private property in trees with this particular affliction. Such protection of private property is gained at the payment of a great risk of very considerable social acrimony within the locality. Personally I think that this kind of thing is the most striking rebuttal of Dr. W. H. R. Rivers' theory of Melanesian communism that these societies offer. Before I left Tewara I could often place a particular palm— " that's gangosa," another " that's incontinence of urine and of semen ", another " that's cerebral malaria and meningitis ". It is not considered polite to voice such a method of classification publicly. One says only " that's Kisi's tree, isn't it ? " or " that's Sati's ", or " that's Togo's, didn't you once tell me ? " For everyone, of course, is like Magibweli in bearing a burden as well as a private policeman. Not that they feel the burden always. It is the order of society and of the universe, and our pleasant freedom from such unnecessary social complications would appear as a sentimental and an unreal idyll. Disease spells are called *tabu*.

I do not know of bequests of *tabus* by a man to his son and to his sister's son both. It is possible that this occurs ; but the assured fact that different *susu* in Tewara owned non-overlapping *tabus* would indicate this is not so.

To understand this fact let us follow out the theoretical possibility that the *tabus*, like garden magic, might descend down a double line, one patrilineal, one matrilineal ; allowing for the fact that divorce is very frequent indeed, that stepfathers do not normally leave magic to stepchildren, and that complete separation between father and child by a divorced wife is more common than continued attachment. Such patrilineal inheritance is likely to be cut short before many generations.

A strictly kept rule is that a child may not eat of the fruit of a dead father's trees. The abstinence of a parent towards his or her father's trees is enforced on a child in turn. Accordingly, if the same *tabus* were bequeathed by a man to his son and to his sister's son, the former could not use the *tabus* to pilfer the trees of the latter compatibly with keeping the rule of abstinence, nor his son after him. But the patrilineal line would have no comparable protection from the matrilineal line. No subsidiary abstinence exists to protect them. Consequently their only protection is different *tabus*.

In the case of gardeh magic, we found a dogma that would enforce exclusive *susu* inheritance paid lip service, but disregarded in practice. In the case of *tabus*, the abstinence from fruit of a dead father's or grandfather's trees is kept fairly rigidly and ensures exclusive *susu* inheritance.

Again, a man in default of a good monopoly in a disease may protect a tree more precariously by naming it after a family catastrophe in his own family. Thus a man whose brother fell from a *siwabu* tree and was killed, calls his palms *siwabu*, and his private ownership in them is respected. He has inherited a big overseas canoe ; he calls it *siwabu* and he alone has direction over it. If he is eating his food and does not wish to share it, he says " this food is *siwabu* " and none will ask for it or expect a share in it. Most of these names were derived from incidents connected with the deaths of close relatives ; one I knew, however, was derived from an incident in which a man ate some unorthodox food and sustained a severe stomach-ache—whereat he made a dance and song, and recorded the food as his property protection name. He was the humorist of the village, and had a strong incapacity for seriousness, but he was gravely dignified over this matter. This custom is called *kelamoa* ; *niu-lamoa* is a coconut palm with *lamoa* protection. If anyone steals from a tree so protected no proceedings are taken against the thief, even if he or she is detected in the act. But the owner of the tree must cut it down in outraged protest. I am sorry to say that this strong appeal for public sympathy, this somewhat pathetic appeal, does not always meet with a chivalrous response. Sometimes owners of such *lamoa* trees have to cut them down in sullen fury. Even the *tabu* protection, though less often violated, is sometimes dared. The daring criminal puts his own different infection on the tree after stealing, trusting that it will infect the owner if the owner's infection has caught him in the stealing.

Property is best safeguarded by watching over it. The garden is protected in this manner. An actual garden thief is most heartily despised—that is, one that is caught in the act. It is believed that yams can be enticed out of one man's garden into another man's by the latter's magic. Everyone, the most respectable included, practise magic to steal the crops of other persons' gardens in this way. It is done every year by all gardeners, in private, as a matter of course. The yams are believed to emerge from the gardens and walk about in the night. Then they can be enticed away from their home garden by magical incantations. Stealing here is believed to be done by magic alone. The person who steals in the flesh from another person's garden is not despised for stealing as such, but for stealing in a clumsy, inefficient, and ridiculously pride for-swearing manner. It is base to admit such poverty, as is admitted by garden stealers in the flesh. It is degradation to eat into one's stock of seed yams, not setting aside seed enough for a reasonably good garden. One then becomes the native beach-comber, object of scorn to all, and the typical beach-comber act is garden stealing in the flesh. Hence, all good citizens steal by magical methods which are believed to be both more consonant with pride and also more efficient on a large scale.

There is only the most embryonic germ of government by chieftainship. In each locality there are one or two persons of outstanding influence. Such leadership occurs when a man of unusual character happens to be born into a rich inheritance of magical ritual power. Such a man was Alo of my own village of the Green Parrot folk. He was to be heard now and again in *guguia*, the public admonishing of a member of his own village. He would commonly talk for half-an-hour or so in loud, angry staccato sentences. The other *tai sinabwadi*, big men, of the village took no part, but listened quietly. On these occasions one of the big men commonly whispered to me in a reverential tone, *i guguia*, he is laying down the law, and motioned to me to sit down and be silent. There was complete silence, no reply or repartee, although obviously one or two persons and a small party of sympathisers were seething in revolt and being most severely tongue-lashed. Such a man as Alo can take risks in public admonishing of offenders because his sorcery is reputed to be the strongest, his knowledge of ritual the best in his locality. He can dare defiance with an impunity not granted to other men. Such a man provides the only germ of good government in Dobu. His influence in matters of morals does not extend beyond his own village, except as far as to Those-resulting-from marriage in his own village. I have described Alo at work admonishing Togo in another place. It was a dignified lecturing of Togo on his bad ways, not a screaming dismissal with obscenity as I saw a lesser man accord to Kopu when he quarrelled with his wife, an owner of the village. Togo got out of the village as speedily as Kopu, nevertheless. Alo had the usual sanction of a united kin group behind him in sympathy in dealing with an outsider, a resultant-from-marriage. In the case of a quarrel confined between owners of the village, Alo had no sanction behind his lecturing, however. He said his say, the quarrel stilling to hear it, but after he was done the quarrel might go on, and Alo became a private individual again. Nevertheless, without sanction of any kind, he alone had silence for his speech, however decisive against one of the conflicting parties, and he often carried his point.

Other villages of Alo's locality were not so ruled, however. There was no other outstanding man. All old men get more respect than young men from their juniors. But the decisions of three or four elder men are more conflicting, less decisively clear, and useless in the case of a dispute between village owners. The village group may mobilise easily against a badly behaved resultant-from-marriage without any good leadership, but only with angry recrimination, obscenity and the like, vindictive without any redeeming note of calmer legality. In case of quarrel within the circle of village owners, such ill-led villages resolve into opposing parties. This actually happens in the majority of villages, but not so anarchically in a village that has an outstanding man of Alo's quality. Alo was the greatest magician—that is to say, governor and administrator of native law. His power was all to the good, as he was, in public, fair and just. All cases were not referred to him, even within his village. Thus Kopu's expulsion was done by another. A great deal of Alo's power was due not only to his force of character and his inheritance of magic by primogeniture, but also to the fact that his mother had been prolific and his grandmother before him. He was the eldest of the eldest line, but his blood brothers and sisters formed the village majority. Kopu's wife was one of the *susu* not connected with Alo's line by a known genealogy. On such rare circumstance as the combination of a strong personality with inheritance of magic in a family conspicuous for its magical knowledge, and with prolific descendants, does the barest show of legality in Dobu depend.

Alo's influence extended over his whole locality of several villages for fixing the sailing dates for overseas expeditions when the whole locality acted at one time. He had the best inheritance of the magical ritual necessary for overseas sailing. Such influence over several villages is a pure function of magical specialization however. In the same locality an old woman of another village than mine came to the fore as the one rain-maker in the locality. Her importance increased in time of drought, just as Alo's did in time of large overseas expeditions. There were no pigs in this locality, but I know that in a different locality one old woman fixed the times when all the villages of the locality went on a big drive in a wild pig hunt. She possessed the magical ritual efficacious and necessary to lucky pig-hunting.

Alo, himself, was a law breaker when he married within his own village, two of his blood brothers deserting the village for two months or so in protest. In his private capacity, as opposed to his public capacity, he was as the others.

VIII

THE CASE OF YOGALU

One of the most firmly founded facts of the social organization is that the mother's brother constantly gives gifts of wealth and of magic to his sister's son, who inherits all at death. A cross-cousin owner exacts magic not so given him but given to his mother's brother's son from that son after the mother's brother's death, so that 'Inosi in describing his relationship to Alo said always " my mother's brother's child, Alo ; hence magic for overseas expeditions he gives me without fee ". (It will be recalled that Alo was his locality's specialist in this magic—hence the emphasis upon it.) In return for gifts the sister's son helps the mother's brother in gardening, in sailing his canoe overseas, and the like.

The case of Yogalu is an interesting inversion of the normal situation. Yogalu, a middle-aged man, was poor in material wealth. His sister's son, a child of four or five years old, was rich, and gave wealth to Yogalu, to a middle-aged man. This situation is a good instance of the emphasis upon reciprocity.

Yogalu was a native of Bwaioa, a locality overseas from Tewara. He fought with the husband of Magile of Tewara over Magile, and killed him. He married Magile. Then he left Bwaioa and settled in his wife's village. As is the custom in such cases, he was adopted by the village in the Tewara locality that was of the same totem as his village in the far off locality of his birth. He was by birth of a White Pigeon village of Bwaioa. He became by adoption a member of the White Pigeon village of Tewara. For some time he and Magile oscillated in the usual manner between his White Pigeon village of adoption and her Green Parrot village. Then a succession of deaths in the White Pigeon village frightened the pair away. They remained permanently in the Green Parrot village, Magile's place. Yogalu could do this, as his kin of the White Pigeon were adopted kin and not as demanding as real kin.

Mwedi also a native of Bwaioa, had married into Tewara. She was by birth a woman of a White Pigeon village of Bwaioa, one different from Yogalu's, however. She left Bwaioa and settled in her husband's place, the Green Parrot village of Tewara. Like Yogalu she became an adopted member of the White Pigeon village of the Tewara locality. Mwedi and her husband oscillated regularly between the Green Parrot and the White Pigeon villages—conforming more to custom than Yogalu and Magile in this particular. Yogalu, however, was always associated with the White Pigeon owners in their economic exchanges with other villages. In this respect, both Yogalu and Mwedi conformed.

These two cases of marriage between two different localities,

moreover localities of two widely sea-separated districts, found
in one small village must not be taken as typical. Tewara
locality was dying out at a very rapid rate. There land was
plentiful, living easier, the land-owners unable to work all the
island, and the population too small now to continue to practise
the normal endogamy of the locality grouping, and yet mate all
its members without village incest, marriage within the village.
A few marriages in a locality are not endogamous within the
locality. The rule applies only to the great majority of marriages.
In the case of Tewara decline of population is very serious
indeed, and, unlike all the other Dobuan speaking districts,
Tewara has a surplus of land and a shortage of possible mates
for marriage.

Mwedi had married into the richest family in Tewara. Her
five-year-old son, Mulubeos, was therefore rich with gifts from
his father. So Mulubeos gave land and some coconut and
betelnut palms to his mother's adoptive brother, Yogalu.
These trees Yogalu would enjoy the fruits of, but at Yogalu's
death Mulubeos would inherit the land back, all the richer for
Yogalu's work in planting. In this manner, strangers were
brought into the social system in another locality than their
own by birth.

Neither Yogalu nor Mwedi ever went visiting to Bwaioa, their
distant home. They had renounced their inheritance there.
Their marriages were the two best and least troubled in Tewara.
The demands of the kin had been well lost with the rewards
from the kin also. Both Yogalu and Mwedi had gifts of
necessities from the place of their wife and husband respectively.
Tewara as an underpopulated locality, could afford to be
generous to Those-resulting-from-marriage who were rifted
apart from their kin.

IX

LEGEND OF THE SAIDO SERE AND SOME GENERAL CONSIDERATIONS

Young girls bathing, their gaze goes upwards.
" I for my husband Mr. Groundward-Branch."
" And I for mine Mr. Middle-Branch."
" I for my husband Mr. Middle-Branch above yours."
" And for mine Mr. Top-Shoot-Frizzling-in-the-Roasting."
The girls bathe and climb villagewards. They sleep. It
dawns. Again they descend to bathe, they four.

"I for my husband Mr. Groundward-Branch."

"For mine Mr. Middle-Branch-below."

"For mine Mr. Middle-Branch-above."

"My husband Mr. Top-Shoot-Frizzling-in-the-Roasting."

Again the girls climb. They sleep. It dawns. They remain at home.

"I go my brothers. You remain, and the women I shall see." The Groundward Branch from his brothers he fell away and down (as leaves fall when sere and fruit when ripe). So he came down. He bathed, he anointed himself, he combed his hair, he painted his face. His personal basket he carried. He ascended villageward.

An old woman. Torches of dried coconut leaf he brushed against rustling. "My grandson, my coconut palm you may climb." His personal basket he set down. He climbed the palm, he pulled down a nut. He descended. In his descent "You turn about, head downwards, feet up, face in to trunk." He did so. She kicked him.

A steep cliff, cliff down he fell.

Again they sleep in the Saido tree. "My brother I go. You remain and the women I shall see."

He fell away and down (as leaves fall when sere, and fruit when ripe). So came Middle-Branch-below descending. He bathed, he anointed himself, he combed his hair, a fresh pubic leaf he donned, he painted his face. His personal pouch he carried and he ascended villageward.

Torches stacked he brushed against rustling. "O my grandson, my coconut palm you may climb." His pouch he set down, he climbed, a nut he cut off. The nut it fell. He descended. "You turn about, head down, feet up, face inwards to trunk of palm." She kicked him.

Cliff down he fell.

(To cut the legend's repetition, Middle-Branch-above did exactly as his brothers, Middle-Branch-below and Groundward Branch had done and met with the same fate.)

They lie. With his brothers they lie, the three dead. It dawns again. The youngest, Top-Shoot-Frizzling-in-the-Roasting fell away and down (as fall leaves when sere, and fruit when ripe).

(Cutting repetition again—a thing never done by the native—and using a general term not used by the native.) He performed his toilet. He ascended villagewards. Torches stacked he brushed against rustling.

" O my grandson, my coconut palm you may climb." He set down his pouch, he climbed, he plucked a nut. " You descend." He looked down. At the cliff foot he saw his three brothers dead. " You turn about head down, feet up, face in to trunk."

" That will I not." He jumped to ground. He descended his brothers to them. A long *Digitaria sanguinalis* grass stalk [1] he charmed with magic. He distended the nose of one with it.

" Ash-i-e ! Who you ? You would awaken us. Go ! You may cease and we may sleep."

Another man—he distended the nose.

" Ash-i-e ! Who you ? You would waken me. You may cease and we may sleep."

Again another man he distended the nose.

" Ash-i-e ! Who you ? Go ! You may cease. Let us sleep."

They arise. They ascend. The torches stacked they strip avoiding rustling them. They remove them, ascend her house.

The old woman she says, " Long ago did I not kill you." They roast her in the earth-oven. Her pigs, her dogs they kill. Together they roast them, together in the earth-oven. They eat. They go.

" Where long ago the woman she named me as her husband, me Groundward-Branch ? "

" I am she." He goes with her, his wife.

" Where long ago the woman she named me as her husband, me Middle-Branch-below ? "

" I." He goes with her, his wife.

" Where long ago the woman she named me as her husband, me Middle-Branch-above ? "

" I." He goes with her, his wife.

The youngest :

" Where long ago the woman she named as her husband, me Top-Shoot-Frizzling-in-the-Roasting."

" I."

The elders on the floor they sleep. The youngest on the house loft floor. With their wives they sleep. The eldest's wife gave birth to a child. He, the father, Groundward Branch, goes. He nets fish at sea.

Another man. With the other owners of the village he stays in the temporary house in the garden. He steals (i.e. commits

---

[1] Always used in restoration of the dead to life in the legends.

adultery) with the wife of Groundward Branch. Her lice he delouses. The woman's child sees the man delousing her. They appear back in the village, the fishers.

The father, he comes. Hibiscus he placed in his hair. The child gave it away. He said, " My father, you run quickly. My mother her lice he delouses in the garden."

" Ya ! Owners of the village these. I, I was netting fish."

Their mother, dead. Her leaves fallen, bare. Night falls. They sleep. It dawns. They go, brothers together, their mother to her. Beneath their mother they lie. Saido stripped of her sere leaf, her children lying below her is happy.

The Saido tree is deciduous. Its large broad leaves turn brilliant scarlet before falling. Its nuts taste somewhat like salted peanuts and are almond shaped.

The legend chronicles the falling of the Saido leaves. It tells how the Saido branches walked abroad, met with ill-fate from an old witch woman, except the youngest brother who restored his elder brothers by magic powerful in restoring life. They burnt and ate the witch, found the women who had spoken of them as their husbands, and married them.

Then the eldest branch's wife committed adultery, village incest with another owner of the village. The branch brothers deserted the village together, and went back to their mother's place, beneath the Saido tree.

I quote the one legend only in this place. It is the legendary equivalent of the cases of Kopu and his wife, and of Alo, Emu and Bobo that I saw.

It may be added that the pattern of the neighbouring Trobriand Islands is closely related to that of Dobu. According to Dr. Malinowski incest with a clan " sister " who is not a real sister or else parallel cousin traceable by geneaological record is there also customary. " To use a somewhat loose comparison, it figures in the tribal life of the Trobrianders much in the same way as that in which adultery figures in French novels. There is no moral indignation or horror about it, but the transgression encroaches upon an important institution and cannot be officially regarded as permissible." Unofficially it is admired and considered the thing to do.

The comparison with French novels is not very loose in the case of Dobu, for the theme enters into Dobuan folklore almost as prominently as it is in its actual occurrence in fact. Such incest is one expression of the conflict between the grouping of the various clan *susu* and the institution of the family by marriage which we have seen to have very wide ramification in Dobu, and which ramifies widely in the Trobriands also.

From this conflict in Dobu comes a state of mutual watch and ward over each other by husband and wife, a state carried to an extreme of indignity as a normal phenomenon. From the conflict comes also frequent attempts at suicide which do not usually even attain to the dignity of being fatal.

From this conflict in the Trobriands our information is full as to this latter suicidal motif. Crimes of passion are frequent, and while most of them are as non-fatal, rather more appear to succeed in attaining fatality than in Dobu.

Marital life based on the relative independence of women secured by legal *susu* right and affected strongly by a conflict between *susu* and marital grouping, elaborated into many ramifications, is a phenomenon removed by a very wide gulf from our own institution. The intensification of the *susu* versus marital grouping conflict by exogamous marriage into villages that are believed to be enemy in their use of the black arts of sorcery and witchcraft against the home village where one's *susu* are village owners, is not a phenomenon remotely similar to any element in our own institution of marriage.

Adultery in Dobu is typically village incest, an affair socially admired, although clandestine and distinctly below board, generally recognized as common, present in the folklore, and so taught to the children. It is a village reaction against exogamous marriage with the enemy, the stranger, the resultant-from-marriage. Neither suicide nor adulteries in this area can be set down as the concern of the human heart bared to the eternal verities. Both alike are the concern of the native heart operating to a culturally and socially determined rhythm of a very particular quality. Thus, where we find jealousy in marriage here, we have a reaction against a kin-group's antagonism to outsiders brought into contact with the kin-group by marriage. Where we find attempted suicide here, we have an expression of desperate appeal from the outsider that often functions in modifying the effects of the kin-group's antagonism towards him or her, or in cases of the suicide's death, towards others. Jealousy, incest, crime of passion, divorce, are all related intimately to the picture of the widower saying farewell to his children for ever that we saw expressed in the widower's song :—

> " Lie awake, lie awake, and talk
> at the midnight hour . . . "

This fact remains true, although adultery in Dobu sometimes

is not between the members of the village kin and suicide is sometimes not committed in the village of the spouse because of marital disagreement there. Adultery, if successful, is the mark of greatness from the individual's point of view. It is easiest in arrangement between members of the village, and such adultery is best protected from revenge. Nevertheless, I knew of cases of adultery that were not in the commoner pattern. When one marries into the enemy, so that a husband is apt to blame his bodily weakness in the morning on his wife's witchcraft during the night, and when suspicion of the black art causing one's sickness falls often on the mother-in-law, a high appreciation of adultery is not altogether unreasonable. But for all that, however highly adultery in general may be evaluated, and despite the fact that it often goes outside the village boundary, it has definitely been drawn into an expression of village solidarity versus the marital grouping's solidarity. Similarly, suicide was sometimes done in the old days by a man or a woman going unarmed into an enemy place and being killed there. But the commoner method still persists—an attempt on one's life in the village of the spouse as a protest against misconduct by the spouse and as a reflection on his or her village. Just as sometimes there is a law-breaker found, as old Sibor living with his children in his widow's village, profiting by the fact that his children formed the village majority, or Alo marrying his village " sister " (*nuuna*), so on occasion adultery passes outside the traditional pattern, on occasion suicide is of a different order. Human nature, always wider in its potentialities than the limited expression it can secure in a social code, breaks through the code ; on the whole, however, the code holds strong.

To the student of native literatures it will be interesting to observe how faithfully the Dobuan unwritten literature of dance, song, and legend, mirrors the social code. It does not depict the law-breaker. Rather it expresses the law impinging on the individual at its most tragic points. The father leaving his children, the husband leaving his wife and returning to his mother's place, both because of the overwhelming power of village solidarity—such are its themes as we have seen it. It is of the same materials as all the world's tragedy, the social code, itself a solidified expression of some elements in human nature and felt as a force within, not merely as an external compulsion, at war with the wider elements in human nature that are denied social expression and validation because of the necessary limitations of cultures ; the magnification of humanity by contrast with the narrower code, itself a solidified expression of some element in human nature, the triumph of the code.

To the student of jurisprudence it will be interesting to observe how the native unwritten literature is itself a conservative force. Together with the ridicule of offenders it is a conservative agent towards the maintenance of the social code. Private rights in property are protected otherwise—by fear of magical sanctions theft is discouraged as in the use of the *tabu* disease incantations, and by appeal to public sympathy as in the *lamoa* custom of naming trees after a family disaster and destroying the trees if a thief pilfers from them. The village solidarity is secured by the village acting as a body in expelling any outsider who has no right in the village. It is this right of expulsion that is presented in the folklore and so taught to the children. Hence adults accept it as a matter of course.

CHAPTER II

THE GARDEN

I

SKETCH OF THE CONCEPT OF RITUAL

When the steep hill slopes of Dobu Island or Tewara Island are yellow with the wilting leaves of the long staked yam vines in the frequent garden patches, the casual European visitor sees little interest in the return of the harvest season. It is true that the yellowing patches perched insecurely on the steep heights and in the hanging valleys are picturesque. They are that, and little more.

To the native his small garden patch is his refuge against hunger in the coming year. He has fasted many times the previous year to save a good supply of seed against this season. He and his wife have brooded over the patch for the year like parents over a sickly child. The garden is more to him than a garden merely. It is a place of ritual. Now with the maturing of the crop his hopes or his fears are coming to fruition. If the season is bad he will not blame the scanty crop on lack of care, but rather he will fear that his ritual has lost some of its potency.

The garden is a sacred place. To understand gardening in Dobu, we must first have understanding, not only of the social organization, but also of the Dobuan conception of creation and of the sacred.

Creation in Dobu is explained by the metamorphosis of some natural thing into another. Language is specialized to express the conception of metamorphosis. Thus *gurewa* means a stone, *egurewa* to become a stone by metamorphosis from something else, *manua* means a bird, *emanua* to become a bird by metamorphosis. Similarly, the prefix *e* placed before any noun signifies metamorphosis into the object signified by the noun. In the beginning of time various human persons *emanua nidi*, changed into birds. Thus birds came to be. Inconsistently enough, various birds hatched eggs from which issued the first human beings upon earth.

In truth, the Dobuan does not push hard upon logic in his account of Creation. He does not notice that one legend conflicts with another. No one Dobuan has ever attempted a composition of the various legends that contain accounts of origins. Metamorphosis provides a ready account of origins provided it is tacitly assumed that A precedes B in one connection, although B precedes A in another connection.

Various human beings changed into tree form, others became spirits such as those who now blow breath from their mouths, so making the winds. From one mango tree the sea issued, and various sea monsters promptly carved the sea channels and straits through the land. Fire came from the pubes of an old woman. Yams came and grew from humans in metamorphosis.

There is no one Creation chant, only a number of separate legends. Many of these legends are family secrets. Many again are known to nearly everyone.

The legends that have within them the account of how humans derive from a bird ancestry are known to the many members of each totem in common. The legend of how the sea issued from a mango tree is possessed by certain families only, but they tell it freely to listeners of other families who wish to hear it. The same is true of the legend of the origin of fire, and of a great number of legends, a few of which deal with origins.

There are other legends again that are closely knit up with ritual. These are kept by the family lines who own them with complete secrecy. Thus only families who perform garden ritual know the legend of how yams originated by metamorphosis from humans. The owners of ritual will tell non-owners and children freely that yams are really human beings in metamorphised form, but not a word more. The names of the first ancestors who changed themselves into yams or who begat children that were yams, not ordinary mortals, are names of power in the ritual to grow yams. Such names are kept secret in the families who own the ritual, together with the legend. Similarly the names of the ancestors whose powers are enlisted in ritual to make love, or to make sorcery, together with the fragmentary legends of the origin of love or of sorcery, are kept secret in the family lines that own the ritual.

The ritual of Dobu consists essentially in the use of incantations in the performance of certain activities such as canoe making and fishing-net making, in agriculture, in soliciting presents of valuables in the annual exchanges made by the long overseas expeditions, in the creating of love, in the making of wind and rain, in the causing and the curing of disease, and in the causing of death. These are the most striking fields in which incantation is used, but it ramifies still more widely. Incantations exist also to strengthen the memory, to inflict mosquito plagues upon others, to exorcise them from oneself, to make coconut and betel palms bear, to create pregnancy and to prevent unwelcome visitors from visiting again.

These incantations are often supplemented by the obligatory use of certain leaves, roots, and fluids, and these auxiliaries are believed to have power in their own right, so that a man who does not know an incantation may boast of the power of the root or the leaf or the fluid which he knows only ; but in most of these cases he is making the best of his ignorance. Were he able to obtain the incantation he would certainly go to great pains in acquiring and memorising it, and he would be prepared to pay for the knowledge fairly heavily as native wealth goes ; for the incantations are the most private of private property. They are always mumbled in a sing-song undertone and never heard by others gratuitously. A pair of men engaged in the learning take the utmost care to prevent eavesdropping, usually resorting to a remote part of the bush for the purpose. For the most part the incantations keep within the family, and different families possess different knowledge. In these days workboys in possession of their earnings for two years or so of indentured labour, sometimes sell an incantation to a friend who is not a close relative, a friend made on a white man's plantation, and in one case I know of, two English pounds, being the wages of four months' indentured labour, passed for a single incantation ; but native wealth cannot buy the knowledge between non-related persons as a rule.

Knowledge of incantation is never given freely, or is never phrased as being given freely. A parent always commands a child's services, a mother's brother always commands a sister's child's services, and gifts of ritual knowledge from elder to youth are looked upon as the reward for these services.

It is the knowledge of the fact that indebtedness for incantations must be worked off heavily at home in the normal course of things, that makes a workboy ready to part with the fruit of four months' indentured labour to another more fortunate friend, in return for an incantation. The youths plan and work for the knowledge. If a younger brother has helped his father or his mother's brother in gardening more than his elder brother, he will probably be given all the ritual knowledge of

his two guardians. The elder brother must reconcile himself
to losing it for ever. One brother does not share such a legacy
with another brother. The system is one of unameliorated
competition, the fruits of success being most jealously guarded
from theft by close secrecy. I had a great deal of difficulty
myself in succeeding in gaining my own knowledge of ritual.
I had to penetrate into what is a close family secret, into what
is the reward of long toil and services even within the family,
and into a secret possession which one brother will not share
with another. I had, moreover, to be trusted by my informant
not to let the knowledge go further than myself. In the native
view, ritual is the truest native wealth, more valuable than house,
canoe, or ornaments. It is the means of sustaining all important
social goods. Its exclusive possession by a few persons brings
them in a small income by its practice for others who do not
own it themselves.

Knowledge of herbs, roots, and saps of trees that are believed
to be auxiliary to incantation, is like incantation itself, kept as
secret as possible within the owning family lines, and secret
by the heir from his non-inheriting brothers and sisters.

Behind this ritual idiom there stands a most rigid and never-
questioned dogma, learnt by every child in infancy, and forced
home by countless instances of everyday usage based upon
it and meaningless without it or in its despite. This dogma, in
general, is that effects are secured by incantation, and that
without incantation such effects cannot come to pass. In its
particular application it is most strongly believed that yams will
not grow, however well the soil is prepared and cared for, without
the due performance of the long drawn-out ritual of gardening
incantations ; canoe lashing will not hold the canoe together
at sea, however firmly the creeper may be wound and fastened,
without the appropriate incantation being performed over its
lashing ; fish nets will not catch fish unless they have been
treated with incantation ; it is impossible to induce an overseas
partner in the annual overseas exchange of gifts to give one a
gift unless one has first prepared his mind and influenced his
susceptibilities with the co-operation of a certain supernatural
being that one directs to one's aid ; and disease is never caused
or never cured but by incantation ; death is caused always
so (death by poison alone excepted) ; " if we call upon the
wind (in incantation) she comes—if we do not call, dead calm."
Love between man and woman is due to incantation, and by
incantation alone can it be called forth. In brief, there is no

natural theory of yam growth, of the powers of canoe lashings or fish nets, of gift exchange in strange places overseas, of disease and death, of wind and rain, of love between man and woman. All these things cannot possibly exist in their own right. All are supernaturally created by the ritual of incantation with the help of the appropriate technological processes in agriculture, canoe making, fishing preparation, and with the help of more mundane wooing in overseas gift exchange and in love-making, but without any such extra work in making wind and rain, disease and death or in their counteracting (apart only from the, practice of bleeding the patient in some cases of illness). This latter type of unaided incantation expresses truly the attitude of the native towards incantation throughout. It is the really important factor in producing an effect. Technology and mundane measures are by no means despised, for they are often essential and are recognized as such ; but it is most firmly believed that agricultural technology alone and gift-giving and serenading alone, as two typical examples, will never grow yams or induce love.

We have already seen that legend in certain cases is closely implicated with ritual. Four generations of human ancestors are known to the native. The generation before that is the generation of Creation by metamorphosis. Its reality is vouched for in legend. The occurrences of Creation do not live in legend alone, however, as events divided strictly from the present by an intervening gulf of time. There is a firm belief in continuity. Although a legendary scene is laid in the time of Creation, its actors still live, their influences still prevail. Thus, an underwater moving rock called Nuakekepaki still menaces and often overturns canoes on the open seas. Legend tells how Nuakekepaki is a deep sea moving rock-man, who, to pay for a wife taken from the land-dwellers, overturned canoes to obtain the valuables they contained, which he duly paid to his mothers-in-law and their brothers as the *kwesi* or bride price. All that can be made of this character is that he is a rock in one aspect, a man in another, and that as a rock he has supernatural qualities. He still overturns canoes to obtain the valuables they contain, apart from his former duty to his parents-in-law in the time of the first ancestors.

Tobwaliton and Tobebeso are two sea monsters that appeared at the creation of the sea and indirectly played a part in connection with its creation. When I was in the

field they were credited with counteracting the attempts
of the local rain-maker, an old woman, to break a long drought
which occurred. A monstrous dog called Weniogwegwe,
that dates from the Creation, still roams in the forest at night,
and many men have seen his great red eyes ; one, I met, had
even given his flank a resounding whack with a paddle. He
is as big as a house and his eyes are like fires. In the time
of the first ancestors men ate food uncooked until a woman
took fire from her pubes and cooked food with it. Still the
kaiana fire issues from the pubes of women, and there is not
a man who has not seen the fire flooding the night with light,
or hovering to and fro in the air—and not slept for hours
after, but huddled about the fire in fear of witchcraft and
death in consequence of it.[1] Kasabwaibwaileta, Bunelala,
Nemwadole, Wanoge and many other characters among the
first ancestors still exist, and exert the same influence that
legend vouches for their having exerted some five generations
ago when existence first came into being and natural history
began.

Many of these characters, supernatural beings all, were
human beings among the first ancestors, many again were
a mysterious fusion of human and sub-human and super-
human. In legend they behave as human, often with
exceptional qualities however ; but they have taken to themselves immortality and other supernatural qualities. They
are not mortals, but *kasa sona*, " born with the sun and the
moon and the earth—we are but newly come " as the term
was interpreted to me. Man of today has power over some,
but not all of these beings, by incantation, nor have these
independent power to resist incantation or to act without it.
When incantation fails, however, or rather is delayed in
succeeding as during a drought, the few of the beings *kasa
sona* who are not called upon in incantation, may be credited
with frustrating the normal course of things. Such was
the work of Tobwaliton and Tobebeso that I referred to above.
A few such beings exist and act independently. So the face
of the ritualist is saved in time of trouble.

The class of independent supernaturals such as Tobwaliton
and Tobebeso, Nuakekepaki, Weniogwegwe, and the *kaiana*
fire from old women's pubes, are referred to freely. The
legends vouching for them are not secret. On the other hand,
the very names of supernaturals such as Bunelala, Nemwadole,

[1] As I have seen many times.

and Wanoge, are close secrets. These are dependent supernaturals, a knowledge of whose names is an important element
in the incantations which force them into the service of the
ritualist. Kasabwaibwaileta is the only such dependent
supernatural whose name and legend is circulated freely.
Nemwadole, Wanoge and a host of others are most secret.
Their names are never pronounced except in inaudible undertone in actual ritual or in the seclusion where one man is
teaching another ritual.

Free use of their names such as I make here would be
felt by the Dobuan magicians as worse than the greatest
blasphemy would be to Christian believers. It combines
the double offence of a slight to the supernatural whose name
must not be taken in vain—in this case not taken at all—and
also a slight to the economic system which is upheld by the
secrecy of powerful information. Such a dual slight in one
stroke is impossible with our comparative separation of Church
and Commerce. Our own term " blasphemy " does not
comprehend the magnitude of the offence.

When a man has power to create love in a woman by
incantation the content of his power is a power over a being
kasa sona, Wanoge, who works under his complusion of ritual
incantation to awaken love for him in the woman desired.
Since many persons do not have this knowledge and power,
he who knows the name Wanoge, the legend of Wanoge, and
the incantation that throws Wanoge into helping him, keeps
all this knowledge most secret. But since he is known to
possess this power by others, they fee him to use it on their
behalf. They, on their part, would look blank if the question
" who is Wanoge " were put to them. If the man in
possession of the ritual heard such a question put to non-
possessors he would be most jealously enraged.

Secrecy in possession is firmly kept, not only because of
the pains taken to gain possession and the economic gains
secured by exclusive possession, but because the world view
of magic is one of contending magical forces. If the ritualist
makes rain by incantation and rain does not come the explanation may be either independent supernaturals such as
Tobwaliton and Tobebeso, as we have seen, or it may be that
another ritualist elsewhere is making drought by incantation.
If the ritualist makes healing by incantation and his patient
dies it is because another ritualist elsewhere is making killing
forces by incantation. If the ritualist uses incantations to

make his yams stay at home in his own garden at night and yet harvests a poor crop, then another ritualist elsewhere has succeeded in enticing his yams to leave his garden by night and enter the other's garden. For one may observe that the other has harvested a good crop. If an enemy ritualist is trying to kill one by incantation of sorcery and one remains in good health, it is because one's own protecting ritual against sorcery which one has been reciting has proved the stronger. All good luck is due to one's ritual being stronger than the ritual of others, which is aimed at results contrary to one's own aim. Accordingly it is most important that one should have strong ritual, and that one should not alienate it to others whose aims are likely to be directly contrary to one's own. Hence, secrecy is the only safeguard, it is felt in Dobu.

The ritual is most importantly a form of words addressed to the appropriate supernaturals. It thus does not differ fundamentally from the concept contained in our own religion —namely, that words addressed apparently into vacancy can be heard by more than natural semi-personal Beings and that effects of human interest can be produced with the assistance of such Beings. There is a wide pantheon of such Beings in Dobu. Their attributes include omnipresence ; but they are not omnipotent. They are conceived as having themselves originated certain formulae in the beginning. They gave these formulae to certain of the descendants of their contemporaries, the first ancestors of man. Such men have in these formulae, omnipotence. The Beings are become of their initial and only volition, impotent. They work the will of the possessor of the formula they created and bequeathed. If the human does not use his will and his formula they remain inert, their fires drawn. If two humans use their formula at the same time desiring incompatible services they are at the service of him whose formula is the more authentic, the more perfectly memorized, and the more perfectly handed down without change or loss of content in its transmission from one generation to another.

If then we come upon a ritual addressed to seed yams, let it not be supposed that a man is muttering a form of words to yams merely. He is addressing a Personal Being as truly as we are when we address God. For the yams are personal beings in metamorphized form. If we come upon a ritual addressed to a canoe-lashing creeper let it not be thought that a man is muttering a form of words to a bush creeper merely. The bush creeper is a personal being in meta-morphized form. If we come upon a ritual addressed to winning the heart of a far-off woman let there not be seen a man addressing vacancy, but here the human ritualist, and there omnipresent in vacancy the unseen Supernatural, mediate between the ritualist and the woman of his desire in her place apart. If we find a ritual to make the wind, we must not see a mortal only flinging a spell into the unhearing air, but here the human ritualist and in the spaces the omnipresent every hearing Supernatural who in the beginning ceded his volition to the ancestors of the ritualist by making over the spell to them without hearing which he will blow no great wind in gigantic breaths of air from his mouth, but upon hearing which he must needs do so, unless some other human ritualist who knows his spell better than the first ritualist, commands him to cease.

Here we have the principles of the Dobuan concept of the sacred.

We may now turn directly to the Dobuan garden, with the preliminary knowledge necessary to understand the native gardening procedure in its most unfamiliar aspect.

II

SOCIAL ORGANIZATION IN GARDENING

It has been already shown that a husband owns his own seed, descended from the seed used by his mother, his mother's brother and so back along the distaff line, while a wife owns her own seed of equivalent descent within the ancestral line of her *susu*. It has been shown how at betrothal the mother-in-law, to be, gives her son-in-law, to be, a digging stick saying, " go, make a garden." Then the son-in-law labours gardening with his parents-in-law while the daughter-in-law also labours gardening with her parents-in-law. The parents-in-law thus have privileged inspection of the seed and the growth of the seed of their future proposed resultant-from-marriage. If the seed proves unsatisfactory in quantity or in quality they may decline to allow the marriage to proceed. If the proposed resultant-from-marriage produces a good garden to their satisfaction, then the economic exchanges to validate marriage are initiated. First must come the garden trials.

Not only the proposed son-in-law and proposed daughter-in-law must work with their respective parents-in-law, but also the lad's true brothers and sisters must help him and his future parents-in-law, and the girl's true brothers and sisters must help her and her future parents-in-law. These brothers and sisters of the betrothed pair must, like the betrothed themselves, abstain from food and drink in the presence of their brother's or sister's future parents-in-law.

At this period the children must help not only their future parents-in-law, but also their own parents in gardening. Hence a lad whose brother is about to be married receives the news with depression. It promises such an excess of work that sometimes nowadays a lad in such a position runs away incontinent to seek work with a white man. This procedure enrages his elders, but they can do nothing about it as they are not forewarned of his intention. The old men say that recruited labour has depleted their garden resources ; the seed now saved is less than it was. I do not know whether this is true or not. Certainly the Dobuan area is poor in gardens. Each year the saving of enough seed for the next year is accomplished against the pressure of hunger, and undoubtedly usually was, although the Mission state that bumper native crops, such as are not known now, used to be harvested in the earlier days of the Mission in good seasons. The area, a poor one to begin with, has certainly given a heavy toll of labour indentured to the white man.

When betrothal has changed to marriage the child-in-law with his or her brothers and sisters no longer work the gardens of the parents-in-law and the child-in-law respectively. In the ensuing years the clearing of the bush and the planting are done by co-operative labour and families connected by marriage help one another in their respective gardens in this work. But in the subsequent work of the year each pair, man and wife, work by themselves their two gardens. Unmarried children work as before with their parents only. The work (under surveillance) of child-in-law with his own brothers' and sisters' help is over. Betrothal often lasts two or three years, however, before the economic validations are finally made.

I had little opportunity to examine the social organization of communal labour at bush clearing and planting of the garden, as much of it was over when I first landed in the Dobuan district. I was ignorant of the language and without an interpreter. During my first month there I was treated with hostility. I was not told when gardening was being done, despite my requests. The first night after my landing in Tewara Island at about midday, the men came back from the palolo fishing on the reef fifteen miles away at about 2 in the morning. They were threatening to my face. They went away, climbed the hill, took out their spears, and debated coming to spear me. Finally they put their spears away. From the usual Dobuan custom in regard to unguarded women, and from their jealousy in watching over their women, they suspected me and their women whom they had left on the island of the worst. Hostility was still active while the last remnants of bush clearing and the latest gardens were being planted—now it was believed that I was a spy and a forerunner of white intrusion and interference with native custom, such as Mission and Government accomplish where they settle. Accordingly, I saw but one piece of communal garden work which I stumbled upon by accident. I was, at this time, living alone in a deserted place by the shore. After six weeks or so of this I was granted land in a village on the hill. There I had my hut built. I entered the village without further hostility. I had my own garden land cleared and my own garden made, a month later than the last native garden was made. In my own garden I had two of the chief magicians of my village perform the usual garden ritual; so I witnessed it all without offending others by wandering into their gardens. For, as I found, the garden is entirely private, once communal clearing and planting is over, to man and wife, who may approach each other intimately there. Further by planting my own garden late and having it done strictly according to native custom, I made up leeway that I had been shut out of by hostility towards me when native bush clearing and garden planting was being completed— that is, leeway in seeing the ritual. I saw only the one truly native organization of labour, for nearly everyone in the island came to clear my land and plant it. The ritual done over my garden then, and subsequently, was true to native custom. After planting, the two magicians and myself alone went to my garden for ritual or plain gardening work.

Neddidiway, a widow of the White Pigeon village, had her land cleared and planted by her mother, herself and her sons, by the members of three families of the Brown Eagle village, by two men of the Green Parrot village, and by most of the other members of her own village. Of the members of her own village Togo was absent, Togo, the wastrel when work was forward, and also Yogalu, adopted member of her village, permanently resident in his wife's village. Yogalu's son was present, however, a Green Parrot lad. The other Green Parrot man present was the husband of Mwedi, (Mwedi also of Yogalu's place, also adopted into the White Pigeon village in Tewara) who was there with Mwedi.

Neddidiway's dead husband had been a Brown Eagle man ; hence the presence of over half of the Brown Eagle village. There is therefore co-operation between all members of the one village, aided by many of the village with whom the person who is having the garden made is or was connected by marriage. Husbands may go with their wives, as Tawa, himself not directly connected, went with Mwedi, a village sister (*tasina*) of Neddidiway. On the other hand Wonoloi did not go with her husband, Pogudu of the Brown Eagle village. Pogudu went by himself, he being related to Neddidiway's dead husband, a village brother (*tasina*) of his. Yogalu's son, who was brother's son, *kedeana*, to Neddidiway went in place of Yogalu.

Bush clearing is done by men and women together, the men cutting away the heavier timber, the women pulling and cutting away the slighter growth. Some of the wood is cut and taken away as firewood by the women. The scrub is left to dry in the sun. After it is well dried it is fired by a màn. Planting follows usually the day after firing, the men wielding the digging sticks, the women following behind inserting and covering up the yam seed. The organization of labour is as for bush clearing. Then follows the privacy of the garden. The wife weeds the soil and hills up the plants after they are grown. The husband cuts stakes and trains the yam vines up them. They both brood over the garden with frequent ritual through the year until harvest. The woman digs the harvest. The husband stands sentinel over the wife, playing with the children it may be, at all events making sure of his wife's fidelity, when all the work there is to do is woman's work as in weeding or in digging the yam harvest. For a part of this leisure time he may occupy himself with an adjoining banana patch. The men take care of banana patches in all respects, even weeding them ;

but they are little work compared to the work of the yam garden.

The harvesting is spread over many forenoons. Each forenoon a few baskets of yams are taken home and stored in a family's special food house in the village. There is no display of garden yields. No one pries into anyone else's harvest. At harvest time each married couple keeps rigidly to itself in its own two gardens. Straying children belonging to some one else are driven out if they are ignorant enough to venture in with a stern " what, do you expect something to eat here ". They never stray, except to lead in an anthropologist who wants to take a snapshot—even then they do not escape the sharp rebuke.

The widows and widowers of the gardening year work the gardens of their parents-in-law or elder sisters and brothers-in-law, work without remuneration and akin to the work under surveillance that initiates marriage. They also work the gardens of their dead spouses under surveillance. Their own gardens must be worked by their brothers and sisters or sisters' children.

At harvest time there are ceremonial exchanges of food between villages connected by marriage, and between villages between whom death has just severed a marriage during the year. These exchanges will be described later when we come to discuss the economics of exchange.

III

THE RITUAL OF THE GARDEN

Without the magical ritual no native garden is made. It is believed most strongly that without certain rites and forms of words the seed yams will not multiply and grow. In Dobu Island, where the Mission has stoutly opposed this dogma for nearly forty years, the rites and incantations are still deemed necessary and never omitted. In Tewara Island, where the Mission has not been, I asked how it came about that the Mission whites and their introduced Polynesian teachers grew yam gardens without the incantations. I was met with the retort that, while it was true the Polynesian teachers did not use Dobuan magic, it was not true that they grew good yam crops. Always their crops were nothing or next to nothing. The reason was that they did not know or use the rites and incantations. Thus report has falsified the evidence to sustain the Dobuan dogma.

In the process of witnessing the long drawn-out garden ritual I was offered various explanations of it by various persons. These I shall give first. Once when Magile (the woman who did the woman's ritual in my garden) was charming over a bundle of smouldering green leaves in my garden her son said to me :

" The Trobrianders charm out aloud. Here, on the contrary, we murmur underbreath. The yams hear. They say among themselves ' this is our language—not loud like everyday talk '. You must understand that yams are persons. Alo recently told you of it. If we call aloud the yams say ' how is this—are they fighting among themselves '. But when we charm softly they listen to our speech attentively. They grow big for our calling on them."

In the Trobriands, incantations are chanted aloud. It is not feared that the right to use an incantation may be stolen by an unprivileged overhearer. Right of possession is socially acknowledged and not tampered with by non-possessors. In Dobu, on the contrary, anyone overhearing another charming aloud, can memorise the incantation and use it himself. Eavesdroppers on one man teaching another an incantation aloud, can by successful eavesdropping, steal the magical power. In practice, precautions against eavesdroppers are rigidly maintained. Dobu has a pattern of possible theft that is not known in the Trobriands. The above native statement is a rationalization of this fact in terms of the yams liking soft speech, underbreath, rather than speech aloud.

Alo had recently told me a legend in which the yams figured as persons. I had not known whether this was a figurative device of legend or an expression of a fact of literal belief. The statement of Magile's son, Kinosi, pointed to the latter alternative. Some nights later I said to Alo :

" Kinosi said in the garden yams are persons. How is this ? "

" Yams are persons," said Alo—" what else ? Like women, they give birth to children. As my grandmother gave birth to children, among them my mother, as she gave birth to me and as my daughter will bear children, and they my grand-children, when I am dead—such is also the way of yams."

" But," I said, " how is it yams are persons ? Do persons stay still always ? "

Alo had his counter-statement.

" At night they come forth from the earth and roam about. For this reason, if we approach a garden at night we tread very quietly. Just as if we startle a man with an abrupt shout— or with a dead snake concealed behind our back—he starts back in fear and later is angry—so we approach a garden very quietly at night. We do not dig the harvest when the sun is low in the morning (the usual time for garden work). We wait till the sun has mounted. Then we know they are back. If we dig in the early morning how should we find yams ? Nothing would be there. We do not dig early. It is *bomama* (our sacred prohibition) of the garden."

This statement proved to be no spontaneous argument, but a direct statement of traditional belief. I enquired if the vine and the root tubers walked about at nights entire. My enquiry was cast in all seriousness and received with all seriousness.

" No ! The vines remain. You may see them steadfast any night in the garden. The tubers alone emerge from the ground and walk the bush tracks in the night."

Later I was to learn, in complete accordance with these early statements, that incantations based upon the believed mobility of yams in the night were generally practised. Later, too, I heard several casual references to the nocturnal prowlings of yams. One man peering out of my house into the pouring rain one night said, as an example of this :

" This is the moon of deepest darkness. It is the *kaniana* of the yams. The yams their time. Now they roam in the forest." (*Kaniana* is rain produced as a by-product of certain supernatural events.)

Later I learned again that the comparison between human child-bearing and yam seed fertility is in its most literal sense insisted upon. Each *susu* family line has its own line of seed. It is pictured that one human family line has its one seed family line that will grow for it. But that seed line will not grow for a stranger family line ; just as if the retainers of one house will work for the descendants of the blood of that house, but not for another house, the retainers and their descendants after them. Seed yams are not inherited outside the *susu* or given away outside the *susu*—this fact assumes in native expression an aspect of a human line of descent that is served and can be served only by one certain yam line of descent—the faithful retainers of the human line, faithless to other human family lines.

After I had arrived at this stage, I once said, in the hope that provocation might elucidate matters further, that one man (whom I did not name) had told me that yams were not persons. This statement was strictly untrue. My two informants both assumed the extremely disgusted expression which means emphatic negation, and Alo said curtly and forcibly :

" Yams are persons, with ears. If we charm they hear."

Next day he showed me the ears, organs of hearing, the several tendril buds about the growing point of the vine. The growing point buds are no more ears than an ear of corn is an organ of hearing. In Dobu the ears of the vine are most literally organs of hearing, however.

In the *elowaila*, the winding of the vines about the stick, some only of the plants are charmed. The remainder are wound without further ceremony. I said to Kinosi :

" Some of the plants you charm—others not. What of the others ? How will they grow as big as those charmed ? "

To which Kinosi :

" Seedling yams are as men. They have understood. One says ' that there he charms. What about me ? ' O he is angry and he shoots up strongly."

At a rite with burning green leaves and so producing a cloud of smoke, the charmer's husband said :

" The yams see it. They snuff it in to get its odour. They forsake the *kebudi* (stick for the climbing tendrils), climb over it, and trail down again."

It will be apparent from these various statements that the yams are treated as highly personal beings. The word *tomot* is used freely of them. *Tomot* is the only word that covers man, woman, and child, irrespective of age or sex. It also connotes native as opposed to belonging to the white man when used adjectivally. This latter usage contains the prevalent idea that the white man is " another kind ", not really a human person in the native sense, but a being with different qualities from the native. The Dobuan will class yams with his own people as personal beings, but he excludes white men. In fact, he has indeed the more friendly feeling for the yams.

After bush clearing and burning off, which need not detain our attention, comes planting. The planting always commences from the inland border of the clearing and proceeds seawards. The inland border of the garden is called by a term which I may translate arbitrarily as top-side. The seawards border of the garden is called by a term which I may translate equally arbitrarily as bottom-side. The two other sides we may call side, simply. (The true native terms are *kaikai*, *kunukunuwana* and *nana* respectively—there is no true translation but I have fabricated translations in order to avoid possible later embarrassment.) Long poles which we may call length-sticks (in order to avoid calling them *eketosika*) run from top-side to bottom-side, each about eight feet apart from its neighbour. At right angles to the length sticks from side to side go cross-sticks (otherwise *sigata*). Length-sticks and cross-sticks mark off spaces about eight feet square in regular division of the garden clearing. The seeds are apportioned regularly over the garden, a fixed number, usually from three to four, in each marked-off square. Big yams are rejected for seed as being a waste of good food. Small yams are rejected as being too small to nourish a good crop. Middle-sized yams alone are selected as seed.

At sunrise on the day of planting, the ceremonial begins. Two squares of the number of the garden squares are selected for intensive ceremony. The seaward cross-stick of the centermost square is called the Place of the Magic Peg. Over the cross-stick the centermost square is called the Place of Pouring. About two or three squares inland from the centermost square, and within the same two length-sticks, a square is selected as the Place of the House Platform. Thus :

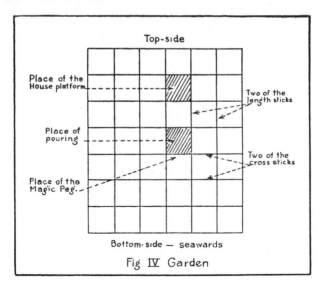

Fig IV Garden

Two small pegs called Boundary Catchers are planted in earth on each side of the cross-stick at the Place of the Magic Peg. The male magican plants these pegs intoning under-breath and inaudibly as he does it :

> Yabowaine
> come down from above
> come break up the earth.
>   my boundary catchers
> break the earth in all directions.
> your breaking up the earth
>   letting light into it,
> my breaking up the earth
>   letting light into it.
> the yams *monolawa, gelaboi*
> my breaking up the earth
>   letting light into it.

In this spell the magican is associated with a certain super-natural termed Yabowaine. Beyond the fact that Yabowaine, like the Christian God, is of the Above, I could discover little about this supernatural. My best informant believed that the supernatural in question was only seen rarely as a small tree snake.

The male ritualist now binds the two pegs, the Boundary Catchers, one on each side of the seaward cross-stick of the Place of Pouring, with *nipuna* creeper, binding each one around and then binding the two together. As he winds the creeper around the pegs he charms :

> Whose belt of red shell discs
> is it that I wind around,
>   I bind around ?
> the woman bulelala
> her belt of red shell discs
>   I bind around
>   I bind around.
> seeing my yams they shout in amazement
> the way of carrying them is a different carrying.
> the way of covering them is a different covering.
>   the shoots spring upwards,
> underground the shoots uncurl,
> many side shoots go outward.

The woman Bulelala was the first woman to plant yams as food. Her spirit survives as a nocturnally active bird. The bird is said to come and hoot across newly made gardens. The bird does exist, but I cannot vouch for its habits. Belts are actually made of intricately plaited *nipuna* creeper, and such belts adorned with discs of a certain red shell are a very highly-valued ornament. Plain *nipuna* unadorned, unplaited, is used in this charm's ritual. The words of the spell trans-form the plain material actually used into a valuable that is being ceremonially bound around the supernatural, Bulelala. This fictitiously costly, actually cheap, sacrifice to Bulelala is followed by a statement of anticipated results. In the first charm, calling upon the supernatural Yabowaine, there was only one line referring to anticipated results—" the yams *monolawa*, *gelaboi*" (two varieties of the larger yams). Now, however, in the second charm a great crop is already specifically mentioned, a crop that will cause shouts of amazement and special devices for carrying and covering it.

The male ritualist now crosses over the Place of the Magic Peg into the Place of Pouring. He prepares the earth for a square yard or so about by breaking up clods and digging into the earth with his hands charming as he does so :

> hill of the rocks,
> hill of the rocks.
> what do I delve, hurl behind me ?
> my feast of young food,
> my assembling of *monolawa*.
> seeing my yams they shout in amazement.
> one *monolawa* is a load set on your head,
> huge *mwamwasipa*
> I hurl from earth belly to earth back.

Monolawa and *mwamwasipa* are larger varieties of yams. The Place of Pouring is alternatively called Earth-Belly. The Place of the Magic Peg is alternatively called Earth-Back. In the last line as the magican intones in a murmur " I hurl from earth belly to earth back " he throws back earth from the Place of Pouring, where he is squatting, towards the Place of the Magic Peg, which he has just left.

While the male ritualist is engaged in this last performance, the female ritualist proceeds seawards to the garden bottom-side, and inland again to the Place of the Magic Peg, striking rocks and the scattered sticks left standing from the bush clearing for future vine supports, with the long leaves of the *pies* shrub. As she walks she charms :

> underneath the turtle
> turns on his side
> they pack up their possessions
> they go far away
> insect eaten leaf,
> sear leaf
> rotted, worm eaten leaf.
> turns on his side
> they pack up their possessions
> they go far away.

At this stage she reaches the seaward fringe of the clearing

and hurls the contaminated *pies* leaves seawards. She takes
fresh *pies* leaves and strikes about anew coming inland.

> my friends where is your food ?
> much food is in my earth's belly.
>   your turning about, your returning,
>   my turning about, my returning.
>   new leaves sprouting on my taro
>   new leaves sprouting on my *ponake* banana,
> I take them in my hand, I release them.

Here she comes back to the Place of the Magic Peg, and on
the two pegs, Boundary Catchers, she lays the *pies* leaves
that she used from the garden bottom-side coming inland.

This spell is in one particular Dobuan pattern. It has
two parts, the first being a removal of contamination, the
second being positive in its direction.

In the first line of the first part of the spell the turtle is
neither an ordinary turtle nor yet a metaphor. He is a supernatural
being conceived as being turtle-like, a turtle with a difference.
He has his special name which like Yabowaine and Bulelala,
is never applied to anything else and never taken as a personal
name by a living person. This name is not taken in vain.
It is a secret name hidden completely from the uninitiate.
To know his name is in large measure to command him.
Hence, his name must never be pronounced except when one
has work for him to do. His name pronounced with the rest
of the words of the spell, and with the correct rites is even
more powerful. It is irresistible. But the mere pro-
nunciation of the names is often enough. (I was cautioned
severely for using the name of the gangosa disease once.
I knew the spell for creating gangosa. I must not use even
the bare name lest " IT " come to command and afflict all
who were present with me with the sad disease of gangosa.
There was no mistaking their fear.)

The secrecy in which the names of the supernaturals are
kept varies. Yabowaine was named by someone to the white
missionaries as the Dobuan equivalent of God in rough native
generalization—and his secrecy has been somewhat damaged
by the association. Bulelala is a name assigned to a certain
night bird, the present embodiment of the spirit of the woman
who first grew yams. This concrete embodiment has led to
the name Bulelala spreading somewhat. Even the partly
uninitiate betray some emotion over the name. The name
of the Turtle of the first spell used by the woman ritualist
is a deep secret, however. So secret also are many of the

names that will be used in the following spells. The names Nebubunebubuero and Nemwadole, had I used them publicly, would have aroused such resentment in my teacher of magic that my learning of magic would have been over. I would have been giving names of power, giving power itself, to those who had no birth-right to such power, but, who had to fee the special practitioners and possessors of such power to exercise it on their behalf.

An essential element in the ritual is the use of the correct leaves, woods or creepers, traditionally associated with the spells. In Dobuan garden ritual these are not conceived as the greatest essential, the core of the magical power. The reason for this is that they are publicly exposed to the view of the uninitiate who help in the communal garden work. They cannot be kept secret, as the names of the supernaturals and the words of the spell are kept secret, and private to the magician. In garden ritual the spell is emphasized as the core of the power of the compulsion over nature exerted by the ritualist. But it is not always so. In the black art, the herbs employed are close secrets. Here the herb is often spoken of as the core of the magician's power.

But even where there is no secret as in the use of *nipuna* creeper to bind the pegs of the Place of the Magic Peg, or in the use of the *pies* leaves by the woman magician in her opening charm, great care is taken to secure the correct leaves or other vegetable product. *Nipuna* creeper and *pies* leaves are not usually difficult to obtain nearby, but other leaves that are used in later ritual are often difficult to find. In such cases, search is made without regard for time spent or labour. One of the best illustrative cases is a certain herb necessary to Trobriand garden magic which the Trobrianders painstakingly collect in Dobuan districts or in Fergusson Island, sixty miles away overseas from their home. The correct herb must be obtained. The ritual is not performed until it is obtained.

The *pies* plant used by the woman magician in her charm :
" underneath the turtle "
is none other than *Cordyline terminalis* more commonly known by its Polynesian name, the *ti* plant. It is a plant that is of ceremonial importance over a wide Oceanic area. In the Admiralty Islands it is used in healing magic, and planted by the grave with a charm breathed into it to lay the spirit of the dead and prevent it causing trouble to the living.

In New Britain it is called *diwai belong tamberan*, the shrub of the spirits of the dead and is planted in the gardens of the magicians.[1] It is allied to the crotons planted over graveyards amongst the Massim, although the Massim use the coloured crotons for this purpose in preference to the green *Cordyline terminalis*. Codrington refers repeatedly to the use of the croton in the Solomons, Banks Islands and New Hebrides. He does not specify the variety, whether *Cordyline terminalis* or one of the coloured varieties. In the area covered by Codrington the plant is used by the ghost societies ceremonially.[2]

In Niue, *Cordyline terminalis* is used ceremonially in first fruits ceremony,[3] and magically to make an unborn child strong.[4] In the Society Group the plant is associated with fire walking,[5] and the same is true of Fiji,[6] and of the Cook Group.[7] It is apparent that this plant has a widely spread ceremonial value in Oceania. From the more utilitarian point of view the root is cooked in the earth oven and eaten in many parts of Polynesia. The leaves are used to flavour taro in Dobu.

We may return from these explanatory by-ways to our main road, the Dobuan ritual in progress. We left the woman magician laying down the leaves of the *ti* plant (*pies*) on the pegs driven in the earth at the seaward edge of the Place of Pouring. She now proceeds across the Place of Pouring and drives a peg in at the inland edge of the Place of Pouring, muttering the Yabowaine charm as the male ritualist had done before her. She winds green *nipuna* creeper about it muttering the Bulelala charm, also as the male ritualist. She breaks up the ground, previously broken in part by the male ritualist, the ground within the Place of Pouring. As she scratches the ground with her hands and breaks it up, she mutters the Hill of the Rocks charm over it, as her male predecessor did before her. The ground clawing with the bare hands, looks somewhat grotesque to the white onlooker,

---

[1] Verbal communication from Mrs. R. Parkinson.
[2] Codrington, *The Melanesians*, p. 83, pp. 210–11. See also Tamate societies, index references.
[3] E. M. Loeb, *History and Traditions of Niue*, Bulletin 32 of Bishop Bernice P. Museum, p. 174.
[4] Percy Smith, *Journal of the Polynesian Society*, vol. xi, p. 203.
[5] Tenira, Henry, ibid., vol. x, p. 53.
[6] Welles, Burke, *The Firewalkers of Fiji*. Frank Leslie's Popular Monthly, 1903, p. 586.
[7] *Journal of the Polynesian Society*, vol. viii, p. 58.

especially, as when I saw it, the soil was very hard even to the sharp pointed digging sticks with which the rest of the garden was done. In this manner and with spell the square of the Place of Pouring is prepared to receive the seed. No digging stick is used upon it.

The male ritualist, who has been squatting nearby while the woman ritualist completes her moves, now rises and proceeds to the Place of the House Platform inland from the Place of Pouring. Here in the centre of the square he plants an upright stick cut from the *siwabu* tree. Then he plants four leaning sticks about it, one from each side of the square, the final effect resembling rifles stacked. He breathes a spell into *nipuna* creeper and fastens the meeting points of the stick pyramid with it, still charming with the same spell—

> whose house platform
> I set up, I bind fast ?
> the man buleima
> his house platform
> I set up, I bind fast.
> the man tulia,
> the man kuyagas
> five posted
> my food five posted
> it shoots upward
> it uncurls underground
> it sends out many side shoots.

The man Buleima, the man Tulia, the man Kuyagas are yam varieties, in ordinary speech called Buleima, Tulia, and Kuyagas simply. This incantation being concluded, the male ritualist's part is done for the day. The woman now slices a large prime variety of red fleshed yam into " eyes ". This is only done with the one variety of yam in Dobu. In Basima, a district of another language bordering Dobu, no slicing of any yam into " eyes " is done. The largest varieties are planted entire. The Basima folk regard the Dobuan custom in this regard with the greatest horror. Their emotion at the idea is exactly comparable to a militant Protestant denunciation of Papist custom. Even in Dobu the slicing is done with apologetic regards to the yam so sliced. As the woman slices the yam she mutters—

> i-oi !
> samu, samuela
> samu, samuela.
> I disembark at walibua
> at the head of the garden
> I cut and her blood
> flows as a stream flows
> spurts as flung sea spray.
> ya !

```
    samu, samuela,
    samu, samuela,
      i-oi !
      samuela.
  kwatea gomanumusa (the variety of yam sliced)
  rises, stands erect.
```

Samuela was the female child of Bulelala, who set her daughter in the earth, where she developed various yam qualities. She went to Wamea in the Amphletts where she was refused food by the people. She left them and went to Walibua near Mt. Koyatabu. There the inhabitants not only refused to give her food but cut her throat and grew her as a yam with a red (blood-coloured) flesh. " I-oi ! " is the native expression of great condolence " you poor thing ". The charm proffers apologies and condolence for the cutting of the seed into " eyes ". This fragment of mythology is not public information in common with ordinary mythology. Like the spell itself it is secret to the owner of the spell. The extraordinary feature about it from the ethnologist's point of view is that Walibua, near Mt. Koyatabu, is exactly where the Basima neighbours of the Dobuans, the folk who express horror at the bare idea of cutting a seed yam into " eyes ", live. The original sin is laid at the door of neighbours, who certainly do not slice yams into eyes at all in these days. There is evidently an imperative need to put the original fault on to someone else, preferably someone else whose custom one does not approve of as being different.

The woman magician next breathes a spell into two or three water gourds containing sea water, and pours the water over the heaped seed yams and sliced " eyes " which she and an assistant have heaped on the Place of Pouring. The slicing performance was done in the Place of Pouring—the woman magician must be pictured as still being there. She continues charming as she pours the water, mixing it with a little mud as she pours it, to make a fine silt that will adhere to the yam seed. The spell breathed into the water gourds and continued while the water is being poured runs—

```
      murua octopus
    from its inner cave
    it thrusts a left arm out
  on the left side it lies, head inland,
    it thrusts a right arm out
    comes over and down, lies down.
    the rich man my friends,
    the rich women my friends,
    my heap of harvest home
    my feast of new food.
```

This charm bears the name by which the Green Parrot clan's system of garden ritual is known as a system. Different totemic clans have each their different system of garden magic. I know only that of the Green Parrot clan in full. It is the system I am giving here. The difference in the magic of other totems is mainly in minor points. They all use Yabowaine and Bunelala charms, they all use a charm involving the use of the *pies* plant (*ti* plant). They all use ritual associated with the Pleiades. They all use ritual based upon the belief in the nocturnal prowling of the growing yams. They have the major elements in common. But the above charm is an especial and exclusive possession of the Green Parrot people. The fact of such differences functions in native theory in the derived belief that the lines of seed used by one totem will not grow in response to the systems of magic used by other totems. Hence seed alienated from a person of one totem to a person of another totem will not grow. The only cases in which a person of one totem is likely to wish to give his seed to a person of another totem is in the father-child relationship or in the husband-wife relationship. Seed does not pass between persons so connected in point of fact. It follows logically that if a man without magical knowledge wants his seed yams charmed he cannot engage and fee a practitioner of any other totem than his own for the purpose ; similarly for a woman. Above all a person cannot logically engage a relative-in-law to do such ritual work except where the less approved marriage within the totem has occurred. As we have already seen, in point of fact, the theory breaks down in the case of the father-child relationship, for the father often passes on his garden magic to his child. This is half subversive practice, however. Just so the logical deduction that a man's separate seed yams must be charmed by a practitioner of his own totem is honoured as much in the breach as in the observance in actual practice, as I know from several instances. Planting the new gardens takes place not long after harvesting the old year's crop. The man's seed is kept apart, the woman's seed apart each from his and her own previous year's garden respectively for the month or two intervening between the old and the new year. The rest of the crop from the man's garden and the woman's garden is stored in common in the family yam house for eating. Furthermore it is said, that a woman is responsible for her garden's contribution, a man for his garden's contribution towards the family food, and that divorce may be based on the failure of the garden of one of the pair. I heard for myself quarrels between man and wife where such responsibility was assumed. It is based on separate ownership of seed and land, for husband and wife work together both in the husband's and in the wife's garden.

The theory of totemic monopoly of the only magic adapted to its yam seed may then be set aside as a survival which is honoured in the breach. It is an attempt to confine inheritance of garden magic and the paid services of garden magic within the totem, by making totemic magic necessary to totemic seed (which actually does not go outside the totem). It is an attempt which has maintained a theory, although practice conflicts directly with it, flouting it—an interesting phase in the legal conflict between the *susu* and the marital grouping.

We left our woman magician charming with the spell Murua (Woodlark Island) octopus, and pouring charmed salt water over the seed in the Place of Pouring. Connected with this spell, and as secret as the spell itself, is a mythological fragment. A woman of the time of the first ancestors whose name was Anabuyueta bore a many-armed son (who subsequently turned out to be an octopus). She set him in fresh water when he curled up and very nearly died. Accordingly he was set in the salt water. There he swam away and made his home in a rock cave of the deep sea floor. Anabuyueta went out to the deep sea to visit him, taking with her some seed yams. There on the sea floor she planted them and charmed them so that they grew. "To-day if we plant in the sea they die. But the seed of the yams grown by Anabuyueta in the sea is the seed we of the Green Parrot totem use to-day—and it is indeed no ordinary seed—but descends from the sea garden of the Murua Octopus." In this manner the charm recalls to the seed yams to be planted the astounding feat of their yam ancestors in growing in the sea. The salt water poured on them is an additional reminder. This magic stimulates the seed to great efforts.

The woman magician now moves from the Place of Pouring to the Place of the House Platform, taking four seed yams with her. She plants one at the foot of each of the four sticks of the stick pyramid, muttering the spell Bulelala, the spell of the first woman to plant yams, as she does so

> whose belt of red shell discs
> is it that I wind around, etc.

as it was uttered earlier in the ritual in the planting of the pegs.

The ritual of the planting is now done—half an hour or more has passed with the workers sitting about silently affecting to take no notice of the proceedings, later comers arriving ; now talk breaks out freely, the digging sticks are sharpened, the men lead down the length stick lanes from landward fringe to seaward fringe with long digging sticks, the seed is distributed, the women follow behind squatting, delving with short sticks and planting the seed. The brick-like soil breaks with hard work only. No worker may cross a length stick—all work is from inland head to seaward foot within the eight-foot lanes formed by the length sticks. The work goes on till mid-day if twelve or so take part. Then the owner of the garden gives the workers the *niaura*, the food given for communal garden work ; they eat and disperse.

The prohibition on working from side to side is a ritual one. I dug with a digging stick in my own garden, and unknowingly crossed a length stick (i.e. a stick going from Topside to Bottom-side of the garden). I was promptly brought back and told to cross only the cross-sticks if I wished for a good crop.

I think that this ritual which precedes planting is self-explanatory. It recalls the early history of yams that have descended in the Green Parrot totem from their first birth from human beings in the time of the ancestors (Samuela, daughter of Bulelala, a woman ancestress, being cut up and planted as a red yam). It is believed that the yams are personal beings who hear the spells directed towards them and must needs respond. Of the Green Parrot peoples' seed it is believed that it was once grown successfully in the sea by strong magic, a part of the strength of which is now lost to man, since yams cannot now be so grown. And it is roundly asserted by every native that if yam seed is not treated with one of the totemic systems of magic it will not grow. Yam seed is personal and must be treated deferentially. Indeed, the gross overstatement that seed will not grow unless treated with the totemic system of magic that matches the totem within which the seed is inherited is made. But I heard of no one who ever acted in despite of the wider dogma that yam seed untreated by some magic will not grow. There has been no such motive for questioning it such as that involved in the *susu* versus marital grouping conflict which has

FISH NET DRYING

FISHING IN SHALLOWS

repudiated the overstatement about totemic matching of magic and seed.

The garden ritual now halts for a time. The men go away on overseas expeditions, leaving their women to attend to weeding. Then comes the time of stick cutting, stick planting in the garden, and the training of the growing vines about the sticks. Several of the first vines to be twined are done with the incantation—

> kapali ! kapali
> twisting around !
> he laughs with joy.
> I with my leaves
> my shoot long in the budding point
> my shoot broad in the leaf.
> kapali, kapali
> twisting around
> he laughs with joy.
> I with my garden darkened with foliage
> I with my leaves.
> kapali, kapali
> twisting around
> he laughs with joy.

The *kapali* is a large species of spider. The suggestion is that the yam vines continue to work up and around the sticks as a *kapali* web-weaving. We must leave the point open as to whether Kapali is a supernatural being, or whether the spell merely makes a comparison between vine twining and a natural spider's web weaving. This point I shall discuss later with further examples.

Following the vine twining on the sticks there comes a series of rites where the green leaves of various trees are burned in the Place of Pouring. This burning produces clouds of dense smoke which drift over the garden. I do not wish to fatigue my reader with a glut of ritual so I shall abbreviate this portion of my notes and state that the trees are noted for dense masses of foliage or for unusually large seed and that the ritual introduces the particular leaf burnt to the yams by placing reference to one and reference to the other side by side as much as to say : " Now allow me to introduce you to each other."

The charm used with nokonoko [1] leaves refers to a nokonoko of Sawatupwa in the middle of the garden, Sawatupwa, the home of all mysteries. The nokonoko tree is said to be dark with foliage. Then the yams are mentioned. In point of fact all that is in the middle of the garden is a smoking bundle

[1] *Vigna marina* (Merrill).

of leaves.   The charm used with *bilubilu* [1] leaves refers to yam leaves shaking in the night wind off Garea.   When siwabu [2] leaves are burnt the siwabu stick that rises erect in the Place of the House Platform is said to be heavy in leaf (in fact it is dead) and the yams, as is usual in the garden charms, are already harvested and in this case stored in the food house.   The constant declaration of a great harvest attained and already garnered are compellingly reminiscent of the speeches of Parliamentary candidates in a general election.   My best informant remarked to me that the yams imitate the heavy foliage of the trees and the plants introduced to them in this matter.   Since the yams are personal there is no reason why they should not do so.   It should be noted that there is no thought of any supernatural being such as Yabowaine, Bulelala, or Samuela involved here—only imitation of one thing by another under the compulsion of the spell.

After vine twining and the series of leaf burning rites come three *luugu*, Entrances.   The Entrances are walks round the garden by the magician who breathes a spell into his hand and places his hand repeatedly on the vines as he walks.   Siwabudoi, the first Entrance, follows closely the pattern of the last burning of leaves spell, when siwabu leaves are burned.   Immediately after the magic employed in an Entrance is done the magician must leave the garden and return home.

Tatapeno, the second Entrance, runs :

> come tatapeno
> from your sand-hole
> he swells up
> yams they shout in amazement to see
> yams of a different kind.
> he swells up
> my feast of young food
> my heaped up food.

Tatapeno is a small sea habitant that lives between high and low water mark.   His sting can cause severe limb swelling. He is only an inch or so in length, but he builds a great sand mound over him " like the mound-building bush hen " said my informant.   The yams are commanded indirectly by the citation of his example.

Shortly after the Tatapeno Entrance, the women acting collectively take the " grandmothers " from the gardens. Grandmother yams are the rotted seed yams after they have produced their offspring.   They are distinguished not only

---

[1] *Hernandia peltata* (Meissn).   [2] *Calophyllum inophyllum*, L.

from fresh seed yams and yams of the ordinary crop, but also from the " spirit " yams—yam vines which grow wild without setting any seed at the roots.   Spirits do not reproduce ; also they are not very important in Dobuan feeling—hence the term.   The women take the grandmother yams from the soil, carry them to the seashore and hurl them into the sea with the cry—

> o turtle, your food,
> o whale, your food,
> o dugong, your food,
> o porpoise, your food ;

my young yams you leap up and down as the porpoise in the sea, lifting up and letting down, lifting up and letting down the earth above you.   His size you imitate.

This formula, unlike the magic in general, is public.   Unlike the magic in general it is not couched in esoteric language. Amongst the Basima people, neighbours of the Dobuans, the same formula is used as a private spell, couched in the usual esoteric language of spells.

The plants are now earthed up.

Then the leaves of the scented *ane* [1] are laid on the earth above each plant by the women with an incantation for keeping cold the womb of the woman Nebubunebubuero and the wombs of the yams cold also, so that they hunch up for the cold and hunch outwards—or in our own speech grow knobby. If the ground gets hot they do not grow as they do when the ground is cold.   The *ane* is associated with the anointing and dressing after bathing, and hence with the measures for keeping cool. Nebubunebubuero is a supernatural.

A month or so later a similar ceremony with the leaves of the scented *keginae* and with a similar incantation is performed.   In between these rites the last Entrance, Nemwadole, is performed.   About the same time occurs the taking of the first fruits from the ground, a small yam or two from each vine.

Towards the end of March or in early April there comes a time of low tides with masses of driftwood floating inshore. The driftwood brings with it a small fish that comes, like the palolo worm, only once yearly.

This is an automatic annual event which the natives foretell to within a week accurately.   The Nemwadole Entrance proceeds this event and is believed to cause it.   This powerful spell runs :

[1] Nothopanax.

> i-oi !
> nemwadole !
> i-oi !
> your journey far over
> from your budibudi
> across your sea
> you journey far and make port
> from the seaward end of my garden
> I draw you to me,
> I with my leaves
> I with my darkening wealth of foliage
> I with my sea driftwood
> I with my sea floating pumice,
> turn about, come nemwadole.
> yams they shout to see,
> yams carried with difficulty.

Nemwadole is said to have lived, a lone woman, in a solitary forest cave. There she bore two children, the Gomanumusa yam and the Muyoi yam. Her spirit is thought to come shorewards and to enter the garden ; the mwedole fish is its carrier over the sea. With her arrival come great banks of floating driftwood and pumice. Budibudi is a bay near Vakuta in the south Trobriands.

After an Entrance spell has been pronounced the magician is very careful to make no sound. No work is done and he or she gets away quickly. If a noise is made it is said that the charm will fly away to the next garden. Charms have an extraordinary quality of mobility. A charm at the bottom of the storing place of the canoe, the *geboboi*, is said to rise up through the food placed upon it. The Entrances are conveyed from mouth to vine by the hand, touching first one then the other, and are said to sink slowly down the vine and into the root provided no noise is made. Given the noise, the charm will fly away elsewhere. A wind charm, of course, has to fly—and a considerable distance at that—all the way to the Lusançay group for a north-westerly for example, to the farthest land known in the north-west.

April is the month of the first fruits. From middle November to April we have followed the garden ritual faithfully. From now on we shall take some of the salient points only.

After the yams have been cajoled into growing sufficiently it is felt that it is time to forbid their nightly prowling, lest they come home in the morning into the wrong garden. There is a series of charms called *sone* which aim at seducing yams from a neighbour's garden into one's own. The danger from *sone* has to be averted. The top shoot is bent over,

bound to the main stem, and the following incantation
pronounced :

> where stands the kasiara palm ?
> in the belly of my garden
> at the foot of my place of the house platform
>   he stands.
> he will stand inflexible, unbending,
>   he stands unmoved.
> the smashers of wood smash,
> the hurlers of stones hurl,
>   they remain unmoved.
> the loud stampers of earth they stamp
>   they remain unmoved.
> he remains, he remains
>   inflexible, unbending.
> the yam kulia
> he remains inflexible, unbending.
> he remains, he remains unmoved
>   in the belly of my garden.

(So also of other yams, their names and the concluding three
lines repeated as a litany to each name in turn.)

After this formula it is safe to crack wood, throw stones,
and stamp in the garden without fear of the yams running
away in the night. My informant pointed out that there
was no kasiara palm in his garden (as indeed I had perceived).
It was a way of ritual " We compare one thing to another ".
The kasiara palm is the hardest wood in the bush. It is used
for spear making and for house floors. It stands erect in
a storm when all else bends.

It will be perceived by my reader that there is an antinomy
of sorts in the magic that I have recorded. On the one hand,
in some spells supernaturals such as Yabowaine, Bulelala,
the woman Nebubunebubuero, and the spirit Nemwadole
are called upon to act. On the other hand in the spells that
accompany burning of green leaves in the garden it is explicitly
stated that the yams are commanded to imitate the thick growth
associated with the plants from which the leaves are plucked.
There is a little reference to a mystical tree, the nokonoko
tree of Sawatuwpa in one such spell, but it is not stressed
greatly. Similarly, are the yams commanded to stand fast
as the kasiara palm stands fast ? Or does a mystical double
or a mystical quality of the nokonoko, etc., leaves and of the
kasiara palm enter into the yams ?

I asked concerning the mound building shell-fish, Tatapeno
--does he come from the inter-tidal space, climb or fly to the
garden and enter the yam growing soil in body ? Or in spirit ?
Or in effluence ? Does the twining spider, Kapali, enter the
twining yam tendril in spirit or in effluence ? Is Samuela

really present in the red yam that is sliced into " eyes " ?
What of Murua Octopus that once had a sea floor garden ?
It was clear that no one had asked such a question of a magician
before. My magician was quick of wit, and grasped exactly
what I meant. He knew that the woman's cry at the hurling
of the grandmother yams seawards said explicitly—

" My young yams you leap up and down *as* the porpoise
in the sea. His size you *imitate*."

He was perplexed and said once of Tatapeno, the shell-
fish : " No, enough, we compare one thing to another—the
yams hear and imitate—it is enough." So also of Kapali,
the Spider. Murua Octopus stays in the sea like Tatapeno,
Kapali in his web in the bush.

" Nemwadole then ? "

" That is a different matter—her spirit comes to our calling.
Did you not see the driftwood come inshore as I predicted ? "
Yabowaine and Bulelala, Nebubunebubuero are all like
Nemwadole—spirits all.

But then I had been told that the Turtle of the charm
with the *pies* (ti) leaves was a supernatural. Again on
another occasion my magician said distinctly that the Shell
Fish, Tatapeno, came in spirit double form right into the
garden.

In disease-causing magic there are spirit doubles of the
hornbill, of the rock limpet, of certain shell-fish, of the brown
eagle, of various trees, that are firmly believed actually to
enter the body. Ligatures are usually bound above the
afflicted spot to prevent further entry of the zoological or
botanical spiritual double into the more vital parts of the body.
In such cases a disease is described as the entry of the hornbill
into the body, or whatever bird, fish, beast, or tree is appropriate
to the disease. In the same way the feeling in regard to garden
magic inclines somewhat to regard Turtle, Shell-fish, Spider,
Kasiara Palm as real effluences that enter the yams and infuse
their qualities into them. I should say that this is the feeling,
but it is not formulated and expressed clearly in native thought
except in the case of the etiology of disease in human beings.
The eaten-away nose in gangosa is said to be caused by the
entry of the spiritual double of the hornbill with its swollen
rending beak (by analogy nose) into the nose of the victim.
Here we have belief in the real entry of a real spirit double.
My magician wobbled, and now ascribed real entry, now
denied it to the Shell-fish, the Spider, the Kasiara Palm, and

the rest into the yams. He did not think to look to the belief in the case of disease for guidance.

We must not be too logic-chopping in our questions, however. The real answer is that the veil that separates sympathetic magic as such (where one thing is compared to another and one imitates the other under the compulsion of the spell) from sympathetic magic where a supernatural effluence or double passes from one and enters the other, is but the flimsiest of veils. The general pattern of Dobuan magic, as a whole, is putting a supernatural to work on the task. But, as my magician said, where the yams are personal and dependent, as they are, they can be compelled to imitate. Either way will do equally well.

Samuela, before I forget her, is present in the red yams sliced into " eyes " as any human ancestress is present in her descendants,[1] said my magician. As for Samuela, he was not informed of her exact whereabouts.

Gardening times are regulated by the position of Pleiades in the sky. (I intend to speak of Pleiades as singular, not as plural, to express the native concept of a personal being.) When he rises at about fifteen degrees angle with the ocean the bush is cleared—at about thirty degrees the land is planted. He climbs from the north-eastern to the south-western sky, sets in the south-west, and is unseen for over a month. Then, when he rises in the north-east, harvest time is come. Orion and Pleiades are down together unseen after falling in the west. In this time each is supposed to pole his canoe round the sea rim from the south-west to the north-east, and the two are said to meet in the north-east behind the cloud bank on the horizon before Pleiades rises again there before Orion.

In order to ensure this annual procedure of Orion and Pleiades, and to bring the harvest home duly, they are sunken in the west by ritual. Several stalks of tabuwara, a wild maize that possibly crossed New Guinea with tobacco from the western Spanish settlements, are slowly hammered down into the earth two at a time—a big garden may have three pairs hammered down with three repetitions of the formula—

> the man pleiades
> the man *yuyuwe* (tail of orion)
> we cover your meeting together,
> your sliding downward.
> they slide downwards.

[1] There is no belief in reincarnation—only in the transmission of a common blood in the distaff line.

we cover your setting, your setting, your meeting together,
    they set.
the yam *kulia*, the yam *yamsu*
sleep faded, withered in leaf
they cry out to see you
they carry you slowly, heavily.

One further charm incites the yams to burrow downwards deeply. The stem near the roots is held between the toes and shaken to emphasize the injunction.

The final charm before digging is that uttered into the coconut oil with which the body is anointed in preparation for the event. The charm makes disparaging statements about the ragged and outward grass skirts of a certain woman, praises the speaker's chiefly rank (using the speech of the Trobriands to do this, for rank is not present in Dobu), his appearance and his friends, and incites the yams to abandon the garden of the owner of the disreputable grass skirts and enter the speaker's garden—the ritualist beckoning them to come with both hands.

This final charm is one of many *sone* that are directed towards alienating yams from another person's garden and bring them into one's own. This power is thoroughly believed in, the mobility of yams in response to incantation is undoubted, and only precautions such as the kasiara charm directing the yams to stand fast, and frequent counter attack serve to maintain a man's composure in the face of the alienating charms that he knows his neighbours are directing against his garden. I have not recorded many of these alienating charms, but I know that many exist, and are in regular employment—even by the best people. In most ritual certain leaves are believed to be necessary, either for burning or for laying about the place of the charm ; and I was shown the plant essential to the *sone* by Yogalu, the old man that I least suspected of villainy. This particular form of beggar-my-neighbour is essential. It is not a matter of form, but actually does carry an atmosphere of extreme distance towards neighbours with it. It is all secret, of course. It is carried on against one another even by the owners of the village, within the village. If one man has a better crop than his neighbours, they believe that he has stolen their yams from their gardens by his strong *sone*, yam-alienating magic. Accordingly it is believed that having a better garden crop than one's neighbours is a cause of disease and death. It is a frequent diagnosis. There is no competitive display of the harvests of different gardens.

Harvest crops are taken home privately, a little at a time. They are stored inside a private yam house, and any curiosity regarding a neighbour's crop is taken with the greatest resentment as an insulting intrusion. All such curiosity is vented by stealth.

Now that we have concluded the ritual of the garden, let us examine some general considerations. First it may be laid down that knowing the secret name of the supernatural, knowing the secret spell, having the right herb to use in the accompanying ritual, are all of such importance that not one of them may be falsified. If we ask ourselves which element is most important from the point of view of theorizing about magic we pose a false problem. All of them are most important in the sense that not one may be neglected. If we ask ourselves which is important in native conversation we have a different problem. Here the herb is unimportant in public garden ritual because it is no secret, whereas the herb is important in the *sone*, alienating other person's yam magic, and in all the black art, because it is a deep secret. Secrecy, privacy of possession is the important thing. It is good to keep secret and private a stronger magic than one's neighbours have. Then one will get better results than they. Then if one is making rain by magic and they are trying to stop rain by magic they will not prevail. Then, if one is trying to alienate their yams from their gardens and they are reciprocating the attempted injury, they will not prevail. Then, if they try to kill one or make one sick, one's own cures are stronger than their deviltries. Hence secrecy and privacy in possession are so valued. If one's magic is most excellent and a good monopoly, others will fee one to use it on their behalf. The better the monopoly, the higher the fee. But to say that the herb is more important in the black art than in garden ritual of a public kind is not to say that it is unimportant in public garden ritual ; nor is it equivalent to saying that the secret name of the supernatural and the secret spell are unimportant in the black art. From the point of view of indispensability name, spell, and herb are as important in the one case as in the other—with a few exceptions. Certain herbs without spells or supernaturals' secret names, are believed to be efficacious in producing sterility and in poisoning enemies. These are not clearly distinguished from the herbs that are an element in the complete magical performance. They are family secrets also. And they colour the whole magical outlook, so that when a man says mysteriously " a certain vegetable product I know " he may refer either to a secret herb that is used without a spell, or to a secret herb that is used with a spell. From the point of view of indispensability in most cases, but not in all, the name of the supernaturals, the spell, and the herb are coequal in importance. From the point of view of secrecy the case is sometimes otherwise. A theory that would emphasize one element as the root of magic in Dobu would condemn itself at the very beginning.

Equally rash would it be to say that the mere power of words is the prime element in the magic. It is a great element, but not absolute, for usually the words have not power as such, but through their action on a supernatural. Nevertheless, the supernaturals fade so faintly from the Dobuan scene, their influence is so taken for granted, and the forms of words as such assume such over-weening value in native eyes that it is easy to say that no one cares a brass button whether the words have power through a mediate supernatural or in their own right—the power is the thing.

The words of Dobuan magic are not words of ordinary speech. They form a secret esoteric language, a language of power. It will be noted that in the spells the power over the supernaturals or over the yams, themselves supernaturals, is not used with a bludgeon. We have found no charm where the magician says : " Come on yams, now grow, and be snappy about it." The truth is that it is realized that crops are capricious. Like wind and rain and many other things produced by magic, there is room for ill fate. If the yams are persons they are not persons to be too roughly coerced, domineered over. The magician does not lay rough hands upon the slave. He handles him with ritualistic displacement. When he cuts a seed yam into " eyes " he offers condolence and apologies. When he wishes the growing vine to produce thick foliage he delicately calls to its attention various thick foliaged trees and shrubs. When he wishes the tuber to grow large he delicately refers to the mound-raising shell-fish, Tatapeno. When he wishes the yam to grow knobby he speaks of the cold womb of Nebubunebubuero and of hunching up with cold. When he wishes his yams to cease nocturnal roaming he speaks with gentle hints of the stead-fastness of the kasiara palm. Enough of this, however. The point will be clear. The literary mechanics of the spell is well in accord with all proper feeling towards supernaturals, even towards coerced supernaturals.

There is no direct circumlocution about the spells that summon Nemwadole with her floating sea driftwood, and that sink Pleiades below the horizon. These spells work infallibly year in and year out. If we recall these spells we may see clearly how certainties are used to ballast the great uncertainty——the success or the failure of the crops of the year. The rains are never certain in this area. In the season that I planted my garden in Dobu the rains of the north-west season were delayed about two months, and the gardens were very nearly damaged irrecoverably before the belated rains came. I found that the natives were aware of the danger of a total loss of the crops through drought in the growing season ; but once the crops were saved differences in the crops of different persons were ascribed to differences in the strength of the magic of the gardeners, particularly to differences in the strength of the *sone*. The drought itself, by one account, was caused by different localities planting their gardens at different times. The late planters delayed the normal seasonal round, inter fering with those who planted at the correct time. Although there is no direct circumlocution in summoning Nemwadole or in sinking the Pleiades, both of these acts are themselves acts of displacement, indirect buttresses of the final issue—the crop of the year. They are no exception to the general rule of politeness to the yams.

NOTES

1. The Dobuan concept of space is that of a huge garden clearing. Just as the garden has its inland border *kaikai*, its seaward border *kunukunuwana*, and its sides *nana*, so also has space in its widest extension. East and west extremities of space are called *nana*. Farthest north and farthest south known I never heard called *kunukunuwana* and *kaikai* respectively, but the universal verbal usage indicates that this is what they would be termed if the substantive forms corresponding to *nana* for east and west, were used. To go far to the north at sea is always phrased as to go seawards, i.e. towards the *kunukunuwana* of space. To go far to the south at sea is always phrased as to go inland, i.e. towards the *kaikai* of space. The use of *nana* for extreme east and extreme west explains why going far to the south at sea should be termed going inland, a puzzling usage until the concept of space as being like a huge garden is grasped.

2. *Kaniana*, a concept that I have mentioned in the text, requires further explanation. It is rain magically caused by young yam crops roaming in the bush, by an overseas canoe voyage, by the death of a person gifted in magical knowledge, by war expeditions or as a by-product of the power of magic not specifically directed to rain-making. If rains are over frequent and the natives are chafing at it interfering with their plans they cannot blame the local rain-maker, an old woman. She has many alibis. Thus Kinosi once said to me disgustedly on a rainy day : " Is it, I wonder, that the men of the Amphletts are starting on their *kula* overseas expedition, or is it that old woman (the local rainmaker) is being nasty ? " Kinosi's mother once came home from a canoe trip to Fergusson Island in falling rain. Kinosi said to her : " *kaniaio*—your

voyage caused rain," smilingly. She smilingly replied : " *kaniagu*—my voyage caused rain ". *Kaniana* in the Trobriands is called *kariyala* ; *vide* B. Malinowski, *Argonauts of the Western Pacific*, p. 422.

3. The drought that I witnessed was attributed to several causes :—

(*a*) the rain-maker said my shooting birds frightened the rain clouds away. This was believed for a short time in her village. It was never accepted in my village, the members of which always secured some of my bag for their eating. They wanted me to go on shooting undeterred.

(*b*) Different places planting their gardens at different times, so interfering with the normal seasonal cycle which is reckoned popularly in terms of garden growth ; conflicts of rain-making magic owing to some places wanting it for their garden growth whereas late gardeners wanted to stave off rains until they had finished bush clearing, scrub burning, and planting.

(*c*) The independent sea supernaturals, Tobwaliton and Tobebeso, having thwarted the rain-maker's magic.

(*d*) The men of the Lusançay Islands to the north-west (in which Islands the spirit that blows the no'th-west monsoon from its mouth is believed to live) had by their magic prevented the monsoon with its rains from coming at the usual time in order that they might extend their season of diving for the valuable Trocus shell.

As the drought became more and more serious, the old rain-maker was to be seen almost daily bathing in the sea, muttering incantations. Her daughter kept her mother's head clean shaven by frequent shaving with obsidian glass (other women let their hair grow). The rain-maker must be scrupulously clean, washed and shaven all over, hair of head, armpits, and pubic hair being removed lest she shelter a little dirt inimical to rain.

CHAPTER III

THE BLACK ART

I

DISEASE INFLICTION

Human beings in general are more vitally interested in other human beings than in their material surroundings. They often ascribe a personal quality to objects that are not personal. Thus it is difficult for us to realize that a Dobuan conceives a garden vegetable as personal and believes words and gestures to be effective in growing it, whereas he regards a canoe as impersonal and does not believe that his canoe can be launched or beached by words and gestures. To us the garden vegetable is impersonal, almost as impersonal as the canoe. Although we distinguish a vegetable as a living thing we do not normally use words and gestures to grow it. The Dobuan has an equal difficulty in conceiving the world as the de-personalized plaything of one Great Person, who is three Persons in One. In brief the projection of an absorbing interest in human personality into the world is done differently in different cultures.

In Dobu not only is personality immanent in yams, and also present in various supernatural persons who are under the control of men wishing to grow yams, but disease, sickness, and death are ascribed to persons, as in the dogma found in our own society in the religion that was largely formulated out of the older attitudes by Mrs. Eddy. Here, again, the importance is laid upon living persons who manipulate the supernaturals for their own ends.

In our discussion of social organization in Dobu we have examined the relationships between living persons in the area. Since personality is carried over into the garden, and into the creating and curing of disease and serious illness, we must expect that Dobuan thought and practice about gardening and about medicine will follow the tenor of personal relationships in Dobu. In gardening we have seen this to be true. It is no exaggeration to say that the Dobuan attitude towards garden yams is in some important respects similar to the attitude of the Dobuan man towards his wife. The

wife like yams is spoken of as property. Just as it is considered
good form to try to " steal " other men's wives whenever
possible, so in gardening the current view is that every man
should try to entice the yams, greatly desired personal beings
in metamorphized form, from other persons' gardens. Just
as a man keeps close watch upon his wife to ensure her fidelity
as far as is possible, so also a Dobuan native keeps close watch
upon the garden. It is impossible to induce a native to leave
his or her garden unattended. The garden must literally
be brooded over, with constant repetition of magic nearly all
the year. I have given the main charms for the garden but
not the number of times each charm must be repeated. The
kasiara charm for keeping the yams steadfast in the garden
is not used too early in the growing season, or it is said the
yams will be rebellious at the too early curtailment of their
night prowling liberties, and refuse to grow. But once the
kasiara charm is used it is repeated often as the garden owner
becomes nervous about the *sone*, the charms used to alienate
the yams from the garden by other men. Towards the last
months of the garden season especially the use of the *sone*
on other persons' gardens and the use of protective charms
on one's own garden multiplies. Jealousy towards everyone
else intensifies. The whole atmosphere is most closely related
to the jealous watch over each other of man and wife. The
attitudes of man and wife are themselves related not only
to the social structure, but also to the magical world view.
One of the most frequent words used in Dobu is the verb
meaning " to try out ". It is used almost always of magic.
The first thing the learner of magic must do is " try it out ".
Then naturally he continues trying it out. The try out is
the competitive pitting of one's own magic against the magic
of others. All the sex intercourse that occurs in Dobu is,
in the native belief, the product of the successful making of
desire by the magic for making desire. The great man is
he whose magic is the strongest. The path of ambition is the
path of " trying out " magic one has acquired. The magic
for making desire is in all cases directed towards securing a
girl or a married woman from the competition of others.
Similarly a part of the magic for securing yams is directed
towards securing personal beings, yams, from the competition
of others. Always it is " try it out " against some obstacle
that will be a real test.

A reputation in Dobu is built upon successful magic.

He whose yam crops are good, whose success in obtaining favours from the other sex is conspicuous, whose health has been better than the health of his enemies, will become known. The magician who practises his art for payment has inherited a traditional magical " good-will ", or " practice ". But amongst such magicians some will stand out as having been more socially successful than others. Social success is desired by everyone. In personal relationships it consists in having seduced many women, in having been a great adulterer. Good gardening is phrased in equivalent terms. Since yams are personal beings the best gardeners are those who have seduced yams most successfully from the majority of poorer gardeners. Since health and ill-health are due to the personal activities of human persons only, the healthy person is he who has powerful magic, the sick or deformed or dying person is he who has weak magic. It is assumed throughout that social success is necessarily gained at the expense of others. The healthy person is he who has defended himself from the black art of others in his pursuit of social success at the expense of others. The sick, deformed, and dying are those whose magic has not been as strong as that of those others who have felt themselves injured by their social climbing.

In this society it is not possible to say that the attitudes of the social organization are created by the attitudes of the magical outlook, or that the attitudes of the magical outlook are created by the attitudes of the social organization. It is, however, possible to show a unity of feeling throughout. Jealousy of possession is the keynote to the culture. In social organization this jealousy is found in a conflict between the kin and the marital groupings. In gardening this jealousy obtains between gardeners. All illness and disease and death are attributed to jealousy, and provoke recrimination. It is also possible to show that poverty and a great pressure of population upon land accords well with the prevalent tone of jealousy of possession. But here again it is not possible to say whether poverty has created the jealousy or vice versâ. Either point of view could be put forward. Accordance is all that can be demonstrated, and in truth it is probable that the more accordance there is in the elements of a culture the stronger an intensification of the mutually agreeable elements will result. They will react upon one another.

In Dobu the race is conceived as going to the strong. For the permanently deformed or permanently sickly there is little or no sympathy. At first the ethnologist is greatly surprised at the use of the words he takes to mean good and bad. " Here comes a bad man " says one's canoe paddler with great emphasis on the " bad " as another canoe comes up. The ethnologist looks with interest, thinking to find a moral reprobate. But no—it is a miserably deformed person. After this type of incident happens many times it is realized that to be a bad person is to be a deformed or incurably sick person. To be a good person is what we mean when we say to have a good person. Such a man is good irrespective of his morality. If he is an accomplished adulterer and a successful thief, who has won all the conflicts that arose from these activities, then he is not merely good, but very good. Deformed and incurably sick persons are those who have not won in the conflicts (of sorcery) that arose from the anti-social acts which all those not deformed or sickly pride themselves on having accomplished without bodily hurt from hostile sorcery.

The successful thief is not necessarily such a wicked person as may be imagined from the term. It must be remembered that a person who harvests a better crop of yams than his neighbours thinks of himself, and is thought of, as a successful thief. We have already seen that this stealing is magical— actual garden stealing in the flesh is despised.

Introduced diseases such as measles (which kills natives), tuberculosis, influenza, dysentery, are recognized by the natives as being of introduced origin. Tauwau is the mythological creator of the white race and of European artefacts. Tauwau placed a devil of his, a supernatural being, in the hot springs of Dede in Bwaioa. When this supernatural being emerges from the hot springs a wave of introduced epidemic disease strikes the country. Any white man may be referred to as a *tauwau*, a bearer of introduced diseases, as the typical feeling behind the term necessitates its correct translation. I never heard the theory, however, that this devil is made to work by white sorcery. As far as I could tell the Tauwau devil is supposed to work independently—but I did not see any time of introduced epidemic. There was measles killing many in the Trobriands, but I did not know the Trobrianders well enough to ascertain their feeling. Dr. Malinowski refers to the *tauwau* as *tauva'u*.[1] The Dobuan character is notably more outspoken in

[1] B. Malinowski, *Argonauts of the Western Pacific*, George Routledge and Sons, Ltd., 1922, p. 76. In the Duau dialect of Dobuan the term becomes *tauhau*. I have heard from a visitor to Dobu a theory that Tauhau is a Dobuan culture hero symbolic of a Polynesian immigration !

unpleasant matters than the Trobriand—and I have a more outspoken account of the term.

Disease and modes of death that are indigenous are well known and catalogued by the native. Their production and infliction upon near neighbours is one of the customary occupations of the people. Underneath the surface of native life there is a constant silent war, a small circle of close kindred alone placing trust in one another. The whole life of the people is strongly coloured by a thorough absence of trust in neighbours and the practice of treachery beneath a show of friendliness. Every person goes in fear of the secret war, and on frequent occasion the fear breaks through the surface.

A man imitating the effects of a cruel disease with obvious enjoyment in his believed power of inflicting it on his neighbour, telling with éclat how his incantation may be placed on a pregnant woman and how it will kill the child within her, and bring about her end in torture, imitating her struggles and her groans in convulsion on the ground, or shrieking in convulsion as he illustrates the agonies of a disease that eats away the skin and leaves a deformity of such a red mass of streaming and streaked jelly where was once a human face, as I saw at least twice, and could scarcely look at as the man tried to turn his head away, is a vile enough object. This debonair and faithful imitation of the worst effects of disease or death is the ordinary procedure adopted in the teaching of black magic. It illustrates what can be done with the incantation ; it is done with fidelity, and with a satisfied conviction of the power to produce such effects and of having produced them on previous occasions. The natives followed their customary procedure in giving me secret knowledge. Thus a man giving me a simple for curing a disease would always chew and swallow some of it in my sight, and call my attention to his doing it. The fact behind this is that treacherous poisoning is a common enough custom. A native will never accept food except from a few people that he knows and trusts, people who accept his food. So in acquiring knowledge of the black art I observed and was shown the customary formalities, as in acquiring knowledge of simples. I went with my informant to a far-away and desolate spot on the shore. We bathed, to cleanse ourselves after the recital of the incantation, and we refrained from returning to the village till late in the day. . . . Further I bound myself to lock the notes of these incantations away and not to scan them idly. If I wanted to use the power on a stranger I might scan them. On his part my native informant followed custom in his somewhat hideous pantomine of the agony of the trouble that the incantation had the power of inflicting.

My medicine man had a very good " bed-side manner ", as I found when I summoned in his curing incantation for a fever that I had. He actually did exert considerable compelling power over me in the way of a will to feel better. So in teaching me incantations for killing he communicated a thoroughly villainous atmosphere with equal pride in his power and with some inevitable contagion of feeling, for anything to the contrary had to be dissembled on my part.

Every disease is held to be caused by a *tabu*. *Tabu* denotes an incantation, expressing black hatred in an extremely ugly form, which has the power of inflicting disease. Each disease has its own *tabu* or incantation. Every man and woman knows from one to five *tabus*—I made a census of *tabus* and their possessors in Tewara—how they are distributed and held is common knowledge. Thus Neddidiway, a middle-aged widow with two children, knew the *tabus* for incontinence of urine and incontinence of semen ; Megibweli, an extremely old and once cannibalistic rain-maker,[1] knew the *tabu* for elephantiasis ; a man who gave me his knowledge of *tabu* knew gangosa, paralysis, tertiary yaws, and wasting in hookworm. The traditional conservatism of the magical world is illustrated by the fact that no one knows or practises *tabus* to create introduced epidemic disease. They are a department apart, outside the scope of sorcery, though they have been present in Dobu for nearly half a century.

The *tabus* are commonly used to protect private property in trees situated away from the village. They are also used, however, in the ordinary course of private feuds. The use of the disease-causing incantations on the *didila*, a dry coconut palm frond tied about a protected tree as a sign of its giving abode to a malevolent charm, creates some resemblance between the Dobuan *tabu* and the Samoan hieroglyphic *tapui*.[2]

The names of the great majority of the *tabus* are the names of certain shell-fish, insects, birds, and animals with the prefix *lo*. A few are the names of trees with the prefix *lo* ; and there are a few further *tabus* outside these categories. The prefix *lo* is used elsewhere in terminology—thus *lo-mwali*

---

[1] Rain-makers are female.
[2] Margaret Mead, *Social Organisation of Manu'a*, p. 120.

is to obtain *mwali* or armshells, *lo-bagura* is to get food from *bagura*, the garden.   By equivalence *lo-binama* is to get *binama*, the hornbill, *lo-moata* is to get *moata*, the snake.   To get the hornbill is to get gangosa, to get the snake is to get paralysis. The unfolding of this somewhat grotesque terminology will be apparent later.

The incantation that causes *gangosa* is known as *Kalena Sigasiga*.   We may consider it in detail.

> *kalena sigasiga*
> hornbill dweller of siga siga   (Place-name)
> hornbill dweller of siga siga
> in the *lowana* tree top
>> he cuts he cuts
>> he rends open
>>
>> he rends standing
>> he rends flying
>> from the nose
>> from the temples
>> he rends standing
>> he rends flying.
>
> hornbill dweller of sawatupa   (Place-name)
> in the *lowana* tree top
>> he slices up
>> he cuts, he cuts
>> he rends open
>> from the throat
>> from the hip
>> from the root of the tongue
>> he rends open
>> he rends flying
>
> hornbill dweller of darubia   (Place-name)
> in the *lowana* tree top
>> he slices up,
>> he booms crying droning
>> he cuts, he cuts
>> he rends open
>> he rends open
>> he rends flying
>
> hornbill dweller of sisiyana   (Place-name)
> in the *lowana* tree top
>> he slices up
>> he booms, crying droning
>> he cuts, he cuts
>> he rends open
>> he rends flying
>> from the side of the body
>> from the back of the neck
>> from the root of the tongue
>> from the temples
>> he rends flying
>> he rends standing.
>
> hornbill dweller of solamanake   (Place-name)
> in the *lowana* tree top
>> he slices up
>> he booms crying droning
>> he cuts, he cuts
>> he rends open.

hornbill dweller of tokuku   (Place-name)
  in the *lowana* tree top
    he booms, crying droning
    he rends open
    he rends flying
    he crouches bent up
    he crouches holding his back
    he crouches arms twined in front of him
    from the back of the neck
    from the root of the tongue.

hornbill dweller of lamona   (Place-name)
  in the *lowana* tree top
    he booms crying droning
    he rends open
    he rends flying
    he crouches bent up
    he crouches hands over his kidneys
    he crouches head bent in arms turned about it
    he crouches double twined.

hornbill dweller of koiyawabu   (Place-name)
  in the *lowana* tree top
    he slices up
    he booms, crying droning
      he rends open
      he rends flying
    from the back of the neck
    from the navel
    from the small of the back
      he rends open
      he rends standing

hornbill dweller of koyatabu   (Place-name)
  in the *lowana* tree top
    he slices up
    he booms crying, droning
    he cuts, he cuts
    he rends open
    he rends flying
    he crouches bent
    he crouches hand over kidneys
    from the root of the tongue
    from the throat
    from the kidneys
    from the entrails
    he rends open
    he rends flying

    kebadidi   (Place-name)
  woman nebagieta   (name of a supernatural)
  your skin my skin
  my vision deceives me
    your shadow
    your spirit
  I conceal away
  they stagger back falteringly stricken
they crouch heads twined in outstretched arms
  wailing, shrieking
    it flies hither
  quickly it flies hither.

First we may consider the native attitude to an incantation such as the above. The attitude is essentially one of great fear. My informant insisted in giving me the charm that no word of it could be uttered anywhere near an inhabited place. It had to be uttered on a far and desolate shore as I have said above. We had to cleanse ourselves in the sea after its ritual, and we had to refrain from going near the village for hours afterwards. I had to cease using my informant's name. Thereafter I observed this prohibition carefully, calling him *igu esoi*, " my partner of a day long sojourn apart," whenever I called to him or referred to him to others.

" Do not say that name idly " several men cautioned me, I having used the term *lobinama* in my house in speech with them. " If we crack a twig, it hears, if we whisper, it hears." My informant for the charm had cautioned me before. Once I knew the incantation I was not to use its name carelessly, lest it come and afflict me or persons near me with gangosa. The group of men did not know for certain whether I knew the charm or no, but they suspected as much, and were not anxious to take risks. The hornbill of gangosa is not an ordinary material hornbill. It is a monstrous being, active in many places at once. Hence, hornbill of Sigasiga, of Sawatupa, of Darubia, of Sisiyana and of the many places quoted, from the centre of Normanby Island in the south to Mt. Koyatabu on the north-east of Fergusson Island. Like other supernatural agents it is not subject to the limitations of time and space.

I wished once to leave my goods unattended in a barrack at Basima to allow my personal boys to come up the hill with me to a dance. At that time I did not know the *tabu* incantations. I feigned that I did and feigned to be about to put one on my goods to protect them. My boys bolted precipitously into the night and I heard later that several families living between fifty and a hundred yards from the barrack left their houses on the beach and went to their houses high on the hill on account of it.

From this digression on the native attitude we may return to the incantation itself. Despite the ubiquity of the hornbill double of gangosa in time and space there is the very material touch of " in the Lowana tree-top ". The great beak of the hornbill which he uses in hacking out tree hollows, accounts for his body-rending powers. The boom of the hornbill in the bush was compared by my informant with the thick nasal utterance that I had heard from a mutual acquaintance who had no nose, the entire organ having been eaten away by gangosa. The references " he crouches up, etc.," refer not to the hornbill, but to the victim, and are introduced towards the final strophes. The final strophe, introducing a change of treatment, reveals the mythical foundation, the reference to the first ancestors which we have found characteristically in the garden ritual. The final strophe conceals the spirit of the woman Nebagieta in the object that is to carry the charm. She is first seen in the flesh, then error of vision is declared, her shadow, her spirit is summoned and flies to command.

The spirit of Nebagieta is said to live in a cave near 'Ebadidi in the central hills of Fergusson Island. She wore a rough jagged nose and she gave birth to a hornbill, the hornbill of all hornbills. She was the creator of gangosa by incantation, and she ordered her offspring to try it out on a village ; whereat the entire village contracted gangosa. The spell calls on the hornbill and also upon the spirit of the mother, and the latter is affirmed to be concealed in the object charmed.

The charm is uttered into an object—the *didila* or *didina* (the term changing according as the dry coconut frond is bound on to a betel nut or a coconut palm). It may also be uttered into a creeper twined across a track, or any other object. The pronouncer of the incantations chews ginger, stands three or four feet away from the object charmed and utters the charm in short staccato phrases with a vicious spitting of ginger on to the object charmed, punctuating each phrase (roughly as I have phrased it), and taking care that his shadow falls behind and not in front of him.

It is worth noting that the great beak of the hornbill is connected with a disease that eats away the nose in the typical gangosa case. Great beak and eaten-away nose is a fair antithesis. To get the hornbill is to get gangosa. To get the snake is to get paralysis. Here again, in lithe snake and paralysed limb is a similar antithesis. Other charms go by likeness rather than antithesis, however, as will appear later.

I shall not detail other incantations, for those I know follow the same pattern as that of *Kalena sigasiga*. In the incantation that causes paralysis, snake dweller of Kulada, snake of Bwakela, snake of Giuri, snake of Tokuku, snake of Lamona, snake of Koiyawabu, snake of Doweta, snake of Dilia, snake of Selewegia, and snake of Diu lead the strophes—peering out from his cave or crevice. The last strophe summons a slippery fish termed *tonewa* into the object charmed. (There is no mythical ancestry cited in the last strophe of this paralysis charm, or in the charm for tertiary yaws ; of the three I worked out in detail it is found in the gangosa charm only.) The snake Double is commanded to twine about the arm bands and leg bands of the victim, to twist the limb about, to stiffen it. There is a refrain of " I cut thighs, chest, arms, temples, throat, hips to the roots "—the utterer of the charm here dividing the work between the snake Double and himself.

Tertiary yaws is *lobwaloga*. *Bwaloga* is a rock limpet. My informant took one from a rock, pointed to its ugly oval " foot " and said that it resembled the open sores of tertiary yaws. The *bwaloga* of Kapoka, of Ulogu, of Sawaiowas, of Koyatabu, of Dilia, of Garea is commanded to crumble the arm like rotted wood, to rot the leg, to twist and stiffen and line the limbs with sores. The leg is commanded to burst open, the wattle tree of Bwebweso (abode of the spirits of the dead) burst open its seed pods, and the names of two deep sea fish, one of almost comically ugly appearance, the other of vile appearance, are named.

The term for catching a *tabu*, a disease, is *enunulatui*. Charms such as these cause all disease, and conversely wherever a diseased person is found there are accounts of his or her success with the other sex, or success in trade, or success in the garden—in which case an envious and more backward rival has intervened as is the custom ; or the diseased person may have stolen from a tree protected by a *tabu*. Again, a man will put a *tabu* on a woman who has refused his advances, improper or otherwise.

My personal boy contracted *lomague* while on the sea. He got *mague*—a shell-fish, the sting of which kills—a child was killed so in my vicinity in Basima. In other words he had a swelling in his arm due to exposure to the sun (the heat beating down on the open canoe) and paddling. He was in some fear—the *mague* had entered his arm, not a shell-fish in material form, but its double of the *tabu*. He had counter incantation performed. He then had his arm ligatured tightly near the arm-pit. This was to prevent " it " from entering his body. If " it " entered beyond the arm-pit he was a dead man. Such is the spiritual yet semi-material nature of the pantheon of demons, that the natives command by incantation and direct upon their neighbours who had excelled them in some native pursuit, or angered them otherwise, and with which they protect private property in trees remote from the village. It would be unthinkable to *tabu* a tree in the village. Everyone would contract the disease by propinquity to it.

The following are some of the names of other diseases—

Native name.	Disease.	Demon involved.
Lobwebwai .	Cerebral malaria and meningitis.	The white-headed Osprey.
Logumo . .	Inflammation of the gums.	The paper wasp.
Lokwalawa .	Intestinal trouble .	The shark.
Logaga . .	Toothache . .	A small flying sea-water insect.
Loiaio . .	Elephantiasis . .	A swollen-looking shell.
Lomagawau .	Intestinal " eating out "	A small eagle that lives on snakes exclusively.
Losakasakalulu	Goose-flesh . .	Porcupine fish.
Losakwara .	Wasting in hookworm .	Sakwara is a tree, the leaves of which wilt with remarkable rapidity when plucked.

There are many other names I have which I do not understand as I do not know the fauna, names of shell-fish and fish mainly, and I have not seen the diseases they name.

In another class there are *sosomwakumwakupwa* incontinence of urine, *lomolo* incontinence of semen, and one or two others that appear to have no connection with fauna or flora-- incantations that dispense with such natural aids. *Lobonu* ulcers (*bonu* being the ordinary term for ulcer), *lobutobuto*, leg "asleep", and several minor troubles have not their incantations perhaps—they are of minor importance and no one prides himself or herself on being able to inflict them. *Lolawa*, boils, has its incantation, however.

The Doubles may be exorcized out of the charmed object by the man who summons them ; only he who knows the incantation to summon a zoological or a botanical Double knows also the incantation to exorcize it. As each *tabu* is a separate incantation so also each exorcism is a separate incantation, and a *tabu* and its exorcism go together, never apart. The exorcizing spells are termed *lolas*. Different families own their different *tabus* and *lolases*—so it is possible to protect private property. There is not too much over-lapping in their possession in a community. In order to get at his own private tree a man must first exorcize the charm he has put upon it. The exorcisms are also used to cure disease. Women take watergourds to a person who knows the *tabu* and exorcism of the disease from which one or their kin is suffering, the person breathes the exorcism into the water, and the women return to bathe the invalid with it. This procedure is often to be seen.

The exorcism for gangosa is a repeated injunction to the spirit to fly away. " They fly away, they go, they fly away quickly." The plural " they " is due to *putautaona*. *Putautaona* is said to occur when one man coming on another man's property protected by the sign of the *tabu* is not deterred thereby. He superimposes his own *tabu* on the owner's *tabu*. He then uses the exorcism of his own *tabu* and names at the beginning of his exorcism the names of the *tabus* which he knows the owner of the tree possesses, as well as the name of his own *tabu*. In treating sickness every care is taken to obtain the exorcism proper to the disease. Here, however, the superimposing of a second *tabu* is evidently thought to make a difference. At the same time I do not believe that *putautaona* is very consistently practised. In point of fact there is usually tremendous respect for and fear of any *tabu* protected tree. I was told of definite cases of *putautaona* and stealing from a *tabu* protected tree ; but they occurred in time of famine and drought when the poorer persons, who had few or no trees, were driven by urgent necessity, careless of risk. *Putautaona* is, however, typical of the " try it out " competitive feeling about magic.

After the thief has put his own disease on the tree, on top of the different disease put on originally by the owner, and used the exorcism for his own disease, modified by the addition of the names of the tree owner's disease charms, he (or she) climbs the tree and steals. Then after stealing the thief re-imposes his or her own disease spell without exorcism, as it is believed that a *didila* or a *didina*, the dried coconut frond tied about the tree trunk, will slip to the ground if it is left untenanted by a disease. Hence the rightful owner of a tree, in exorcizing his own disease charm, names other disease charms also and uses the plural form—a precaution against stealing having occurred.

Here we see that the strong thieving tendency of the natives sometimes breaks through their own very great fear of sorcery, and makes a subversion of magical dogma in doing so. The dogma is most strongly stated that only the exorcism proper to gangosa will drive out the effects of the gangosa spell when they are contracted, only the exorcism proper to tertiary yaws will drive out the effects of the tertiary yaws spell when they are contracted, and so on. A person afflicted with gangosa is never treated with the exorcism for tertiary yaws or vice versa. But in stealing, a tree affected with gangosa may be exorcized with the exorcism for tertiary yaws or some other disease, the exorcism being modified by the addition of supplementary references to other diseases than that for which it is the true and traditional exorcism as used invariably in treating actual cases of disease.

The words used in the *tabu* are avoided in the exorcism— most conspicuously; different places entirely than those used in its summons are advised for the Double's retreat. The *tabu* is exorcized from all about, the *lolas* intoner turning over stray stones and sticks, digging up loose earth, and exorcizing in all crannies and crevices with anxious care, gently striking the objects of his exorcism with a rhythmical series of blows from a short stick he wields, in this way punctuating the phrases of the *lolas* (much as the phrases of the *tabu* were punctuated with spitting of ginger).

The following is the text of the *lolas* for gangosa, the exorcism for the *tabu* cited in full above :—

(Place-name)	dutuna you fly to
	dutuna you fly nesting there
(Place-name)	nabana you flee to
	tabu lobinama
	I leave the village in ignorance of an impending attack
	they fly away, they go.
(Place-name)	kapoka you flee to
	tabu losilai (paralysis)
	tabu lobinama (gangosa)
	I leave the village in ignorance of an impending attack
	they fly away, they go.
	magibweli you flee to (a cave near the extreme east of tewara)
	mwaniwara you flee to (the extreme easterly point of the island)
(Place-name)	tuesia you flee to
	tabu lobinama
	I leave the village in ignorance of an impending attack
	they fly away, they go.
	my *didila* from its tip (lit. " eye ")
	my rock from its edges
	my scraper away of rubbish from its edge
	they fly away they go
	yewau
	throw away refuse.
(Place-name)	uloga you flee to
	tabu lobinama
	tabu losilai
	I leave the village in ignorance of an impending attack
	they fly away, they go.

and so over several stanzas with little variation to a conclusion with nothing variant except the verb *butubutu*, to stamp heavily in going, and an explicit exorcism of *putautaona*.

The exorcism of paralysis commands the *lomwata* to fly away (a flying snake, this Double) and finally, after much repetition of verbs of flight, helps its exit by reference to small shell-fish that scatter from the rocks at a man's approach and by reference to the eggs of two seashore birds, *Yodudu* and *Legiagia*, eggs which no native has ever succeeded in finding. The Double is referred to as *makamakaiau*, the word for spirit used of the spirit of the human dead.

The exorcism for tertiary yaws is similar in its tenor. I learnt no new thing from it after carefully working it out. So much as we have learnt is the etiology and treatment of indigenous disease. I have considered it somewhat exclusively from the point of view of tree protection. When the charms are used in feuds the customary procedure is to breathe the spell into a bush creeper about the track that the intended victim is known to be ascending. The sorcerer then retreats into hiding nearby to assure himself of his victim coming into bodily contact with the creeper. After such contact has been made the sorcerer takes the creeper with him, keeps it in his hut, and ultimately burns it over a fire.

When the exorcism is breathed into water with which an afflicted person is to be bathed for curing, there is no striking of stray stones and sticks lying near with a tapping stick wielded by the exorcist. The exorcist as already stated does not usually approach his patient. Water gourds are carried to him. He breathes the charm into the water in the gourd, closes up the gourd and gives it to the patient's kinswoman, who has come to him. She returns and bathes the patient with the water. In all manner of its operation the spell is given a local habitation with which the person to be afflicted by it must come into bodily contact. All the disease spells, it is believed, lead inevitably to death, unless the diseased patient is treated with the correct exorcism. This exorcism may recover the patient entirely. Often it only prevents death, not deformity. Since many of the indigenous diseases cause deformity rather than death, the curative exorcisms are automatically credited with more power than they deserve.

II

TEACHER AND PUPIL

In discussing further the relationship between teacher of spells of the black art and learner we shall not confine ourselves to the *tabu* spells. Here the teacher is the mother's brother of the learner. (See discussion of the improbability of father teaching son *tabu* spells, pp. 80–2.) In other spells of the black art, which we are now approaching, with very few exceptions the teacher is either the father, the mother's brother, or elder Boundary Man cross-cousin of the learner. Without seniority, Boundary Man would hardly have a knowledge superior to that of his Owner cross-cousin.

Any spell of black magic, the *tabus* included, is taught in several sessions. The greatest care is taken that the spell is learnt word perfect. The pupil strengthens his memory by a charm to assure learning correctly. This charm is done with a process known as *tolu*. Four holes are scooped close to one another in a straight inland-seaward line on a slope. When water is found in the most inland hole some of it is used for drinking, a spell being uttered during the drinking. This spell is directed towards clearing the stomach of digested and partly digested food. Then a channel is made from this hole to the next seaward one so that water flows down it. Water from this hole is used for drinking, the drinker muttering a spell designed to ensure removing the blood from his stomach as he drinks. The process is repeated and at the next hole the spell is designed to remove water from the stomach. The process repeated again leads to the last most seaward hole, where the spell used is designed to make certain that the stomach is now absolutely empty (despite the last draughts of water, which are, of course, not considered in a sacred performance). The stomach is now in a receptive condition to hold magic. As in the Trobriands it is the seat of memory.

Once the pupil has declared himself satisfied that he knows the incantation perfectly he must undergo a most serious ordeal. The teacher must place the spell on an object and bring it into contact with his pupil's body. If the pupil has learned the spell and the exorcism word-perfect this attempt at infection cannot succeed ; for his magic is the same as, and equal in power to, that which is used against him. If this is the case the pupil's magic is believed to be the complete and perfect prophylactic. But if the pupil does not retain his firm memory of the spell and exorcism then his magic is inferior, will not resist the attack, and the unfortunate pupil will contract the disease. Some youths are afraid of learning sorcery, but the great majority realize that it should be done, and face the ordeal bravely.

The next step is a further obligatory test. The pupil who, as is usual, has survived the ordeal, must now " try out " the spell on someone else, someone not too closely related to him. Theoretically it should be the first person he encounters, but actually one man told me that it was customary to avoid encountering close relatives and friends until the test had been made. It is singular that, despite this emphasis on testing, " trying out," of hocus pocus, nevertheless every native swears that the hocus pocus is powerful, and lively fears, quarrels, secret vendettas, and sometimes undisguised murders flow from the belief in its strong efficacy. The concept of proof is not sufficiently stringent. Once in a while a man uses a spell on another and the other happens to sicken shortly after. Meanwhile, when the owner of the spell teaches it to another he always says : " I used it on one man ; the day after, it took effect, and he died immediately." A statement that is a lie is used always in warranting the efficacy of the spell. It is a social lie, socially always used in the circumstances, a manner of lie that descends from father to son or from mother's brother to sister's son quite irrespective of the actual experience of any one generation in the use of the spell ; and quite surely the faith in the force of magic is such that it is really a faith which is impervious to individual experience, or individual conceptions of proof in ordinary secular affairs. The fact that magic can enjoin an obligatory test case such as that incumbent upon the young learner of sorcery, and yet have the faith in it undimmed by such testing, is curious. And yet again it is not so curious. For sickness, disease, and death are common enough. No other explanation of them than the sorcery and witchcraft used by living persons near by, for they must be near by, exists. The neophyte whose own test of his own spell yields a negative result will not betray any feeling of inferiority over it, except by boasting beyond the limits of reason, as is commonly done in teaching the spell again.

I do not know if failure is ever even self-admitted. If so it would be the last secret of the Dobuan soul, and in view of the obvious success of others as measured by the sicknesses and deaths that occur, the mainspring of fear. What is certain is that fear far beyond reason is actually present.

Testing out of magic is not confined to black magic, as we have seen. It is the first step invariably. The testing of the pupil by the teacher is the individual departure.

III

WITCHCRAFT AND SORCERY

Death is caused by witchcraft, sorcery, poisoning, suicide, or by actual assault. There is no concept of accident. Falling from coconut palms or other trees is due to witchcraft; similarly of other accidents.

When the Tewara men were in the Amphletts on an overseas voyage they went for the night to a small sandbank near by to obtain sea-birds' eggs. The canoe was not well beached. It floated off in the night, the supports of the outrigger boom smashed, and outrigger boom and canoe sank separately. Fortunately both were washed up on a sand-bar within swimming distance. Every man blamed the flying witches. " They charm so that we sleep like the dead and do not guard our canoe. They lay no hand on the canoe. They say ' you go to sea ' and the canoe goes." Some of the men blamed their own women of Tewara, declaring that their habits were vile. Some blamed the women of Gumasila, who were jealous, presumably, of their taking sea-birds' eggs from an island near Gumasila.

Witchcraft is the woman's prerogative, sorcery the man's. A witch does all of her work in spirit form while her body sleeps, but only at the bidding of the fully conscious and fully awake woman and as the result of her spells, it is said. Not only is all that we term accident as opposed to sickness ascribed exclusively to witchcraft, but a particular way of causing illness and death is the monopoly of women. This method is that of spirit abstraction from the victim.

The man, as sorcerer, has the monopoly of causing sickness and death by using spells on the personal leavings of the victim. When the diviner of the person responsible for an illness beards a witch he says : " Restore X's spirit to him " ; when he beards a man he says : " Produce X's personal leavings that you have in your house." Such personal leavings may be remains of food, excreta, footprints in sand, body dirt, or a bush creeper with a malevolent charm first breathed into it which the sorcerer watched his victim brush against and which he subsequently took to his house to treat further.

Moving among the men mainly I soon became aware of a convention. Death is always referred to the *werebana*. That village is weeds and grass, that island is uninhabited now—

the flying witches. Yet these same men in reality feared sorcery as much as witchcraft, all had their killing powers, and little by little I heard of what they had done with them. By convention only, death is referred to the women's activities. Underneath the convention was the knowledge that men themselves had a great hand in it—only this is not referred to by men, except in great confidence that usually betrays itself first in a panic and is pressed home from the panic by the field worker. The sorcery of other places is referred to freely—the sorcerers there, the danger of poison in the food offered one.

The women do not seem to have enough solidarity to turn the tables and to blame all death upon the *barau*, the male practitioner, as they might. Instead, they voice the general convention—the flying witches are responsible. The diviner takes no notice of this convention of speech. He is as likely to divine a sorcerer as a witch in any concrete case of illness.

The women, however, have a counter convention established. No woman will admit to a man that she knows a witchcraft spell. The men have the benefit of a general alibi. But a man will admit to his wife that he knows death-dealing spells, whereas she will not reciprocate. The women have the benefit of an individual alibi. The diviner, and all persons discarding courtesy of speech, take no more account of the women's alibi than of the men's. Courtesy of speech in direct conversation matters greatly in Dobu. If *A* tells *B* that *B*'s greatest friend is vile, *B* replies : " Yes, he is vile." *B* may take secret measures to revenge himself on *A*, but in conversation there is never any controversy in such a matter.

The Dobuan men are quite certain that the women of the Trobriands do not practice witchcraft spells, as they are equally certain that their own women do so practise. Accordingly the men of Dobu feel safer in the Trobriands among a strange people of a strange speech than they do in their own homes—in direct and striking contrast to their greater fear in the Amphletts and in parts of Fergusson Island than in their own homes, and in contrast also to their greater fear in other Dobuan districts than in their own home districts. I saw this most clearly for myself ; there was no doubt about their attitudes—considerable fear at home, sharpened greatly in all strange places, but blunted in the Trobriands. Whether this great certainty of feeling is founded on a solid fact that women in Dobu do practise witchcraft spells, or merely on acceptance of the Trobriand freedom from Dobuan-like fears, I should be loath to say. I have worked with the men intimately and I know that the diviner's discarding of the convention clearing the male sex is correct. I know the men complain about the lying they believe there is in the women's convention. But only a woman working with women could tell what the facts are—whether they are really innocent or whether they are putting up a convention counter to the men's. Personally I suspect the latter. The women certainly own *tabus*. A few men say themselves that they penetrated beneath the women's convention and actually got witchcraft spells from women by threatening them with violence. Such men are few, and may be telling the truth or not. The probability is that women do own spells, however. The witch charged as a witch by the diviner summoned to a sick person does not deny witchcraft any more often than a sorcerer in a similar position denies sorcery. Such denials are few in all, for a reason that we shall discuss later. It would be unreasonable that women should suffer so without benefit when spells may be so easily made from the natural expression of hate. Innovation in spells occurs despite native belief to the contrary. In the *kula* magic we shall meet Tauwau, the culture hero who created galvanized iron roofs, nailed houses, bully beef in tins, and European diseases. Side by side with Tauwau in the magic are lines that are as old as any. Sometimes *kaiana*, fire vented forth from the pubes of flying witches, is seen at night. Then the village gathers together around its fires, which are kept burning all night, and none retires to the house to sleep. The entire village became more than usually dormant in the afternoon on such occasions. On other occasions a woman would wake from a nightmare convinced that the flying witches were chasing her spirit and were just outside baulked by her spirit's good luck in getting home before them. Then the night would be hideous with a ghastly yelling or alternate high and low shrieking, expressing such fear in its very sound as to be contagious enough to myself who knew its origin. Next day sometimes the woman and her husband were outwardly serene and I had to get the whole story from someone else. But sometimes the woman or her husband would be shaken and ill and drawn in appearance all day, confined to the mat—in which case I dosed the patient with salts or quinine according to taste.

Because of danger from witch or sorcerer it is not advisable to go alone. Frequently in broad daylight I was warned not to do it. " You go alone " in surprise and in dissuasion. In strange places they looked after me well. Once in Raputat of Sanaroa I went with three natives, fresh from the canoe under the hot sun, to bathe in a cool spring ten minutes away from the shore. Two bathed and went away on an errand. One remained. I was resting in my bathing V's and not going back. My native hung about chewing a stem of grass and gazing at the distance. This lasted a long while. Finally I said : " It's all right, Kisian, I know the track now." " No, I shall wait for you. New Guinea vile—witchcraft, sorcery is here." That is typical. Even at home it is rare for anyone to be alone except on adultery or stealing bent ; and often adultery and stealing are co-operative ventures, two men going together. Many means of death exist by day. Only in the night, however, bats are abroad. If a bat approaches a house, crying aloud, panic rises. They pale quite visibly, talk stops abruptly ; and on several occasions it happened when natives were in my house by night, they said " *werebana* " in an undertone, sat saying nothing for five or ten minutes, and then as soon as was decent got up and slunk away. The night is a little more feared than the day because it is the time for sleep when the spirits of the sleepers go abroad in the pursuit of the black art. Most of the black art of the daytime is done in the flesh. But fear of the night work is only slightly greater than fear of the day work.

The situation created by witchcraft beliefs in marriage we have already treated. The members of village *x* may refer freely to their fear of certain women of village *y*, until inter-marriage takes place. Then comment is forced underground, as it is a great insult to " call witchcraft " within a husband's range of gaining report of comment upon his close relatives in law or upon his wife. All men have a nervousness of their wives' complicity, and a fear of mothers-in-law. Only the most reckless will say privily of another man : " It would appear that last night he slept with his wife—but did he sleep with his wife ? Or was she far away ? With an empty skin at his side he slept."

I may add that as well as witches who are mortal women (*werebana*) there are also sea witches (*gelaboi*) who have no present human embodiment.

IV

METHODS OF DIVINATION

Divining is usually done by water-gazing or crystal-gazing. In the former case water is put into a wooden bowl and hibiscus flowers thrown on the water. The diviner charms : " the water is water no longer." He cuts the water-in-changed-nature open. At the bottom of the cut he sees the spirit of the witch who has abstracted the spirit of his patient and who now has it concealed, or the spirit of the sorcerer who has the *sumwana*, body leavings of the patient and now has them concealed. Volcanic crystals may be used instead of water.

Spirit abstraction by a *gelaboi* may be indicated by the patient making delirious or semi-delirious statements about canoes at sea, canoes used by these spiritual *gelaboi*. Great attention is paid to the patient's ravings if there are any.

If the patient runs about in delirium then again his *sumwana* has been taken by a sorcerer. The sorcerer in such case has bound up the *sumwana*, winding it about in some receptacle with bush creeper. This winding is compared to the way in which the tree oppossum, Cuscus, winds its tail around branches and darts about apparently aimlessly. The sorcerer's winding of *sumwana* has made the patient run about like the oppossum.

The diviner may bend forward the middle finger of the patient, grasping it tightly at the first joint. If the tip of the finger does not flush then spirit abstraction by a witch has occurred. If it does flush then the patient's *sumwana* has been taken by a sorcerer.

Again the diviner may tell by the body odour of the patient the sex of the person responsible. None could define how this was done.

These measures of noting the symptoms of delirium, or of trying the finger bending or the smelling tests, precede the water or crystal gazing which finally determines the exact identity of the person responsible for the illness. The attention paid to delirium narrows down the circle of people within which the diviner's judgment may operate, but the other two tests leave him free by their nebulousness. Flushing or no flushing in the finger bent is rarely so obvious as to rule out subjective appraisal of the results, a subjective factor that is even more obvious in the smelling test.

Unless the agent revealed is a *gelaboi*, a *yatala* or, as it is also called, a *bwokumatana* follows. The diviner summons the village, a member of which he has " seen " in his water-gazing. The person divined is charged with the deed by the diviner. Then follows a promise of cessation of enmity and of active black magic by the witch or the sorcerer charged, provided her or his just complaint against the patient is remedied by the patient immediately. The patient pays the black magician and the diviner, and recovers—unless unremedied grudges undivined as yet still exist elsewhere.

After a death the kin of the dead divine whose grudge killed their kinsman by watching the corpse as the mourners file by one by one as is the custom. When the guilty person passes the corpse it is believed to twitch in one place or another. So strong is this belief that twitches are probably often fancied. In any case common fact is often relied on rather than the pure magic of divination. If one man has sought out another's company too much and for no reason that appears customary, and the latter dies, suspicion falls on his unexplained companion. False friendship is suspected. I heard from three different sources : " If we wish to kill a man we approach him, we eat, drink, sleep, work, and rest with him, it may be for several moons, and we wait our time ; we *kawagosiana*, call him friend." It will be recalled that the black art is believed to be in-effective at a distance as it is conducted by men. Men have to work in the flesh. Even witches are believed to confine their work to within the locality to which they belong.

It is realized by the Dobuan that relationship considerations debar certain persons who might be responsible for the death from mourning, so that divination by the corpse is not perfect. As well as consideration of unreasonable companionship there is consideration of possible grudges left unhealed. Then again the possibility of poison in food eaten is canvassed. I have heard these considerations being turned over in the heat that followed the sudden death of a father and child together without marks of violence. Every meal for several days back was considered in detail. So also of companions of the pair, and old hostilities. It was all done in my presence in about ten minutes, provoked by the sudden reception of the news by two men related to the dead.

Divination in Dobu is practised by everyone without magic, and by a special class with more authority and with magic.

V

The Diviner at Work

Alo's second wife of the Brown Eagle village died. Alo performed the mourning observances for a year, and shortly after his mourning was done and he returned to his own Green Parrot village, he fell seriously ill.

Bwai of the place Bwaioa, two days' journey away, was summoned, as diviner. Bwai duly performed the water-gazing divinatory rite, and saw at the bottom of the wooden dish Alo's recently deceased wife's mother. He pointed out that Alo had failed to give her her due of bananas (in an obligatory gift to his mother-in-law incumbent on the widower a year after the death of his wife). Bwai had probably made discreet inquiries before doing his divining, as the sequel proved. No objection to his divination was offered. A summons for the *bwokumatana* or *yatala* went out to the Brown Eagle people. They filed passed Alo one by one, each protesting innocence. When Alo's late wife's mother came she was given no time to protest. Bwai accused her of witchcraft from the evidence of his water-divining, and asked her if Alo had not a bad debt to her which he had been obdurate in paying. She admitted that Alo had declined to pay her her just due, and she admitted anger and witchcraft against him. She assured Alo that he would not die, at least by her witchcraft, if the bananas were paid her at once. She would restore his spirit to him the moment the bananas were received by her. He would not die while she lived. But if she herself died, he would also be likely to die at the same time (with a veiled threat and a shrewd warning against his undertaking future sorcery reprisals against her).

Alo's kin pointed out forcibly to the witch mother-in-law and her kin that not so long ago the witch's daughter had died. They had felled a sago tree, worked it, cooked the sago and brought it to the witch and her kin for their eating. If Alo were to die now, the return gift would be due. The witch and her kin would have to fell a sago tree, work and cook sago for them to eat. The diviner had put the entire matter on a sound business footing. Alo rapidly put on several stone in weight and recovered. I did not see the affair. The above is Alo's account of it.

When the diviner makes a just charge, as that which Bwai

made in the case of Alo bewitched by his late wife's mother, there is little thought of sorcery or witchcraft reprisals being made by the sick person on recovery. It is held that the black art has been practised fairly, its justice has been made public, justice has been appeased, and the affair is over. If the sick person does not recover, but dies, his death is not attributed to the anger of a witch who has been publicly exposed and publicly appeased and placated, but to someone else who up till death supervened was undetected and unplacated.

The working of this system may be examined in much more detail in my forthcoming study of the natives of the Admiralty Islands. There illness and death are attributed not to human agents, but to spirits. There I was able to examine the system in detail unhampered by the very small size of the village as in Dobu, and by fear of Government interference as in Dobu. But the causes of illness and death are often exactly as in the case of Alo. The Admiralty Island diviner proceeds on almost exactly the same lines as the Dobuan diviner, Bwai. I saw a great deal of illness and some deaths as an eye-witness in the Admiralties and I know that the system is closely related to the Dobuan, even although the agents in the Admiralties are usually the spirits of the dead and only rarely living sorcerers, whereas in Dobu the agents are usually living persons and more rarely the purely spiritual sea witches. It will be seen that the system is a very good one in maintaining native custom and economic honesty.

Just as we have seen the *tabus*, spells to cause disease, used most typically in the protection of private property in trees, so now we see witchcraft used most typically to enforce economic obligations. *Tabus* and witchcraft and sorcery may also be used in feuds. That I shall discuss in more detail later. Meanwhile it should be appreciated that there is a very strong legal background to the use of the black art. The natives understand how our own legal system is imposed with the help of rifles perfectly. They say typically : " You have your rifles—we have *tabu*, witchcraft, and sorcery, our weapons." Behind this statement is the knowledge that the native weapons are used to maintain native law, as well as in private feuds—a thing that I knew, as also my informants. " If we are caught using our weapons to maintain our just rights by the white Government it gaols us."

VI

THE DIVINER REFUSES TO WORK

The case of Hill Man's sorcery occurred in a locality which I did not know at all well but which I passed through three or four times in the course of a month. The people of this locality were very far removed from my home in Tewara and little report of me from Alo, Tawa, Kisi, Kopu, and the rest of my best known associates had penetrated to its people. Once as I passed through I asked if there had been a *bwoko-matana* anywhere lately. One woman in a large village where a native church stood answered me without suspicion of my intentions, saying there had been a *bwokomatana* for her sick father the night before. On hearing this statement Hill Man arose from his hut and followed me as I moved on to the next village, where I intended to make further inquiries (one always asks in the next village in Dobu, not too much at first in the actual village of occurrence). I turned and asked Hill Man if the *bwokomatana* had picked on anybody. No, nobody. Only he himself and the sick man with his wife were in the *bwokomatana*. (This proved to be true. No diviner had come. The sick man had made his own charge against Hill Man ; Hill Man had consistently and stoutly denied the charge of sorcery before all the village.) He himself, Hill Man, was the sick man's true blood brother, not a village " brother " (*tasi-yaiobara-na*) merely. No evidence of sorcery had been revealed. It was God's handiwork. (I knew that this was not native belief in any real sense.)

At this statement I became angry and charged him directly with deliberate lying. What was he following me for anyway ? Hill Man became uneasy and took my accusation of lying to refer to his statement that he was not the sick man's true brother. He repeated, reiterated that he was the sick man's true brother, still following me. As I approached the next village he turned and went back.

Everyone in the next village said that Hill Man was no brother of the sick man. Hill Man had married into the village where I had found him. His home was high on the hill, not on the shore. Hill Man had lied unnecessarily and protested far too much. Obviously he was under public suspicion of causing the sick man's illness.

I returned to the sick man's house. There I asked of

his daughter her father's relationship to Hill Man. She replied that Hill Man was distantly related by having married into the same village that her father had married into. He came from the hill in Dobu. She replied quickly, just a second or two too quickly to get a prompting from another woman who had overheard Hill Man talking to me, and who prompted her : " Hill Man is your father's blood brother from the one womb." The prompting fell a second after the daughter's quick reply—the prompter looked unabashed as usual. The sick person's house was half the village away from the house where Hill Man sat—itself the soundest evidence of distance of relationship. I told the too slow prompter to set aside deceit of such clumsy nature. The sick man lay in his hut somewhat emaciated. He had not eaten or had any bowel movement for a fortnight. He was incontinent of urine. He could hardly speak. I said to his wife : " He will recover, don't you think ? " Loudly, so that her sick husband heard distinctly, she said : " As likely not."

I then emerged from the hut—the sick man had not stirred from where he lay within it for the fortnight—and went over to Hill Man. Hill Man, without being questioned, swore profusely that he was a Mission man believing in God only (a lie—as every Dobuan native combines going to church or sending his children to church for fear of antagonizing the Mission, with the full practice of old pre-Christian custom in which he believes fully and thoroughly and not as a matter of policy merely). He went on to say that he was a native of Bwaioa, some three miles away across the sea. (This was another lie. He came from high on the hill in Dobu, hence his name Hill Man. Bwaioa has no villages high in the hills. It is a flat foreshore.)

I put on a show of fierce resentment of Hill Man's lies. Hill Man turned aside and brow-beat a woman for having told me too much, not the woman who had told me anything, but the unfortunate would-be prompter. He swore to me that he knew no sorcery (another lie—even twenty-year old boys know some sorcery ; all my servants, young boys of no social importance, knew sorcery spells and had told me of them). He reaffirmed that he was the sick man's true blood brother.

As I went home I told one man in a neighbouring locality of the affair. " Hill Man is a feared and over threatening sorcerer," he said. " He never comes near my village.

I never go near his. Long ago we quarrelled. I said if he came near my place he would taste of my sorcery. He retaliated in kind."

I sent rice with jam, tea with sugar, and a heavy dose of salts to the sick man. He pulled up, and left his hut for the first time in the fortnight the day after his first treatment. I kept on treating him and rapidly he recovered. His family sent me occasional baskets of yams in return.

The sick man and his family still would tell me nothing specific. They were much afraid of Hill Man. I used friendliness, and found it unavailing. But one day Hill Man happened to be away on an overseas canoe expedition. I got the family of the sick man alone, used cajolery, and I mingled with the cajolery some vague threats of Government and Mission getting *them* for sorcery if they would disclose nothing. My time was short in their place and I had to resort to rough and ready methods. The full story emerged, however. The sick man while still well had ordered Hill Man off his land. Hill Man had no legal right on it, and obeyed, but in a quarrelsome mood over his eviction. Sometime later the evictor, owner of the land, whom we may call X, was working in his garden. X required stakes to train his yam vines upon, and he wandered alone on the bush-covered hillside seeking and cutting good stakes. In the deep bush he encountered Hill Man, also alone and there for no legitimate purpose. What actually transpired I could not obtain from either one concerned. X became too agitated to talk of it, and would not talk. Hill Man, of course, maintained, in an almost equally agitated state, a stream of lies about everything and anything. X ran back to his garden, left all his tools lying in it, having scattered the stakes he had cut somewhere in the bush near where he had met Hill Man. He entered his hut and collapsed on its floor saying : " I encountered Hill Man in the bush." From that time it was that he ceased to eat, his bowels did not function normally, his urine was incontinent, he did not speak. He was forcibly given drink. So he lay in his hut without moving from it until a fortnight later, when I found him emaciated and half dead. Hill Man meanwhile denied vigorously having used sorcery on X. But no one believed Hill Man. Everyone was in fear of him. X's family offered payment to diviners. No diviner would take up the case. It was known that the charge would have to be put against Hill Man. It was known that Hill Man would not admit it, as it was not sorcery used by Hill Man to enforce his rights, sorcery that would not lead to a vendetta between X and Hill Man if X recovered. Hill Man could not risk the help towards X's recovery that he would have to give if he publicly admitted his use of the black art and publicly renounced it.

I am not a physician skilled in diagnosis but I do not believe that there was much organic trouble with X. There was no bodily sign of any trouble, and he mended too rapidly for his trouble to have been hookworm, which often causes great emaciation. Salts, rice, and tea, and someone to intimidate Hill Man, brought him round at once. I talked to Hill Man afterwards, telling him to cease his lies immediately. I was so disgusted with them that I would see him put into gaol for sorcery if I had another one of them. My medicine was more powerful than his black art, and he had better cease it in this case if he wished to remain a free man. Hill Man became as meek as he had been truculent.

What X's statement " I encountered Hill Man in the bush " in the light of X's quarrel with Hill Man over his land, and X's illness meant to the natives I knew from a talk that I had heard told by my best sorcery instructor a considerable time before I ever met X or Hill Man.

Christopher (a *nom de plume* for my informant) was one night alone with me in my hut. Christopher let fall a hint of a piece of work in the black art quite accidentally. I followed it up and with some pressure got it out of him. He began with reluctance, but soon his eyes were half starting from his head and he was rolling and writhing on the floor of my hut in active description of a thing too vigorous for words to do justice to—obviously re-living the scene he described with a thoroughly ugly intensity.

A man had said to Christopher's wife's mother's brother, a noted sorcerer :

" You are always on the sea and without new garden food."

Any such statement derogatory to a man's garden is as great an insult as can be hurled. The garden is knit up with the ceremonial of the sacred—any impugning of it is to blaspheme against a man's gods.

The wife's mother's brother (whom we may call Y) said nothing. Within himself he said " later on ". Later he spoke to Christopher. " You will not betray me." " How should I—I who have married your sister's daughter."

Y drank a great quantity of salt water to parch his throat and keep himself safe from swallowing his own black spells with his saliva. He chewed great quantities of ginger and *gau* to make his body hot and heat up the spells to an effective killing temperature.

The intended victim, all unknowing, went alone to his garden in the early morning. Y and Christopher set out, the sorcerer with his assistant and watch-dog. The two performed the *logau*, a charm which is believed to make the man who utters it invisible. Christopher circled three times round the foot of a convenient coco-nut palm while he did the *logau*. Y and Christopher could see each other, being both charmed together. Others could not see them. Nevertheless, Christopher climbed the palm to keep watch against possible intruders. From this height he also directed the movements of Y by signs towards the unconscious solitary gardener.

Y moved in concealment, charming with spells towards the gardener and charming his sorcerer's lime spatula. Then with the gardener facing him, and nearby where he crouched concealed, he burst forth with the sorcerer's screaming shout. Christopher saw the gardener fall to the ground and lie writhing convulsively under the sorcerer's attentions. (Christopher had a painful filarial swelling in his groin approaching bursting point—but here he hurled himself down on the floor of my hut and writhed, groaning horribly—re-living the scene in his excitement.)

The sorcerer feinted to rap his victim gently over the body with his lime spatula. The body lay still. He cut open the body with the charmed spatula, removed entrails, heart, and lungs, and tapped the body again with the spatula, restoring its appearance to apparent wholeness (here my informant speaks from what he apparently believes his own eyes saw in the cleared garden space below). The sorcerer's attentions here left the body of the victim, and transferred to charming the lime spatula anew. The body rose. Y said " You name me ". The body mumbled incoherently and received a feint at a gentle rap on the temples from the spatula. Again " You name me " aggressively. Again an incoherent mumble, and another feinted rap. So a third time. Y said " You go ". The man went to the village, and arrived raving, leaving his personal goods and tools in the garden. His children went to bring them. The man lay down writhing, groaning, and calling on his abstracted vital parts by name—

by this time it was mid-day. So he lay that day and night. Next day the sun climbed to its zenith and he lay dead.

Such is the account of the watch-dog in the case. At one stage he informed me that the lime spatula did not actually strike the body of the victim, but threatened striking and approached the skin closely only. At another stage he said it cut the skin. Other informants later confirmed the view that it did not strike the skin in such sorcerer's procedure, nevertheless it cut the skin. On subsequent questioning Christopher clung to the view that the spatula did not strike the skin, but it was evident that he had some magical striking, magical cutting, and later magical restoring of skin in mind. He was not vacillating between opposing views in his own mind, but only struggling for words to express his conception. So firm was his belief that he used the language of an eye witness of the removal of the entrails, heart, and lungs of the victim.

It is clear that the sorcerer's procedure is hypnotic in nature, the fear apparently being paralysing. I have seen a man blanch—get ready to run and threaten death in reprisal at the threat of sorcery, fear that lasted until the threat was proved otherwise directed, despite my expressed intention to deal with the threatener. The fear of the sorcerer is tremendous in its strength.

I believe that Christopher's account of his adventure as his wife's mother's brother's watch-dog was no fabrication. He had no need to implicate himself so closely if he was spinning a tale. I have never seen a human being so possessed with emotion as my informant, yet retaining his sanity. He appeared to see everything that he described once again, and I felt towards him much as I did towards a man that ran amuck with a spear in my village and raved, threatening to cut my throat and eat me, stuffing rubbish into his mouth to illustrate his intention, after I got him disarmed and was proceeding to truss him up. My informant was equally ugly in manner, and more powerfully so in that he was not in any pathological state. He was, however, so strongly excited that I would be inclined to connect the running amuck, which is a well-known occurrence and which I witnessed three times during my stay, with the state of mind engendered by witchcraft and sorcery. During his recital with much bodily imitation I kept my attention closely on him and on a possible weapon in case he went out of all reason.

His tale checks up with other information, less detailed and more ambiguous, but unquestionably referring to the same practice that Christopher describes. Since this information comes from Motu, Mailu, and the North-Eastern Division, far scattered areas of Papua,[1] we have a very good check on him. He was a most reliable informant and most trustworthy.

VII

CONSIDERING THE DIVINER

I shall consider the diviner first from the point of view of justice. I do not pretend that sorcery cannot be used unjustly. But I do most certainly insist that the diviner's craft is one in which native justice must be paid scrupulous regard, and in which scrupulous regard to such justice is paid. The diviner who did not ply his divining within just bounds would have had a short life in the old days. Now he has still the benefit of this good tradition, and as sorcery still goes on undiminished, he still believes that he is under the check of his fellows.

Consider theoretically that Bwai, the diviner from Bwaioa, had selected his witch unwisely in the case of Alo's illness. I have heard that in rare cases an unsatisfactory divining has occurred. Then the person unjustly accused of causing the illness and his or her relatives violently oppose the diviner—" their minds towards throat cutting ", as one informant phrased the situation.

Or the diviner might be conceived to make the other possible mistake of accusing a person such as Hill Man, a person in the wrong to whom no just propitiation could be made, between whom and his victim no reconciliation could be effected.

I have only three good accounts of divining ; but it is worthy of notice that Bwai made no mistake and acted rather shrewdly ; and that further a large fee (by native standards) is always given the diviner. An advance on the fee was sent out to summon a diviner by the relatives of X, the victim of Hill Man, but no diviner would touch it. (This all occurred well before I knew of the case and had no possible connection with me or with any other white influence.)

The diviners are not fanatics gazing altogether too

[1] See pp. 284–7 for discussion of this.

religiously, or fee seekers gazing altogether too arbitrarily into a bowl of water or into a volcanic crystal. They apparently know all that is necessary to make their work socially acceptable. In other words they administer native justice as well as is possible in terms of the fact that illness alone brings investigation to the fore.

My third account of divining does not belie these conclusions in the slightest. Two weeks after one of the Bobo-Emu duels (between abandoned wife and new wife of Alo) Bobo fell very ill and her flesh wasted on her bones until it looked almost like a hide hanging loosely on a frame. The diviner was called in and did his divining unbeknown to me until afterwards. Bobo owed no one debts. She was now divorced, her mother and her children were living, her father long dead. Neither marriage exchanges of property, nor exchanges following a death were in point. In Dobu economic exchanges are not very frequent and the diviner cannot very often select unpaid debts as the cause of illness. In Manus of the Admiralties economic exchanges are due constantly, owing to a tremendous elaboration of exchange, so that the diviner is seldom at a loss. Bobo's only enemies were Alo, her deserting husband, and Emu, her successor in his house. It is considered right and reasonable that Bobo and Emu should fight with stones and knives under such circumstances. Consequently the diviner did not select Emu as the witch responsible. Alo was somewhat uneasy about the issue of the divination. He questioned Bobo's village sisters closely and tried to " pump " the small children of the village for hours.

The diviner, it appeared, had fallen back on a non-human explanation. The witch responsible was a sea witch, a *gelaboi*, the type that has no human embodiment. After securing this result from water-gazing, the diviner performed a circular dance with its magical song designed to get the abstracted spirit of his patient back from the *gelaboi*. The diviner is always summoned in from another locality than that of the patient, in order to secure impartiality and his own subsequent safety. In consequence I did not obtain the ritual used.

It is interesting to note that *gelaboi* is the Trobriand term. A comparison of Trobriand beliefs and Dobuan beliefs reveals that the concept of *gelaboi* is almost certainly Trobriand. Dobuans meeting disaster at sea attribute the blame to human women, as we have seen in the case cited of the Tewara canoe accident that happened during my stay. Dr. Malinowski has shown that the Trobrianders attribute such disasters to the *gelaboi*. They have a far greater development of the concept than exists in Dobu. It would appear that the diviner hard pressed falls back on a way of escape opened up by the ideas of a neighbouring culture.

I did not know Bobo's family well enough to know whether they were satisfied. 'Inosi, my servant, was not. He said the diviner would probably communicate the name of the human witch later and with more secrecy to Bobo's family. So there was some feeling at least that the trouble had not been thoroughly met.

I regret that I can cite but three cases only. Owing to Administration having made sorcery or witchcraft a criminal offence in Papua the ethnologist is very considerably impeded. A search of the literature will reveal that not a single case of divination with all the personal implications involved has ever been recorded before from Papua, although various methods of divination in their formal aspects have been recorded from various places. This is entirely explicable, for obtaining material is beset with the greatest difficulties.

I do not believe that the diviner touches a case after death has supervened, in order to divine the direction vendetta should take. The diviner is a well known and generally respected practitioner. The profession could hardly survive if it took up proceedings that placed it in the greatest danger. There is no disguising of the diviner, such as that which is said in West Africa to conceal his identity, and allow post mortem divination by him compatible with his personal safety.

Moreover means of divination after a death are used by non-professionals, by the near kin of the dead for the purpose of vendetta. The magic in divination is decidedly secondary to the amount of private judgment displayed in it. Where there is the fire of sorcery or witchcraft there has been very often the smoke of quarrel. In Dobu granted the quarrel the subsequent black magic is practically assured. Everyone knows gossip of local dissensions. There is no strife over small points in such an atmosphere. In all small matters there is an over great show of cordial agreement, the sincerity of which is a sincere appreciation of the sorcery milieu rather than anything else.

VIII

THE SORCERER IN ACTION

I find in my notes one instance of some play with the sorcery of *sumwana*, personal leavings. This, however, is not at all a gruesome story. Aines and Peter were one day far from home, and outside their own locality, cutting *sakwara* sticks for house building. They killed the domestic pig of Luilo, under the impression that it was wild bush pig. Discovering their mistake they concealed the dead pig in the bush and went home quickly hoping to escape discovery. Luilo hunted for his pig and finally found it when it was partially decomposed. Meanwhile he had ascertained that the only outsiders who had been about the locality had been Aines and Peter. On finding his pig with tell-tale spear wounds near cut *sakwara* trees, he set out to watch Aines and Peter. He collected sand fresh with their foot-prints. He then went to Aines and Peter and demanded pay for his pig—or he would work the *sumwana* sorcery on their sand tracks. Aines and Peter paid up, a handsome recompense.

Such men are not men acting contrary to native ideas of justice. But because the braver man acting with justice and openly, is open, he is the sorcerer that Administration usually hears about, secures, and is likely to imprison—for exactly the wrong type of sorcery. The anti-social type of sorcerer is just the kind where neither openness by the sorcerer, before acting or after acting, nor the work of the diviner, is possible. Owing to native antagonism to Administration interfering with sorcery there is surprisingly little betrayal, however. This is in part resentment of over-lordship, in part, prospective fear of the sorcerer returning from prison after his term with what everyone would regard as a just score to settle.

I give below the statements of an important conversation which I had with my mentor, Christopher, after four and a half months of his company. We went to a solitary place— a bare rock slab on the edge of a great cliff, on a day when the New Guinea mainland showed up clearly in the distance. Christopher chanted the names of the spells for making the charmer invisible. I took out my note book, and wrote four names. The fifth I forgot, and I could not get it out of him again.

I asked for details—*Akasaoleole* or *Duntna Moligogona*, which he had sung over rapidly and had come out intending to give me—was to make a man invisible for stealing purposes. I could use it in Sydney and take what I liked from the shops without fear of detection. He had stolen often with it and never been caught—cooked pig and what not.

Then *Sineboganbaura* ?—That was to make a man invisible from the flying witches in time of shipwreck.

Then *Mokakasi* ?—That was to enable a man to strike and kill a woman with her children in the garden (remaining invisible the while as in the stealing aid). The sorcerer's charm.

And *Sekaikaiawana* ?—Like *Mokakasi*.

Here I took down *Akasaoleole* and had it interpreted from the magical language into the normal language of every day speech.

Then we talked idly—and I said :

" *Mokakasi* ?—I will write that down."

He gave it me somewhat reluctantly, looking at me strangely. Then after, before I had time to ask for its interpretation, he said : " My friend, I lied ; it is not a *logau*—but a *yauboda*." He got up, strung a creeper across the path charmed in spitting on to it—showed me how a woman or a man or child coming along the track would breast it or take it in the stomach and push it to the side—crawled into a bush near by, concealed himself—how he would wait till the person passed by.

He came out, took the creeper in hand, charming briefly as he did so. Then he told me how he would smoke it all day on the smoking shelf and at night crumble it in his hand and burn it on a firestick. He illustrated how meanwhile he would feign sickness, lying contorted and groaning horribly. He said he would eat nothing that day or night—if he did his stomach would get cold—it was necessary that his body should be hot—in the morning the man would be dead, the mourners would come wailing and find him washed, bathed all over, anointed with oil, his face painted and all in best array--so he would eat. But all day and night his closest relatives would think him dying.

He told me how it could be done to a child, or to a pregnant woman, how the child would die within her and how she would die from it.

IN THE EARLY MORNING SUN

DOBUAN HOUSE

Then I went over the charm in detail—

```
              crab
        inside your earth cave
          your throat clogs up
              (as the crab clogs up his hole)
          your body fat congeals
          your foot crouches bends
          your seat of the voice rots
          your heel gives under you standing
          your seat of urine secretion clogs up
          your tongue hangs out with spue vomiting
          your intestines flow out your anus.
```

All this in the esoteric language where *lakua*, crab, becomes *mokakasi*, for example.

Then he took the creeper and repeated the formula again for unloosing it after the victim's body had been seen to brush it aside—

```
        your throat (i.e. mind) I roll up
        your heart I crumble up
        I crumble up striking dead
        your throat (seat of mind) I roll up
```

rolling the creeper compact in his hand. Again he illustrated the smoking of it, the feigned illness and groaning on his part, the burning of the rolled up creeper at night.

I waited silent a while. He said: " Two men I killed so". " For what reason ? " I asked.

He told me how his father-in-law, a noted and feared sorcerer, had given him the charm, how a certain man had acted in a vain and proud manner. He had said: " That— he does not know *mokakasi*. His father-in-law has not given it him." So I said: " Very well—you slight me in proud fashion—later I will kill you." He beached his canoe at Muria. I twined the *dutu* creeper on the track—charmed it and hid. He brushed it aside—I saw it. I lay feigning sickness all day and night—I did not do so in the village— I remained in the bush. I did not eat. He fell sick. Next morning he was dead."

" And the other man ? " I asked.

" That was overseas exchange. He (naming the man) got from my debtor the necklace which my debtor should have given me in return for an armshell I had given him before. I did in like manner to him. Next day he was dead."

" You gave them the poison," I said, using the term for the sorcerer's poisoning tactics.

" That," he said " is different, another method."

" You combined the methods ? " I said.

" No," he said, " the poison is given without magic. That was a child I killed."

" Why ? " I said.

" My father told me of the poison, it is *budobudo*, plenty of it grows by the sea. The day after to-morrow we shall go and I shall instruct you in it. *I wanted to try it out.* We draw the sap from it. I took a coco-nut, drank from it, squeezed the sap into it, the remainder, and closed it up. Next day I gave it to the child, saying : " I have drunk of it, you may drink." She fell ill at mid-day. In the night she died."

" She was of X—— village."

" No, her village is grass and weeds."

" L——," I said, naming his father's village.

" Yes," he said, " my classificatory cross-cousin, father's village sister's daughter. My father poisoned her mother with the *budobudo*. I poisoned the orphan later."

" What was the trouble ? " I said.

" She bewitched my father, he felt weak—he killed her and his body grew strong again."

" You chew *mwadi* (ginger) ? " he asked.

" No," I said. " Not generally. I have chewed it."

" It sharpens the charm," he said, " we spit with it."

" You combine the charm and the *budobudo*," I said.

" No," he replied. " If we like we do. It is not necessary. The *budobudo* was different—that was a child. The charm was different—that was two men—in one moon one man ; two moons later, the second." (Later) " The Boyowans use *soki*. Here we who know this secret, use *budobudo*."

Christopher gave me some plant food to eat when he returned to the village. Fresh from his revelations I hesitated just one second before eating, although the food came from his wife's pot. He noticed it, for his eyes bulged with a queer expression. He was wondering, as I was, how far we really trusted each other.

The fear of being poisoned dominates native life. Food or tobacco is not accepted except within a small circle. The woman of the house when cooking does not leave the pot and go away for as long as a half minute even. The antithesis " The Boyowans (Trobriands) use *soki* ; here we who know the secret use *budobudo* " was merely an expression of the moment. For at a later time Christopher told me that he had caught a *soki* fish, and had it now concealed in a private hiding place in the bush. It is a globe fish with a gall which contains a swift and fatal poison.   Despite the fear of accepting food or drink, poisoned, from false friends, mistakes are sometimes made.

To act in a proud or in any way overbearing manner is regarded as a great crime in Dobu.   It is resented most keenly. The economic situation regarding overseas exchange as mentioned in Christopher's account will be more fully explained later when we discuss *wabuwabu* in the *kula*.   The practice of " trying out " sorcery or poison we have already mentioned in the section on Teacher and Pupil.

IX

An Evaluation of Claims

It is apparent that we must pause to consider how effective the black art of Dobu actually is in attaining its objects.   It must be remembered that magic is an element of social prestige. The magician will inevitably claim results when he sells a spell or a magical technique for payment or when he hands it down to his heir.   The rainmaker will tell of droughts broken, the gardener will tell of great harvests.   The sorcerer in handing on a *tabu* will tell of persons who contracted a disease from his *tabu*.   Such beliefs are patently false.   Whatever else suggestion may do I have heard no evidence that it can produce yaws or gangosa or elephantiasis, the objects of the *tabus*.

Now sorcery in general is but a part of the magical complex, and subject to the same limitations.   Let us examine first the alleged poison used by Christopher, the sap of the tree *budobudo*.   I secured specimens which were identified by Kew Botanical Gardens, through the courtesy of the Botany Department of the University of Sydney, Australia, as *Cerbera odollam*, Hamilt.   *Cerbera odollam* has been analysed by M. Greshoff.[1]   I give a translation of the relevant passage :

Cerbera Odollam Hamilt.

" As experience has long since taught that the poisonous qualities of this plant are situated in its seeds, these were taken as a starting point of our chemical research.   30 grams of pulverized seed were extracted with spirits containing

[1] *Erste Verslag van vet Onderzock Naar de Planten stoffen van Nederlandsch Indie* (Batavia, 1890), Hoofstuck iv, pp. 70–6.

acetic acid, and examined with Stas-Otto's method ; it then
appeared that already from the acid liquid a poisonous substance is shaken out by ether. This substance, injected into
a toad, caused violent spasms followed by tetanus with
opisthotonus ; disruption of the connection between the brain
and the spinal marrow did not stop the tetanic spasms. A
quantity, corresponding to 2 grams of seed, of the substance
shaken out by ether, was injected into a chicken weighing
500 grams ; the voluntary movements soon became slower
and then ceased entirely ; the animal lay on its side, its head
drooping, its breathing irregular and not noticeably increased ;
the animal remained in any position that was given to it and
was apparently very much intoxicated ; now and then spasmodic
motions were noticed. Slowly the chicken recovered entirely.

*   *   *   *   *   *

Its taste is poignant, a little bitter, biting, and rather
persistent. As appears from animal experiments it is a strong
heart poison. This poison like odolline is deposited only
in the seed-cores of the Cerbera. · The slightly bitter bark
and the tasteless leaves possess no toxic capacities whatsoever.

*   *   *   *   *   *

Concerning this family a large number of data can be
found in the literature of Indian plants. As poisonous plant
and medicinal herb it is mentioned in the earliest dispatches
concerning Java which were carried over to Europe by the
Portuguese and the Dutch. In the *Philosophical Transactions*
of March, 1666 (p. 417), under the " Enquiries for East Indies ",
the following question is put : " Whether there be such a
vegetable in Java called *Mangas Bravas* that is so poisonous
that it kills presently and for which no remedy has yet been
found ? " Judging by the name, it is our plant to which
here is referred, although the possibility exists that the *Antiaris
toxicaria* Lesch., the ill-famed Upas-tree, is meant, which
originally was confused with the Cerbera (Horsfield Plant,
Java, p. 53). This same confusion may also be the reason
that the perfectly unpoisonous milk-juice of the Cerbera is
called by Lindley and other authors " the most poisonous
of all Apocyneae ".

On a similar error is based the widely spread belief, that
the deadly poison lies in the fat oil from the seeds, of which
Hasskarl (l, *c*. p. 24, no. 173) says : " If this oil is drunk, the
head is affected and death will be the immediate result ; if

a small quantity is taken, a vehement blood-diarrhœa will quickly ensue."

This is only in so far true, as part of the poisonous substance can come *with* the oil, but, as is obvious from the experiment just described, the oil in itself is completely innocuous. No more is there any poisonous element in the bark and the leaves, which were introduced into the medical practice by Waitz (*Pract. Waarn.*, p. 7) and which correspond in their effects with senna-leaves, " without any disagreeable or harmful after-effects " ; Rumphius already called the juice squeezed from the fresh bark of *C. lactaria* an excellent laxative. The only poisonous part of the plant are the seed-cores, which, by the way, show a rather close resemblance to almonds. Their deadly effects have been clearly and repeatedly observed in Java and were already known to Rumphius. Horsfield once witnessed the workings of a small quantity (a scruple of the utmost part) upon a Javanese woman, who had swallowed them from curiosity ; she became delirious and could not distinguish the persons and objects in her immediate surroundings ; her power of speech, however, she retained ; she remained in this condition for five hours (Filet, *De planten in den bot. tuin te Weltevreden*, p. 64). A poisoning with the seeds is also mentioned in the *Geneeskunddig tydschrift voor Ned. Indie*, vol. 7 (1859), p. 158. Furthermore, widespread rumour has it that in the South-Preanger Cerbera is still used for criminal purposes, the truth of which, however, the existing state of knowledge does not guarantee. (In the beach-dessah's of Djampang Koelon the only lamp-oil used is still always the Minjak Bintaroh.)

Before this Cerbera has already figured in chemical research. In part x, p. 505, of the *Geneeskundig tydschrift voor Ned. Indie*, an analysis (by Altheer) of the milk-juice is described ; it was found to contain caoutchouc (19·7%), resin (3%) and gum (0·59%), but no toxic principle whatsoever ; when experimenting on a dog, 32 gr. of milk-juice had no harmful effects. Teysmann, in referring to his negative result, remarked that the native never considered the milk-juice as poisonous. De Vry thought originally that the seeds contained Thevetine, but later on he found that Cergerine was different from this in that it lacked a colour-reaction with sulphuric acid."

Now there is no doubt that Christopher stated that the milk-juice, the milky sap of *budobudo*, was what he had used for his believed poisoning tactics mixed with coco-nut juice. There could hardly have been any motive for lying and yet lying so near to what might have been truth. The milk sap does not show up in prepared coco-nut milk or on a prepared yam, he said, because of its appropriate milky colour.

To check the remotest possibility of my having confused my dried specimens I examined the literature in detail and checked the identification of *budobudo* as *Cerbera odollam* in every detail that I had observed of the tree in New Guinea, an observation that had not been casual. There can be no doubt whatever of the facts of the identification.

As a check on Christopher's truth-telling, the poisonous element in the seed cores is stated by Greshoff to be " very hard to dissolve in water, even a 1,000 fold quantity of boiling water is not sufficient ". Further the seed cores are coloured and could not be well disguised.

It is evident that the milky sap of *budobudo*,[1] believed to be a poison by Christopher is not poisonous. Hence his account of how he killed a child with it cannot be accepted. In the same way his claimed killing of two men by magical spells cannot be accepted. The statement that all three died the day after he proceeded against them is obviously a lie of prestige. (Even in the case of Hill Man's sorcery where Hill Man met his victim face to face in the bush, and the thing was not done from concealment as in Christopher's two spell bindings, the victim, apparently suffering from suggestion, had been two weeks indisposed when I encountered him.) Doubtless natural deaths occurred in three cases of those that Christopher had proceeded against magically beforehand, possibly months beforehand.

Certain poisons are known to everyone. Derris, a vegetable poison in the roots of a tall liana, is used publicly for stupefying fish. The gall of a globe fish called *soki* is a poison more deadly than *tuva*. These two poisons are known to everyone. But apart from these two there are many simples believed to be poisonous that are family secrets, just as spells are. *Budobudo*, told to me by Christopher in the last material quoted, is just such a family secret.

Such secrets are not obtained easily by the white man. The native usually gives a facile lie or preserves silence on the matter. The literature on the area has no instance of such clear truth-telling in it, as Christopher gave to me.

[1] The same tree is also called *butobuto* in the Phillipines.

I think it is clear that he did give me a traditional secret simple without reticence or lying. *Cerbera odollam*, Hamilt., clearly is a tree that produces a poison traditionally recognized as such in southern Asia by the natives. In Dobu, at least in Christopher's case, knowledge of its properties has not been handed down quite faithfully. It is apparently one case of the loss of a useful art, the sap being now believed to be a poison. From this incident, however, I may demonstrate that Christopher probably told me the truth in his other accounts of the black art with only the customary lies of prestige.

After my initiation into the black art as it is practised in Dobu, I pin my faith to the kind of sorcery Hill Man used on *X*, and Christopher's wife's mother's brother in company with Christopher used on the gardener. In this type of sorcery (for the further proof of which see Appendix II), the sorcerer fronts his victim, who actually knows for certain that trouble has come upon him. I refer to the method by which the victim's internal organs are removed [*sic*] by the sorcerer in person, and in full fleshly person.

For the rest, witchcraft, sorcery upon body leavings, *tabus*, and the secret poisons are for the most part ineffective psychologically. For the most part their use in feuds is most secret.

In a few cases threats before execution occur. Unwelcome conduct may be taken as the equivalent of a specific threat. In such cases of known trouble impending both parties must live at a very high tension. The victim does not know of the sorcerer's intention unless by threat or threatening behaviour in advance. There is no pattern of anonymous message after execution ; complete anonymity is sedulously preserved in most cases. There is no belief that the diviner is necessarily right and that one must be found out if one is successful.

If a threat of execution can be averted by payment, such payment is usually made, as Aines and Peter paid Luilo about double the value of his slaughtered pig.

X

GENERAL ATTITUDES

To sum up, the black art is used not only for collecting bad debts and enforcing economic obligation, in vendetta to avenge one's own sickness or one's kinsman's death, to wipe out any serious insult offered to one, and for the sake of " trying it out " to see how it works. It is also used generally " to cast down the mighty from their seat ". There is great resentment of any conspicuously successful man in Dobu. There is respect for old age and for primogeniture, but nothing except anger for any differences in success due to ability.

The black art is used against an over successful gardener, since he is believed to have stolen other person's yams from their gardens by magic. The black art is used against rivals who interfere with one's own success in overseas exchange, where armshells are exchanged for necklaces ; a long time elapses between gift and counter gift, giving a rival a chance to cut in. Such cutting in is not rare as we shall see later. There is real competition here since the most prized valuables are not numerous enough for every one to handle them. Even a man who has too many domestic pigs is in danger—his greater wealth is regarded as an affront.

The desirable man in Dobu is he who has been more successful than his fellows in gardening, overseas exchange of valuables, in the pigs he has and even more importantly in the number of women he has seduced (this last is of course a case of real competition). It is interesting to note how our distinction between real competition where one man's gain is another's loss, and rivalry where all may gain, but not at one another's expense, is not made in Dobu. All matters of economics fall under the real competition concept. But with all this success the desirable man must be sound in body and in health. In other words the desirable man is he who has sought and gained the dangerous values unhurt by the black art of his rivals, who have used their sorcery against his success. He is the *tai bobo'ana*, the desirable man.

A man who is not conspicuously successful, but who has a sound body is neither *bobo'ana* nor *tokumali*. And in the rare cases where a deformed person remains socially successful Dobuans hesitate to use the term *tokumali*, which applies to nearly all hurt persons.

By means of a theory which makes the most prized social values so dangerous it is possible to explain a great many cases of disease and death. We have here a good blanket explanation for the misfortunes of men.

The diseased or deformed man in Dobu normally falls back in the scale. He is not a success with women, or with overseas exchanges ; whether from infirmity or from fear of further disaster or from both, his economic status is normally low.

The diviner does not use this diagnosis of disease or deformity or death in his divining, probably because there is no just reason why a too rich man should give away some of his wealth to the one particular rival only whom the diviner might select as causing illness. This diagnosis is popular, not professional.

The concepts good and bad in the purely moral sense do not exist in Dobu. If it were said : " He did not mourn his wife, he is a *tai tokumali*," what would this mean ? For a cripple, a person with tertiary yaws, with gangosa or what not *tokumali* is practically always used, irrespective of whether that person is now conforming to the Dobuan code of what is safe conduct or not. Some serious departure from pleasing others in the past life of the cripple is assumed—hence his physical trouble. The exact departure can almost always be named. So if a man who did not mourn his wife were called *tokumali* there would be implicit in the term, some anticipation of proceedings against him that might be expected to damage his health.

In point of fact I have never heard that sorcery proceedings are actually taken against the non-conformist widower by his late wife's relatives. They are incensed and taunt him if they meet him. They remark on him disparagingly to everyone. He gets a bad name. But that is all. Consonantly it is never said "he did not mourn his wife ; he is a *tai tokumali* ". *Tokumali* is too strong a term here.

I may remark that the translator of the Bible into Dobuan, the Rev. W. E. Bromilow, D.D., has made *bobo'ana* and *tokumali* the equivalents of moral good and bad. There is a real difficulty here, as the Dobuan categories are not closely related to our own. Such translation is linguistically unsound, but there is nothing else that could have been done than to try to change the meaning of the terms. This is not impossible provided that the true native use of the terms is specifically guarded against. The fact that the *tokumali* do not get into the Dobuan spirit land adds a fine touch of trouble after death as well as trouble during mortality. But the attitude towards the deformed and the diseased in Dobu is hardly Christian.

I have a further discussion of as yet unstressed facts of the black art in appendices.

CHAPTER IV

The Spirits of the Dead

I have discussed the black art in Dobu before the discussion of economic exchanges owing to a profound colouring of the latter by the former. It may not seem clear why I should also interpose a chapter on beliefs regarding the spirits of the dead in this place. The reason is one that is particularly apropos in any treatment of a Melanesian culture. In Melanesia generally if misfortune is not attributed to the black art it is attributed to the spirits of the dead. It is reasonable therefore to turn from the black art to its possible substitute.

We have seen that a few spirits of the first ancestors of man are conceived as the familiars who do the magician's bidding. The existence of these familiars is an assumption of spiritual immortality in itself. Magic in Dobu pre-supposes the doctrine of immortality, usually one of the basic doctrines of religion.

We have seen that witchcraft in Dobu is conceived as the witch woman sending forth her spirit with murderous intent during her sleep ; and that nightmare is usually inter-preted as a witchcraft episode in which the spirit of the sleeper who has the nightmare has been in great danger from hostile spirits, the spirits of all concerned having gone forth from their human habitations of skin and bone.

We have seen again that the diviner in diagnosing a case of illness may say that the sea witches, *gelaboi*, have come to shore by canoe and caused it ; and that these sea witches, unlike most witch spirits, have no skin and bone residence to enter at will. This difference between *gelaboi* and land witches is not firmly insisted upon by the Dobuans, as it might be, however. They do not really grasp and welcome the *gelaboi* as purely spiritual agents. When the diviner gives a prognosis of sea witch caused illness, I know that some think he is lying to put them off the scent. The question of whether the *gelaboi* are the spirits of the dead does not occur naturally to the Dobuan. He will say that these sea witches are spirits of some of the dead, a minority that has found no rest in the spirit home. Not that the existence of the *gelaboi* is a lie. But he is not comfortable in the idea that the dead can do any damage. Damage is done so preponderantly by the living, that this latter conception will not tolerate a rival conception easily.

In one Dobuan district there is a belief that the spirit of a person who has died with a swollen stomach is dangerous. It seeks to enter the body of another person, to cause him to die with a swollen stomach also. Infection with such a disease is due in the first place to the person going to a place where some time before he had killed a man or woman. Everywhere where Dobuan is spoken it is believed that if the killer returns to the place of the killed the blood of the killed will enter his body and swell it until he dies ; and death with a swollen body is interpreted as having been caused so. But only amongst the Dobuans of one particular district is it believed that the spirit of a person so dying will enter the bodies of others still living and cause them to die so also.

In this Dobuan district, when an individual lies seriously ill with swollen stomach, he is tied hand and foot before he is dead. " He has breathing, his mouth works in speech, crying for compassion, shrieking, shouting. He is as one alive ; but he is dead. Only the blood in him, the blood of one he slew that has entered him, breathes, moves his mouth in speech. You think it is a man breathing, speaking. It is not. It is blood. He is tied hand and foot. He is taken to a cave in the cliffs, a cave opening on the sea with a small inland aperture. He is put through the aperture, and a stone is rolled over it. There he is left unburied, crying and calling in vain, a dead man though in semblance alive." A magician makes fast the stone rolled over the aperture with magic to lay the spirit. Then the magician and an assistant conceal themselves close by. Later the magician sees the spirit leave the body and emerge from the cave by the stone-sealed aperture. As it emerges he rushes to the aperture and holds a cooking pot perforated with a small trap hole in its bottom upside down over the spirit. The spirit enters the opening of the cooking pot and emerges from the small trap hole in its bottom held close to him by the magician. As it emerges so the magician cuts the spirit. So it cannot enter others and kill them in like manner. So the spirit of the blood of the killed is laid.

Nevertheless the fear of such a spirit is considerable. Such a spirit is obliged to enter and infect its next-of-kin only, the surviving members of its own *susu*. Accordingly, if shortly after such a death, someone not related to the dead falls ill, it is customary to say to the spirit of him who died in this manner : " Am I your sister or your brother ? What relative of yours am I ? Go away, enter your own relative. You are making a mistake in coming to this house." But such a spirit, though it properly infects and enters one of its *susu* kin, is also believed to enter and infect anyone who owed the dead a debt and had not paid it by the time of the creditor dying. This belief applies to death by blood, by swollen stomach only. In the other Dobuan districts the belief of the district that alone practises premature exposure has penetrated somewhat. It has caused a current saying : " Spirits of the dead are filth ; they hurt men and women." In other Dobuan districts, those dying of a swollen stomach are allowed to die. But then they are buried in great haste with nothing of the usual interval for mourning. Generally speaking other districts have no fear of the spirits of the dead. Such spirits are regarded as powerless against the living. One kind of death only causes a bad spirit which is felt as being dangerous in the extreme in but one district.

The Dobuans of this same district have a custom of carrying on the vendetta in more spiritual terms, also in cases of ordinary death. They keep the corpse in a specially built hut for over a week. A cooking pot is put over the head of the corpse, and the brothers and sisters of the dead sleep by the corpse, one or two with an arm twined about the pot. " The air becomes foul with decomposing corpse ; they are not allowed to spit. If one spat the hand of brother would turn against brother to slay him." The spirit of the sorcerer or the witch who was responsible for the killing is expected to come back to dance over its killed or to eat of the corpse. A magical trap is laid to catch this spirit and so to kill the skin and bone habitation of this spirit.

Every person is believed to have a bodily and a ghostly self. This ghostly self survives after the body is rotted in the grave and the skull alone retained of it in the house of the next-of-kin. It is the reflection seen in a pool—the only mirror before the white man came—and in a mirror. It is related to the shadow in a way that the native refuses to define clearly. Sometimes he says that the shadow goes to Bwebweso, the Mountain of the Spirits in Normanby Island, sometimes he says not, thinking of the shadow's difference from the spirit. On the whole, however, the shadow is a form the spirit may take ; and a native would sometimes comment in a tone that left no doubt as to its spiritual quality on my great shadow cast on my mosquito net by my Tilley lamp as I sat at night at my table writing. Again, a native takes great care to keep his shadow clear of an object upon which he is placing an evil incantation. The spirit is reflection and shadow ; but more importantly and more decisively it is the shapes that are seen in dreams. In sleep the spirit goes forth ; the spirits of witches and sorcerers go on their evil errands, the spirits of the sleeper sometimes go to Bwebweso, the Hill of the Dead, and there hold conversation with the dead. There are magicians, *tokenobeku*, who have power over their spirits to send them forth thus. Not only witchcraft is carried on by women who have incantations that charge their spirits with death-dealing errands, and *tokenobeku* possess incantations that send their spirits to Bwebweso to meet the dead, but lovers also send their spirits forth to play upon the spirit of the loved one ; and persons wake up shrieking and howling from nightmare cast in witchcraft terms.

A sleeper's spirit that visits Bwebweso must not eat of the Dokanikani banana there, or it will never return to the home of the living. Dokanikani was an evil ogre of early times ; the banana named after her is quite truly an inferior banana as I discovered for myself. Sometimes a sleeper will find betel nut in the hut in the morning unaccounted for—his spirit has brought it from Bwebweso (I understand that such strokes of good fortune are rare).

If a corpse becomes infested with lice the spirit has taken a wrong turning on the track to Mt. Bwebweso and gone to Koiakutu, the Hill of Lice, in error.

For several nights after a death cooked yams are left in the hut. In the morning a mark is detected on them—" yes the spirit has eaten of them." So for several nights and several mornings ; then no mark is seen one morning—" he has left us for Bwebweso." [1] The spirit does not gain admittance among the dead till the corpse is " cooked ", i.e. a little decayed ; for the spirits would refuse to believe that too fresh a spirit came from a true corpse. In this way thought

[1] There are jumping-off places where the spirits leave the land for the sea on the Bwebweso facing extreme points of each Dobuan island.

Night falls. They rise up. They go to the gardens. He does nothing but cut himself about the hands. Midnight, they cook food. The men go to sea, fishing. Dawn comes. They wash. They go to lie with the women, to sleep.

He takes his wife with him to the garden. He fells trees. His wife sleeps. The sun rises, climbs. They come out searching for them with torches lit. They say : " The spirits of sorcerers and witches might have killed you." They take man and wife home with them.

They rise at nightfall. They go to the gardens. He remains at home and sleeps. At dawn they come to their houses to sleep.

He asks of them :

" Where leads this path ? "

" To the People of the Sewed-on Wings."

He finds their village. They go to the forest edge of the village clearing. They spread their wings and fly. He follows on foot. There is no track to be found. He pushes through the jungle slowly. He arrives at their gardens. Their work is done. They spread their wings and fly home. He follows toilsomely through the jungle. His stomach is muddy (i.e. he is angry).

In the houses they blow up the fires. They eat. They fly up and hang to the roof poles to sleep. The women call : " Come up and lie with us." " How if I fall ? " He says : " So that is their fashion."

Next morning :

" Where leads this path ? "

" To the village of the Earth Piercing Buttocks." He arrives. They say to him : " Let us go and garden." Their elongated buttocks stick into the ground.

He flees along the path.

He come to the village of the Weave-weave fish nets. The sun is low. Men, women, and children are at work weaving fish nets. They prepare to sleep. They grip the nets in their toes and weave in their sleep. All next day they weave. They prepare to sleep. They grip the nets in their toes, sleep and weave.

Next morning :

" Where leads this path ? "

" To the Adorners of Armshells."

All day they ornament armshells. Next day all day they ornament armshells. Next day again. He became fatigued.

" Where leads this path ? "

" To Those who Fell Canoes."

Men, women, and small children fell trees for canoes. There he marries. His wife bears a male child. They say : " Let us take the new canoe on its trial run."

Dried up banana leaves they pluck.

They pluck the body hairs from pigs, from dogs. They charm a shell trumpet. They close up the charm inside it. They paddle along the shore. They open the shell trumpet and blow on it.

Kwe ! Kwe ! Kwe ! (the pigs' hairs are pigs grunting).

Bwau ! Bwau ! Bwau ! (the dogs' hairs are dogs barking).

The dried banana leaf is heaps of ripe bananas.

The man fells his canoe, sews his sail, plaits his ropes, shapes his gaff.

" When do you sail ? "

" The day after to-morrow."

" With your child ? "

" Alone. Soon I return."

His wife's brother brings dried banana leaves, dried coco-nut leaves, yam leaves. They pluck pigs' hairs and bind the canoe parts together with them. A pig's jaw bones they bind on the outrigger boom sticks.

They charm the shell trumpet, set the sand on the outrigger for the firesticks. He charms ginger, wraps it up, gives it to his sister's husband. He instructs him to chew the ginger at sea and spit it towards the land of the spirits of the killed and roasted in the earth oven. At sea he turns to face the spirit land. He spits the ginger towards it. The spirit land sinks below the horizon. His mother is sweeping. The children are playing. One child :

" Mother, a war canoe comes quickly from their country."

It is their mother's year of *matabora* (prohibition on going to the seashore during mourning).

The brother approaches Silasila (a village of Bwaioa). The mother remains. The rest go to the shore. The canoe drives on to the beach under sail. He blows the shell trumpet.

Pigs—Kwe ! Kwe ! Kwe !

Dogs—Bwau ! Bwau ! Bwau !

Mothers, brothers, sisters, fathers' sisters, mothers' brothers' wives, mothers' brothers, fathers' sisters' husbands, cross-cousins, they wail. They carry pigs and dogs. They kill them and eat the *keaweawasina* (food killed on return of absentee).

This legend was heard by the whole company solemnly—
one laugh when the shut mouths burst open at the snake. At
its close everyone was silent. Then Kopu : " Had we the
charm we could turn all the Trobrianders into the pigs
and dogs."

Togo (very solemnly and quickly) :

" But indeed no—we could take the skulls of the dead—
blow on the trumpet and our dead would be restored to us."

When the body is interred betel nut is closed in its hand.
This is to be given to the gate-keeper of Bwebweso, Sinebomatu, who will then let the spirits pass. The legend of the
origin of death runs :—

Sinebomatu, the woman of the north-east wind, with
her granddaughter, they go to bathe. The grandmother
goes seawards down a stream. Her skin she peels off. She
throws it away. She comes inland her granddaughter to her.
Her granddaughter wails, she says : " My grandmother an
aged woman, you a different woman." She says : " No, I
enough your grandmother."

" You lie. You another woman. My grandmother an
aged woman." She says : " You wail. I return, my skin
I bring."

Her skin she brought it. Like a shirt she donned it again.
She returns. She says : " You wailed. My skin I brought.
When you grow old you will die. If wailing you had set
aside and we had gone village-wards when you grow old you
had stripped your wrinkled skin."

Snake, monitor lizard, crab, lobster a part of her skin
they ate. They strip their old skins, live for ever ; we enough
we die.

I suggested to the owner of this legend that it was filched
from the Trobriands. He told me it came from his mother's
mother, and from her mother before her. The Trobrianders
were thieves to possess it, and liars to claim it as their own.
Later I found it all over Fergusson claimed as its own by each
tribe, one legend common in sets of legends that were as various
as the languages (of which there are five or six). The Dobuan
version is peculiar in owning Sinebomatu, the Woman of
the North-east Wind.

At the portals of Bwebweso Sinebomatu by day, and
Kekewage by night guard a huge shrub of the fragrant *kemwata*
or *ane* (Kekewage is the husband). They scrutinize new
arriving spirits, get their betel nut from them and pass them

on if they fulfil the requirements of not being diseased or too " fresh ". As each new arrival is passed, from a palm overhead falls a coco-nut. A different variety of nut falls according to the totem of the entrant to the spirit world ; there is a well-known list of such varieties and their totem allocation for the purpose.

Sinebomatu, Woman of the North-east Wind and Kekewage, her husband and fellow janitor of the portals, adopt children who have died before their parents pending a parent's death—" who would care for them in Bwebweso ? "

With the exceptions noted the Dobuans believe that the spirits stay quietly in their places for ever, not troubling mortal men. The life of the spirits is conceived as thin and shadowy —in no sense does it offer any single advantage over this earthly life. It is as in Euripides :

> " If any earthly place there be
> Dearer to life than mortality
> The land of the dark hath hold thereof
> And mist is under and mist is above
> And we float on legends for ever." [1]

That is as true to a Dobuan savage as it was to Euripides. It is expressed in the dance song of the dance re-appearing, the first dance after mourning is over :

> " I go hillwards to Bwebweso
> By Dokwabu's white pandanus flower
> I go hillwards to Bwebweso.
> The white, white pandanus flower,
> From the palm I have climbed
> I look out upon the path behind me,
> I mourn for Dobu.

So the feelings of the spirit of the dead are bodied forth in the dance when the village kin of the dead dance bearing the skull of the dead at the feast *dugumalala*. So the kin in sympathy escort the spirit of the dead to its home in Bwebweso. The word *bwebweso* itself means extinguished. A fire or a lantern goes out, *i kweu* or *i bweso*. In dance or in ritual, thought of the spirit enters in, but without fear, without un-kindness as in the Fergusson Island neighbours of Dobu. Occasional isolated teachings are handed down, such as one that a woman with old sunken breasts in Bwebweso is really a maiden, while a firm, young breasted woman is an old, decayed woman. One should be careful to woo the former rather than the latter—in Bwebweso. The life of the spirit after

---

[1] In Professor Gilbert Murray's rendering.

death is so pictured as a Rip Van Winkle-like adventure.

Mt. Bwebweso is an extinct volcano, but whether the Dobuans call it extinguished with special reference to it as a land form, or as a home of the dead who died by diseases we do not know. The home of the dead who were killed in action, described in the legend Tokebanibani told above (pp. 182-86), had as its guardians Iaboaine and his consort Sinekili, Woman Cleaner. Iaboaine is the same as the Yabwayna mentioned as the god of wars by Malinowski in his introduction (p. xvi). He is also the same as the Yabowaine invoked in a charm of the agricultural ritual mentioned on p. 111. The disease with the symptom of a swollen stomach mentioned on p. 179 is probably shistosomiasis, marked in more discriminating terms by spleenomegaly, a greatly enlarged liver and a parasitic protozoan infection in the liver cells and in the portal veinous system. The Dobuans thought that it was caused by one of the *iaboaineao,* the ghosts of those killed in action, and in particular by a ghost of a former enemy who introduced a double of his blood into food accepted in his village from his survivors. Malinowski terms Iaboaine an alleged high god, but it has not been claimed that he was believed to be a supreme god. As may be noticed from the legend of the home of Iaboaine, Woman Cleaner, and the *iaboaineao,* they were believed to go up into the clouds and down to earth. Their home was not believed to be in any landmark.

CHAPTER V

ECONOMICS

I

MARITAL EXCHANGES

Marriage in Dobu is inaugurated and maintained by a number of gift exchanges. Betel nut is first sent by the prospective groom or by his parents to the girl's parents. If this gift is accepted it is an indication of acceptance of the proposed marriage. If it is rejected the marriage is off.

The groom and his kin hunt oppossum (*Cuscus*) towards harvest time. Oppossum and yams are given as gifts to the bride's relatives. These return the gift with yams only.

The groom and his kin also go forth on the *kula*. Regardless of future impediment to their *kula*, they must accumulate armshells, many of them, and a spondylus shell necklace or two to give as a present to the bride's relatives as the *kwesi*, or bride price. The bride's relatives need not return the equivalent of these gifts in any haste. In fact the return is often years delayed, the overseas partners of the groom and his kin having their return equally delayed. A prospective groom does not inform his *kula* partner of his need of *kula* valuables for internal exchanges, or he would be refused them.

While the marriage is in being a series of repeated gift exchanges take place between the two villages party to the union.

A killed pig or a portion of it may go from the mother's brother of one spouse to the mother's brother of the other. It is carried by a woman of the village that gives it and set down in the other village. There the recipient cuts it up and distributes it to the entire village. This gift is variously termed *sebuwana*, *katuesiki*, and *niueta*. If it is given by the husband's mother's brother the entire village of the wife eat of it with the exception of the wife herself. The owners of the village and Those-resulting-from-marriage all partake of it without distinction of clan ; only if the man in whose name and by whose village kinsman it is given is resident at the time in his wife's village, he must abstain with his wife, as must also any other village kinsman of his married into the same village. The same holds true reversed when later the gift is repaid ; i.e. the entire village of the husband eat together with all Those-resulting-from-marriage not of the wife's village, with the exception of the husband himself among the former class, and his wife, if she is resident in her husband's village, among the latter class. The children from the marriage in whose name the gift is exchanged need not abstain as must their parents.

A banana and fish gift is termed *ekekwaro*. The village of the spouse that are giving the gift go to sea and net fish. They cut the finest bananas, called *Ponake*, and cook fish and bananas together into a dish called *ekwasi*. The village receiving the gift net a smaller quantity of fish, cut an inferior banana called *Bworabwora* and cook a smaller *ekwasi*. The *ekwasi* are then exchanged. It is usually an all day affair and it usually takes place by the shore, both villages resorting thither. As in the case of pig gift, husband and wife must abstain from eating of the gifts exchanged in their name. In cooking and eating the villages keep well apart. When the cooked food is exchanged each village carries its own food to its own place. Later on the sides will be reversed in a return match, the other village cooking the larger *ekwasi*.

Gifts of sago and taro are termed *bwanakupwa*. A large supply of food is taken by the donors to the village of the recipients. The recipients keep to one end of the village and cook a smaller quantity of food there. The donors, keeping to the other end of the village, cook their large supply. The food is interchanged and the donors return to eat the gift given them in their own village, carrying it there. The white observer is inclined to marvel how the recipients manage to eat the quantity given them—it is not left to go bad. As before, husband and wife must abstain from touching the food exchange made in the name of their marriage. Later, the sides are reversed in a return match.

Ekekwaro and *bwanakupwa* differ from pig gift in that more ceremony is involved. They occupy the whole day. The men cook, not the women, as in everyday cooking. The alignment is strictly between the owners of the two villages concerned. Those-resulting-from-marriage go elsewhere about their own business. When they return to their spouses in the evening, however, they usually find plenty of food left unconsumed. This they eat.

The custom by which man and wife are debarred from contributing to or eating of ceremonial gifts made to cement their marriage, makes for village communal authority. No one bears his or her own obligations. Marriage ceases to be a private matter.

At any one of the ceremonial exchanges husbands and wives are apart. Some are Those-resulting-from-marriage and have no business at the exchange. Some, including the pair in whose name the exchange is being made, belong to the two villages concerned. Such pairs split up and ignore each other all day. The husband is with his sister, brother, sister's children, and the other *susu* of his village ; the wife is with her brother, sister, sister's children, and the other *susu* of her village. These two parties engaged in exchange sit or stand at extreme ends of the village, preparing and cooking, a wide space in between them. If they look at the other party at all by custom they glare with hostility. For the most part they appear with a studied unconcern not to notice that any other party than their own is in the same village.

They only notice each other when the food, finally cooked, is exchanged. Then, this done, they immediately separate, the visitors carrying their food home. There they may eat.

The importance of the economic system is paramount, the gifts are of great valuables, and the enlisting of the economic system to split the marriage bond, cleaving it asunder by a cross-cutting village *susu* wedge, is one expression of a fact that comes up again whenever a village elder is disciplining a younger ward, reminding him or her of the food obligations fulfilled by the kindred to keep the marriage in being and threatening to drop the obligations in the event of further offence being given, so compelling the kin of the spouse into taking measures for divorce or sorcery for non-fulfilment of food obligations. It is an effective system of control.

Only in rare and extreme cases is a person reminded by his or her kin as to the identity of those who fulfill the economic arrangements of the marriage. From elder to younger it is done when a head-man brings an offender to book. From equal to equal it is an insult that must be swallowed in silence and with respect ; it is never made gratuitously, and it is never received without great mortification.

In this manner the component village *susu* bear one another's marriage obligations, and if they think a marriage for which they pay does not repay them fairly, they set about sorcery or witchcraft as we have already seen, or else wait for a chance of a marital quarrel over suspected adultery to give them opportunity to send the member of the offending village packing out of their village. Resource to the black art is the more direct course.

To revert from discussion of the functioning of the economic forms to the forms themselves, there are at yam harvest small and large exchanges of uncooked yams. A child-in-law usually takes a few baskets of yams to the mother-in-law, *silasila lawa*.

The greater exchange, *pwatukwara*, is between entire villages connected by intermarriage of their members, on behalf of each and every individual member. The true parents-in-law of any single marriage give about half of the gift and receive about half if it in due order of gift and counter-gift. The other half is contributed and received over a village range (owners of the village only). The gift is made by the one side one year and repaid by the other the next. The givers are those who are losing the company of the couple concerned for the ensuing year, the recipients those in the village that receives them that year.

The givers take the yams to the village of the recipients and set it up there on display in large wooden hoppers. The mother-in-law of the incoming resultant-from-marriage takes down the yams after this display, and distributes the half which she does not retain to the other owners of the village. As she hands each owner a basket of gift yams the recipient thanks her politely with the traditional and obligatory formula, " if you kill me by witchcraft, how shall I repay you this gift."

There are also irregular exchanges between father-in-law and son-in-law. One may catch a big fish and give it to the other. Later the former recipient will cook a banana and taro mash with his own hands and redeem the debt. The only indication of this being ceremonial is the sight of a man or two sitting beneath another's house while their host prepares especially fine food and cooks it. A male cook is always an indication of ceremony in Dobu, even although in the inter-island *kula* exchanges the cooks are never male.

After the death of his wife a man is expected to keep up exchanges with her relatives. As the widower has often been hasty to remarry, he has often a double exchange to maintain. This may press hard on his resources. Even although the exchange balances in the long run there may be a serious deficit at any moment, and the exchanges demanded by a dead wife's relatives are frequently productive of such bitterness and coolnesses as the diviner of the black art and of socially difficult situations may uncover.

Success in *wabuwabu* is a matter for pride with many Dobuans. In connection with marriage the term means to initiate a marriage with deliberate intention not to continue it, but to break it off at a point when the marriage exchanges set heavily in one's favour ; then to risk the black art of the angry unrepaid creditors. A life-long avoidance with mutual fear is then set up between the near kin of the parties to the marriage so dissolved in *wabuwabu*. Since it is believed that the black art is dangerous only from possible associates, and since persons of one locality do not trespass in another locality, marriage without the locality is rare. It is known that there is no good deterrent to the ever possible *wabuwabu*, possible enough despite deterrent, within the locality.

On the other hand, relieving the picture of a too grim economic situation marriage exchanges sometimes continue long after the deaths of the married pair. A man's sister's son will continue to exchange with his mother's brother's wife's son, and the sisters' sons of these men with each other again. A man in taking his mother's brother's name, relationship place and inheritance, will continue the marriage exchanges of his mother's brother towards the heirs of the latter's deceased wife. The exchanges become individual, between the two men directly concerned only. Their existence is an interesting comment on the *kula* exchange of armshells and necklaces. Both exchanges are made for the love of exchange primarily.

II

DEATH AND MOURNING EXCHANGES

Death and mourning initiate a long cycle of economic exchanges and feasts. The corpse of an adult is buried by the sister's children, a child's corpse by the mother's brothers.

I saw a child buried in my village, in Tewara, half a chain to the side of my hut. One of the mother's village sisters buried it with the assistance of the mother's brother. The women of the village wailed throughout the proceedings. The father sat far apart not looking on the scene. The corpse was laid below ground on its back in the extended position on a mat. Betel

nut was put into its hand and the hand curled about it. After
the burial, about half a day after death, the sextons [1] were given
cooked yams by the mother of the dead, and an armshell each.
The mother alone went into regular mourning, putting on the
neck rope, *mwagura*, blackening her body, and abstaining from
good food.   The payment of yams to the sextons is called
bwobwore, and of armshells, *kunututu*.

In the event of the death of a married person the widow
or widower goes into mourning in the village of the dead, not
in own village. The survivor is debarred from looking upon the
interment.   The survivor's family pay the *kunututu* to the
grave-diggers, who are more likely to be the sister's sons than
the mother's brothers of the dead. The village of the survivor
pay the *bwobwore* gift to the sister's sons of the dead.

It was in a case of inability to make the *kunututu* payment
for burial, that an event discussed in the social organization
occurred.   The dead husband came from another island.
His widow's kin could not pay an armshell to his kin ; so
instead of the armshell the widow parted with her female child
who went with her dead father's sister to her far away place,
there to stay until she bore a child to replace her father ; that
done she had choice of leaving her child and rejoining her
mother, or staying with her child and not staying in her mother's
place again. I saw the child who was given instead of *kunututu*,
now a full-grown woman, in Sanaroa. Her mother and mother's
mother's brother I knew well in my own village in Tewara.
She stood apart from the groups around not speaking to anyone, but overhearing a man tell me who and what she was—a
lonely figure in a strange place and in a strange situation for this
culture of strong matrilineal descent ; where ordinarily no one
ever enters the village of dead father, but stays ceremonially
on its fringe and lets fall the head—hence it is called the village
of bowing the head, *asa kopuana*. She looked as a Russian
political convict in exile in Siberia might look.

The *bwobwore* gift is not confined to the sexton's payment
just after they have buried the dead and washed themselves
in the sea. Many times through the year after death if the
dead was a man his children cook a banana and taro mash with
a fish or two thrust into it and take it to the sister's children
of the dead. These gifts, without repayment, are called
bwobwore also. They are regarded as the children's payment

---

[1] I use the term sexton to indicate grave-diggers who perform their duties
ceremonially, so stripped of much of its English meaning.

for their father " did he not hold us in his arm ? " the strangers-resulting-from-marriage paying the kin for a member of that kin group having done well by them. The point of the marriage grouping's subservience to the *susu* group is reinforced.

The house of the dead is left standing for the year of death. The widow digs the yams of the dead's garden. His sister's children alone may enter the house of the dead—there they store the yams so harvested. Later, the sister's children inherit these yams when after harvest the house of the dead is torn down and burned.

At the beginning of mourning the kin of the surviving spouse not only pay the sextons with a small *bwobwore* of cooked yams ; they also bring a large gift of uncooked yams, display them in the village of the dead, and the village kin of the dead then distribute them amongst themselves, the true sister's children of the dead securing the greatest share.

To end mourning the kin of the surviving spouse again bring another large gift of uncooked yams. If their kinsman is a widower, his neck cord of mourning is cut, his body charcoal is washed off, his ornaments are replaced with fragrant herbs in them by the kin of his dead spouse who then lead him back to his own village, never to return to theirs. If their kinsman is a widow, her neck cord of mourning is cut, and she is treated as the widower, but in addition the four or five inches longer grass skirt than others wear, which she has had to wear throughout her year of mourning is ceremonially clipped little by little until it is the usual knee length only.

At these big *bwobwore* gifts by the kin of the survivor to the kin of the dead we find three distinct groups sitting apart from one another at the ceremony (if the dead is a man).

(1) The village *susu* of the surviving spouse.

(2) The village *susu* of the dead (and if the dead is a man, a third group).

(3) The children of the dead, and the children of the village brothers of the dead.

If the dead is a woman, group (3) is a part of group (2) necessarily, and is not distinguished from group (2) in behaviour as it is if the dead is a man.

Group (1) give the big gift of uncooked garden yams to group (2) (*bwobwore*).

Group (3) give a much smaller but adequate for one meal, gift of cooked yams to group (1) (*siudana*).

Group (2) repay the gift of group (1) ultimately on the

death of the surviving spouse. Group (3) are not allowed
to eat of the yams given by group (1) to group (2)—this is the
prohibition of eating of the food of their dead fathers' places.
They do not get repaid for their gifts, *siudana*. They are
paying for their father.[1] They are all Boundary men to
group (2) and they bear group (2)'s obligation of giving a little
cooked food to group (1) gratuitously (when group (1) gives
away the major gift to group (2) of uncooked food).

After the first *bwobwore* that initiates mourning and before
the last, which closes it, there are two or three *bwobwore* feasts
between the village of the dead and the village of the survivor
(who is still in mourning in the village of the dead). The
first and last *bwobwore* are all display of a toll paid. But
there are one or two real feasts in the interval between.
I saw one called *miaewaewara*. Such feasts involve sago contributions and fishing by both villages, and also by the children
of the dead (father). The fish and sago are cooked together
by the men, one lot on one fire for the owners of the village
of the dead, one lot on another fire for the owners of the village
of the survivor, as well as for children of the dead of other
villages, i.e. children of brothers, village brothers of the
deceased. Own children of the dead do not eat, nor do children
of the dead's blood brothers.

The food is obtained by communal effort by everyone
present. Ask a native who will eat of it and he will reply
" the owners of the village of the dead only ; all others are
under *tabu* not to eat ". What this means in practice is
that many others eat of food cooked on a different hot stone
oven from that used for the food of the kin of the dead. After
the feast the sisters' sons of the dead helped by contributions
from their true sisters' husbands, distributed bananas to the
classificatory children of the dead and to the village of the
spouse of the survivor, to nearly all who had come to the feast.

The classificatory section of the children of the dead,
group (3), are thus repaid for their previous services in providing cooked food at uncooked yam exchange *bwobwore*.
But the children of the dead (own true children), children
of the village and *susu* of the widower, as distinct from the
children of the widower's classificatory village " brothers ",
continue more private duties in occasionally taking cooked
taro or banana mash to their father's sister's children, debts
of true blood Boundary Man to true blood cross-cousin Owner.

---

[1] But note, several paragraphs below, a qualification.

And though I saw many such gifts given I never saw a single repayment. They are meals of the best food for the blood heirs of the dead given them without repayment by the disinherited (disinherited from our patrilineal viewpoint).

There are also a series of real feasts between the village of the dead and all villages with which it has intermarried. The affinal relatives of the members of the village of the dead are to be found in nearly all the villages of the locality. All these villages now become involved in feasts. The members of such other villages connected with the village of the dead by intermarriage are called *murimuri*. After the death and interment, the *murimuri* come rushing into the village of the dead and with great show of force and violence cut down trees. I have not seen this done, as I have seen everything else I have described up to the present, both in marital exchanges and in death and mourning exchanges. But, shortly after it happened I was shown the fresh stumps of one betel nut palm, two large bread-fruit trees and one *mwagoru* [1] " apple " tree, and told by the *murimuri* themselves that they had done it as is customary. In this particular case the *murimuri* abstained from pig-hunting for two or three months, acting on the decision of the mother of the dead. She and her dead son were the repositories of pig-hunting magic in the locality, and pig-hunting was denied to thirteen villages for a decent time after the death in recognition of the fact. Then the mother of the dead released the restraint, and all the *murimuri* went out together on a pig drive. They came back in triumph with a huge boar which they threw down in front of the house of the dead. As they came into the village of the dead with their bag, shouting, I with them, out rushed the aged lady, the mother of the dead, brushing past me into the bush and wailing " I'm frightened, I'm frightened ". The hunters hurled down the pig unceremoniously, rushed the betel palms of the village, swarmed up them, stripped them bare of nuts, and were away out of the village almost before one realized what was happening. One grabbed a fish net, made to take it, but dropped it as he went. Some of the trees of the village had been cut down some months before with just such show of hostility. The trees left (the majority) had been under an interdict since the death. They are called *yadiyadi*. Their fruit may not be touched by the owners of the village or by anyone else. Now that the *murimuri* have given a large wild

[1] *Eugenia malaccensis*, also termed *Jambos malaccensis*.

pig to the owners of the village of the dead they break the *yadiyadi tabu* and strip the trees with a show of fierce hostility. The spears they carry, coming straight from the hunt, add to the effect. This tree-cutting, pig-giving, tree-plundering, is always done irrespective of whether the dead was concerned with pig-hunting magic or not.

This is the breaking of the *tabu* on the trees of the village after a death there, that is mentioned by Dr. Malinowski in the *Argonauts of the Western Pacific*. The *yadiyadi tabu* Dr. Malinowski terms *gwara* (which is a different *tabu* altogether and one not connected with death). Dr. Malinowski pictures the Trobrianders, coming on the *kula*, breaking the *tabu*. As far as I know that is only Trobriand native statement. Traditionally the *murimuri* went out on a hunt not for pig, but for man. On more than one occasion the men of Dobu Island being *murimuri* and needing a freshly-killed man to give to the village of the dead before they were free to break the *tabu* on the trees there, went out to sea at the sight of the Trobriand canoes coming down to make *kula* with the Dobuan district of Bwaioa half a mile or so away. Then on occasion, a Trobriand native was present at the breaking of a Dobu Island *yadiyadi tabu*—but only in the same capacity as the hunted pig of these peaceful days. Bwaioa, being *kula* partners with the Trobrianders, did not use them so, but found a victim elsewhere. What is certainly true is that *kula* visitors were never welcome in the interval between death and the breaking of the *tabu*, and that its breaking is one of the functions of the affinal relatives of the clan of the dead.

The village of the dead, at sight of the large boar brought in by the *murimuri* went half mad with excitement. Everyone crowded on to view it and comment on its great size, on the old scars of former spear wounds that it bore. Men threw women into the air. In all cases these women were their father's sisters whom men are allowed to treat so on great occasions. The pig was eaten. Some of it was given by the village of the dead to the *murimuri*. In all cases of such gifts, the donor took pig fat, boiled down to grease, poured it over a venerable and old man of the village to whom the gift was given, and smeared and plastered him with it. The venerable old man immediately flew into a great rage, danced in spear-fighting attitudes, cursed the givers of the gift, mentioned their sex organs in highly coloured and unflattering terms, damned their gift as probably having poison concealed in it, and invited them to explain why they had picked on him. One of the donors of the gift went into counter spear-fighting attitudes but did not say anything very insulting, as the matter had already gone to the very borders of ceremonial hostility—it might easily become too dangerous. The old man in such cases washed himself and came back and ate heartily, although in public he had said he was not going to touch the stuff (the donors having gone home shortly after hearing the old man out).

The village of the dead, owners and resident spouses, proceed to cut bananas, make a mash of them with taro, fish, and cook fish to put in the mash. They then take the cooked food to one village of the *murimuri* ; they have food enough for all in the village. The recipients of the food return the donors raw bananas and a few yams, not nearly as great a value as that received. So day by day the village of the dead give feasts of cooked food to all the villages of their *murimuri*, to one village a day. Some days they fish or go to trade for food, as the process is a severe strain upon them. Whenever they give a gift of such food they smear a recipient with sticky food mash. Gradually these one village feasts are finished ; then preparations go hot foot for *sagali*, the great feast. The *murimuri* send in domestic pigs for slaughter. The village of the dead slaughter its own pigs. The village of the dead fasts for a week before to save even more yams. Yams come in from *murimuri* and from the village's own resources. Sago is worked by the village of the dead. Fish are caught, bananas cut. Then all members of other localities who are accustomed to ˙invite members of this particular locality to their *sagalis*, and have treated them generously, are invited.

The food is cooked and shared all round, the master of ceremonies crying " X——, your share this ! He who is dead was a great gardener. He came from his work at dusk. You creep home feebly at noon "

" Y——, your share this ! He who is dead had many domestic pigs. Your sows are barren."

" Z——, your share this ! He who is dead was a master of fish nets. This is how *you* catch fish."

Long after *sagali* the long platform built round the central graveyard stands, the platform that held the food.

In this happy manner the locality pulls together its forces whenever death has stricken one of its important members ; nor is importance centred in a few persons. There are, of course, some wastrels who are not given such honours, but they are a small minority.

By custom the village of the dead at *sagali* give away every bit of food collected, leaving none for themselves. By equally polite custom the recipients leave a little behind to ensure that the village of the dead will have something left to eat.

The gifts of banana and taro mash with fish that precede *sagali* are carried by the men and women of the village of the dead to the village of the *murimuri* to which it is to be given. He who follows such a procession will see a good section of Dobuan custom. The men go in front bearing pots of food on their shoulders, with stripped coco-nut leaf or sago leaf ribs with a hibiscus flower or a piece of white coco-nut on top of each rib stuck jauntily into the food, the women follow behind with pots of food similarly decorated on their heads. Thirty yards from the village of destination a man hands his load over to another and drops out—goes back home. His deceased wife was of the village of destination. On the village boundary three or four stay with their heads down, putting their loads on the ground. Their fathers were of this village and are now dead. Others retrieve their loads and take them on. The rest go in, put down their loads on the platform of a larger house, then retreat a little and seat themselves. The owners of the village sit unconcernedly under their houses apparently brooding over astronomy or some such remote subject. Only one man of the donors joins a group. His wife is of this village and he talks to his parents-in-law, sister-in-law or brother-in-law. Suddenly one of the young men of the donors' party pours food grease over an old man of the village. Immediately there is commotion between the two. The young man gets out of the way. Before it has died down the owners of the village have flung down counter gifts of newly plucked green bananas, a few yams. Everyone remains sitting down. The donors of the cooked food now observe their own remote broodings. Finally they pick up the bananas and yams and file away—those who have remained all this time on the outskirts of the village, leading.

III

THE ESSENTIALS OF THE OVERSEAS EXCHANGES

The *kula* is a system of exchanges between a circle of islands, of which Dobu is one, maintained by about two annual overseas expeditions by each island. It is international, taking within its main circuit five different linguistic areas. The exchanges are not in continuous operation as the routine of the gardening would be interfered with too much. In Dobu, for instance, it is a mortal insult for one man to say to another " you are always on the sea, and without new garden food ". Gardening is the supreme occupation. In great part, as we have seen, the attention demanded by the garden is due to certain magical beliefs. A man must stand by his garden to protect it by magic when there is obviously no need for him to do anything else with it. If a man is away on the sea once the new yams are well formed and growing in his garden, his neighbours are believed to be able to attract his crop away by magic into their own gardens. If a neighbour says " you are always on the sea and without new garden food ", it is tantamount to saying " you've been away leaving your garden unprotected, and I've taken advantage of you by my magic ".

The Dobuans make their overseas expeditions while the gardens are yet newly planted before the yam vines are more than a few inches long. The expeditions cease shortly after the time for staking the vines. The time for the voyages falls in March and April normally. These are the months just before the north-west monsoon gathers its full force ; it is still variable and usually not continuous. Sailing is possible both to the north and to the south, but it is not yet over-dangerous as in the stormier period that follows. Overseas sailing is avoided during the more dangerous months of the later north-west monsoon, during the cool season (cold by native standards) of the south-east monsoon and during the calms that occur in between the monsoons in late November, December, and January. Fear of the sea, and fear of magical garden pillage make for fair weather sailing.

The *kula* has already been described by Seligman and Malinowski. Dr. Seligman discusses the institution briefly with the assistance of reports from missionaries and Government officers, and from its trading aspect only. Dr. Malinowski has described the entire range of the institution from his own first-hand observation most meticulously and accurately in his very fine study, *Argonauts of the Western Pacific*.

In its trading aspects the *kula* ring may be divided into a northern section and a southern section. The northern section covers the Trobriands, the Marshall Bennets, Murua

(Woodlark Island) and Panamoti. In this area the greatly
valued ornaments, armshells made from Trocus shell, are
found and made. Here again the finest and most seaworthy
canoes in these eastern waters are made—in the Marshall
Bennets. Here further, the greenstone that circulates all
over the eastern archipelago and for hundreds of miles west
down the coast of Papua is quarried—in Murua. In this
northern section no pottery is made.

The southern section of the main *kula* ring covers three
nationals, the Amphletts, Dobu, and Tubetube. This section
is the section of potters, for all three, as distinct from
the northern internationals, make pottery. Tubetube, in
the south, is the port which receives the finest spondylus
shell, which is made up into necklaces (together with the
armshells above mentioned, the most valued possessions
of the natives of all groups). This spondylus shell is known
to be manufactured in Rossel Island to the extreme east, and
in Port Morseby far to the west. Tubetube, the southernmost pottery district of the *kula* ring, receives this shell both
from west and east. If we diagram this situation we have
the following (see p. 203).

The northern section exchanges its surplus of armshells for
spondylus shell necklaces from Tubetube. Dobu is the nearest
receiving station to Tubetube, and although Tubetube canoes
go to Murua they always go by way of Duau, a Dobuan
district. Tubetube canoes never go to the Trobriands or
Trobriand canoes to Tubetube. Hence Dobu receives armshells from the Trobriands, and exchanges these armshells
for the spondylus shell necklaces that the Tubetube men
bring north. The Tubetube men do not carry their spondylus
shell necklaces to Murua ; the explanation of this is, I believe,
that since they must call in Dobu on their trade route to Murua,
Dobu has become a shunting station that diverts the entire
stream of spondylus shell necklaces to the Trobriands in
exchange for Trobriand armshells. Dobuan canoes go to
the Amphletts, to the Trobriands, and to Tubetube. The
three pottery-making internationals, Amphletts, Dobu, and
Tubetube, being comparatively close together, carry the
exchange route of the northern ornament for the southern
ornament.

Murua, cut off from direct obtaining of spondylus shell
for its armshells, despite its exchange voyage with Tubetube,
sends its armshells to the Trobriands, thence to Dobu. The

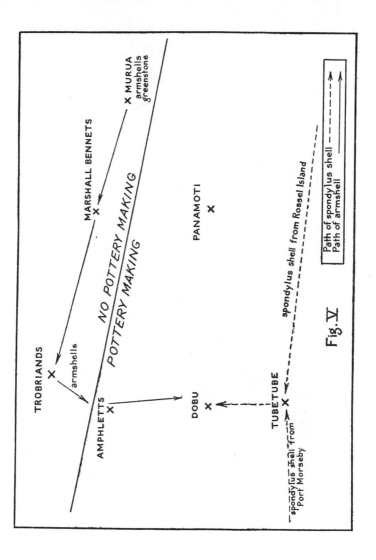

Fig. V

return value in spondylus shells comes from Dobu to the Trobriands, thence to Murua.

Thus the exchange of newly manufactured ornaments takes place as follows:

(1) Concentration of the northern armshell ornament in the Trobriands.

(2) Concentration of the southern spondylus shell ornament in Dobu.

(3) Exchange between Dobu and the Trobriands.

(4) The Trobriands recoup those other districts of the northern area, who contributed to the concentration in the Trobriands, with their share of the southern ornament obtained in exchange.

(5) Dobu recoups Tubetube for the southern ornament concentrated in Dobu with most of the northern ornaments received in exchange.

I have described this process as if I had observed it. Actually I have not, for I saw no newly manufactured spondylus shells coming up from the south, and I do not know how damaged this supply may be nowadays by white influence. And although I saw new armshells coming south through the Amphletts to Dobu, I did not see them coming from Murua to the Trobriands.

The course of newly manufactured ornaments, however, is determined by the set course of old ornaments of long standing. These do not stop still. Armshells always go from Murua to the Trobriands and thence via Dobu to Tubetube. Spondylus shell necklaces always go from Tubetube via Dobu to the Trobriands and thence to Murua.

This course is reasonable for newly manufactured ornaments also. Dobu, as the first port of call for Tubetube canoes, necessarily wants the southern ornament and necessarily gets it—for Tubetube uses Dobu as a port to get to Murua, and could have its trade route cut by provoking Dobuan opposition, by refusing to exchange. The peacemaking ceremony in this area consists essentially in one party exchanging its particular ornament for the ornament of the other party. Refusal to make such exchange between Dobu and Tubetube would mean war and the isolation of Tubetube from the northern archipelago.

The *kula* is essentially the continued exchange of all such ornaments, old and new. Since spondylus shell goes from Tubetube via Dobu via Trobriands to Murua and armshells go from Murua via Trobriands via Dobu to Tubetube, new and old alike, there would be a great concentration of spondylus shell in Murua and of armshells in Tubetube were nothing done about it. Actually this is prevented by the Tubetube men taking armshells to Murua annually, coals to Newcastle from the point of view of the areas of production of the ornaments, and the Murua men taking spondylus shell necklaces to Tubetube annually, coals to Newcastle again.

The non-economic character of the *kula* institution appears in bold relief in considering how Tubetube men take a valuable to its centre of production, and Murua men do so likewise annually with long sea voyages and great expenditure of time and energy.

Were the *kula* an economic exchange merely, the northern non-pottery section would export its surplus only of newly manufactured armshells annually, while the southern pottery section would export an equivalent surplus of newly manufactured spondylus shell necklaces only, in repayment of the armshells received. In this manner both north and south could possess an equal division of the ornamental products of north and south respectively.

Actually this equal division exists ; it is effected by exchanges. But actually also, the love of exchange has so dominated native life that the northern non-pottery division proceeds annually to export *all* its armshells, new, middle-aged, and old, and the southern pottery division exports annually *all* its spondylus shell necklaces, new, middle-aged, and old, in return. Then Tubetube, the southernmost pottery district secures its spondylus shell necklaces, previously exported by the western route through Dobu, Amphletts and Trobriands, back by the eastern route from Murua. Murua of the non-pottery district secures the northern armshells, previously exported by the western route, back by the eastern route from Tubetube. On the west *all* the northern ornaments go south, *all* the southern ornaments go north. On the east the northern non-pottery district, Murua, recovers all the northern ornaments, while Tubetube recovers all the southern ornaments. Such recovery may take several years of annual expeditions before every ornament has gone full circle. So all the important and valuable ornaments of the five main internationals of the *kula* ring go round the mulberry bush.

In practice the exchange involves the giving of credit and the need for honesty in meeting a debt. On the western side the armshells go from the Trobriands south to Dobu annually, some months before the spondylus shell necklaces go from Dobu north to the Trobriands in repayment, although spondylus shell necklaces often go north from Dobu to the Amphletts a few months before armshells come south from the Amphletts to Dobu in repayment. It must be understood that the entire circuit does not revolve in a regular procession from one district to the next, then to the next, and so on, every year. Each year's overseas expeditions cease with an approximately equal number of armshells and spondylus shell necklaces everywhere. By the next year's recurrence of the time for sailing, the north will have an extra balance of armshells, the south of spondylus shell by reason of the year's work in fishing for shell. But this extra balance from one year's fishing is little compared with the great stock in circulation, a stock representing the fishing of generations of shell fishers.

It should be realized that the love of exchange is one of the great characters of Melanesian culture. In most Melanesian areas separate geographical districts practise different art-crafts, and exchange their diverse products amongst themselves. This exchange is not always confined to the demands of utility. Thus some villages of the Admiralty Islands which do not make pottery exchange their own produce for stores of pots which far exceed the number they can use. The tribes that live in the sea lagoons a quarter to half a mile out from the shore in houses built on piles, cook their food in fresh water from the land. The hill-top tribes, who come down from the hills to trade with the sea lagoon dwellers at a morning market on the uninhabited swampy coast, cook their food in sea water. At the market the sea dwellers barter their fishing catch for the garden products of the hill dwellers. The fishers, who have no gardens, exchange their produce with the gardeners, who do no fishing. Intoxicated with great love of exchange, they exchange even the water of their respective dwelling places and carry it home for the boiling of their food.

This exchange of waters used to boil food helps to maintain the customary market meeting every morning. Despite enmities, and commercial grudges, food must always be cooked, and cooked in the correct kind of water.

In similar manner the *kula* exchange of ornamental valuables, useless enough in itself, helps to maintain annual exchanges of other objects that serve more utilitarian ends. I do not intend any view that such development of useless exchange is indispensable to the maintainence of the useful exchange. The useful exchange might maintain itself alone. Only in such a place as the *kula* ring, where suspicion of the black art of strange people runs rife, where enmity is likely to flare up easily, the over-development of exchange is a very good counter against the over-development of international enmity.

This over-development of exchange flows from a system of exchange founded on utility. The northern non-pottery section of the *kula* ring imports pots from the southern section. Pots of the Amphletts are used for boiling food in the Trobriands, in the Marshall Bennets, in Murua, as sepulchral pottery in Murua, and also for boiling food in the northern Dobuan districts of Tewara, Sanaroa, and Bwaioa. The southern Dobuan districts of Dobu Island and Duau use mainly the pottery made in Duau. The Dobuan district of Duau does not export pottery to the northern non-pottery making internationals, however. Tubetube supplies Murua. Greenstone is quarried in Murua, and polished in a few special villages of the Trobriands with sand specially imported for the purpose from Fergusson Island, fifty or sixty miles away to the south. The largest and finest adze blades are not used. They, like the armshells and spondylus shell necklaces, go round and round the *kula* ring in perpetual exchange ; some, however, are used in barter with districts outside the *kula* ring, as are some of the armshells also. The smaller adze blades are used. Murua which quarries the stone, does no woodwork, other than canoe-making. The adzes find use in woodwork in the Trobriands. They also find use in sago pith cutting in Dobu (they are still used so in Dobu, and cannot be purchased readily for this reason). Dobu exports sago to the Trobriands and also to the Amphletts—these places having no sago. Like Muruan greenstone adzes, Trobriand woodwork, wooden bowls, drums, and lime spatulas particularly, circulate all over the ring. Amphlett pots and Tubetube pots circulate over great portions of the ring. Dobuan sago over a smaller portion. Dobuan face paint and paint for the teeth also circulate far. In this manner different areas have special products, and by exchange, all areas are supplied with a selection of the products of each area.

Tubetube, according to Dr. Seligman, lives by making pottery and nose ornaments, and by importing the spondylus shell into the *kula* ring from without. All its material culture otherwise is imported, even its canoes, which it obtains from the north-east section of the *kula* ring.

Similarly the Amphletts live by their pottery. They have to import the clay from Fergusson Island. This done, their pots supply them with Trobriand-made drums, wooden bowls, lime gourds and lime spatulas, bananas, yams, and coco-nuts from the Trobriands, greenstone adzes from Murua, sago, coco-nuts, and face and teeth paint from Dobu, nose ornaments from Tubetube. Their islands are wretchedly barren and deficient in food ; the islanders are dependent on outside food supplies.

Necessary utilitarian exchange thus obtains in the *kula* ring. It is all done without direct barter. An expedition going out to seek ornamental valuables, e.g. a Dobuan canoe going to the Trobriands to seek armshells, takes large quantities of sago—representing solid unremitting work by all the families of the men who are the crew of the canoe. This sago they offer as a present to their Trobriand hosts, from whom they desire armshells. The armshells are given them some days later and also some of the special Trobriand products. There is often fair equivalence between the present given by guest to host, and that returned from host to guest some days later. But no haggling or questioning of equivalence is permitted. The armshell is, of course, given on credit and must be repaid some months later by a spondylus shell necklace.

This pleasant method of utilitarian exchange flows from a mental concentration on the non-utilitarian exchanges of ornaments which involve a far longer credit than the few days' credit which elapse between present and counter present of utilities.

I have discussed the Dobuan use of the black art, the Dobuan fear of it, the fear of strangers and strange places, the fear of the sea, before I came to discuss the *kula*, because it will be apparent that the pleasant methods of overseas exchange of utilities contrast strongly with what might be expected of a people whose fear is great enough to lead one to think that silent trade, the most elementary form of barter, might well be their only method. It is likely enough that overseas exchange for the sake of gain merely would not be

OLD SIBOR, FATHER OF HIS VILLAGE AND RESIDENT IN IT

COMING FROM THE GARDEN

effective enough to withstand the sorcery-filled atmosphere of mutual suspicion between the internationals. Since sorcery and suspicion are so important, and so disruptive of relationship with strangers in general, overseas exchanges with certain special strangers must acquire at least corresponding importance to survive. Here is the fitness of the exchange for exchange's sake of the most valuable ornaments, armshells and spondylus shell necklaces—an exchange that is like an annually repeated peacemaking ceremony (actually the means of cementing peace when peacemaking is done after war, but, if war has not broken the regular procedure, recurring annually regularly), an exchange that encourages competitive attempts at power, upon success in which pride is reared or upon failure in which pride is cast down, a useless exchange, upon which native energies are traditionally centred. Behind this annual peacemaking ceremony with the stranger, otherwise the sorcerer and the enemy, ordinary utilitarian exchange is accomplished easily and without friction as a side issue. A great premium on exchange for its own sake, sets up extensive non-utilitarian exchanges that enlist stronger motives than desire for utilitarian gain merely against the great antagonistic disruptive forces of the black art, the fear of the sea, and the fear of strangers and strange places.

The peacemaking function of the exchange, as set against strong disruptive hostilities, has not been greatly stressed in the theoretical discussion of the *kula*, except in one article, by M. Raymond Lenoir in *L'Anthropologie*.[1] M. Lenoir further appears to suppose that the magical ritual of the entire *kula* ring is communal, is connected with totemism, and is the basis of an international social group, to which young persons are admitted by initiation. Nothing could be further from the truth, and at the same time so near the truth as to what occurs with the tribes of Australia. The magical ritual of Dobu used in the *kula* differs in great part from that of the Trobriands, as will appear below. Totemism is not important in establishing international exchange partnerships between the pairs of individuals who exchange. There are no collective totemic rituals in the area. There is no ceremony of initiation. The young person, who is given *kula* magic by his father or his mother's brother, is taught it in complete privacy lest others overhear it and steal it. One neighbour

---

[1] " Les Expeditions Maritimes, Institution Sociale en Melanesie Occidentale," *L'Anthropologie*, vol. xxxiv, pp. 387–410.

is jealous of another in the acquisition of ornamental valuables in the places to which they journey together. It is true that the owner of the canoe performs certain ritual for the entire canoe's crew. But the important charms and spells in the *kula* are those calculated to influence overseas strangers or partners to be generous in giving. These, no man does for another. Each man hopes that his own magic for this purpose is stronger than that of his fellows ; each man hopes to secure for himself supremacy and pride of place. That is why it is said of the valuables " many men died because of them ". Such men are believed to have been killed by the sorcery of their own canoe fellows, who were enraged at another obtaining so much more success than they, maybe obtaining the very valuable that one other considered his right (as in the case of the man Christopher told me he killed by sorcery over trouble of this kind—see p. 169). M. Lenoir has missed the point. Jealousy and striving for pride of place does not occur powerfully between two organized groups standing over against each other. Such jealousy and striving, leading often to the use of the black art on each other, takes place power-fully within the *uvalaku*, *kula* fleet, within the one tribal group, even within the small group that form a single canoe crew.

Through all M. Lenoir's misconceptions he has, however, grasped the fact that the exchange of the ornaments, useless in itself, makes strongly for peaceful relationships between potentially hostile internationals. It is a good point.

Providentially enough a great love of exchange for its own sake regardless of utility, is a strong protection to trade in an area rent by fear of the black art, suspicion, and hostility.

IV

OVERSEAS EXPEDITION

When I went with the overseas canoes of Tewara, a small detachment going before the main Dobuan fleet, to the south Trobriands, we took ten full days on the water to cover the sailing distance there and back, one hundred and twenty miles in all. The canoes hugged the lee of the reef all the way. Every night before twilight we beached the canoes on a coral outcrop of the reef, and slept there the night. If we

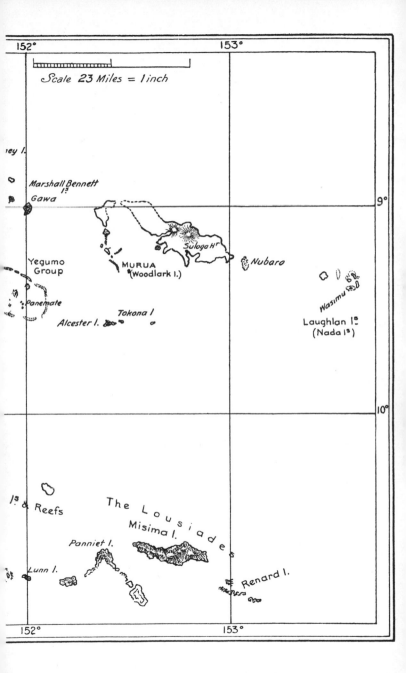

had made good time, and had come upon the only large coral outcrop for miles early in the afternoon, we stopped and camped, lest we might be forced to spend a night at sea. This was no concession to my presence. It was their custom and their usual timidity. The delays irked me. Later, when in the Admiralties, I crossed open seas by canoe, exposed to the full Pacific swell and without any reef to hug, at the rate of forty miles a day, sailing by daylight or by night indifferently, I realized fully that even if the Dobuans were Argonauts of a kind, they were very indifferent sailors. They sail overseas in time of long calms and occasional winds.

All the long times that we lay becalmed and unsheltered under the sun, cries rung intermittently, but regularly, across the water :

O, north-west wind, native of Gilibwai, native of Kibu, native of Sikokolo, native of Nubiam, clutch *lamusi*, the sail new woven of fine pandanus leaf, the misbehaving child of your husband.

ge ! ge ! ge ! ge ! ge ! ge ! ge ! ge ! ge ! ge ! ge !

O, north-west wind, native of Gilibwai, native of Kibu, native of Sikokolo, native of Nubiam, our yams are done, our water is done. Come, O, north-west wind, the sail *lamusi* new woven of fine pandanus leaf, take him in wedlock.

ge ! ge ! ge ! ge ! ge ! ge ! ge ! ge ! ge ! ge ! ge !

I did not obtain full understanding of these cries until later, on an expedition to Sanaroa, when we drifted in a calm all day, till close upon evening—the same type of cry rang out all day again :

O, north-west wind, native of Kitava, native of Kibu, native of Kitalubululu, let us anchor at Siyawawa. You are my cross-cousin. Hear and come to me.

ge ! ge ! ge ! ge ! ge ! ge ! ge ! ge ! ge ! ge ! ge !

O, north-west wind, native of Kibu, native of Gilibwai, native of Nubiam, native of Sikokolo, who is stealing your husband away from you, your husband *lamusi*, the sail new woven of fine pandanus leaf.

ge ! ge ! ge ! ge ! ge ! ge ! ge ! ge ! ge ! ge ! ge !

These cries may only be uttered from the stern, the part of the canoe nearest to the wind-quarter that is invoked. I heard a man begin to start a cry from the bows and promptly check himself as committing an error. On the Sanaroa trip I had my best informant in the same canoe with me, and he gave me an explanation.

" The wind is a person ; if we cry on her she comes ; but if we remain silent, dead calm, men likewise ; if I cry ' my cross-cousin ' she answers ' yes ', she comes."

Later on, I followed up this statement. My informant said " long ago, when I was a child, I asked my grandmother —' the winds, whence and how they come,' and as she answered me, I answer you ". I was then told the legends of the winds, telling how in the time of the first ancestors the winds were natives engaged in various adventures, with other of the ancestors, and how now they lived as supernatural persons in the various wind-quarters, emerging to blow their breaths from their mouths over the sea when called upon. If they were not called upon they never did anything, but remained inert.

I have quoted the cries for the north-west wind only, so I may confine myself to the legend embodying the belief in that wind only. Yarata is the name of the north-west wind.

" Yarata, a pregnant woman, her place Yowana. She gave birth to a female child, whom she named Bwarakwaiyoyo. In the garden she set it in a taro plant. There she grew to maidenhood, so beautiful she that all other girls were forsaken by the youths on her account.

With her women companions, sisters, and female cousins, Bwarakwaiyoyo goes paddling to sea in search of shellfish. They arrive at Yawaigili (a small atoll between Yowana and Tuma in the Lusancay group, the extreme north-westerly land known in Dobu). The women dive for shellfish, bring them, cook them in the earth oven, eat and sleep. While Bwarakwaiyoyo still sleeps they rise stealthily and paddle away, leaving her marooned on the small reef outcrop. Her mother, Yarata, blows over the ocean in search of her lost daughter. She discovers her and brings her back to Yowana.

There Bwarakwaiyoyo marries and bears a male child. The child comes to manhood and sets sail to Kavataria (Trobriands) on the *kula*, a fleet of twenty canoes in his company.

Bwarakwaiyoyo, in revenge for her being marooned on Yawaigili by the jealous malice of her companions, blows violently out to sea, and every canoe with the exception of her son's is capsized. The sharks eat the crews.

Such is the legend. But still when the north-westerly blows gently, Yarata is blowing the breath from her mouth, a light continuous wind. When the north-westerly wind brings up a squall, Bwarakwaiyoyo is blowing in anger. In the overseas canoes the men call upon Yarata. If Bwarak-waiyoyo comes blowing they face the black swell of squall, with whipped white sea at its foot, in its rapid advance and mutter the warding-off ritual, fearful of the traditional anger that was enkindled at Yawaigili and is not even now averted, although now Bwarakwaiyoyo does not blow, except at a magician's behest. As the warding-off magic is muttered, ginger is spat in the direction of the squall. This I saw, for we encountered one violent squall at sea.

The canoe cries are not ordinary incantations. They are in the Trobriand language of the Lusançay Archipelago to the north-west, where the wind called upon lives. Thus they are not in the usual esoteric speech of incantation, and they are not muttered under breath, as usual, and so kept as private property. The reason for this is that the true incantation for wind and rain is exclusively woman's property and the men in their overseas sailing, without a true wind-maker with them, have only a makeshift to fall back upon. The makeshift was easier to get at and understand than the secret ritual, but I found later that it was in exactly the same pattern as the secret ritual employing a being *kasa sona*, and it embodies, of course, the same dogma that no effect comes from anything but incantation. The lying becalmed in the canoes was a very tiresome business, and hot enough to drive one nearly comatose for hours at a time, so that often I wished the semi-incantations would hasten a little in producing the desired effect. Delay in securing an effect never troubles the native belief one jot, however ; it is all in the day's work. While this magic is being made, as it is made unremittingly in time of calm, no paddling is done. The canoe lies as motion-less as seaweed. For its future progress complete reliance is placed in the magic. As all sailing is done in time of calm with occasional wind only, a great strain is placed upon the magic.

Some of the more timid become scared of a choppy sea, that chops only half-way up the canoe side. They mutter magic at it to make it cease being choppy.

The canoes of Dobu do not have the huge spread of sail that the canoes of Kitava use. They are heavier than the fast light canoes of Murua. Their pattern of construction is that of the Trobriand canoe.

The Dobuans are not a seafaring people by love or by ability. Even their true wind magic is possessed by their women. Old women control the winds for rainmaking purposes. Old women possess the incantations for making and for lulling hurricanes. They keep this superior magic closely to themselves, and the men admit that the women possess the ritual that is most needed by sailors. The women cannot make the *kula*. They are jealous of it, and are gifted with the power that can break it. They are not of the kind that easily allow their men a free hand upon the seas or in strange ports.

V

THE RITUAL OF THE KULA

The armshells of the north, which pass south in the *kula* exchange on the western side of the ring, are called *mwali*. The spondylus shell necklaces of the south which pass north on the western side of the ring, are called *bagi*.

The southerners must go north on an expedition to solicit *mwali*. They carry no *bagi*, but in the case of the Dobuans, presents of sago and face paint only. Later, the northerners will go south to solicit *bagi*, carrying as presents the special products of their Trobriand home, carven woodwork, lime gourds, and the like. An equivalent practice prevails between the Amphletts and the Trobriands, south to north, and between the Amphletts and the Dobuans, north to south. So also are the relations between Dobu and Tubetube.

It is a convention that a gift given by A to B when B comes overseas to A's village will be returned by a gift of the other kind (a *bagi* for a *mwali* or vice versa), but of equivalent size and value when A comes overseas to B's village later in the year. On the whole, fair dealing prevails ; but a man is never sure of it, and occasionally his overseas partner does not or cannot return a fair equivalent ; there is ample room for good luck or ill. Partnerships between the most powerful men who exchange the finest valuables are the most stable. But the majority of partnerships are not more stable than marriage partnerships in Dobu. They frequently break up, and new partnerships are contracted owing to one of the partners failing to meet his just obligations. One man usually has three or four partners in different places.

A man is judged *esaesa*, rich man, or not, by the size of the valuables which he keeps in continuous possession and exchange in the *kula*. His reputation in native eyes is in very great measure estimated by his success in it. Such success in the *kula* exchange is not believed to flow from any natural causes. To the native, the giving to him of a most valuable present by a man of a strange place, the giving of such extensive credit, such reliance placed in his commercial honesty, is an annually repeated miracle. Knowing what we do know of the high value the Dobuan places upon successful theft and analogous anti-social practice, we may sympathize sincerely with his view that the trust reposed in him in the *kula* is a miracle of magic, a result of a power that is not natural or human, except in so far as the results of magic are natural or human. Knowing also Dobuan distrust of, and lack of hospitality to strangers, his fear of strange sorcery, the fact that he is given hospitality and fed by his host, his *kula* partner abroad, may well be viewed, as he views it, as one of the strange miracles of magic. If he, in return, does not cheat his creditor, and offers food and hospitality for many days to his *kula* partner and creditor when his partner visits him in his home, then he may well put down such exceptional behaviour towards one not of his blood to the powers of his partner's magic over him.

Success in the *kula* exchange is believed to depend much on the personal appearance of the man engaging in it. Such appearance is in part natural, in part supernaturally enhanced. In native thought, courtship of women and courtship of a *kula* partner are closely bound together. In both cases a fine person is held to be requisite ; in the ritual of the *kula* as in the ritual of love the same fine-scented *lamalama*[1] leaves are used, and in both cases the frequent misfortune of a skin ruined by ringworm is conceived as the greatest obstacle to be overcome. In the *kula*, although the ordinary native remedies for a bad skin, and the ordinary toilet enhancements of black unguent for the face, betel nut for a red mouth and coco-nut oil for the body, are exploited carefully to the full, success is held to flow primarily from the ritual. The end of the ritual is to secure *mwali* or *bagi*, but its more proximate end is to create that personal beauty which is the prime requisite to success. One who knows the ritual attains personal beauty by mystical means, ritual means, ringworm, and ulcers or not ; one who does not know the ritual does not attain the mystical beauty which is so much more important than natural beauty that without the ritual a fine skin and person may go in despite, and failure result.

[1] Lamalama is *Scaevola fructuscens*, also called *Scaevola Konigii Vahl*.

In an examination of the *kula* ritual we must first deal with the legend of Kasabwaibwaileta, the legendary foundation of the ritual. It runs :

Kasabwaibwaileta

The twenty-nine villages of Tewara and Uwamo equip each one a canoe ; Kasabwaibwaileta, a man of diseased skin covered with sores—inside his skin a handsome man—his canoe *Kegawagoa*. The fleet prepares for sailing ; Kasabwaibwaileta has sago cooked between banana leaves on circles of white hot stones ; they eat ; he cries " let us go ".

They lash down the sea mats on the *geboboi* (structure built in mid-canoe to hold food, mats, and gifts) ; they set their stone axes on their shoulders ; they climb to their villages ; they sleep.

Before sunrise, Boluba, mother of Kasabwaibwaileta, descends to Mulia to bring water ; she charms the water in the water-gourd. She says to her son " a small unripe coco-nut you cut down, green betel nut you wrap up, green bananas you cut ". He does this ; she utters a spell over the coco-nut, the betel nut, the green bananas. She gives him the water-gourd containing the water she has charmed ; he pours the water on the prow ; he takes the fruit she has charmed.

They set sail ; at sea Kasabwaibwaileta performs the *tunaseana* ; the others eat—he does not eat. *Kegawagoa* outstrips the fleet ; the men of the *Kegawagoa* canoe sail round Siyawawa, Sanaroa, Udaudana, Raputat ; they *wabuwabu*.

At this stage I must interrupt the movement of the legend in order to make it intelligible. The legend preserves the names of the twenty-nine villages of Tewara and Uwamo, adjoining small islands. This list of names I have omitted. Now, only four villages are left with only forty living persons, men, women, and children, in them. The charmed water is poured on the canoe prow to make the canoe fast, to enable it to outstrip the rest of the fleet. The *tunaseana* is a charm performed by the canoe-owner at sea ; with a *tabu* of not eating until after nightfall associated with it. Siyawawa, Sanoroa, Udaudana, Raputat are the names of villages in Sanaroa Island.

To *wabuwabu* is to get many spondylus shell necklaces from different places, different villages in the south on security of the same one armshell left at home in the north, or vice versa, many armshells from the north on a security that cannot meet them, promising the one valuable which one possesses to many different persons of different places in return for their gifts that are being solicited. It is sharp practice, but not complete confidence trickstering.

" Suppose I, Kisian of Tewara, go to the Trobriands and secure an armshell named Monitor Lizard. I then go to Sanaroa and in four different places secure four different shell necklaces, promising each man who gives me a shell necklace, Monitor Lizard, in return later. I, Kisian, do not have to be very specific in my promise. It will be conveyed by implication and assumption for the most part. Later, when four men appear in my home at Tewara each expecting Monitor Lizard, only one will get it. The other three are not defrauded permanently, however. They are furious, it is true, and their exchange is blocked for the year. Next year, when I, Kisian, go again to the Trobriands I shall represent that I have four necklaces at home waiting for those who will give me four armshells. I obtain more armshells than I obtained previously, and pay my debts a year late. The three men who did not get Monitor Lizard are at a disadvantage in my place, Tewara. Later when they return to their homes they are too far off to be dangerous to me. They are likely to attempt to kill their successful rival, who did get the armshell, Monitor Lizard, by the black art. That is true enough. But that is their own business. I have become a great man by enlarging my exchanges at the expense of blocking theirs for a year. I cannot afford to block their exchange for too long, or my exchanges will never be trusted by anyone again. I am honest in the final issue."

To *wabuwabu* successfully is a great achievement. It causes the black art to operate, but not against the man who does the *wabuwabu*. It is because of the frequency of the *wabuwabu* practice that a man who secures a fine valuable is often enviously hated by his compatriots who had an equal, but a temporarily unmet, claim upon it. He is in favour, high in prestige, and they are cast down, shamed for the year, although they had as legitimate an expectation of successfully securing a return for their credit as their luckier rival. Hence it is said of the *kula* valuables : " many men died on their account." So also are interpreted the deaths of men on *kula* expeditions. Their graves on small coral reef outcrops are remembered and chronicled on the seas. They were sorcerised by their luckless rivals indignant at their success. And sorcery actually is used frequently by a man, who has failed to get a valuable, upon another man who has obtained it successfully, when both men were induced to give credit on the strength of their belief. (See account given by Christopher, pp. 169.)

A temporary lapse of commercial honour may occur not only as the result of previous *wabuwabu*, but also when a man has given a *kula* valuable as part of the bride-price and has not received a return gift promptly from his affinal relatives. *Wabuwabu* is the kind of sharp practice that is possible without entailing too serious consequences, a kind in which the Dobuan delights. Hence the great mythical hero of the *kula* necessarily succeeds in performing it. To return to the legend :

Again they sail, the fleet, to Wamea and Gumawana[1] ; brown eagle, first to arrive of the fleet, sees a canoe beached at Wamea ; he says " The *tautauna*[2] men are here "—as it turned out, Kasabwaibwaileta. He had sailed by Basima and Dilia, turned east and come to shore long before the others. The men of *Kegawagoa* again they *wabuwabu*. Humming bird in the bows blows on the shell trumpet again and again.

They set up masts, haul up sail—away to Vakuta[3] ; again *Kegawagoa* arrives with the rest of the fleet not in sight and behind. They go to their partners ; Kasabwaibwaileta remains under his mat in the canoe. His cross-cousin goes to *pokala*[4] Gomakarakedakeda[5] ; many bananas, much betelnut he throws down. They would not give it him ; night falls.

Kasabwaibwaileta rises ; he charms and his diseased skin falls from him ; he emerges a most handsome man. He does not bathe, comb his hair, or paint his face—without this he is most handsome. He charms the green coco-nut ; it grows and ripens ; he charms the green bananas ; they grow and ripen ; he charms the green betel nut ; it ripens.

In the night he goes to the house of the partner of his cross-cousin ; only the daughter of the house is there. He gives her the gifts, instructing her not to unwrap the betelnut, but to give it to her father so. To-morrow he will return. Her heart is trembling for the handsome stranger ; he returns to his canoe, he resumes his sore-covered skin.

The next morning the men go again to their partners ;

---

[1] Places of the Amphletts.
[2] Bwaioa.
[3] South Trobriands.
[4] Offer solicitary presents to the possessor of an ornamental valuable desired from him.
[5] Name of a particular spondylus shell necklace.

Kasabwaibwaileta himself remains under his mat. The possessors do not give Gomakarakedakeda ; night falls.

Kasabwaibwaileta charms, his diseased skin falls from him ; he goes to the house of the partner of his cross-cousin ; his beauty, the charmed potency of his gifts, his beauty move them. Their hearts tremble with desire for him. They give him Gomakarakedakeda.

He returns to his mat unseen ; he resumes his diseased skin. On his head beneath an ulcer he places the necklace wound up.

They sail to Gabuwana.[1] They cook pig in the earth oven. Kasabwaibwaileta calls his grandson ; " you louse my hair "—his grandson louses ; he lifts up the ulcer. He exclaims " Gomakarakedakeda ". " No " says Kasabwaibwaileta, " that is a Tewara *bagi* I carry." The child louses.

Secretly he informs his father " Kasabwaibwaileta Gomakarakedakeda he carries ". " E ! sore skin ! foul skin ! it is impossible." " My father I saw it. I loused his hair. Beneath the ulcer he has it concealed."

With his brothers they plot together ; the women go to bring water ; the men follow ; they muddy the water. They prepare to sail ; they say " Kasabwaibwaileta, go, bring water ". He sits down and waits for the mud to settle ; he blows mucus from his nose ; it turns to rocks. Meanwhile, they have sailed away ; he rises with the water ; he sees them forsaking him ; he seizes great rocks and hurls them at the canoe ; the canoe zigzags and escapes. These rocks are still to be seen—rock islands just south of Gabuwana and one far removed and beyond the Amphletts—Gurewaiya.

Kasabwaibwaileta wails ; night falls ; the stars appear. He charms a *kaiawana* tree into growth. One branch puts out to the north-west wind, one branch puts out to the south wind, one branch puts out to the south-west wind, one branch puts out to the south-east wind, one branch puts out to the north-east wind. On the branch of the north-east wind he treads ; he charms ; a *sagusagu* palm grows on the branch of the north-east wind. He climbs ; he stays.

Kibi (a constellation) comes near. " My friend I embark with you." " It is not possible. Goods many I have shipped in my canoe."

Gomayawa (Pleiades) comes near. " My friend, I embark with you." " Come, embark." " *Pwopwosa* he embarks,

---

[1] A coral outcrop on the reef near the south Trobriands.

kalitabu he embarks, *sinasinate* he embarks, *memwai* he embarks, *ali*[1] he embarks. The star his arm-band "pandanus" streamer (of shells) he fastened on. (The names are of sea-shells not identified—*sinasinate*, however, is the sea-urchin. They remain in the sky to-day, imaged as a streamer worn in the arm-band of Pleiades, as the pandanus float, so worn by a man at a dance.) He hopped ; he crossed Mwaniwara, he went inland, Lalaiya, Tanubweala, Tribut. (Places of Tewara).

Kasabwaibwaileta disembarks. He stays with the sky people ; he marries. His wife bears him a child. The children play *kenokinoki*. One throws a spear into *kalitabu*. He lifts it up. He says "niwaroa".[2] Kasabwaibwaileta sees Tribut far below on the earth. (*Niwaroa* is the word for Tribut of Tewara in the language of Megarewa, the sky people).

It dawns ; he feigns illness ; his wife goes to the garden ; he prepares a rope ; he fastens the necklace to the rope ; a child holds the rope in the heavens ; he descends the necklace. As he descends it breaks, the necklace, a small part here below, a larger part the child pulls up to the heavens. It swings out in a storm to Woodlark Island, to Sud-est. The child coils it up. Kasabwaibwaileta lands in a betel palm, *magilode*. His mother is sweeping below ; he throws down a betel nut ; it strikes her ; she finds him.

His relatives are engaged in a funerary feast for him. They build a house at Tribut, according to his instructions ; he charms the house, hitting it with an axe, while they are inside. He charms, changing them into birds, knocking on the four sides of the house in turn, they fleeing to the opposite sides in turn, their feathers growing each time. He allotted the birds their foods (details abbreviated).

Scrub hen, his mother formerly, and Yodudu, his wife, are still friendly to men and stay about close to the village, unlike other birds.

Kasabwaibwaileta adorns himself in armshells and neck-laces. He goes by Tanubweala, Lalaiya, Pwosipwosimo, Kedatete, Magisewa to Mwaniwara (east point of Tewara). He wails for Tribut. He dives ; at Woodlark Island he emerges from his dive.

Kenokinoki is a game at piercing rolling sections of banana tree stem with spears—in the legend the child's spear opens

---

[1] Names of shell fish.   [2] A linguistic touch.

one of the shells of Pleiades' arm-band. Gomakarakedakeda, the fabulously long necklace, sweeping from the heavens to Woodlark Island and down to Sud-est in a storm, means monitor lizard on the path, *gomakara* being the monitor lizard and *keda*, a path.

It is believed that *gomakara*, the monitor lizard, trumpets at home in Tewara when the men receive gifts abroad. The women staying at home hear the sound and send round word that their men folk have secured valuables. Not any monitor lizard may give this omen—only the monitor lizard of Tribut— legendary home of Kasabwaibwaileta in Tewara and now uninhabited.

The main point of the legend that is brought out in the *kula* ritual is that a man of evil and diseased skin sheds his sore-covered skin, emerges a handsome man and profits by it to secure a necklace of a fabulous size; this will become more apparent when we come to consider the ritual in detail. The monitor lizard has a certain artistic relevance to the tale, because it is believed that he sheds his old skin periodically and emerges young again.

The skin of *gomakara*, the monitor lizard, is used as the tympanum for the native drum. While the overseas expedition is in progress dancing is rigidly prohibited, both to the men on the expedition and to the women at home. The drums are put away. They may be brought out at the conclusion of a successful expedition, however. This was done at the conclusion of the *kula* trip I made in Sanaroa. Whether it was done on the conclusion of the *kula* trip to Vakuta I do not know, as the night before sailing home I was north near Sinaketa. Perhaps that is why the trumpeting of *gomakara* announces a successful termination of the expedition, and the women are informed of it beforehand. When I made the *kula* in the canoes of the Tewara folk and we stayed in Gumasila in the Amphletts, the local men and women of Gumawana danced all night. I said to an old man of Tewara, who stayed with me a long while, " Why do you not go to the dance, Yogalu ? " The old man was offended. He said " Had I wished to do so long ago I had gone ". Then after a pause " Magile (his wife) would insult me. She would say I had been happy ". At the dance I found none of the Tewara men ; on the other hand two young Tewara women who were accompanying their husbands to the Trobriands were there. Later I learned that no man on the *kula* can go near a dance, and if his wife is left at home she cannot express any happiness at home. Men on the *kula* and wives at home cannot sing, dance, yodel, or tell legends. Apparently the two young married women at the dance in Gumawana were taking advantage of an unusual situation for which there was no customary rule. Their presence in the *kula* canoes was exceptional and due to relationship duties connected with a mourning feast in the Trobriands.

Kisi, a propros of the *tabus* enforced during a *kula* expedition, recalled an old event :

" Long ago we were in Vakuta and Tolibwogwo (Dr. Malinowski) said ' whose canoes are those ? ' They said ' from Tewara '. ' Let them come and relate the legend of Kasabwaibwaileta to me.' We answered ' *Bomama* ' (our sacred prohibition). So also in the gardens. When we are engaged in garden ritual as when we are engaged in the *kula* ritual we do not play, we do not sing, we do not yodel, we do not relate legends. If in the garden we behave so the seed yams say ' what charm is this ? Once before was a good charm—but this, what is this ? ' The seed yams mistake our speech. They do not grow."

When I was with the *kula* canoes this *bomama* was observed. Once the object of the expedition was attained, however, the prohibition was not in force. On the homeward voyage when we had put in at Gabuwana, the scene of Kasabwaibwaileta's marooning, I woke up in the middle of the night to hear a legend in full swing, and at the conclusion of the Sanaroa expedition there was a dance.

One way of marking the attainment of an object is an infringement of a prohibition obligatory in the process of attaining it. Thus Dobuan marriage ceremony consists most importantly of eating and drinking in the sight of the mother-in-law, this action being rigidly prohibited throughout the engagement stage. It is possibly this reasoning that finds grounds for belief in the attainment of the *kula* when *gomakara*, the drum tympanum in potentiality, trumpets. The drum tympanum in actuality is necessarily debarred from announcing the tidings, for legend relates how in the time of the first ancestors, drums sounded of their own volition, but someone carried one under sea water, and now they have to be beaten to produce sound.

The monitor lizard is of no use to the Dobuans other than as a potential drum tympanum. Drums are never used except for a dance. Whether the fabulous spondylus shell necklace of the great legend of the *kula* is called " Monitor Lizard on the Path" because of the *tabus* associated with the *kula*, the omens, or because like Kasabwaibwaileta he is believed to shed his old skin and emerge new and handsome, I do not know. There is a possible chain of free association. I am not merely indulging in such association, however ; for I wish to emphasize that the ritual of Dobu does carry with it sacred prohibitions that tend towards seriousness, perhaps even glumness, as in the case of the Puritan Sabbath amongst ourselves.

Kibi and the Pleiades are spoken of by Kasbwaibwaileta as my friend. Three constellations, Kibi, Pleiades, and Yuyuna (tail of Orion), are the only stars singled out by the natives for attention and naming.[1] The garden calendar is closely connected with their annual passage across the sky. Clearing the bush takes place when Pleiades is in the north-eastern sky at an angle of about fifteen degrees above the horizon. This is about October. Before harvest is due Pleiades, followed by Orion, sinks in the south-west and is not seen for a time. Pleiades [2] is said to pole his canoe round the horizon from south-west to north-east, Orion following him in like manner in this time of invisibility. The two meet in their canoes. Then Pleiades rises in the north-east over Woodlark Island— and it is harvest time. Clearing and planting follow again when Pleiades climbs somewhat. The *kula* expeditions take place shortly after the bush clearing and planting of seed-yams. Hence Kasbwaibwaileta mounts a *sagusagu* palm grown by magic on the branch of the north-east wind of a magically grown tree. Pleiades has mounted in the north-east.

In accordance with all Dobuan theory the heroes or villains of legends still are alive, living supernaturals still capable of producing effects whether of themselves or under magical compulsion. The sky people living near the stars, with whom Kasbwaibwaileta inter-married, still live there. Kasabwaibwaileta still lives. So also we saw before in considering the legend of the origin of fire, the *kaiana* fire still issues from the pubes of women. Kasabwaibwaileta, as a still living supernatural, is of the greatest importance in the Dobuan *kula* ritual. Unlike the names of other supernaturals important as magical familiars, his name is not secret. His legend is

---

[1] Venus is also named, however.
[2] I use the singular to express the native conception.

not only not secret, but the Dobuans consider it as their most important legend and tell it *ad nauseam* with unfailing verve and grand gesticulation.

The ritual proceedings open with the charming of the *seuseula,* the sea-mat, which is to cover food and valuables shipped in the *geboboi,* the structure erected in mid-canoe to hold the *pokala,* solicitary gifts. The *toni-waga,* owner of the canoe, rises early in the morning and performs this rite in private. He chews ginger and spits it on to the mat with this incantation, each *toni-waga* performing the rite for his own canoe.

> heavily the *kuloia* [1] cries
> by the shore at mulia.
> your cry is of the sunrise and morning,
> my cry is of the first dawning half-light.
> *mwali* over the elbow,
>   fine *karumoi* [2]
> my cry is of the first dawning half-light
>   from my sea-mat
> from inside my *geboboi*
> from the nose of the canoe
> I cry out, I cry out in the morning.
> over the top board of my canoe
>   the spray wetting
> I strike it, I thrust it back returning.
> my embarking, many embarking,
> their *kune* [3] to me with my wife
>   with my child
> the report, the tidings of us is a different tidings. [4]

At the same early morning hour as the *toni-waga* descends to charm the sea-mat, his wife goes into the forest and gently draws up the root of a certain plant, charming as she does so. The charm declares that the speaker's root (naming her husband) is the *sibukaka* root, dwells on the thunder that his voyage will awaken in the heavens, the privy whisperings of the charmer to the owners of *mwali* or *bagi,* the shaking effect that he will produce in the eager bodies of his partner, his partner's wife and child, and finally how they will dream in the night of him and rise from the dream.

The woman comes away, leaving the root lying. At mid-day she goes with her husband, they collect it together, and it is placed in the man's lime gourd against his chewing it with betel nut just before he meets his *kula* partner abroad.

Then follows the riual halt. Once when I made the *kula* to the Trobriands we entered the canoes and pulled over

---

[1] A bird, unidentified.
[2] Spondylus shell.
[3] Dobuan term for *kula.*
[4] i.e. we have a better reputation than other persons.

to Uwamo, an uninhabited island next door. It took us about half an hour to reach there. We then spent the afternoon sitting solemnly on the beach, ignoring the fair wind that could have taken us to our first overseas halt in the Amphletts easily before night-fall. We slept on the beach and next morning drifted at sea in a calm till a breeze took us to Wata, an uninhabited outlying island of the Amphletts, late in the afternoon.

There is an alternative form of the ritual halt practised in Tewara, however ; it is followed when the canoes go south, rather than north. After the *toni-waga* and his wife collect the charmed root at midday, those going on the expedition descend to the beach and sit solemnly beside the canoes on the beach all the afternoon. A fair wind was blowing on this occasion ; but according to ritual custom it had to be ignored, despite the risk of a calm next day. As dusk fell everyone rose and re-climbed the hill to the village, remarking that the wind, which still set fair, had been impossible. Next morning early, we put to sea in a calm and did not get to Sanaroa, with a very light breeze, until close on midnight, a fifteen-hour voyage that would have been possible in four or five hours the afternoon before, when the ritual halt was observed.

It does not make any difference to custom how the winds may be. The ritual halt may occur with a grand wind for sailing blowing, and next day the canoes may put to sea in a calm, drift under the sun all day and catch a capful of wind in the evening. For good or bad the ritual must go forward. The preliminary halt on an adjoining uninhabited shore, or on the shore below the village, is intended to take the voyagers away from their everyday occupation, leave them solemnly by themselves and clear their minds of distractions. Next day they cannot return to everyday matters—the ritual is in swing and out to sea they must go.

Early next morning the *toni-waga* places two yams and a coco-nut at the bottom of the empty *geboboi*, and in charming them speaks of Kasabwaibwaileta's having charmed his *pokala*, of Kasabwaibwaileta's placing them so, of his own placing—then follow several verbs of method of placing ; and as the magical tour de force, *karumoi*, long soulava necklaces, green-stone blades, and a repetition of the same verbs of methods of placing—not yams and coco-nut now, but *karumoi*, *bagi*, greenstone blades. The conversion of the solicitary gifts into valuables of the *kula* is ritually completed before the expedition is begun. All the solicitary gifts, yams, sago, coco-nuts, are placed rapidly on top of the charmed yams and coco-nut in the *geboboi*. The charm is said to rise up and permeate the entire *geboboi* and its contents.

If the preliminary halt has been in complete isolation from the village—on a neighbouring but isolated shore or island or sandbank, there is no *tunaseana* in the canoe at sea next day. If, on the other hand, the preliminary halt has been merely a sitting on the shore from midday to dusk, on the shore below the village, and a return up the hill to the village at night, the *tunaseana* must be performed in the canoe the next day.

There is no early eating on the day of embarkation, if the *tunaseana* is to be performed. The *toni-waga* cannot eat till night-fall. He charms the *tunaseana* in the canoe and his companions eat a little food each in the afternoon. First must come his charm :

> O, foot of the *geboboi*, cover of the *geboboi*,
>   wenio of silana
>   barking, barking,
> I shout you back,
>   your return.
> they take up, they stack in the bush
>   the *nanoa* [1]
> they tread the hill-ridge
> they pluck the scented *ane*
> the canoe's resting log stamped on with cursing.
> they shade their eyes looking far to sea
>   they look nearby.
> from the end of my outrigger float
> from the foot of my sternboard
>   the howling infant *lelebuyo*
> they fall away, they go back mourning
>   they go from out my sea-mat
>   they float away.
>
>   *   *   *   *   *
>
>   with my evening star
> the star that accuses of meanness rises
>   by the steep side of gabuwana
>   the evening star
> the star that accuses of meanness rises
>   my friends
> your fish is a different dish
>   many at my back.
>   my fish, *sulua*.
> I with my *kune* [2] of very great valuables only,
>   my *kune* of very great valuables only.
> *karumoi* from stretched out finger tip to mid-breast.
>   the food brought out wading in the sea.
>   my *kune*
>   of very great valuables only.

---

[1] Canoe launching logs.
[2] Dobuan term synonymous with the Trobriand term kula.

```
      man kasabwaibwaileta
you go to the steep cliff side
      you dress
the man miaropa (naming himself)
      he goes to kokua
      by the bay he dresses
the thunder tidings of my coming rolls
      and crashes
      it crashes.
over kedagwaba the new moon
      turns its back.
    they call crying on it
    they call crying on it
      they are happy
      on their bwaima ¹
on the extreme edge of the outward going support
    they look out on the path
      they look for us
      they look for me
        they look.
```

After the charm is done the men may eat a little food, the *toni-waga*, the charmer, refraining from eating till nightfall.

With this charm we are further into the magical wood. The simplicity of the earlier charms is done. First it must be noted that the charm is in a fairly common two-part pattern. The first part is the *egoyainina*, the naming and hurling away of evil. The second part, beginning " with my evening star " is the *ebwainina* and naming and superimposing of good. The charms are uttered inaudibly by the charmer in a mumbled sing-song. In between *egoyainina* and *ebwainina* the charmer ceases his sing-song mumble and says distinctly and loudly : " May the mouth of X—— be stopped up, the evil mouth of X——." X—— in the charm I heard at sea was the charmer's own brother. After this remark, to which nobody pays any attention, the charm is resumed in the *ebwainina* part. The remark about someone named left behind is invariably interposed in the same form between *egoyainina* and *ebwainina*. I asked about it and was told : " O, he will be saying, ' I hope they have bad luck with their *kula*.' "

The *egoyainina*, naming and hurling away of evil, is a charm to take the place of complete isolation in the ritual halt. Its wording therefore interprets the purpose of the complete preliminary halt, for which it is a substitute, used only when there has been partial isolation in the ritual halt.

Wenio is a legendary dog of huge stature—he is here symbolic of barking dogs in general. The women stack up the *nanoa*, or launching logs, but not until the canoes are out

¹ House platform.

of sight at sea. Children and infants are held to have a bad influence on the expedition. When we were engaged in the ritual halt, sitting on the beach at Tewara before the return to the village for the night before embarkation, I was taken to task by the head-man for talking to youths and children and allowing them behind my back. Hence it appears that the preliminary ritual halt is to separate the *kula* adventurers from dogs, women, and children, and all those liable to curse the expedition. So much for the removal of evil.

Coming to the *ebwainina*, the star that accuses of meanness is Kubwana, Venus, who used to shine in the day, and the sun in the night ; but neither Kubwana or the sun lit up properly under these conditions, and the present order had to be adopted. Venus is always watching people at their evening meal, looking into the cooking pots, and is spoken of as " the root of greed ". Sulua is said to be a fish of very fine appearance—he has not his equal in the sea. The charmer here compares himself with his friends in his own favour. Fish, bird, and tree are linked totems, but Sulua is not totemic to my knowledge.

The food referred to may be that put into the *geboboi* as *pokala*, or that which may be eaten when the charm is done. Both of these are carried out to the canoes by women wading in the sea. Kokua is a bay near Vakuta, where the Dobuans dress up before going to meet their northern partners. The new moon's rising is usually looked for, and children salute it with whooping. It cannot be done, however, while a man of importance is eating his evening meal. The concluding lines refer to the charmer's *kula* partner looking out for his approach with eagerness—evidently as children for a new moon rising. It is a symbol for happiness, the whooping at the new moon.

The canoes land at an entirely isolated spot not too far away from their final destination for the concluding and most important ritual. This is the private but ceremonial washing off the sweat of the voyage and the anointing for an international occasion. The incantations for this occasion are the most valued in the *kula* magic, to a native among his richest posssessions and the object of his greatest pride. No more the *toni-waga*, owner of the canoe, performs incantations for the entire canoe. Even in the *tunaseana* last quoted he names himself only, side by side with the supernatural,

Kasabwaibwaileta, the star spoken of as " the star of greed ", is quoted with citation of *his* superior " fish ", *his* different and greater *kune*. Now no man charms in the presence of another or for another. It is every man for himself and every man hoping for more success than his fellows. Those who know the following charms feel their superiority ; these charms are such that one man will not sell them to another for pay. Knowledge of them secures pre-eminence in the exchanges, a pre-eminence coveted above the possible pay for a charm :

> the bathing place of woodlark island I approach,
> I draw away from you
> I approach close to you.
> your wife crosses over and comes down to me, your child.
> your back that fronted me is turned about,
> your child's back does not front me
> my skin is that of a man of rank,
> my features are those of a man of rank.
> I draw away from you.
> I approach close to you.
> they float away from me,
> they float close to me.

This formula is uttered while the charmer stands in the sea alone, apart, and beats himself over shoulders and body with the leaves of the *lamalama* tree,[1] the leaves used in love charms also. He has three bundles, one for each formula, and he throws one away as each formula is ended.

The noteworthy point about this incantation is that it is not directed to the charmer's *kula* partner, who will give him a *kula* valuable soon. It is directed to Kasabwaibwaileta, now of Woodlark Island (after the dive from Mwaniwara in eastern Tewara).[2] Hence " the bathing place of woodlark island I approach ", though in fact no canoe from Dobu goes near Woodlark Island (Murua).

" If Kasabwaibwaileta turns his back upon us "—so runs the more esoteric talk of everyday, " we get no *mwali* and no *bagi*. Our hosts give them to the men of other places. But if he turns around, fronts us and laughs, our canoes sink beneath the weight of *mwali* and *bagi*. Long ago our forefathers abandoned him on Gabuwana." It is this effect of turning Kasabwaibwaileta's back around that the incantation has for its object. This object secured, there follows the second charm of the ritual washing with self-striking. of *lamalama* leaves upon the body of the ritualist.

---

[1] *Scaevola fructuscens* (Konigi Vahl).
[2] See conclusion of the Kasabwaibwaileta legend.

Dawn over woodlark island, the sun casting off its coating of night,
your breaking forth from covering as the sun breaking forth from darkness,
my breaking forth from covering as the sun breaking forth from darkness,
your fine skin breaking forth from the evil peeling from your body,
my fine skin breaking forth from the evil peeling from my body.
my skin is that of a man of rank.
              long *bagi*
bagi closed and kept long in the bound up basket.
Your fine skin breaking forth from the evil peeling from your body,
my fine skin breaking forth from the evil peeling
                    from my body
                    from my hip
              from the skin of my skull
                    peeling off
              to my feet it descends
              I hurl it from me,
              to the tips of my hand it descends
              I hurl it from me.

" You must know " said my *toni-waga*, giving me the charm
alone in the bush (lest others overhear and steal it), " that it
is Kasabwaibwaileta that doffs his skin." " And you how ? "
I said. " That is the speech of ritual merely." Nevertheless,
the charm is believed to make the charmer beautiful and
attractive and irresistible to his partner.

The third charm of the ceremonial bathing may be abbreviated. It introduces a new mythological person, Tauwau
in place of Kasabwaibwaileta ; Tauwau and the charmer bathe
and produce thunder with their footsteps in well alternated
lines, then the charm goes on to boast that the anointing
is rightly done, the charmer's words too persuasive for refusal,
and the effect of the charmer on the susceptibilities of his
partner with his wife and child sitting, awaiting him, on the
house platform, is pictured as overwhelming. Tauwau is
a mythological person of recent extraction, being the maker
of all the white man's artcrafts in one capacity, the being
responsible for leaving a pair of subordinate beings to spread
white man's diseases in another, and originally a native of
Tewara who made the *kula*, but had a feud with Kasabwaibwaileta and left Tewara for the white man's country in a third
capacity. One may presume that it is in the first and third
capacity only that he is named in the final incantation, and that
he is an accretion to the charm.

These three formulæ are done privately, each man going
a different way. The last *lamalama* leaves are thrown away,
a fresh pubic leaf is donned, and painting the face and
anointing the body with coco-nut oil is carried forward. The
canoes pull in leisurely to their destination, the crews dis-
embark, and go to their partners.

It is firmly believed that thunder and rain are produced by the arrival of an overseas canoe. Such atmospheric indications are called *kaniana* ; hence the reference to footsteps of thunder in the final charm.

This ritual performance with its prohibitions on dancing, singing, yodelling, or telling of legends, with its preliminary halt to secure isolation from profane events, and with the special *tunaseana* incantation when the preliminary halt is whittled down to an afternoon instead of the full afternoon and night of solemn isolation, is thus very largely a declaration of anticipated results in an esoteric speech ; but most importantly it is a speech of power over a spiritual being, Kasabwaibwaileta, on the influencing of whom success depends. Of the class of beings *kasa sona*, Kasabwaibwaileta is one ; and the ritual is primarily an appeal to him, and a mystical sharing of the ritualist in his legendary vouched-for power of overcoming a bad appearance and making himself irresistible to his *kula* partner by his beauty of appearance. The ritual is felt as a mystery by the native. It is removed from the profane and it bears some of the typical marks of the sacred.

Without this ritual performance a native believes that he will not be able to induce his partner to give him a *kula* valuable, for which, according to native fairness in the exchange of presents, a due return will be made later. Such is the dogma that gives the ritual its importance.

It is very difficult to discover who knows the ritual and who does not. One man does not mention another's ignorance at peril of feud possibly ending in fatality to one or the other. Nevertheless, I ascertained of five older men in my village that three knew the three ritual charms of the ceremonial bathing, two did not. One of those who did not know the charms was given away by his son, my personal cook-boy. The boy pretended to have learned the bathing charms, the final charms of the overseas expedition, but to have forgotten them in part. Would I repeat them so that his memory might be refreshed. I agreed that I would if he could first substantiate his statement by repeating a line or even less. He could not. From this ruse it followed that his father, Yogalu, did not know the charms, for I knew he denied no ritual to his son—and the boy would never have run the gauntlet of asking me for them rather than his father. The three men who did know the charms were brothers, one of whom taught me them, assured me of his brothers' knowledge, and of the ignorance of the fifth man. The same three brothers did not have knowledge of any *tabus* or sorcery in common. Their *tabus* were different, obtained from different of their mother's brothers separately. Only one inherited any garden magic ; he sold some of the garden charms to the wife of one of his brothers and was paid a tenth of her next harvest for it " to make the charm pointed ", i.e. powerful. The three had the important *kula* charms in common, however, an unusual community of magic between brothers. The three were together in the knowledge with their cross-cousin, instead of one brother alone possessing magic in common with his cross-cousin—the normal distribution for most magic.

It is significant that, as I saw for myself on the expeditions, of these five older men of the village, the three brothers who knew the ritual also ran the most important exchanges. They had more partners and handled more valuable ornaments in exchange than the two other men who were ignorant of the magic. The magic is believed to be necessary to success. Success is largely a matter of self confidence and poise in wooing an overseas partner with assurance and in demanding the best against other competitors, who also seek the best, and who continually attempt to make new partners if other men than their old partners have better ornaments in their possession than their old partners have. Knowing the magic actually does seem to help considerably—not knowing it seems to detract from a person's chances. The belief in the potency and necessity of magical knowledge appears in the *kula* to to create its own reality, at least in some measure.

If we may permit ourselves a flight of fancy and in imagination plunge our own society into a Dobuan atmosphere, the facts are as if the most profitable business undertakings amongst ourselves were reserved exclusively for those families that knew the mumbo-jumbo that secured the assistance of Dives, while those that knew but a small part of the mumbo-jumbo did not dare to engage in other than the less profitable class of business undertakings ; and this state of affairs were caused by a firm and solid dogma that the return which it was possible to secure was dependent on the control exerted over Dives, and upon nothing else, since ordinary qualities are common to everyone. We must allow, however, for the discordant fact that the passage of native wealth is notably different from our own in the conception that it is gained by beauty of person, so that Dives in his true capacity must be also the god of male personal beauty, and not have the ambiguous standing that private appreciation and ritual damnation place him in amongst ourselves. It is clear, I trust, that this belief would so establish a status, separate the leaders from the led without any ups and downs due to non-traditional traits, and enable wealth that cannot go all around equally to be distributed unequally by inducing an inferiority feeling in the unfortunates who do not know the mumbo-jumbo that is so effective over Dives. We should, however, have to believe firmly in Dives and very firmly in incantations. Calling the spells mumbo-jumbo, for example, would be Bolshevism.

I do not wish to pretend that the status of the five older men I knew best, is typical of all Dobu. Generally it is true that the magical leaders are the social leaders in everything. But there are many outsiders too, who are contemptuous, or pretend to be so, of all charms they do not know, who believe in the substitutes they have picked up, who refuse to acknowledge any inferiority, and who " try out " a substitute magic of some kind that is only a vestige of the full traditional magic. As everywhere, there are conformists and non-conformists by temperament ; and Dobu is the last place in the world where strict conformity might be expected.

It is interesting to note how the native explains the truly great faith of his overseas partner in him in giving him an ornament of the greatest value on credit, subject to repayment by an ornament of equivalent value and of the other variety some months later, as due to magic analogous to love magic which he exercises over his partner. It is true enough that it takes love to prevail against the native atmosphere of bad dealing with strangers, it takes love to endure *wabuwabu* without fearing it for ever in the future. As St. Paul put it, " love suffereth long and is kind." The native theory is not bad ; but it is the love of exchanging valuables, the love of exchange carried on in an extreme state of exchange intoxication, and not really a personal love towards a *kula* partner dandy such as the *kula* magic invokes, which is the force at work in this great and widely ramifying institution.

NOTES

1. *Bomana* is a term inflected with pronominal suffixes of possession. Thus *bomana*, his sacred prohibition to secure magical power or the sacred prohibition, etc., but, *bomagu*, my sacred prohibition ; *bomama*, our sacred prohibition. It is a *tabu* to secure power of a magical nature. It is probably the word *mana* in a modified form, combining as it does the concepts of *tabu* and power secured thereby.

2. To turn to the comparisons that have been instituted between the *potlatch* and the *kula* : it will be apparent that *wabuwabu* is sharp practice unlike anything recorded of the *potlatch*. Sometimes I believe that *wabuwabu* leads to actual non-payment of credits received. At least, when I went to Sanaroa to the south I was introduced to a prominent native, who had a large necklace believed to be free for him to give to me if he liked me, and liked the prospect of getting my very fine armshell which I had in Tewara (having obtained it some time before from the Trobriands), in exchange. My Tewara friends helped me with all their might to open up an exchange with this Sanaroa native policeman. He behaved so politely with a veneer of mission acquired courtesy that I was amazed to find a Dobuan behaving so remarkably like a Polynesian. He had a fowl slain and gave it me, although, as is the custom in an inter-Dobuan *kula* exchange, I gave no propitiatory gifts—only the promise of an exchange (and some small gift when later he visited me at home in my place as an understood thing that is never mentioned). He did not give me the necklace. He meditated over it all day. Then he announced that an Amphlett partner of his had played badly by him. This Amphlett man owed him an armshell long overdue, long unpaid. So long overdue was it that he intended to drop the man altogether in future. But while he had a valuable necklace in his possession he wanted to keep it for some months as a bait. Perhaps the hope of acquiring it would lure his absconding debtor into paying the debt, as nothing else could. Not that if the debt were paid the absconding one would realize his hope. Never again would he be given a second chance to abscond. He would give me the necklace, but only later on if I came for it again. As earnest of good faith, he gave me a minor valuable of the *kula*, a *sapisapi* shell belt, a ceremonial valuable that is inferior to armshell or necklace, as *basi*. *Basi* is a preliminary gift which obliges one to wait for a later gift of a superior valuable, and to hold one's own valuable in reserve against what is yet to come. My accepting *basi* meant that later I would get a necklace which again would precede my giving my armshell in return for it, together with an inferior valuable such as ceremonial greenstone axe blade in return for my *basi*.

At this announcement the evening ended in the best Dobuan manner. The moment the Sanaroa policeman had thrown down the *sapisapi* belt as *basi* and ceased speaking his speech of decision, a Tewara man took up the *basi* gift. My Tewara friends seated beside me on the Sanaroa man's house platform rose and said quietly, but urgently, " Come away." We all arose, and stalked away in injured pride, I somewhat amused but acting my part—no farewell greeting, and no more commerce with the Sanaroa policeman, though someone had the *basi* gift.

The unfortunate Sanaroa policeman, amazed at his fellow Dobuans taking a white man's part so viciously against him, followed in our wake. He poured out long streams of sentences to Alo's back, which was rearmost, Alo answering everything in an occasional sarcastically toned reply of " O " (yes). The Sanaroa man got nothing more than a rare and brief " O " to his voluble expostulations all the way to the seashore. When we arrived there everyone sat about, cutting him dead, no one would speak to him, he stood forlorn and finally went back home without farewell or any rapprochement whatever. Everyone remained vicious for some time.

At a later date his *basi* gift was returned to him by a canoe going from Tewara to Sanaroa on other business than the *kula*.

It appears that credit in the *kula* is sometimes damaged by worse sharp practice than the *wabuwabu* even. This was my impression of it. I only had two *kula* trips, one north and one south, in which I had experience of the *kula* as a participant. But I think that if I had carried it on over a long period as a participant I would have discovered much more of this type of situation that I found in Sanaroa. No Tewara man pretended that such hold-ups were rare. But naturally no man would recount his own misadventures. Pride is too centred in *kula* success for a native to recount such a story of himself as I have told of myself. And were I a native, and a man seeking to make an enemy of me asked me what had happened to my *kula* with the policeman of Sanaroa, even many years afterwards, then I would recognize an insult that was a deliberate challenge to the utmost. This pride, however, is not as the pride of the *potlatch* giver. Far from it. It is based on great having, not on generous giving. All giving is for equal return, and all fallen pride and shame is for loss of equal return.

Chapter VI

SEX

I

Native Theory of Sex

Without a love charm to arouse and create desire, desire does not exist according to the native theory. Men and women mate only because men are constantly exerting magical power over women, and women over men. If a youth's steps lead to a strange house at night where from inside an invitation on a jew's harp or a bamboo flute is playing, and the youth does not know who the girl is or what her appearance may be, nevertheless she has seen him and used magic upon him. Why else would his inclination go out to the unknown stranger? Even when, as more often, the identity of the girl of the house approached is known, it is her magic on the youth or his on her that allows desire its way.

I do not know many love charms. There are many, but I encountered great difficulty in acquiring knowledge. The Dobuans are almost pathologically jealous. The men believed that I had no seductive qualities for their women as long as I knew no love magic. A man without love magic is not a real man, only half a man. Because of their jealousy, and of their disapproval of mixed blood unions and of mixed blood children, they were determined to keep me without love magic. Their determination was the stronger because the women were jealous of the fact that the men were my informants, and that the male sex only profited from my inquiries. One night and one night only, the women in a body induced the men to get out, and my hut was filled with women all anxious to give information and acquire tobacco. Three or four times Kadi, Alo's daughter, seized a chance when no men were about, to slip into my hut and tell me gossip. She could not do so under Alo's eye, or when Kinosi, my personal boy, was about as one of the two was usually. Kinosi had married her and divorced her for infidelity. The two practised complete avoidance. Once Kadi, young and divorced, and Nela, Kinosi's elder married half-sister, came in when the village was otherwise deserted. On these

occasions the situation felt very electrically charged, as such
furtive visiting would have led to furious quarrels if it had
been detected ; no Dobuan woman makes such visit normally
except on sex intent.   No Dobuan man would not take advantage of it.   In my case, the women were expressing a feminine
protest against masculine monopoly in giving information,
but they were very tense in doing it, and only Kadi and Nela
succeeding in finding about four opportunities in as many
months.   The old women came more freely with the men
on occasion.

Towards the end of my stay I succeeded in acquiring one
love charm.   It is called *Kawaganutu*.   The forlorn lover lies
under his mat the last thing at night with a glowing fire stick
in one hand and an unlighted stick in the other.   He rubs
the tips of the two together, sending down a shower of sparks
and intoning as he does so :

> I knock
> I knock
> my spirit
> my double
> your go forth
> > (names the loved one)
> you lie with her
> you return.
> our sleeping mat
> we shall lie upon
> > at midnight
> do I see rightly, or I err
> > your spirit
> > your double.
> your mind is shaken for me.
> you wail for me in the dusk
> you wail for me at the dawn.
> > wanoge, the woman wanoge
> > > at midnight
> > rising and sitting erect
> > > my wailing,
> > > for me you are wailing.
> where is a resting place for your rest ?
> > where is food for your eating ?
> where is a sleeping place for your slumber ?
> for me you are loath to go forth in the
> > > morning
> > > to the garden or shell fishing.
> for me your wistful smacking of lips.
> > I sleep alone
> > I sleep with my wife.
> > I mourn for you,
> > sighing for you,
> > > my wife.

At dawn when the sleeper wakes he hurls his mat from
him with a loud shout "*wekani !*"   The absent beloved is
believed to start convulsively at this moment and to come.

The incantation calls upon a being *kasa sona*, Wanoge. Her name is most secret, her legend not known.

The charm is used not only in love affairs, but in recalling an absentee who has left a place for a time. I left Tewara to go to Bwaidoga at Christmas, '27, and it came out when I returned that the charm had been directed at me by the head-man. He secured my boots and a comb of mine to breathe the charm into. As usual the children did not keep the secret.

Other love creating ritual is connected with *Koiwaga*. By one account *Koiwaga* is a tree near Bwebweso, the home of the spirits of the dead. Its sap is potent as a love charm when placed on the body. It is fine scented. There is said to be one tree only—and it is not a tree as the trees of the bush—but a woman. Long ago she changed her form into a tree, to the help of all men since. In my notes I find record of a short conversation : " Why do you not take its seed and plant it here ? Bwebweso mountain is very far away."

" How ? As if it were a tree of the forest ? It is a woman." The tree's sap is the woman weeping for her lover who, in his hardness of heart, changed her from her human form into the form of a tree. There are various talismans said to be taken from this tree, but, I think, no more authentic than the wood of the Cross on which Christ was crucified still obtainable by pilgrims to the Holy Land.

By another account *Koiwaga* is a magical waterfall on Bwebweso mountain, the bereft woman having been transformed into a weeping water trickle. It is certain that much love magic derives from the *Koiwaga* beliefs.

Other love-creating magic again employs the *lamalama* leaves (*scaevola konigii vahl* or *fructuscens*) that are used also to influence a *kula* partner. In the love ritual, unlike the use in the *kula*, each leaf is divided down the mid-rib to symbolize unity in division. The charmed leaves are placed beneath the magic-maker's head as he or she sleeps. In all love-magic the spirit of the magician is exhorted to go forth in the night to influence the spirit of the beloved one. We saw this in *Kawaganutu*. In *Koiwaga* the association of the being *kasa sona* with Bwebweso expresses a like spiritual significance. The use of the charmed *lamalama* leaves under the head of the sleeping charmer is associated with the same concept. An old Dobuan dance song expresses the appropriateness of *lamalama* leaves and spirit influence.

> Woman of the North-East Wind
> Charging them on their way
> " Spirits you behave yourselves
> You behave, behave yourselves."
> The *lamalama* leaves I pluck.
> The maidens of Mumugwa
> As they sit sigh desire for me,
> " Spirits, you behave yourselves."

Here Woman of the North-East Wind, guardian of the portals of the home of the spirits of the dead, is portrayed as warning the spirits to be good as they enter Bwebweso. One spirit plucks *lamalama* to use love magic on the living maidens of Mumugwa, a real village near Bwebweso.

Love-creating magic has a clearer purely spiritual alliance than any magic in Dobu. It is in truth a far more spiritual technique than that of the black art for example, and this fact is expressed in its content, its alliance with thought of Bwebweso. Just as the lover magician can send forth his spirit to his loved one during his sleep, so also some magicians can send forth their spirit to enter Bwebweso and hold converse with the spirits of the dead while the magician sleeps.

In practice, however, love magic like black magic must be " tried out " competitively on its acquisition. It is no great trial to try it on a disengaged maiden. It should be tried to test it against the love magic of other men. Hence, the proof of love magic lies in the success of attempted seduction ; where another man's love magic has obtained him a wife there is a good field for experimenting with the strength of one's own differently derived magic. " Try it out " is always the first and the last word that must be said of Dobuan magic. The ladder of social ambition is that of successful magic.

II

NATIVE THEORY OF PROCREATION

There is no ignorance of the part played by the male in procreation in Dobu. Semen is believed to be voided coco-nut milk which has passed through the body of the male, and is ejected at the point of orgasm. This voided coco-nut milk semen is believed to fertilize the woman, causing the blood within her, which when unfertilized comes away in monthly menstrual flow, to coagulate and form the fœtus. A man drinking coco-nut milk to make himself potent is liable to have obscene jests made at the expense of his action. " My coco-nut milk " is the term meaning " my bastard child ".

The Dobuans know the Trobriand belief that procreation is from the reincarnation of spirits of the dead, not from the biological father. They say bluntly that the Trobrianders lie. The subject is not brought up between Trobrianders and Dobuans as it has been the subject of anger and quarrel too often in the past. My Dobuan friends warned me not to mention the matter in the Trobriands before I went there. Once I was there I deliberately made the experiment. The Trobrianders asserted the spiritual belief, just as Dr. Malinowski has published it. But the head of every Dobuan in the room in which I brought the matter up, immediately was turned away from me towards the wall. They affected not to hear the conversation; but afterwards when they had me alone they were furious with me.

With the exception of the part played by the seminal fluid, Dr. Malinowski's rendering of the Trobriand ideas on the physiology of sex applies also to the Dobuan state of knowledge.

It may be noted that in Dobu as in the Trobriands there is complete freedom for sex intercourse before marriage, and this freedom is used freely. Nevertheless, unmarried girls rarely bear bastards. In the community I know well enough to be certain of my facts, one child in about twelve in all was a bastard. This is partly related to the fact that a pregnant girl may become married before child-birth. Furthermore, means of securing abortion are effective, and are in general practice both by the married and by the unmarried. For a girl to bear a child out of wedlock is a great disgrace, easily as great a disgrace as it was amongst ourselves in Mid-Victorian days or in old Puritan New England. It may be true that conception is less frequent where a girl has many different lovers and mixes them freely and frequently. Nevertheless, sometimes the unmarried girls of Dobu become pregnant; I was told of definite cases. In these cases abortion is resorted to. One of the abortifacients is the dried root of the *ketomatasekera* tree (" entering-eye-squirting " tree). From this tree I preserved dried specimens which were identified by Kew Botanical Gardens as *Excoecaria Agallocha*. This tree is called River Poison Tree in Southern Asia. It is feared by wood cutters in Malaysia, in Cambodia, and in Southern India because if the tree is cut the sap is liable to squirt into the eyes of the wood cutter and blind them permanently. Hence come the botanical term *Excoecaria*, and also the Dobuan term " entering-eye-squirting " tree. The sap of *Excoecaria* is known to be a poison in Dobu. I was warned from snapping off a branch as I once made to do unwittingly, the warning coming from Alo. For use as an abortifacient a section of the root of this tree about eight or nine inches long, is smoked over the fire until it is shrivelled to about a two-inch length. It is then chewed and eaten. It is said to be a good abortifacient without any conspicuous weakening effect upon the woman. For using it once, Kadi, Alo's daughter, was severely beaten about the body with a club by her mother's brother, Kopu. A man feels that he has a right to a male heir from the womb of his sister's daughter. His right is socially recognized, and may be corporally enforced.

There are also other abortifacients. One root I was initiated into the secret of by Kopu and his wife, Nela ; Nela chewed and swallowed its thick outer layer, chewed and threw away its inner core, under my inspection inside my hut in the presence of her mother and her husband. At the time of chewing she was full breasted. Twenty-four hours later I noticed that she was absolutely flat breasted, her breasts like small flat plates. I called Kopu aside and commented on this. " That is the way of its evil—always," he said carelessly. Nela was not pregnant at the time. She had had one child which died. In all the rest of her ten or twelve years of married life she had secured abortion for all her pregnancies—I could not discover their number as I was on very ticklish ground. She chewed the root in my presence, since it is the custom to do so in giving a secret herb. The giver chews to show that the gift is no treacherous poison. The gift was for reward in this case. Unfortunately, my specimens of this plant were not identified.

These roots are used to procure abortion without the use of any magical incantation. As in the case of the *budobudo* poison (*Cerbera Manghas* or *Odallam*) they are believed to be naturally efficient. The idea of using magic with them is scorned.

There is at present a very great decline in the population of Dobu. Taking away the young men as a labour force for the white man has depleted native garden resources and made life harder to support than ever. Added to this there is a great and prevalent discontent with the payment of tax and tithe. I have not the slightest doubt that the decline in population is in a large measure deliberate race suicide, and for pardonable and comprehensible reasons. A man does

GIRL WITH HER YOUNG BROTHER AS CHAPERONE

CEREMONIAL COOKING

not flog his sister's daughter for using an abortifacient as easily in the Missionised area as Kopu flogged Kadi in solitary non-missionised Tewara. The new white authority is undermining the old native authority, and not reproducing its more intimate powers.

It is recognized that pregnancy may follow directly from sex intercourse. It is also known that it does not necessarily follow. There is no special magic for creating it. It is customary to use the same magic as is used to make coco-nut and betel nut palms bear fruit, to secure human pregnancy. Children are not as greatly desired these days as they were in the old days when the need of keeping up the fighting strength of the village was urgent and imperative. The spells used to create pregnancy are the one isolated instance of magic directed towards an effect which it is recognized may occur also naturally. It may be noted that the Trobriand ignorance of naturalistic conception prevents such an anomaly in the general theory of magic as it exists in the Trobriands. Whether the spiritualistic theory of conception in the Trobriands is a buttress of magical practice such as the spiritualistic theories of creating love or sex desire, or wind, and so on, are buttresses of Dobuan magical practice is unfortunately not certain. The Dobuan faith in magic proves that it can put up with a theoretical anomaly with ease.

And it will be clear that the Trobriand theory might have arisen with facility from a state of society such as exists in Dobu, particularly if rank were introduced in Dobu to make a legal conflict between *susu* and marital grouping more spectacular and its decision more widely known and accepted. The Trobriand turn of the wheel has not taken place in Dobu, however, whether from the kinship or from the magical direction of social pressure.

III

DOMINANT SEX ATTITUDES

The general attitude towards sex is in essentials that which in the present day and generation is termed Mid-Victorianism. It might be expected that complete pre-nuptial freedom in sex would breed a cleaner, less prudish outlook than that which we know as Victorian. The case is not so, however. Perfect freedom before marriage is associated in Dobu with a general attitude towards sex that can only be described as dirty, lascivious, and obscene below the surface, and rigidly decorous and euphemistic above the surface. The Dobuans fit exactly Havelock Ellis' remark, " To the people of the nineteenth century it was shocking to make vice anything but pretty, and virtue anything but comfortably happy. They considered it immoral, even punishable." [1] In Dobu adultery is considered pretty, and a very fine achievement. Virtue in marriage is the dullness of a fool. As it was in our own nineteenth century, sex is considered as fundamentally unspeakable, but nevertheless, as an intriguing lascivious achievement. It is remarkable how consistently shame, prudishness, and severe public censorship go together with a high valuation of the breaking of such restraint. Shame, prudishness, and severe puritanical attitudes seem to be the best breeding ground for the concept of adulterous cut-and-run episodes as most highly desirable.

There exists a minimum of decent language for sex in Dobu. The custom by which the youths go out to sleep with the girls of miscellaneous houses every night is called *loiawe*. That is a decent word although, as everyone knows, the youths have intercourse with the girls. The youths questioned, deny sex intercourse vigorously. By etiquette one is never allowed to mention a man's sex life to his face, and the questioner regarding the habits of the *loiawe*, is violating all native etiquette. By puritanical etiquette the questioner is necessarily told that the *loiawe* is chaste. The observer, who is not a missionary, soon learns how " chaste " the *loiawe* is. First come reports from youths that they never, never have intercourse in their *loiawe* ; but they are better than the generation before them, now married. That generation got the unmarried girls pregnant. Then a youth is going away for the night. His outspoken old father calls out to his departing thirteen or fourteen year old " with your penis O ". The youth looks as deprecating as he can. There is a dance song :

> " the cock is crowing
> my sweetheart embrace me
> dawn breaks hitherward
> your embraces are sweet to me
> my sweetheart embrace me."

picturing the situation which enjoins that an unmarried

[1] Havelock Ellis in the *Mentor* for January, 1930, p. 54.

youth must flee home undetected at dawn. Another dance song runs :

> naked, naked are you
> the morning star, the morning star speeds
> enough, naked be you.
> the morning star, the morning star speeds
> the widow woman of Bwatete
> your going away parallel with the shore for teasing
> enough naked be you.

where a youth is pictured in *loiawe* with an older woman, a widow—an object for teasing. Still another dance song begins :

> how did you come to spoil me

depicting a girl become pregnant, reproaching her lover for her condition.

It is clear from the sidelights that the *loiawe* is not the chaste affair it is made out to be to the direct questioner. The emphasis on chastity is due to a Victorian-like prudery of convention in speech, and in speech only.

To the anthropologist in his less specialized rôle, as an observer of the general social situation, it is interesting to observe how the Missionary accepts the stock lie of convention and believes the *loiawe* to be as chaste as universal native statement assures him it is. The Dobuan native is from the simple, faithful, pure, and good light of honest faith, a good soul, truthful and puritan in heart and in action.

Let now our anthropologist see his native through the Trader's eyes. The old, experienced, native-speaking, with-native-woman-living, Trader knows his man better. He knows just what native is living with and having sex intercourse with his own mother, nothing being done about it by the village concerned. He knows just where a youth on *loiawe* bent found the man of the house away fishing by night and was compelled by the wife of the house to have intercourse with her as a necessary preliminary to his being allowed to have intercourse with the daughter of the house. He knows just who, in attempting to rape a woman, had his penis broken by the woman, damaged irrecoverably for life. He knows that the would-be raper was indicted before Government and imprisoned for his attempt at rape, but his information about the damaged penis comes indirectly from another male native that the would-be raper, released from prison, has subsequently attempted homosexual relations with, and been betrayed by as to his unfortunate state, so that it has become quiet subterranean gossip amongst the native women. He knows how new fashions of speech spring up and die away amongst the native women so that at one time it is the fashion for a woman who does not hear what another is saying aright to ask for its repetition by saying " your pubic hair " ; whereas at other times it will be a different slang that will be employed in the same situation. The Trader is usually entirely correct, and gets to know more than the anthropologist can about such doings. He also discovers from the woman or women of his own how a Dobuan woman may teach her daughter that the way to keep a man faithful is to keep him as exhausted as may be possible.

Loiawe is a decent term in ordinary, everyday use. So also is *kenolua*, to lie two together, the ordinary euphemism for intercourse. *Kenoduma*, to lie apart, is the euphemism for sleeping in the same hut but without intercourse. All speech that is not euphemistic is obscene, however. All direct physiological terms belong to the *bake*, the obscene language that is used in abuse, and used rarely. It is impossible to speak of female homosexuality without using a word of the *bake*, *ginebwabwada*. The word for intercourse is a word of the *bake*. I once asked a man why he gave sago to X, since everyone agreed that X was an anti-social person, who never did his share of communal work, and since, true to character, X had skulked apart when everyone else was engaged in communal sago working. " If I did not give to him he would *bake* me." It is a weapon that can always be used as an insult without starting a feud in sorcery or witchcraft, but it is felt severely and comparatively rarely practised. My best informant was considerably troubled at my using the word for intercourse in a serious and not in a foul sense. He finally insisted on coining a word and if I must refer to the subject I was to use the coined word. Thereafter we used the word for grandparent as if it were a verb with mutual understanding ; but it did not clear the atmosphere substantially. I obtained a long list of *bake* terms from white sources, and tried them on my head-man seriatim to show him that I knew them one night. It had a most unexpected effect. I never saw him so scared. He was trembling violently in every limb before I finished, his teeth even were going and he said faintly : " You will not betray us, you will not." The only conclusion I could form was that the very complete set of acts which are considered perversions embodied among other terms in the *bake* probably had considerable foundation in fact, especially since the word for intercourse itself is a term of the *bake*.

Physiological reference apart from the *bake* is not much used in speech. Old women who have borne children are allowed by custom to refer freely to male or female sex organs impersonally in obscene legends that are not felt as obscene in their mouths, but only in the mouths of younger sexually active persons. Young male children go about freely shouting "with your penis" and replying "with your testicles", at each other. But, again sexually mature youths do not use such language. By convention, participants in sex activity must practise such an extreme of decorum as to publicly banish sex out of existence. Privately two or three young men often interchange private obscenities that send them off into long roars of obscene sounding laughter. I was not admitted into any such obscene fraternity, however, and I know nothing of the very private obscenity of the young men. Married men do not indulge in this practice, and such men were my best informants.

A man is allowed to maintain a joking relationship with his father's sister and with his father's sister's daughter ; but the joking never approaches the *bake* in its direct physiological terminology. "How and why should I give my tobacco to a grass skirt" is the current type of joking reference that a man normally uses to a woman who is his joking relative. Body-handling such a woman takes place only on rare festive occasions, and speech never touches her more intimately than a reference to her breasts or to her grass skirt such as is not permitted, mild as it is, to any woman other than a joking relative. There is nothing in Dobu of as fully fledged joking as the Trobriand "it is well that the nephew should lie with his father's sister", although the joking takes place between the same relatives in Dobu as in the Trobriands.

A common euphemism for intercourse in the Dobuan is *tokumali* used as a verb. As an adjective the same word means diseased or evil or bad.

Bake is used in cases of extreme quarrel between man and wife. A man in my vicinity suspecting his wife of adultery said to her : "Go, have intercourse with the wild boars of the bush," using the *bake* word for intercourse, no euphemism. His wife took poison, the poison used for stunning fish. The fear of *bake* and suicidal tendencies flowing directly from it make parents-in-law particularly protective of their own child and particularly sensitive to the moods of their child-in-law, even to the extreme of a very ready irritability towards him. The fact that attempted suicide usually follows *bake* between husband and wife is fairly indicative of the shame that is felt at direct reference to sex life. Shame only, not suicidal attempts, flows from *bake* between persons who are not husband and wife.

It is a fact that intercourse between husband and wife is not thought fitting after child-birth until the infant is weaned. The wife and mother is kept apart from her husband for a month after she gives birth—in her own village of birth ; the husband meanwhile stays in his own village. At the end of the month apart there is still supposed to be no intercourse before weaning. From this *tabu* comes the motive for such action as a man holding his infant over the fire to die from shock, also a motive for the use of abortifacients. I had the greatest difficulty in discovering that this *tabu* was observed. Those I questioned were so utterly prudish that they declined to discuss the matter. At last I got two or three ashamed admissions that the case was so.

When I first broached the subject of abortifacients to Nela, with her husband's, Kopu's, connivance, an extremely prudish attitude was also shown. Nela, seated on top of a large flat rock outside my hut, literally bristled at the mention of the matter like a wild cat in defence of its young. Kopu's bringing her to hear such improper suggestions made the matter grave. Eventually it went through well, however. Once it was agreed to Nela lost her initial horror.

No man ever witnesses child-birth. I could get no in-information on the subject except a pantomime of one man imitating an old woman stroking down another man who imitated a pregnant woman. The men's enjoyment of the pantomime was illuminating. The impersonator of pregnancy groaned and shrieked in a mockery of pain, the midwife impersonator stroked down the back and the hips of the seated straddle-legged pregnant one, and all the men gathered round roared with laughter at the pantomime release of their *tabu*.

The height of prudishness occurs in uncovering for the natural functions. After I had known him several months as my intimate neighbour I once stumbled on Alo in the act of re-covering himself with his pubic leaf. He was already sufficiently covered to be decent by the time I saw him. But I had evidently disturbed him, for he was completely enraged, too enraged to speak to me for the rest of that day. Even in an overseas canoe carrying a male crew only, a man goes over the side out of sight in the stern, and on the outrigger side, merely to micturate. On the *kula* a canoe crew or two will sleep on a small coral reef outcrop of about a chain and half diameter, and as I was with them, and saw for myself, one man will always take the greatest care never to be exposed in sight of another.

Coupled with this great shame of the bodily organs, this great prudishness in speech and these violent reactions to obscene abuse, goes a lascivious delight in cut-and-run adulteries and seductions.

Whenever a woman alone in the bush hears a rustling sound approaching she runs for the village at top speed. If she remains careless of the intruder, and the intruder happens to be a man, he knows that she, by the very act of not running, has welcomed his approach. She may feign to run at the last minute when it is too late. The man then seizes her and a feint of violent seizure is performed. At one stage of my field work I believed that this was rape. It is not, however. All men agree that a women seized so never cries out or screams, or tells her husband afterwards. Three or four times I startled a woman in the bush. Always they were off like startled hares before I saw them. Once I went straight to the village and found an old woman panting there from her quick run up the hill. She had loitered behind her companions gathering bush windfalls. It is clear enough that a woman seized is a woman who does not care to get away, with some possible rare exceptions. One informant told me that standing intercourse in the posterior position was the rule in such encounters in order to enable the pair to break away quickly in case of intrusion.

It is because of this custom of casual bush encounters that a husband in Dobu tends to fall into the habit of mentally timing his wife when she goes off in performance of the natural functions. Extreme jealousy takes the form of the husband who insists on going with his wife into the bush when she goes to exercise the natural functions. Such action shocks Dobuan prudish feeling profoundly. It is pathological, but it represents the form that pathology in Dobu is likely to assume.

Tempting a woman into adultery by secret offer of an armshell is also sometimes done. Sometimes two men are associated in the seduction of a woman covertly in the bush. One stands sentinel while the other has connection with the woman. Then the rôles of the men are reversed. Two youths are sometimes also associated in a *loiawe*. Such action is not normal, however. The normal pattern is competition between the men with rivalry and jealousy and no alliances.

There is a high valuation placed upon sex by men and by women alike. There are words for all manner of sex play that are preliminary to intercourse normally, although some exist in some individuals as perversions. Free pre-nuptial sex affairs in almost unlimited number place a premium upon skilful technique as an avenue to marriage. Marriage itself, and jealousy in trying to preserve its limitation of fidelity, are the general rule. Polygamy was very rare and does not exist nowadays. In the old times it occurred not only rarely, but with much bad feeling between the two wives of one man, who kept strictly each in her own separate village, except to fight each other by arranged duel on occasion, the duels being of a semi-serious nature resulting in minor wounds.

Persons who have not ringworm skin object to mating with persons whose skins are disfigured with ringworm, and whose body odour is evil from ringworm. Ringworm is one of the great calamities of Dobuan life. It is impossible to say whether the dark skin or the light skin is most admired. Both exist in extreme forms and both are admired. Albinoidism is an even worse fate than ringworm. A man who runs amuck may have difficulty in finding a wife. And to close the list, old men do not marry with young women, or old women with young men. White men present the only cases of corpulence known to the natives. Corpulence is regarded with disgust. All defects are defects against marriage, not by any means inhibitory of casual sex encounters, as also in the Trobriands where Dr. Malinowski has discussed the fact that albinos, whom no one would marry, frequently bear children.

The freedom in sex does not appear to encourage neuroses of sexual content. I did not see or hear of any one such case in Dobu, although in the Admiralties which has a prudish sex life without individual freedom, I both saw and heard of many. There were aberrant persons in Dobu, but apart from pathological jealousy in a few cases aberration took non-sexual paths. The most interesting fact of Dobuan sex life, however, is the fact that complete pre-nuptial freedom is accompanied with the utmost prudishness and shame in speech and in social convention, a most interesting divorce of action and theory, and one striking case to be placed beside other such divorces of action and theory as we have already seen in Dobu.

In married life, however, the prevalent prudishness and shame accord very well with the concept of the prettiness of petty cut-and-run adulteries. Here theory and action are in reasonably congenial company. Despite the premium on unfaithfulness and its counterpart, jealousy, there are some marriages that are happily contracted and happily preserved. They are a small minority but it would be unfair not to mention them.

A case of a marriage for love despite the cost was that of Obediah. He married within the prohibited degree, his cross-cousin. In her place, his dead father's place, he had to live on the outskirts of the village, unable to enter it. Worse still she had a very inadequate stock of seed yams and an inconspicuous garden. In marrying her Obediah was marrying hunger. His kin refused their sanction, warning him of inevitable hunger. He outraged his own kin, who refused to give public recognition to the marriage. He could not enter the village of his wife's kin to speak to them, though he lived on the outskirts of their village for the beginning of his married life rather than with his own kin. He had only his wife, and she was an economic drag on him, and a source of real unmitigated hunger to gnaw him constantly. Yet he married her, and clave to her. One Sunday I know his kin fed Obediah, but with insult to accompany the food, such insult as is usually intolerable to a Dobuan native, insult directed against his wife and his marriage ; and none the more tolerable in that it was merely true statement of fact.

CHAPTER VII

DANCE AND SONG

The Dobuans do not dance very often. The group that
I lived amongst danced only for three nights in five months.
There is no great dancing season at harvest time as in Basima,
Fergusson Island, Goodenough Island, and in the Trobriands.
I was in Dobu Island for a month while harvesting the year's
crop was going on—but there was no dancing. The village
is not specialized for dancing. There is a central graveyard
—ringed about by huts—no central dance plaza as in a
Trobriand village.

The Basima neighbours of Dobu on Fergusson Island
are great dancers, for ever dancing. The dour Dobuans
despise them—" the root of laughter they ; and the men talk
freely in public with the wives of their friends ".

There are some special dances for special events such
as the dance with the skull of the dead, already referred to.
At *sagali*, the culminating mourning feast, there is a special
dance in which croton leaves are held quivering in the hands
of the dancers. These two forms of dance I did not see.

In the ordinary dance such as I saw at the end of sago
working in preparation for the *kula*, and at the conclusion
of a *kula* expedition to Sanaroa, and also, the same form of
dance amongst the Basima people at harvest, the men form
a circle, facing inwards, and stand beating their drums and
singing a dance song. The women trip around the outside
of the ring. Towards the conclusion of a dance the drum
beats quicken, the women's pace increases and one or two
men break into the interior of the drum circle to time a conclusion. There is a brief respite. Then the drummers take
up a new song, a new dance. So the dance goes on usually
all night long.

The Basima form is very little different. The circle of
drummers bend down to a squatting position, hissing at the
conclusion of a dance. The Amphlett form is also very little
different. There, when the drums quicken the time, the women
cease tripping round the outside of the circle of men, but
face in towards the inner circle and rise and fall to the rhythm,

bending from the knees and swinging their arms. They keep the entire torso otherwise entirely still, and very statuesque they look.

Such differences in form are minute, but it is very humorous to watch Dobuan men trying to imitate the Basima conclusion, or Dobuan women trying to imitate the statuesque Amphlett conclusion. They are hopeless at imitating it properly and can only give a burlesque.

The interesting point is the dance song. Every Dobuan is a song-maker. Any interesting event calls forth a number of songs. There is very little imitation, very little use of poetic verbal counters. The form is more or less stereotyped as in our sonnet form; and there is as much emphasis on originality of content and of words used for expression as in our own literary tradition. The song-maker is proud of his creation, proud of its originality, and he has rights to prevent others from using his song, at least for a while. The song-maker must give his permission before his song is used for the dance. Later on it may gain currency in far-away places, for the songs are sung everywhere, on canoes and about the land after they have been danced to. Many of the songs are love songs actually first used in love-making. Serenading is the normal preliminary step in wooing.

ku eona be nuanaia	tell her to bear in mind
badilai gomwagwaia	at badilai bay
lawelawe ku eonai	the beloved (married to another) tell her
ku eona be nuanai	tell her to bear in mind.

'u eona be nuanaia	tell her to bear in mind
maide kalikalikebe	with her serving companion
kewa kewo i gelubi	let him bring a canoe and embark
i talakedekededama	that we meet on the way
lawelawe 'u eonai	the beloved (married to another) tell her.

The form of this song is fairly typical (I use letters to represent line units, not rhymes as in formal description of our own poetry)

a
b
c
a

these first four lines making the *kalena* or " root " of the song. Then follows :

a
d
e
f
c

these latter five lines making the *sipwana* or " tied on piece "
of the song.

It may be noted how *a*, the first line of the " root ", is a coda
which begins and ends the root and begins also the tied on
piece. Once the coda is announced, both in the root and in
the tied on piece, the lines proceed without repetition, each
line striking off a new phrase until the last line of each part
is due. Thus we have *b c* in the root, and *d e f* in the tied
on piece. Then the tied on piece is closed with *c*, another
line of the root than the line first used as a coda, *a*. It will
be seen that this is a fairly sophisticated pattern. That is to
say, its use demands a very good command of phrasing if the
pattern is not to interfere with the attempt to say something
and to express it well.

It has often been said that the demands of rhythm or of
symmetry in repeated phrase elements tend to reduce primitive
poetry to nonsense phrases of the " hey nonny, nonny " type,
so that probably most primitive poetry cannot be interpreted
into English. It does not make sense in any language other
than the non-symbolic, meaningless language of rhythm.
Dobuan poetry is not primitive in this sense. It is certainly
the poetry of a primitive people. But the Dobuan has learned
to grapple with the problem. He has accomplished a solution
of rhythmic demands, the demands of symmetry in repeated
elements and the maintenance of the statement of an idea
in simple everyday language. Every word in the above song
is a simple everyday word. Only one word, *gelu*, to embark,
is furbished up by the addition of a meaningless suffix, bi,
which is probably suggested by the fact that the last word
of the preceding line ends in *be*. With the word *gelu* so extended the line " kewa kewo i gelu-bi " has exactly the same
number of syllables as the other lines of the tied on piece
" maide kalikalikebe " and " lawelawe 'u eonai ", and one
syllable less than the other two lines " 'u eona be nuanaia "
and " i talekedekededama ". Notice also how the coda of the
root is stripped of its final syllable when it ends the root. So :

> *lawelawe ku eonai*
> *ku eona be nuanai*

have exactly the same number of syllables, the same rhythmic
stresses, and the same last syllable, *nai*, to both lines (*nuanai*
being clipped from *nuanaia*).

In brief we have a close regard to rhythm, formal pattern,
assonance, and meaningful statement ; and all the distortion

of language in the song is confined to adding one meaningless assonance syllable to one word. For the only other change, the clipping of *nuanaia*, to *nuanai*, is just such a clipping as is often done in everyday speech.

The formal pattern is not absolutely stereotyped. The following song has a three-line root and a four-line tied on piece :

bomatu kana numega	from the cliff of the north-east
gaura dobutu doro	the cave booms seawards
bomatu kana numega	from the cliff of the north-east.
eiagu kenokeno	my sister-in-law sleeping
kana kuia gisigis	his red hair
ya keno lonuwenaia	I slept dreaming of it
bomatu hana numega	from the cliff of the north-east.

Here we have the form :

                    a
                    b
                    a

                    c
                    d
                    e
                    a

where a coda, *a*, is used for the opening and closing of the root and for the closing of the tied on piece. No assonance is used. There is no word clipping. There is no variation upon the words of everyday speech. The articulation between the root and the tied on piece is not obvious. It may be intended that the sound of the sea booming awakened the dreamer, or else that the woman of the song is thinking of her man of the red hair being abroad on a sea voyage. The coda, *a*, and line *e* have one syllable more than the other lines *b*, *c* and *d*, which agree in their number of syllables. The rhythmic element in the lines in this song, as in all of them, can only be indicated by the syllabic congruence of the lines. They have no unity in terms of feet as in our own poetry. Thus scansion is as follows :

No unity by scansion exists. There is no concept of rhyme, only occasional assonance.

We have considered two love songs. We may now turn to a song of a different type. It will be recalled that in the Dobuan, the term *tabu* means a charm of the black art efficacious in causing a disease or a disfigurement.

bomatu i toatoa	the east wind is blowing
mwagwa waleanama	fish hawk he swoops down hither
waleawaleanama	swoops, swoops down hither
bomatu i toatoa	the east wind is blowing
segatu 'u kotebe	don your red dance skirt
susuio yagumaradi	your young breasts come newly
tabu i mudalinaia	the tabu will rend them
mwagwa waleanama	fish hawk he swoops downward.

The form is here :

a
b
b modified
a

c
d
e
b

It is a slight variation on the form of the first song cited. There are no abnormal word forms or clippings. Line *b* modified is a part of line *b* as first stated with re-duplication of the part retained—a frequent poetic technique in the Dobuan. There is one word in the song, *yagumaradi*, that I do not know elsewhere, but such negation of my knowledge is not necessarily significant although I speak Dobuan fluently. Unusual, or archaic or foreign words are freely used in many songs, although this song is the first to be cited that opens up such a possibility.

The quality in this song cannot be very well appreciated at sight. More than half the native delight in it lies in the picture of the young girls out for the dance, their beautiful bodies anointed and glistening, and all clad in their spectacular and fine red dance skirts. The native appreciation of youth lies behind the song. Women who have borne children are said to have their beauty spoiled by child-bearing, even though to a European eye they are still beautiful.

The contrasting blackness and gloom of all that pertains to the black art, the characteristic long-drawn out melancholy of mourning that most thoroughly pervades Oceanic life, must be appreciated emotionally before the contrasting elements of youthful dancing, brightness and gloomy resignation to evil that the song evokes, can be fully appreciated. There is one painting of a Tahitian woman by Gaugin that expresses something of this spirit. But neither the emotion of the song nor the emotion of a picture can be conveyed very well or adequately on paper.

i lulu i lululaga	he is singing, singing inland
natuwa lekawaega	from the straights of natuwa
suau i lululaga	black satin bird singing inland.
'lologea i kwaia	at kelologea one lies dead
mwatebu gomagweine	mwatebu, the maiden
kewabum ladiladi	her mourning sweet sounding
i lulu i lululaga	he is singing, singing inland
suau i lululaga	black satin bird singing inland.

This song of mourning is in the form:

a
b
c

d
e
f
a
c

The use of the *l* sound should be noted. Almost the entire song is pervaded with it. Only one line *mwatebu gomagweine* is without it. In the translation the *s* sound replaces it somewhat.

lulu	is to sing
lekawa	is a sea strait
ladiladi	is sweet sounding
but *laga*	is inland.

One word, *kelologea*, a place name, is clipped to *'lologea* in the song. Lines *a* and *b* have one more syllable than lines *c*, *d*, *e* and *f*, which agree. There is no use of uncommon words, although the word *ladiladi* belongs to one Dobuan dialect only. In none of these songs has there been a single meaningless word.

The emotional ending of this song again cannot be rendered. I have not listened to the song of the black satin bird myself as it was a bird very rare in the island in which I lived. But I have sat concealed in the bush, careful not to break in upon the mourner, doing nothing but listen to the musical cadences of mourning (not at death, when mourning is too real to be an art, but afterwards). Most truly Dobuan mourning is as fine as finest bird song. The simile of the song is not tenuous or unjust.

It will be recalled that the widower's song is sung at the expiration of mourning when the widower is about to be parted finally from his children, who must remain in their dead mother's place. Their father, on the contrary, must never again enter the place of his dead wife and of his living children.

kenolokenologwai	lie awake, lie awake and talk
maniuniuwanina	at the midnight hour
u gimi kenologwai	first lie awake and talk
kenolokenologwai.	lie awake, lie awake and talk.

maiwortu kam gatu	maiwortu your charcoal body covering
mwaniwara kubunaia	by mwaniwara below
tomwai i bwegabwegai	dawn breaks from the night
u gimi kenologwai	first lie awake and talk.

The form is :

a
b
c
a

d
e
f
c

Keno, meaning to lie, is used as a part of many compound words in ordinary speech. In this song it is used with *logwai*. *Gwai* means to talk. The prefix *lo* conveys the meaning of securing or of catching while one can—hence *keno-lo-gwai*, to lie securing an opportunity still for talking.

In the last two lines of the *sipwana*, the tied on piece, an assonance is made between *bwegai* and *logwai*. There is also a fairly subtle reference. The following morning before the widower is led out of his dead wife's village never to return, his body is washed from its black charcoal covering, anointed and adorned—hence " dawn breaks from the night " refers not only to the time of his departure, but also to the manner of it ; his black charcoal body covering is compared to the night. His shedding of his body charcoal would be referred to as *oona i bwegabwegai*, his body appears out from it, just as dawn appears out of night is *tomwa i bwegabwegai*. There is some reduplication of words in this song. *Kenologwai* is reduplicated in its first two parts. So is *bwega*. Dawn breaks is ordinarily *tomwai i bwega* merely. *Bwega* is not reduplicated as *bwegabwega*, as ordinarily it might be reduplicated, but as *bwegabwegai*. Thus an assonance is made with *kenologwai* and also with *tomwai*. Reduplication is used in ordinary speech to signify continuity, in the present or in the past, or the present passing over into the future. This is just what the song intends to convey. The reduplication is musical, but it is not a musical *tour de force* at the expense of meaning in this song.

To one who has seen how the village bury their dead when death has stricken a child or a person still in his or her prime, how the entire village seems to lose its manhood and carry the dead to the grave as if they were cowering under a whipping, how afraid they are of the night in the nights that follow, and how finally they recover their equilibrium in a series of feasts, the song of the dance re-appearing when dancing is once more permitted at the final feast, *sagali*, carries some feeling with it. The spirit is pictured on its way to Bwebweso, the home of the dead. It is fête day in Dobu.

bwebweso lagalaga	I go hillwards to bwebweso
dokwabu saliwina	by dokwabu's white sagusagu flower
bwebweso lagalaga	I go hillwards to bwebweso.
saliwisaliwina	the white, white sagusagu flower
saliwega ya mwera	from the palm I have climbed
ya keseasearu	I look out upon the path behind me,
dobu ya mweroroi	I mourn for dobu.

The form is :

a
b
a

c
d
e
f

This form is aberrant in that the tied on piece has not the coda. The feeling for expression of a statement has broken through the usual formal demands, and the lines of the *sipwana* move steadily towards a conclusion that carries its own sufficient sense of finality of statement. If the repetition of the coda in the root is poetically justifiable, as I think it is, there is not a word wasted. All the words are those of simple everyday speech. Every line has exactly the same number of syllables except the last line. This line is one syllable short, a technique that adds much to its convincing use as a closure.

All the songs are not as simple to me as those quoted. I have cited for analysis only examples of songs that employ one or the other of the two dialects of Dobuan which I speak and understand. But there are four of five local dialects and there are many songs which contain a word or two which I have never heard used colloquially. They are in many cases colloquialisms of another dialect, in a few cases introduced words of another language used for rhythmical purposes ; and also in some cases they are archaic. The speed with which words may become archaic in Dobu is extraordinary. Old men use at least from three to five words in a hundred that young and middle-aged men never use. A few differences in vocabulary cling to the old invariably and universally, as Victorian manners in dress cling to a very few of the old amongst ourselves. So that if an invisible person is overheard using a certain term in Dobu the hearer may know immediately that the speaker is a grandfather. Certain terms indicate a local dialect and the place of the speaker ; and just as certainly other terms indicate age of the speaker within the one local dialect.

I do not know all the dialects. Even less so do I know all the terms of the very old in the various differing dialects. Those who sing songs which contain archaic words, words in process of disuse but still retained by the aged of other dialects, usually know what the words mean, because they are interested in the meaning of dance songs ; but very frequently they cannot characterize the uncommon word as to its origin in place or in time. There are several possibilities always, and it requires more academic interest than the natives possess to unravel them. But it must be emphasized that the presence of such words, difficult to me, does not mean at all that the songs contain jingles, music for music's sake. That they do not. My difficulty is only with one or two words in a song containing, from fifteen to twenty words in all. I cannot place such a word. My native informant cannot place it ; nevertheless, they know that it has an exact connotation and they usually know exactly what that connotation is. With this explanation I pass to such songs, where for a word or two I may be utterly dependent on my informant's rendering of a term obscure to me. There is no evidence to prove that such terms proper to other places are used by a song-maker in a place where the term is not colloquial. I only heard three or four songs coined by the people of my own place ; they kept entirely within the limits of their own dialect and age generation usage of terms. It is probable that the songs containing an element or two foreign to me are of foreign origin, for dance songs spread all over Dobu. The differences between the dialects are not sufficiently great to cause more than sporadic non-comprehension of occasional terms.

kana kwadima panamoti	o star of panamoti
kebwaga i oleole	the south night wind ascends
panamoti kana kwadima.	o star of panamoti.
bwaruada ya tolaiane	at bwaruada I disembark
kwadima egweguguia	star peering in the cooking pot
i saisai oleole	he rises and ascends
panamoti kana kwadima.	star of panamoti.

The form is :

a
b
a

c
d
e
a

The words *tolaiane* and *egweguguia* are not colloquial in my dialect.

The song records a canoe voyage to Panamoti in the east. Star of Panamoti is Venus, the evening star.

damasi budibudi	the deep sea palolo
kasa butu yoyoi	the village shakes from our running
butu yoyoinaia.	shakes from our running thither.
da geba doroebe	look there seawards
nabudibudiega	from their deep sea place
maina laulauolu	with yellow sunset glow.
kasa butu yoyoi.	the village shakes from our running.

The form is :

a
b
b modified.

c
d
e
b

yoyoi and *da geba* are terms not colloquial to me.

The palolo worms come once a year on to the reef about the time of the change of the monsoon, " the palolo rule over the south-east monsoon ; we take them from the reef, we cook and eat them ; next morning, dead calm ; then the north-west monsoon comes." The palolo come in early November. It is a great day to the natives as the palolo is good eating, and signals the end of the south-east cool season which is generally disliked. The palolo correspond to our first spring flowers symbolically. For while the white man enjoys the cool season the native will describe it as wintry, a bad time and a time for huddling over the fire.

The following song is addressed by a Dobuan wooer to a woman of the Mountain, i.e. to a Basima woman. The Basima tongue differs characteristically from the Dobuan in that it is pronounced with a constant rising and falling inflection which is absolutely regular, a phrase rising, a phrase falling, and so repeated indefinitely :

kenagumo i wanea	my speech goes to your house floor
mukwai do gwali mumu	your flute you breathe to singing
do gwaligwali mumu	you breathe to singing, singing,
ya bwaubwau wanea.	I cry unto your house floor.
koiyakoiya kenanina	the speech of the mountain
i mwagamwaga i guma	refreshes like wind rising and falling
mukwai do gwali mumu	your flute you breathe to singing
kenagu i wanea.	my speech goes to your house floor.

The comparison of the rising and falling inflection of the speech of the Mountain to refreshing gusts of cool wind coming and going is a deftly turned compliment, and a fair simile.

The line *i mwagamwaga i guma* is not colloquial to me. *Wanea* is a Basima word. So also in the construction that uses *mumu* I suspect. This song is, I think, a bastard combination of Dobuan and Basima constructions, predominantly Dobuan. It is addressed by a Dobuan to a Basima woman. It is a compliment to her and to her language, and a few words of the " speech of the mountain " are inserted consonantly.

The form is :

```
a
b
b modified
a modified

c
d
e
a
```

tube gibwogebwobwoi	swim in close formation
siwabu i damanaia	siwabu is sunken
wa da tube gibwobwoi.	you swim in close formation.
bwebwesala ina saru	the bird bwebwesala's island
ta enaienaiida	we ask of one another
wa da tube gibwobwoi	you swim in close formation.

This song is in the form :

```
a
b
a modified

c
d
a modified
```

It is a song that was made during my stay by Alo. His canoe, Siwabu, was beached one night on a coral outcrop. Whilst all were sleeping the canoe floated off undetected. The flying witches had laid deep sleep upon all, then floated the canoe off. Such was every man's immediate thought once the loss was discovered. It was still night, but the men swam off searching. At first they swam in different ways. Then as they became frightened one sang out : " Let us swim all close together—the witches are at work." They swam to a neighbouring sandbank, home of the sea bird—*bwebwesala*. There they found their canoe stranded but with the outrigger broken off and drifted somewhere. In the morning they located the outrigger also.

From this song I learnt how the song-maker has property rights over his song. He must give permission for its use in the dance. The song was danced to at the end of the *kula* at Sanaroa, Alo being present and consenting. Like many songs it records history. There are many war songs that chronicle victories and defeats.

Form is subordinated to matter, as an assembling of the forms already demonstrated shows. We have discussed :

```
a               a          a                     a
b        a      b          b          a          b        a       a
c        b      b (mod.)   b (mod.)   b          c        b       b
a        a      a          a          c          a        a       a

a               c          c          d          d        c       c
d        c      d          d          e          e        d       d
e        d      e          e          f          f        e       e
f        e      f          b          a          c        f       a
c        a      b                     c
```

```
                          a
              a           b
              b           b (mod.)
              b (mod.)    a
                                       a
                                 and finally b
              c           c                  a
              d           d
              e           e                  c
              b           a                  d
                                             a
```

Thus, in a chance selection of songs, we actually do not find any two forms exactly alike. There is only a general common pattern, no rule of thumb pattern, no over great constraint of matter by form. Form is present in syllabic congruence of the lines, in the universal division of the song into the root and the tied on piece, and in the use of the coda. We need not discuss other songs in examination of literary structure. Those already examined are an unselected group. A number of others will be set down for their own interest in an appendix. Some of them throw some ethnological light on the byways of the culture.

CHAPTER VIII

LEGEND

Legends are not frequently told in Dobu. They are not nearly as popular as dance songs. They are told occasionally to satisfy curiosity on a specific point or, and more often, to while away a casual hour. On occasions of dignity brief and pithy legendary references are often made.

We have already seen that legend validates magic and that the characters of legend are often the spiritual agents which magic operates. Thus Kasabwaibwaileta, originally a great ancestral hero of the *kula*, is a spiritual being to-day, mentioned in *kula* magic directed towards enlisting the good will of a *kula* partner. A part of the *kula* magic is directed towards Kasabwaibwaileta specifically. " If Kasabwaibwaileta turns his back on us we get no *mwali* and *bagi* . . . but if he turns around, fronts us and laughs, our canoes sink beneath the weight of *mwali* and *bagi*." Hence there is magic to influence Kasabwaibwaileta, as well as the employment of Kasabwaibwaileta's name, and the magical imitation of his example of stripping off his diseased skin, to influence more directly one's *kula* partner.

One dance song runs :

i kita lebwalebwaga	he looks down the steep place
boiboi wa kawali	at night at your crawling
i kita lebwa lebwaga.	he looks down the steep place.
walada ya kesiwe	in walada pool I bathe
bwaileta kana bwas	kasabwaibwaileta his pool
ya tube numanumai	I swim drinking of it
i kita lebwalebwaga	he looks down the steep place

Walada is a pool in the coral outcrop, Gabuwana, one of the last reef outcrops on the voyage from Dobu to the Trobriands. There in the legend Kasabwaibwaileta was marooned by his canoe crew. From there he ascended to the sky on a star constellation.

In the song Kasabwaibwaileta is imaged as looking down on Gabuwana from such a height that everyone seems to be crawling there. He still exists and still matters.

We have already seen further that Kasabwaibwaileta is almost the only public supernatural of magic whose legend is a public legend, whose name is public information. Other supernaturals of magic have but pithy fragmentary legends that are secret [1]; but together with Kasabwaibwaileta we must place all the supernaturals of the winds such as Yarata, the north-west wind, in that their legends are public.

It follows that the great majority of public legends do not validate magic primarily. This function applies to the Kasabwaibwaileta legend and to the legends of the winds only. Other legends deal with the time of the first ancestors and the origins of things in supernatural terms without reference to the supernaturals of magic.

Legend in Dobu, while it refers to a historic past, does not refer to the past only. Just as Kasabwaibwaileta was important in the past and is in the present, so also fire was first obtained from a woman's pubes in the past and still bright floods of light of indeterminate origin in the night are said to be fire issuing from witch women's pubes. There is no sharp distinction between past and present in Dobuan legend.

We have seen how a span of about four generations only divides the Dobuan from the time of the first ancestors, the time of legend, and we have seen how this gulf is not stressed, so that a continuity of legend-like performances by the characters of legends is still expected and firmly believed in, read into the facts of nature.

First we may uncover the tale of Tobwaliton and Tobebeso, two supernatural fish monsters, who were credited with defeating the efforts of the local rain-maker in time of drought, when I was in the field, although an uninformed collector of legends might believe that they belonged merely to the time of the beginning of the world and of the first ancestors.

A mango tree stood rooted in Sawatupa (a place of Normanby Island near Mt. Bwebweso). They sleep, a man and his dog. Also his wife. Early dawn. He asks his wife, " You roast food and we (exclusive i.e. man and dog) go." She roasts food and gives it them. They eat. He and his dog they go, stand in the bush.

Inside the mango tree a fish wriggles. It comes out of a crevice. The man does not know what it is—perhaps a sorcerer? Perhaps a witch? He takes it. He gives it to an old woman. She roasts it. He says : " You eat it, try it out ; perhaps you will die ; perhaps not."

---

[1] Often not worthy of the name legend, and often missing from the tradition as it is handed down.

The dog takes a piece of the fish and runs off with it. The owner of the dog speaks harshly to it. He says : " Presently it will die." The old woman roasts it, eats it, finishes it.

The sun at afternoon she climbs into her house. She sleeps like one dead. Night falls. All sleep. It dawns. They say : " Women, you go parallel with the shore, go and see. Perhaps she is dead, perhaps she is well."

They go parallel with the shore. They call: " Respected old woman, you stand up." (Aside they say : " Perhaps she is dead, perhaps she is well.")

She stands up, she says : " Good food you gave me. What do you bring now ? To-morrow early you go and cut down the mango tree."

Next day they take stone axes. They go, they cut. All day they cut. The sun sets. They leave the tree and go to sleep. The tree closes up, it completes its skin (i.e. bark and wood) re-gathering it to itself. It closes up shut (as if uncut).

They sleep. It dawns. They return. They say : " Yai, how ? Yesterday we cut it and to-day how is it ? It is completely closed up again."

Again they cut. One slab of wood they cut out. A woman carried it on her head to the village. She says : " My board for resting upon." They cut. The sun sets, they leave it. They sleep.

It closes up again. It closes to—all but one piece, one without its mate (of a pair of pieces). Agape and the piece lacking. It says : " Ya ! Where my skin. Altogether I have collected it and one piece not. O, it is done. I am lacking ".

They sleep. It dawns. They go, " Ya ! there he has closed himself up all but one piece. Who yesterday carried a piece away on her head ? " " The small woman, she carried a piece away on her head. She went with it to the village." " Eh ! Likewise, we'll burn the wood cut out." They cut, they burn the cut wood. It falls night. They leave it and go villagewards.

It tries to close up. It is deficient finally. It is impossible. It dawns. They come. They say : " Yes, likewise."

(Cutting and burning the cut-out wood is repeated with good effect for some days until the tree is nearly cut through.)

The tree its width uncut is now small. They say : " You women who are evil in appearance stand on the tree's seaward side ; you other women who are handsome stand on the tree's inland side." They cut. The tree crashed sea-wards. It took up the evil-looking women, bounced back inland, flung the evil-looking women inland, took up the handsome women, crashed seawards and flung the handsome women seawards and into the Trobriands (100 miles away overseas, I may interpolate). Broad feet, paralysed feet, swelled skins and ankles, inland. Good looking women sea-wards to the Trobriands.

Here I must interrupt the movement of the legend to remark that this supernatural tree is conceived as rooted in Normanby Island and, after its felling, stretching all the way to the Trobriands. It did not kill all the ugly women by falling on them as was intended. They were placed seawards and it was felled for a seaward fall. All the good-looking women were put inland out of the way. But the tree defeated all intention by scattering the ugly women inland and the handsome women seawards and into the Trobriands. It is curious to find in a legend current in Dobu such a frank admission that the most handsome women in the area are they of the Trobriands, and that in comparison their own women of the Central Massim, including the Dobuan, are not nearly as handsome. It is true, and admitted frankly enough in the legend.

Good-looking women seawards to the Trobriands.

From the felled mango tree stretching from Normanby Island to the Trobriands, from its root water poured forth, water, water, water, and water again, covering the tree from sight, making the ocean above it.

Tobwaliton said to Tobebeso: "My friend, you remain, I go, the mango tree to walk along". Tobebeso himself was a fool. He gripped the root, the mango tree quivered. As it lay Tobwaliton walked on it. He returned and said: "My friend, you are mad. Stop it. Let me walk along it first. Afterwards you may grip it and make it shake."

Sword fish appeared. He passed over the sea making it calm. The fish *watuatuke* said: "My friend, you stay; let me go first and the islands of our grandchildren let me set down." *Watuatuke* fish goes. Madalabuna Island, Nedaonara Island, Tewara, Sanaroa, Domdom, Legumatabu, Segata, Kwaluia, Lesopi, Kotukotu, Iagaina, Similagaga, Wadana Islands he made and completed. He turned about to the Bwaidogu side. Samarai, Kwato, 'Anuabada. He came to Mt. Solomanaki. He meant to cut right through it. He lay on top instead. He wriggled, cut a lake. Inside the lake are now many fish. So he finished land making.

The water poured forth from the mango-tree root. They became afraid lest it engulf everything, and their efforts in vain. Their sister said : " E ! presently my grass skirt I shall take off and you shall see my pubes." She doffed her skirt. Vulva she had none. A *kalitabu* shell she took ; she charmed it ; lay it between her legs. With it they closed up the tree. The water flow ceased.

The woman said : " Done ". They said : " Yes, good, it is finished." They took charcoal. They blackened their bodies over with it. They dived into the water. The deep sea mist covered.

She charmed them. They became sharks and *kokoko* fish. They asked to come back to shore. She refused them harshly.

They, angry, made the sea bitter. Long ago we drank sea water and it was good. Shark and *kokoko* fish embittered it. Now enough it is bitter ever. We throw it away. And shark and *kokoko* fish still eat men.

It will be appreciated that this legend is a very mine of information. It tells of the origin of fish and of the sea, why Trobriand women are better looking than D'Entrecastreaux women, why sharks and one other fish (unidentified) eat men when they can, why the sea is bitter, how islands were made, how there came to be fish in the crater lake of Mt. Solomanaki, so high above sea-level.

The mango-tree is believed to lie still under the wide seas (unrotted, of course). " This is not legend just," said my informant vigorously, " this is everyday speech absolutely verified. Some legends we hear with our ears only, but this thing we have seen. Near Sawatupa, the root lies. We have seen the place. Our canoes are under *tabu* not to approach it closely at peril of the root opening again, more water coming forth, and the sea rising to engulf the level land and the highest hills."

My informant was exaggerating a little. For legends " heard with our ears only " are few. They do exist. But the great majority of legends are confirmed in just such " everyday speech " or sight. Tobebeso and Tobwaliton came back to frustrate the rain-maker. There is a *tabu* on approaching the site of the mango-tree root. The wonders of legend are not past. The world is still young. Much magic is told of in legend that is not done nowadays. But every now and again a man or a woman claims to be able to do such extraordinary magic as is done by the actors of legends.

My reader may have noticed how in the opening of the legend quoted above a strong solidarity between a man and his dog is evident. He tells his wife to cook food for us, exclusive, i.e. for himself and his dog. Later on, fish, being then unknown and suspected of possibly being poisonous to eat, he gives it callously to an old woman to eat and is enraged at his dog running off with a portion. The unfortunate animal may die.

It would be incorrect if it were concluded that this is merely a joke. It is not. A man normally cares more for his dog than for mere acquaintances. Also cases of a man spearing his wife out of affection for his dog, which she had treated shabbily over food, have come before the white courts. Not that a dog is not eaten in the last resort—that is always the case. There is a relationship term in Dobu to express the particular relationship between a man and his dog, a term that cannot be used in any other connection. I do not mean that wife-spearing is frequent. But it will be apparent that the man-dog relationship is socially important. In one aspect it has the point of helping the man to maintain his social value against woman's power in a matrilineal society. Women do not own dogs. The unfortunate animals have become involved in marital disagreements. In quarrels the man may break his wife's cooking pots ; she may be unkind to his dog.

To illustrate the fact that the events of legend are not left pigeon-holed in the past in Dobu, I shall cite two more legends. The remainder of the legends I shall give in a later publication, where the emphasis will be upon Dobuan texts with interlinear translation.

First we may take the legend of Nuakekepaki :—

The fleet of the men of Dede speeds. They say : " Where shall we drop sail ? " " At Tewara we shall drop sail, and lie with the women of Tewara. Handsome women are they, women of Tewara." They go. They would lie with the women. The women are unwilling. It dawns. They sail off to Gumawana.

(The same action then follows for the fleets of the men of Sanaroa and of the men of Waruma respectively.)

Nuakekepaki speaks : " I go, I shall see the women." They all said, Dede men, Sanaroa men, Waruma men, the same thing. I eavesdropped. All said, " They are beauties, Tewara women." His belt of *sapisapi* shell he donned, his armbands, his nose bone he inserted, his earrings, his pouch he fastened. A great rock moving under the sea is the house of Nuakekepaki.

(The owners of the village, youths like Kinosi, go to lie with the girls. They disperse scatteredly.) He comes to the edge of the village clearing. All the youths enter the houses of the girls and the place is clear. He comes out. He calls up : " Open the house that I may ascend." " Who are you ? " He did not name himself. " Open the house that I may ascend." " Who are you ? " He did not name himself. " Open, that I may enter." She opens the house. " You may come in, let us lie together." He says, " Not so ; you collect your belongings."

She collects them. She dons her best skirt, rolls up her mat, plucks off betel-nut. They go, they two. The woman says : " Lead the way." The man leads. They pass through Dilikaiai, Mwatuia, Guiaboga, here (Kubwagai), Kwatobwa, and descend to the strait, Gadimotu.

The woman asks : " Where is our canoe ? " " No canoe for us ; come, we put out to sea." The woman slipped off her skirts. He said : " Don't." Her mouth fell open.

They enter the underwater moving rock. It speeds away. They go by Yauyana straits. There the woman stays with her new husband's sisters They stay. Later on they go. A big overseas canoe sailed by the Tubetube men they capsize. They collect all the wealth it carries. (So they wreck other canoes and collect the wealth they carry, necklaces and arm-shells, *bagi* and *mwali*.) They return. They net fish, smoke them on a smoking shelf.

It dawns. They collect their wealth (fruits of high seas' piracy), *bagi* and *mwali*. Yams, bananas, pig, and fish they put up in baskets. With all his many relatives Nuakekepaki prepares for a feast. They go Nuakekepaki with his new wife and all his relatives. They enter Tewara (by a submarine rock voyage). They climb to her village. Her mother is wailing for her death.

She calls up to the house : " My mother." Her father replies (from inside the house) : " Who are you, who are you that call up so lightly ? Take your light speech from here. She who while she lived called ' my mother ' was a great beauty." [1]

---

[1] The father evidently thought a classificatory term of relationship was being used. Note his objection to it.

She says: " My mother, it is I." She (the mother) opens the house. She flings her arms about her. She says: " How whence are you come, my child; ye-e-e-e! " She cries over her.

She says: " My mother, as if my man lived on the heights. He is a deep-sea dweller. His name is Nuakekepaki. With our (exclusive) mothers we (exclusive) are come."

It dawns. They go down to the shore. They send yams, bananas, fish, pig up to the village. They cook there the feast given by the man to the woman's relatives (to publicly contract marriage).

It dawns. The woman's relatives give a return feast to the man's kin.

" Let us collect our baskets." They take their baskets and go down. They embark and go to their place. Husband and wife remain behind here (i.e. in Tewara). He refused his kin (the right to take him and his wife with them).

The woman becomes pregnant. She bears a child. He grows.

One day she says (to her husband) : " You go, fish with nets. With my child we (exclusive) go to collect food from the garden." They go, mother and child, to the garden. They snap off sugar cane, pull up taro, dig yams, and cut down bananas.

A man appears, an Owner of the village (*toni-kasa*, woman's classificatory brother). He says: " Where goes your husband ? " She says: " The man nets fish." He (the *toni-kasa*) gives her betel-nut, gives her tobacco. (This is never done by man to woman not of the same *susu* except for favours expected and granted by acceptance.)

The husband appears back in the village. The child informs his father. " Oh, an Owner of the village ! Very well, she's his wife. How ? As if it were my village ? "

His brothers come for him. He embarked and left.

Here we have again the motive of the helpless position of the man in his wife's place when she commits village " incest ", intercourse with a classificatory and village brother. Nuakekepaki has already been given some prominence in Dr. Malinowski's *Argonauts of the Pacific*. His underwater swift-moving rock is still one of the terrors of the seas to all the bold sailors who hug the reef between Dobu and the Trobriands, coming and going once or twice a year. Still Nuakekepaki is believed to capsize canoes in order to pirate their valued freight of *kula* arm-shells or necklaces. He began doing it in order to collect the *kwesi*, the valuables given by the man's kin to the woman's kin to publicly contract marriage. His marriage went the way of many marriages to-day. No one suggests that he is now repeating his matrimonial adventures. At least I do not know that any young marriageable women day-dream of his possible advances ; although such a fixation is quite possible in some rare soul. Someone occasionally breaks out with legend-based expectations or prophesies. But on the seas Nuakekepaki is a constant trouble. I once tried the rash experiment of looking astern from the stern, and exclaiming, " Nuakekepaki ! " Immediately every man's head slewed round in alarm, every paddle hung nerveless. No one thought that I was not warranted in being nervous. They all became nervous, too. Piracy for collecting a bride price has become piracy for the sake of piracy.

The last legend that we shall consider here is that of Weniogwegwe, the Great Dog.

Tokedokeket (a horrid ogre of terrifying appearance) ravaged the country far and wide. Many died a gruesome death. The rest fled to a remote island.

One woman is left alone. She goes on gardening. Tokedokeket appears daily whenever she cooks food, demands it, and gets it.

The woman grows fainter and fainter with hunger. One night in a dream her mother's spirit comes and instructs her to find Weniogwegwe, the great Dog, under the rubbish in a certain spot near the garden.

Next day the woman lifts the rubbish and discovers Weniogwegwe.

" Who are you ? " says Weniogwegwe.

" I am your master, one whose voice you hear and obey."

She cooks food in the garden, first carefully covering Weniogwegwe from sight with her grass skirt.

Tokedokeket appears as usual. " Give me my food." She gives it to him. (Weniogwegwe) Gr-r-r-r !

Tokedokeket takes to his heels, Weniogwegwe gives chase. Tokedokeket arrives near his home. His wife opens out her legs for intercourse. " No, we must run." They run into their house and close the door, blocking it up.

Weniogwegwe takes a stem of cat's-tail (in the Dobuan still called Wenio's tail) and leaves it projecting outside their door. Tokedokeket and his wife have no food and water but they dare not venture out. Every time they peer out they see Wenio's tail.

"You micturate, I must drink." "You defecate, I must eat," they say one to the other. Wenio's tail remains there. They die miserably in their hut.

The solitary woman sends up smoke signals. The refugees who had fled to the isolated island return. Weniogwegwe meets them. They offer him a spondylus shell necklace. He declines it contemptuously, "a binding for firewood." They offer him an armshell. He spurns it, "a woman's head-rest to carry loads upon". They offer him a ceremonial (too fine for use) greenstone axe-blade. He refuses "a splitter of wood". He asks for a wife. They give him a woman.

Weniogwegwe still roams in the bush of a dark night. He is as big as a house, his eyes are like glowing embers. One man I met had thwacked him on his huge flank with a paddle, and Weniogwegwe fled leaving him unmolested. But usually he is liable to devour a man that he meets. He is a source of some fear at nights, but only away from the village.

The Trobrianders believe in him to the extent that they know of him. Every year when the Trobriand *kula* canoes approach the Dobuan district of Bwaioa, the owner of each canoe utters the charm :—

> Floating spirit of the earthquake,
> (Nikiniki being earthquake)
> Duduba, Kirakira (names of birds),
> Thy fury ebbs away, O man of Dobu
> (and many like expressions until we come to)
> The dog plays about,
> The dog is docile.[1]

This spell abates the fury of the Dobuan man and of the Great Dog together. Its opening lines contain some Dobuan terms and towards the close we have reference to our supernatural friend, Weniogwegwe. He is not a supernatural accessory to magic. He is not controlled by magic for useful ends. He is merely guarded against in the Trobriand *kula* spell as also in the *tunaseana*[2] of the Dobuan *kula* magic. We see that public legend enjoys a supernatural world of its own that has only occasional contact with magic. Most Dobuan magic uses supernaturals whose very names are close secrets, whose legends are secret, and fragments or nothing, even so.

---

[1] For the complete charm see *Argonauts of the Western Pacific*, pp. 347–8.
[2] See page 226.

The supernaturals of public legend provide for some emotional situations in Dobu that are not derivative from magic ; not such omnipresent emotional situations as those arising from magic, it is true, but very real and also independent. The most noticeable function of public legend in Dobu is to sustain an interest in the marvellous. It provides occasional excitements other than those secured by magic.

Chapter IX

THE INDIVIDUAL IN THE SOCIAL PATTERN

Up to the present we have outlined the social pattern in its various departments, using individual cases to illustrate the pattern. Now we may envisage a typical individual in his progression through the culture, taking the case of a male.

At his own birth a male is for the first and the last time present at a birth. He is unavoidably present. Thereafter his presence in any house where a woman is in labour is avoidable, and he is excluded.

The child is born in the house of his mother's mother. The man does not approach the house while his wife is in labour or for the month following the birth of the child. Mother and child remain naked in the hut of the former's mother for a month after birth, only a few women of the mother's *susu* being permitted to enter. During this time mother and child lie on a long bunk under which a fire is kept going continuously. This custom is called " roasting of the mother and child ". The child is suckled by its mother. If its mother is deficient in milk the child suffers ; there is no custom of procuring a wet nurse.

After the month of " roasting " the man joins his wife and child in one of their respective houses. Now, until weaning of the child, the man is prohibited from intercourse with his wife. The child makes its entry into the world as a definite barrier to the intimacy between man and wife. The male child is not the man's heir. If the wife is barren or uses abortifacients, it is not her husband who may legally object, but her mother's brother who may flog her. Her son is his heir.

In consequence child-birth is often a delicate issue between husband and wife. It is my strong impression that while intercourse between husband and wife is prohibited until the child is weaned, other methods than that calculated to make the woman pregnant again are used. What is certain is that children are often weaned too young, the mother smearing a nauseous mixture on the nipples. They are fed early on partly masticated yams.

So, generally speaking, we may envisage our infant as wanted by the head male of its mother's *susu*, unwanted on the whole by the father, and usually not wanted by the mother. The mother is said to lose her beauty in child-bearing. To her own chagrin she is at a discount thereafter in love affairs. Discipline between elder and younger generations within the *susu* is essential to the continuance of the Dobuan people, and any antagonism to the legal status of the *susu* by white Mission or Government will lead naturally to depopulation.

The infant as he grows is made ashamed of allowing his natural functions free play in public. He achieves decorum at a very early age. He is slapped and left to cry without sympathy when he offends his parents upon any count. He runs naked until he is between three and half to four years old, when he is given a pubic leaf and taught to keep it in place. He is of no ceremonial importance except that an exchange of wealth between the kin of his father and the kin of his mother, initiated by the former group, may be said to be in the name of the child. The child is given no feeling of importance or prominence, however, even on this occasion. At any period between five and seven or eight the child has his ear lobes and his nasal septum perforated by his father or by his mother's brother. This is quite informal, and a small child may often be seen running about with only one ear lobe pierced. He is made ashamed to flinch or to cry out under such pain as ear-lobe perforation, but he still cries from " mental hurt " if he is punished for not being obedient or for any such reason. At this stage he not only goes with his parents gardening, but he is also given a small 6 feet square plot as a garden of his own, for his own managing under direction. He is taught small parts of garden magic, charms which he is taught to keep most severely secret. He goes off with a gang of small boys in the afternoon usually. The gang may fish in pools with small lines and hooks. The six- and seven-year-old have been taught fishing charms for the purpose—small charms for small children. Secrecy in keeping these charms, each child to himself, has been strongly stressed. The father normally gives his own child these small charms, showing it at the same time some such typical childish and unimportant trick as how to hypnotize a giant grasshopper with a certain technique, and a certain infant's charm—the lullaby his mother used upon him to put him to sleep when he was younger.

NEW HOUSE BUILDING

MOURNING OVER A CORPSE, THE END OF A HOUSE—THE LOGS IN
FRONT OF IT MARK THE CLOSE OF ITS USE

As the child grows to be about nine and ten years old he comes into a measure of manhood. His nasal septum and ear lobes are pierced. He wears ear-rings and arm-bands. The arm-bands were torture to him when they were forced over his elbows, a slow process for an hour or more—so tight they are. He is taught baby charms no longer, but the real ones of adult life. In three or four years the boy will be a youth courting the girls, and sleeping with one or other of them every night. He now learns real love charms in preparation from his father, and, if he has worked well in his mother's brother's garden, from his mother's brother also. It is no longer safe for the father or the mother to strike the nine-year-old boy. If he is struck, he will imitate his father and mother when they are engaged in a family quarrel. Imitating his father he will break his mother's cooking pots. Imitating his mother he will treat his father's dog harshly. Such abuse of household valuables is too unprofitable to be courted by the parents. The father, at the utmost, may hurl stones viciously at the boy. But the boy ducks and dodges deftly. That also has been a part of his recent training. Any adult may engage in a game of throwing dummy spears at a child, the child returning the compliment. The dummies are pith protected at the point, long but heavy enough reeds like a bulrush stem. They are thrown with greater force and precision by adults, and dodged with great adroitness. The boy learns to throw and to dodge. If it is stones hurled he dodges equally adroitly. There were no shields used in Dobuan warfare.

The boy, although now free from punishment, has been well disciplined in earlier years. He does not run away from gardening work in his parents' and mother's brothers' gardens, or if his elder brother is engaged, in his elder brother's parents'-in-law gardens also.[1] He is well versed in his obligation of keeping magic secret. Nevertheless between the ages of seven and twelve he is a power that is often courted by other stranger adults in secret. Has there been a severe illness or a death in his family or amongst his near relatives, then a diviner has been called in. The result of the divining may not have been made public. In that case various enemies of the ill or dead person will be uneasy, and in fear of the diviner having given their names to the kin of the ill or the dead as witch or sorcerer responsible. They obtain a kinsman or a close friend to try to " pump " the small boy of the family

---

[1] Except to work for a white man.

that summoned in the diviner. I have seen an adult in such case try to pump a small nine- or ten-year-old, for some hours, with I know not what offers of bribing. Again adult strangers may attempt to obtain the nine or ten-year-old's knowledge of love magic. I was awakened by just such a conference under my house wall once at two o'clock in the morning. I eavesdropped from my bed until I was sure what the matter was—the rhythmical repetition of magical formulæ. My astonishment was great to discover young 3 feet nothing teaching 5 ft. 6 in. love charms. At that early hour in the dark night they were too scared to leave the village. The side of my house was the most secluded place.

Again, the boy is a good confidant and go-between in the most private of love affairs. Just because the boy is not personally involved in adult life he is made use of as bribed spy and confidant in affairs of the heart, of magic, and of the underground war of the black art. His mother's brother alone dare flog him, and will not do so unless he takes that august person's coco-nuts or betel-nut without permission.

The boy approaching puberty now chews betel whenever he can get it. He has his teeth blackened with a black paint. He grows his hair long, combs it carefully, paints his face with black paint, oils his body carefully every night. Presently he goes to sleep with his young sweethearts at night. As he goes off after the evening meal his father may call after him, " With your penis, O." The boy is abashed, but goes off stoutly. In truth he is not yet sexually mature, but he knows the facts of sex well enough from sleeping nightly in the same very small hut with his parents. As a seven- to ten-year-old gangster he went about shouting freely to his associates " With your penis, O " or returning " With your testicles, O " ; but now that he is involved and is actually sleeping with the young girls and experimenting with his only half ripened sex impulses this same language does not pass his lips. The pre-pubescent girls of his own age have lain with boys older than he, boys of sixteen or so, on occasion, and consequently are more experienced than he.

The boy, come to puberty, sleeps no more in his parents' house. Every night he must go a-roving to find a girl and a night's resting place. Usually there is a young widower, or more frequently a young man, who has divorced a young wife for adultery nearby. This young man will have a house of his own which he built at his marriage. There the boys, temporarily out of humour for roving and wooing, or out of luck, may sleep. It is felt improper that a youth should stay at home where his parents lie together and where his sister must be left free to receive a lover if one comes that way.

For some years the boy has been learning real magic, that is if he is first-born and in the line of inheritance. At puberty comes the next step. He is taken overseas in the *kula* canoes. He paddles, and learns the art of managing a canoe. He sees strange places. After several such trips his mother's brother will give him a *kula* valuable as a reward for his previous services in canoe manning. He then enters the *kula* in earnest, a young blade of seventeen or so. Nowadays he goes away to work for the white man at this stage. He returns, and marries. His marriage usually goes on the rocks, as divorce follows infidelity, and fidelity is very very rare. Typically his wife will commit adultery with a village " brother ", he with a village " sister ". Both will remarry after their divorce, but not with village " brother " or " sister ". That is forbidden for marriage, therefore good field for adultery.

The infant is the heir desired by the *susu*, not desired by the marital grouping. He marries outside the several *susu* of his village, but commits the greater proportion of his infidelities within the several *susu* of the village ; so expressing in his married life, as in his birth, an antagonism to any marital grouping. At his death his corpse is buried by the several *susu* of his village, his skull is taken by them, and his spirit danced to Bwebweso by them ; and from the obsequies all others who are not of the *susu* of the village are rigidly excluded, his widow and former surviving wives amongst them, his children also. From birth to death the Dobuan is a *susu* dominated individual. *Susu* right is not a legality external to him. It is a part of him, and his emotions are moulded to it. I did not see any one conspicuous instance of father-love between father and son. It is the mother who mourns for the son who goes far away to work for the white man, who pleads with him not to go, and who loves him truly. More than once I saw a boy go away so. The mother, in one case, came out with a package in her hand. As she came near I saw her face working convulsively. She thrust the gift into the boy's hand without looking at him and fled away along the path still not looking lest he see her face. She could not look on his departure. So it usually is. The father was a step-father, as is the case more often than not. He did not care except for losing an economic asset. The blood-father was occupied with another woman and her, some his, children. He was long cut off, in feeling. Father-daughter love I did see, and it conspicuous enough to be greater than mother-daughter love in one instance. But on the whole passionate family attachment does run most strongly where it is legally supported, between mother and child, between brother and sister. It must not be thought that father-son love is the strong silent rebel against the *susu* system. Far from it. The great rebellion is from the often most passionate ties that are contracted in marriage. Brother-sister attachment within one blood family does not react very dangerously against marriage, as I saw in the Admiralty Islands. But in Dobu various *susu* own a local dwelling place. They attribute sorcery, witchcraft to all other local dwelling places. They are brought up as children to fear the places they must later marry into. The children who are members of the several village *susu* are playmates together. They trust one another far more as adults than they trust their respective relatives-in-law. They are organized to make marriage insecure. They are friends and yet not closely enough inter-related to feel as strongly about incest as true brother to true sister. Here the legally extended brother-sister tie acts as a serious intrusion into the marriage ties of the village members, who all reside side by side all their lives, with only alternate year excursions to live with relatives-in-law. Dwelling houses are all close together like tents pitched by a camping party, and, like tents close-pitched, hold secrets badly. It is marriage which pits private passion against an unreceptive village *susu* alliance. And typically marriage dissolves, reforms, dissolves and reforms, and might reform again after dissolution less were the means of suicide more effective. The alliance of village *susu* remains firm, cemented by local land holding, local birth, local death. The children pass out of the father's grasp. The firm, undissolving group possesses them, the dissolving group passes them by. The father does not care as greatly for a grown son as we expect a father to care in our own society. He does appear to care for a grown daughter in some cases. Here we find rebellion, but it is not as institutionally dangerous as is father-son love. It may be objected that I have stressed the inheritance of garden land and magic from father to son as due to strong father-son attachment. I did not, however, discover any conspicuous instance of such attachment between young adult son and father. That fact remains firm ; and I would stress the fact that the division of the inheritance between Boundary Man and his cross-cousin Owner may depend not only on a father's attachment to his son while the latter is yet a child, but possibly even more on the necessity felt for keeping the peace between an adult Boundary Man and an adult cross-cousin Owner when the father of the former, mother's brother of the latter, has passed away from the individualistic and quarrelsome society that is Dobu.

ADDITIONAL NOTES

In correction of some points, the plant called labuwara mentioned at the foot of p. 127 is an undentified cultigen, not uncommon in New Guinea, and is not a species of maize. The account of pre-marital courtship in this chapter is subject to the correction made in Appendix VIII. So is the view of depopulation in this chapter subject to the correction made in the same Appendix. In his work *Polynesian Religion,* pp. 296-311, under a heading "Seasonal Fertility Rites," E. S. Craighill Handy shows that there is definite proof of an association in the native mind of fertility rites with the thought of the return and presence of the spirits of the dead. The amorous parties for adolescents arranged in the Milamala or palolo worm moon in the Trobriand Islands and on Egg Laying Day in the Dobuan Islands are such fertility rites, not that the Dobuans celebrated the return and presence of the spirits of the dead as the Trobriand islanders did. There is a mistaken view, not only in this chapter, but in Malinowski's books on the Trobriands also, that amorous occasions for adolescents were secular, were continuous throughout the year, and were pre-marital courtship. Actually marriages were arranged ones. Again the view that the distinction between the kindred of the *susu* or matrilineage and the family was a cause of divorces may be corrected. The reasons of those who preferred their own arrangements over the prior arrangements made for them by their kindred may have included early deaths of spouses and a number of reasons which were not investigated in detail. It takes more than a few remarks to define or to characterise the Pacific island culture of the neolithic or of the colonial period. A remark on p. 135 that there was jealousy of possession in society or in the culture is not narrowly intended.

DOBU AND BASIMA

The social organisation of the Basima people who live at the seaward foot of Koyatabu, Holy Mountain, on north-east Fergusson Island is matrilineal in clan descent. Marriage residence is virilocal. The term virilocal means simply that wives reside in their husbands' villages—a former term with the same intended meaning was patrilocal. However as some husbands were not also fathers, and as those who were organised in localised matrilineal clans might reside in their maternal uncles' and not in their fathers' villages, the term patrilocal as it was used to refer to wives' residence in their husbands' villages was dropped. The virilocal residence of the Basima may be contrasted with the bi-local residence of the Dobuans; and in the first edition of this book this contrast was made, with brittle marriage and the fear of sorcery amongst the Dobuans attributed to the mixed company resulting from bi-local residence. Today it may be remarked that the bi-local residence of the Dobuans is associated more exactly with wives growing yams on their own clan land and residing on it one year, giving gifts of yams to their husbands' sisters in exchange for gifts of shell currency in such years, and in intercalated years not doing so. In the intercalated years the wives live in their husbands' villages and their husbands' sisters give them gifts of yams in exchange for gifts of shell currency from them.

In Basima the custom of interpreting the cause of deaths by reading signs on the corpse is practised. The procedure is nearly the same as that recorded by Malinowski from the Trobriands, but in a case witnessed the sister and the sister's child alone read the signs. The corpse is buried for only a few hours before it is unearthed for the purpose of sign reading. The signs looked for were one of the following:

PIG WALLOW. The deceased died of owning too many pigs.

GARDEN. The deceased died of owning too good a garden.

FIRESTICKS FOR COOKING. The deceased died of eating something without distributing it to others.

In this way the provocation for the sorcery or witchcraft that killed the deceased is interpreted. The first mark is a pig track with a wallow at its end, the second represents the garden space, the third the usual arrangement of firesticks in cooking.

It is not only in the type of divination after death that Basima resembles the Trobriands. The decorated yam houses resemble those of the Trobriands, and are not found in Dobu or elsewhere in Fergusson Island. The house is built on the ground, not on piles, as in Dobu and in the rest of Fergusson, and is of the Trobriand pattern. Polygamy is common amongst the leading men. There is one chief-supreme in title, over thirty villages—a degree of titular authority utterly foreign to Dobu and to elsewhere in Fergusson. The chief in Basima is only titular chief, however. He works his garden with his own hands and receives no tribute. But he is generally recognized in all villages, and wears more ornaments than is allowed to anyone else. Dobuans in Basima recognize a plant important in Trobriand garden magic, as also in Basima garden magic, growing about the Basima villages—not used in Dobu. Near a Basima village is a legendary hole from which the first ancestors of the village emerged—a tradition familiar to all readers of Dr. Malinowski's works on the Trobriands, but quite unknown in Dobu.

The Dobuan islanders did not practise post-mortem divination and they, unlike the Basima and the Trobrianders, did not dance continuously as a recreation for many nights in the moon following yam crop digging. Agricultural magic in Basima is in part identical with that of the Dobuan Islands. Yabowaine, Nabelita, and Bunelala are the main names involved. The seed *kwatea* are not cut into "eyes" as in Dobu. I brought out this difference with one Dobuan and two Basima men present. They treated the subject as delicately and with the same type of reserve as a non-militant but friendly Protestant and a non-militant but friendly Roman Catholic might possibly treat the topic of intercommunion.

Despite the agreement there is a measure of difference. The legend of the origin of yams describes how a non-gardening first wife burnt down the food house of a gardening second wife, the first gardener, and how the yams prompty fled, half-burnt, overseas to the Trobriands. The ritual is conceived as an Homeric struggle between the gardeners of Basima and the gardeners of the Trobriands for the possession of free-flying yams. Streams near the gardens are magically dammed up with miniature doll's house dams, but with powerful ritual to prevent the yams from this habit of embarking on logs and sticks, going downstream and overseas. Positively, yams are magically charmed to come from overseas on a big fish's back from the Trobriands. The Dobuans, on the other hand, considered that a pool of mobile yam tubers was local to their islands.

That is all there is to this story. As another point, however, it may be mentioned that in the first edition it was remarked in this appendix that the Dobuans dourly said that the Basima were "*Edagi kaledi*," the sources, origins, or roots of laughter. It was remarked also that, if detail of difference in tribal belief in myth and magic were pressed, agriculturalists might make invidious statements about the superiority of their yields to those of the members of another denomination. It was said also that Trobriand and Basima yields possibly were greater than the Dobuan. It is clear from Malinowski's introduction that he paid particular attention to these statements and indeed that he made more of them than was intended by them. With regard to the question of the quantities of agricultural yields, Tewara Island is stony ground, Dobu Island has suffered some depopulation, lowering the yields by the standards of 1891. The loss of yams is proportional to that of labour, but is not the more considerable loss. Normanby Island, the largest Dobuan Island, was not taken into this account. Basima is near Tewara Island. An environment was studied, and not a tribal area. Where it is said that in Basima the chief received no tribute, the statement may be qualified. He received gifts of agricultural produce from his affines in exchange for gifts of shell currency. Such gifts are called tribute by Malinowski, but his translation of the Trobriand Island term for them is not a correct one.

VADA

Christopher's account of sorcery by magical (i.e. hypnotic) cutting open of the body of the victim, abstraction of the vital organs, and closing of the body is confirmed, not only by Christopher's evident truthfulness about the secret poison, but also by several independent reports of such sorcery. None of these reports are satisfactory, but all embody parts of the whole that Christopher gave me.

First I may quote that collected by Dr. C. G. Seligman :

" Ahuia gave the following account of one method of killing people by magic, the sorcerers practising this method being called *vada*, though they were clearly not spirits or other non-human beings.

" One or more (often two or three) men who were sorcerers would follow their intended victim to his garden, or into the bush. There he would be speared and clubbed, and when dead cut to pieces. One end of a length of rope is then looped round the dead man's hand or knee, while the opposite end is steeped in certain ' medicine ' (*gorto*). This ' go along rope make man get up ', i.e. the virtue in the medicine passing along the rope to the dead man would restore him to life. Often the medicine of the sorcerer who first endeavours to revive the dead man is not strong enough. Then his colleagues would be asked to help. The dead man on his revival is dazed, ' he mad,' and knows not where he is, or what has befallen him. He is told that he will die shortly ; he does not subsequently remember this, but manages to return to his village, where his friends know what has happened to him by reason of his feeble, silly condition, though the victim himself does not know, and gives no account of what has occurred." [1]

This report comes from the Koita, a tribe 400 miles from Dobu, south and west along the south coast of Papua. It is evident that Ahuia is detailing the same practice to Dr. Seligman as Christopher detailed to me. Ahuia is described as clan chief, village constable, Government interpreter, a man with a good knowledge of English which he can write intelligibly. He is English trained, and as is evident, has some loyalty to the English in telling what he did about *vada*, since sorcery is punishable. He apparently gave the information with detachment.

Christopher has only some native prestige for his magical power, is not connected with the white man officially. He speaks no English, pidgin or otherwise, and has never been to school or learned writing. He has never been in contact with a missionary, white or coloured. He described a case of *vada* as a participant.

Dr. Seligman's account is as good as might be expected for one not obtained in the native tongue. It is greatly to Dr. Seligman's

[1] C. G. Seligman, *The Melanesians of British New Guinea*, pp. 170–1.

credit that he should have taken the scrupulous care to set down and record an account that appears so impossible on the face of it. It gives the confirmation of Christopher's account that is necessary to prove that the tale is not a lie ; and at the same time we have now a better understanding of the apparent miracle of *vada*. In Dobuan it is not called *vada*. It was called *wawari* by Christopher from the sorcerer's shout as he emerges on to his victim. *Wawari* is also the term for the yells used sometimes at night to scare away the spirits of witches that are believed to be detected approaching the village. From Christopher's eye-witness account we have, as well as know-ledge of the working mechanism of *vada*, the answer to Dr. Seligman's doubts as to whether the *vada* or *vata* is a human or a spiritual agency. It is emphatically a human procedure. What cast most doubt on this fact previously was that spearing and clubbing and restoring the dead to life without leaving any bodily trace, only a dazed madness, is impossible. Yet this is what Ahuia, Dr. Seligman's informant, stated was a fact and a human fact. Naturally enough Dr. Seligman doubts Ahuia's interpretation of what is human.

It is notable that Ahuia's account contains one omission. It is not stated that the sorcerer removes the vital organs of the victim before he is restored to apparent but dazed wholeness. This is found in the *vada* of the Mailu of the Papuan coast, east of the Koita and expressly stated by Dr. Malinowski [1] ; who also states that *vada* is a human process. [2]

Christopher's account is of the same procedure beyond all doubt. It covers the human appearance of the sorcerer in assault upon his victim (Seligman and Malinowski), the removal of vital organs (Malinowski), the restoration to apparent bodily wholeness but dazed madness and forgetfulness (Seligman). Malinowski's account of opening-up of the body, removal of vital organs, and restoration of apparent wholeness to the skin of the body agrees with mine, against what Ahuia told Dr. Seligman of clubbing and spearing and restoration to life. Christopher's eye-witness account betrays a magical opening-up of the body done with a wooden spatula, suitable only for cutting paper.

Dr. Malinowski, while he has recorded the belief in body opening-up, removal of vital organs, and restoration of the body, treats it both in his paper on the Mailu people and in the Argonauts as a super-stition not connected with any practical procedure. He cites the native belief that it is done humanly by a human sorcerer. There his information ends. But the combined evidence from Seligman's study of the Koita, and Malinowski's study of the Mailu, establishes the complete, more detailed participant's account of *vada* that Christopher gave me in Dobu. I had never mentioned either Seligman's or Malinowski's account of *vada* to Christopher or to any other Dobuan native. I had no expectation of finding *vada* in Dobu. I had used no leading question. My account fell from a

[1] B. Malinowski, *Argonauts of the Western Pacific*, p. 42. Also " Natives of Mailu ", *Transactions of the Royal Society of South Australia*, vol. xxxix, 1915, p. 649.
[2] " Natives of Mailu," ibid., p. 648, footnote.

clear sky out of my sorcery mentor's indulging in a violently emotional reminiscence.

From the north-east coast comes another account of *vada*, also. " A somewhat remarkable instance of native superstition is reported by Mr. Oelrichs, Assistant Resident Magistrate, in a district report relative to a murder inquiry held by that officer. Mr. Oelrichs writes :

" ' Rather a curious story regarding the alleged bewitching came out in the course of the examination of some men during the inquiry, and I found it was the general belief in the district (Maisina and Wanigela). When a man dies suddenly, it is supposed that when the deceased was last in the bush he was met by some persons unknown who, it is surmised, live in a swamp ; the man is caught and held by the unknown persons, and a vine twisted round his throat so as to throttle him ; when the victim faints the vine is released, and he is brought round by the application of New Guinea drugs and placed on his feet.

" ' One of the strangers then steps forward and says : " Do you know us ? " If the subject of the inquiry replies " No ", he is again asked : " Will you tell your people what has been done to you ? " Should he reply in the affirmative he is immediately thrown down again, and this time a thorny lawyer vine is forced into his gullet and violently withdrawn so as to tear the root of the tongue. He is again then asked the question, but is, of course, unable to reply ; the man is then badly mauled and allowed to return to his village, where he dies. At his own village he is able to speak on any subject but the one in reference to the treatment he has received.' "

The Resident Magistrate, C. A. W. Monckton, comments :—

" It is hardly necessary to remark that fanciful beliefs of such nature floating through a witness's mind do not tend to clear the point at issue." [1]

The district from which this case comes is inland of Cape Nelson on the north-east coast of Papua. The report covers the human appearance of the sorcerer in assault on his victim (Seligman, Malinowski, and the account from Christopher). It states " the man (i.e. victim) is then badly mauled ", in reference to the extraction of the vital organs (Malinowski and the account from Christopher). It covers the subsequent dazed, forgetful condition of the victim (Seligman and the account from Christopher). Best evidence of all, it includes the true Dobuan formula, as used by the sorcerer, and as given me by Christopher and others—" You name me " in the Dobuan, " Do you know us," in Mr. Oelrichs' communication ; the precaution of the sorcerer against his identity being revealed and a test of how completely his technique has dazed his victim.

Thus, from widely scattered areas of Papua, comes evidence of a common sorcery practice. Seligman, Malinowski and Oelrichs, all three obtained their accounts in pidgin English, the two former admittedly so, the last presumably so, as pidgin is the legal language, if such it can be called. Christopher's account was in a native tongue that I understand perfectly, and was the evidence of an eye-witness, self-incriminating evidence.

[1] Report on British New Guinea for year ending 30th June, 1904, p. 33.

Such covering of separate Koita, Mailu, and Cape Nelson district accounts by Christopher's largely agreeing, but more intelligible account, together with his frankness at many times, but conspicuously with regard to the secret poison, *Cerbera odollam* Hamilt., should be convincing in establishing the facts of the *vada* sorcery in an intelligible manner, not only for Dobu, but also for a great area of the Possession. It remains sorcery, not violence—hence the wholeness of the body of the ill or dying victim, as in the case of Hill Man's victim, whom I inspected in Dobu Island, suffering from the effects of meeting the sorcerer Hill Man in the bush. It is a practice that links up with our knowledge of hypnotism.

I have not been out in the company of a sorcerer on *vada* bent, and I have not seen a victim immediately after a *vada* encounter. But the subject is one difficult to work in great refinement particularly if the anthropologist has been seen anywhere in the Territory—for rumour travels far—in the company of a member of the legal and reforming professions, Administration and Mission. I did my best to make my informants believe that I had little sympathy and no business with these professions, but although I accomplished a great deal in this direction I could not surmount, in the limited time that I had, all the barriers of native reserve. Some things were done without my knowledge although many were revealed. And I would have had to stay longer and had a lucky chance of it occurring within my own small circle before I had seen *vada* more closely.

A practice such as that of *vada* is one practice of the magical complex ; and in a very real sense it is the best paradigm of the magical outlook.

Consider the mental affection known in Siberia and also in Malaysia and Indonesia as Arctic madness. The person suffering from this trouble has a compulsion to imitate anything done in his or her presence ; for example, if the afflicted person is carrying a platter of food a mischievous small boy may pick up an empty platter and drop it to the ground in sight of the afflicted person. Then she also must needs drop the platter, food and all. So in all her actions she is compelled to imitate that done right before her. It is a diseased suggestibility of an extreme nature.

And broadly considered, taking sympathetic magic the world over, it can be summed up as the use of a suggestive technique upon man and upon nature. It treats man and nature as if all existence had Arctic hysteria, and were bound to imitate, as if everything were permeated with a compulsive neurosis of advanced hypnotic suggestibility. Consequently, it is fitting that some such practice as *vada* should be found as the effective element in magic, the point where magic for once does not miss its mark.

ADMINISTRATION AND SORCERY

Papua is under the control of Federal Australia, and is administered by a Governor appointed by the Australian Federal Parliament.

It has been the policy of Administration to attempt to punish sorcery by imprisonment. Now, there is little doubt that when one man grievously assaults another or bodily injures another or murders another because of suspicion of sorcery then Administration should act. But in Papua, Administration has not been content with this. It has attempted to get behind such assault and to punish sorcery whether it lead to assault or not. For some reason Administration has made sorcery a crime, but not witchcraft, although the two procedures are very much the same, the main difference being that the one is performed by men, the other by women.

Historically within our own culture the reverse has been the case. It has been administrative policy to punish witchcraft much more notably than sorcery. Within our own culture an administrative policy making the practice of the black art a crime was the product of a close co-operation between Church and State. The prosecution of witchcraft was bitter, vigorous, far-reaching and more prejudiced against the crime than any secular prejudice would have been.

In Papua of to-day the case is otherwise. It is true that the practice of the black art by males is a crime. It is true that the State sometimes proceeds against it from information against it offered by the Church, which is fighting a not wholly secular battle against magic. But, nevertheless, the punishment is comparatively mild, usually less than a year's imprisonment, and is not more than is fitting to a purely secular view of the murders, assaults, and unsociabilities that occur in a native community in which sorcery is rife.

The Native Ordinance declares : " Sorcery is only deceit, the lies of the sorcerer frighten many people ; therefore, the sorcerer must be punished."

This formulation is even milder than is necessary. We have seen that the *tabus*, the believed secret poison, and probably most of the sorcery stock-in-trade, is a system of belief which allows individuals to have secret ideas that the black magic which they have been broadcasting has taken effect ; whereas, in reality disease and death have in most cases been natural.

Vada is a more serious case, where sorcery probably kills or damages severely, we have seen reason to believe. Thus the Ordinance might well be amended to, " Sorcery is for the most part mistaken belief."

The wording of the Ordinance betrays one misconception, however. Sorcery is not merely deceit, and the sorcerer an exceptional person, who intimidates others who are not sorcerers. This is true in some areas of the world but not, as far as I know, in Papua. In some areas of the world the practitioner of black magic is a different person from the practitioner of white magic, and is more or less in conflict with his better-class, more publicly approved rival. There is nothing of this, however, in Papua, according to present report.

In Papua sorcery is an integral part of the supernatural system of the people. This supernatural system is practised by everyone, and believed in firmly by everyone. Like most supernatural systems it enlists its believers, not by tricks, deceits, and stratagems, but by a more dignified faith in the reality of Unseen Forces, and in the reality of the power of human speech to affect these Unseen Forces, that were " born with the sun and the moon and the earth " in contrast to mortals " we are but newly come ".

If the Ordinance were amended to " sorcery is a part of a supernatural system which causes much social damage and fear, but which is practised in secret by all members of a Papuan community ", the truth would be more fairly represented.

One further truth is that one native never knows certainly what another is doing in sorcery. The practice is as secret as secret poisoning. Consequently the natives must resort to supernatural methods to reveal the supposed identity of a sorcerer or of a witch. Divination is practised for the purpose.

One of the great difficulties of the administration of the law against sorcery is the impossibility of securing reliable evidence against a native. The situation is precisely the same as that which confronted our own ancestors when they set out to indict witchcraft. It must be emphasized that if the natives believe that X has committed sorcery their belief, if they are sure of it, is derived from a magical divination, such as should not be valid before any European law court of the twentieth century. If it is not so derived, and two or three natives bring a charge of sorcery against another, and one of the witnesses claims to have witnessed a transaction between the accused and a sorcerer, or to be the paid sorcerer himself turned King's Evidence, then the Administrative Officer is ill-informed if he does not realize that the complainant and his witnesses are, in at least ninety-five cases out of a hundred, perjured men who are carrying on a feud with an enemy by using Administration as their unconscious accessory. The natives of this area do not regard perjury seriously, and they can but rarely be discovered in it except by one who lives intimately with them. That I have done, and I know their methods. It is for the reasons that I have stated that sorcery charges are but rarely laid before the courts by the natives, although sorcery is in constant and widely ramified practice.

The worst aspect of the law against sorcery is not that it tends to make Administration accessory to native feuds, however, but that it tends to strengthen the practice of sorcery. Magic in general is a very blind fool. After a long drought, when rain-making magic has proved futile, rain at last falls. The rain-making magic is then everywhere acclaimed for its great power. In this same way most sorcery is futile, blind, and proved powerful by a foolish conception of what constitutes proof. I except *vada* only.

In regard to rain-making magic, garden growing magic, and the like it may prove possible to finally ridicule the people out of their faith in their magic. This is gradually happening in some areas exposed to civilization. But, so long as sorcery is a crime, as murder, assault, rape, theft, and the like are crimes, it will hardly prove possible to ridicule the natives away from it. Does not Administration treat it seriously! There is no doubt that it does, and there is equally no doubt that Administration is a powerful ally of the native sorcerer against all would-be educative agencies. A native imprisoned for sorcery will never learn to take the view that he is imprisoned for creating bad social feeling. He and all others inevitably take the view that the white man shares in his conception of sorcery as actually and directly powerful.

Now this, from one anthropological viewpoint, is a good thing. It is well that Administration should support native custom by a little mild legal antagonism, which is not effective in doing more than deepening the native faith in his supernaturals because the law takes them apparently seriously. The price of a few men in gaol for short periods is not too great, considering that it does not touch the universal underworld of sorcery, except most casually. Such action tends to preserve native custom for scientific study, and should be encouraged from this view point.

Nevertheless, although I favour this view point strongly, I have some allegiance also to a contrary view that is derived from the consideration of what is best for white and native contact in the Possession. Contact there has been and there must be; and white ideals must probably replace native ideals sooner or later. Personally, I incline to the view that even if this occurs sooner, as it will if there is not too much friction, then apart from the anthropological view point of preservation of fields for study, it is better so than that it should occur later, with, and because of, unnecessary friction.

Gaoling of sorcerers where all men are sorcerers and liable to indictment at any time is a practice that produces racial friction; and it is debatable whether the preservation of sorcery is worth the friction.

The annual reports of the Administration contain many amusing stories relevant to the attitudes set up by the policy of Administration. One officer reports the following tale. It must be understood that in Papuan pidgin, the language used between Administrative officers and natives, *puri-puri* means sorcery in its main and narrower meaning; also magic in general in its wider meaning. Officers are not concerned with *puri-puri* officially in its wider meaning, and they have rarely an appreciation of what an everyday thing it is in the villages when they are not present. *Puri-puri* in its narrower meaning of the black art is on the contrary one of their official pre-occupations and as such it is used in this tale.

A village constable (native) came to the Station one day and the following conversation took place (the conversation is translated into English, I may remark, in the report).

"You know those two *puri-puri* men you let out of gaol about a week ago, named Andugai and Serawabai?"

" Yes."

" Well, when they returned to my village they *puri-puri* the bush pigs, and the bush pigs have broken into my garden and eaten all my taro. Look, here is some taro half-eaten " (presenting a half-eaten root).

" How do you know Andugai and Serawabai *puri-puri* the bush pigs ? "

" When the two men returned they said : ' This village policeman got us three months in gaol ; we will damage his garden in revenge.' "

" Did anyone hear them say that ? "

" No, but what more reasonable thing could they say, since I was the cause of their imprisonment ? "

" Then you have no witnesses ? "

" No, none."

" How long is it since you have repaired your fence round your garden ? "

" About six months."

He was a very crestfallen man when I told him to go and mend his fence as New Guinea fences would not last six months. Both the village constable and the corporal interpreter were perfectly certain the two *puri-puri* men had done what they stated, and equally convinced that I did not understand " fashion along New Guinea." [1]

The Magistrate, who tells this story tells it as a joke on the natives, the village constable, and the corporal interpreter. But in reality to the well-informed outsider it is rather a joke on the Magistrate and Administration generally. The Magistrate put the *puri-puri* men, Andugai and Serawabai, into gaol on the story that they caused illness, disease, or death [2] by hocus-pocus cock-and-bull methods. Now sorcery exists not only to produce death, disease and illness, but also to magically rob other persons' gardens (*see* section on garden ritual) and also to send the wild bush pigs into other persons' gardens to destroy them (although I did not find this last in Tewara, where I lived and where there were no wild bush pigs left). Where such magic exists no illness, disease, death, poor crop, or destruction of gardens by wild pigs can occur without generating suspicion of sorcery.

Why should a Magistrate act upon one story and not upon another ? Because one story had witnesses, and the other had not can be the only solution. But all evil magic is done in deepest secrecy and privacy and without true witnesses.

I think it will be agreed that the joke is on the Magistrate. Administration by treating sorcery as a crime lays itself open to receive all manner of absurdities and often perjuries. What if the village constable had had his witnesses ? By what logic could the Magistrate have refrained from sending the two sorcerers back to gaol ? By no logic whatsoever I am afraid. But would he have gaoled them again ? Probably not, I am afraid. But by what justice could he justify not doing so ? None whatever, I fear. If he were to let the sorcerers go free he might rationalize his action by saying that a

[1] Report for year ending June, 1911, p. 132.
[2] Unless it was for *vada* and proven *vada*.

Magistrate should not encourage gross superstition. But is not all sorcery such : can a line be drawn between what is and what is not such by a Magistrate ? If it is drawn to debar magical influence on pigs, but not magical influence on human beings, then is not the Magistrate a little inconsistent ?

No one stays long in Papua before he discovers that white men, even the best educated of them, vary in the extent to which they conjecture native knowledge of poisons to be a true or false knowledge, and native sorcery to be powerful or not powerful in actually causing native ill-health. They actually know very little, as they have not been initiated into the native arcana by the natives. Consequently even the best of Magistrates may vary in their estimates of the ills of sorcery. Can a very personal factor be made impersonal in a law against such a phenomenon as sorcery ? Is there any rule to debar a Christian Scientist, for instance, from a Magistrate's position ?

Another good story in the Reports narrates how in a time of great drought in the south-eastern division, a visitor came to the place of drought. He offered to make rain for a fee of a pig and a spondylus shell necklace. He was retained for the purpose. That night surely enough the first rain fell, but not enough of it. Next day the rainmaker, now with tremendous prestige, was importuned to make more rain. Evidently thinking that the labourer had been worthy of his hire already he refused curtly. From the height of his prestige he announced equally curtly that within ten days all the men of the island would be turned into women, and all the women into men.[1]

The men immediately made a sea voyage to Samarai to throw Government action against the impending calamity.

Such magic is no more cock-and-bull magic than most of the magic of sorcery. If Administration takes punitive measures against one it should against the other. I do not know the issue of the above case. But Administration certainly should have let the ten days expire before acting, then pointed the moral, and then have refrained from further action.

It will be apparent from such stories as these two, and there are many such, how the natives and the Administration share in a world of superstition which they both treat seriously. So Administrative action must and does appear to the natives.

I learned Dobuan quickly at the outset and made a journey across Fergusson Island speaking it, before rumour had gone across the Island announcing who I was or where I came from. One woman said I was the spirit of her dead brother come back from the dead. She prophesied, on this basis, a general resurrection of the dead shortly, and told everyone to kill all their pigs and dogs. A wave of this superstition swept over the island and in several tribes the livestock, litters and all, were exterminated. The District Officer of the Administration tracked down the woman prophet who was partly responsible for the state of chaos that he found, livestock exterminated, no gardening being done, houses stored against a siege in fear of the coming resurrection of the spirits. He got her too late, after expectation

[1] Report for the year ending June, 1903, p. 26.

had almost died and chaos was already changing back to normal routine.

I do not think, however, that it was necessarily wise to have kept her in gaol for a month. Superstition could say, and did say, that the power of the white man had intervened, and that inevitably the resurrection of the spirits had been frustrated. Better far to leave such superstition to its own failure—it could not have done much more damage than it had already done, and its more convincing failure might have done good.

It will be seen that there is a case for Administration refusing to touch native superstition. Such a case as that last quoted is on debatable ground, because of the extent of the damage to property done by the owners of their property. But even legally there is some right for an owner to do what he likes to his own property. A Christian Scientist has even a right to refuse to have a doctor attend the serious illness of his child. Sorcery is less debatable ground. It is a traditional system, not the uprising of a new prophecy. It is not questionable that Administration supports belief in it by treating it so seriously as to hold long court cases upon suspected instances of it, and to convict supposed sorcerers to a term in gaol. It is perhaps questionable whether belief in sorcery requires the support of Administration. But considering the very great influence that white contact can and does in many cases exert upon native life, considering that a growing minority of natives, at least, are less convinced of the power of white magic than their fathers were, it is perhaps true that the native belief in sorcery is coming to require the support of Administration more and more, and will continue to do so in the years to come.

Whether Administration will favour this support or not should depend upon its examination of the customs of the Papuan tribes. Owing to the existence of the law against sorcery an investigator known to be associated with Administration can only hope at best to touch the fringes of the customs connected with sorcery. There is a great deal of native feeling against the law, naturally enough, although there need be no opposition to it from the anthropologist anxious to preserve a native sanctuary for scientific purposes. Dobu, which I studied, is just such a good sanctuary scientifically. Whether the Dobuans would be better natives without their own legal sanctions of black magic powerful in enforcing economic honesty, and without their feuds it is difficult to say. They would possibly become more dishonest amongst themselves and more sociable also. Black magic in Dobu tends to nourish honest economics, and much bad feeling. It is undoubtedly an expensive and an imperfect method of maintaining honesty in native economic exchanges. Almost all natives in Dobu Island can read and write Dobuan now. But they are enemies, owing to sorcery distrust, to all persons who do not live so near to them as to be spoken to more easily than to be written to. If black magic were not supported so strongly by Government measures, ostensibly directed against it, it might in time be dispensed with without too much social damage by an education that would include the use of writing for business purposes. Writing could be used in giving a receipt for a payment and such documentary evidence could be preserved against disputes, now settled by black magic, but possible then by legal settlement.

Meanwhile, white legality intrudes somewhat bizarrely into native life and, as I have shown, even throws its weight against the chances of its own reform. Such chances of reform depend greatly upon the measure of consideration that may be accorded to anthropological findings, and to the measure of willingness, unmixed with resentment, that may be given to well-founded criticism. The gulf between *vada* and the rest of sorcery is a gulf that should be recognized. There should be no difference between most sorcery on human beings and sorcery to make pigs do damage for example. Nor does the presence or absence of witnesses mean very much when the law is directed against such a phenomenon as sorcery.

HEAT AND THE BLACK ART

It will have been noted from the material that the sorcerer engaged in sorcery believes that he must keep his body hot and parched ; hence the drinking of salt water, the chewing of the hot ginger, and abstention from food for a while. This ginger chewing is used in the *tabu* as well as in more serious sorcery. It is chewed with many healing incantations, apart from the *tabu* exorcisms which are breathed into water for bathing the patient. With other healing spells it is spat on to the seat of illness. The sight of a magician chewing ginger, spitting it on to the object charmed at intervals, and muttering his spell at the same time is a common one in Dobu. It is not done in garden magic. But it is chewed in some of the magic accessory to the overseas exchange, the *kula*. It is chewed in all the incantations to ward off a squall at sea and spat towards the lowering squall. It is chewed and bespattered over the canoe in lashing it with incantation, in making it speedy and seaworthy by incantation. Moreover, there is believed to be virtue in ginger chewing alone—I saw men who were anxious to get a man who had just run amuck with a spear to chew ginger. I was engaged in deluging his body with cold water, while they were pressing ginger into his mouth—so there was some incompatibility between our theories.

The necessity for a hot body is most stressed for sorcery, however. Witchcraft is also associated with the sign of heat—fire. It is believed that *kaiana* fire issues from the pubes of flying witches as they go through the night. The body of the witch is also unusually " hot ". I first heard of the *kaiana* fire of witchcraft in connection with the legend that relates the origin of fire. This runs as follows :—

An old woman has five grandsons. They go pig-hunting with nets. The old woman takes fire from her vagina and cooks her yams with it. They return. They give her pig. She gives them uncooked food (the cooked food she has eaten herself) They eat.

Again next day they go hunting pigs with nets. Again fire issues from the old woman's pubes, she cooks her food with it. Unseen by her a *kitu* yam—cooked—drops through a crevice and to the ground beneath the house. She replaces the fire in her womb—as she had done the day before. She eats her cooked food. Her grandsons return. They give her pig. She gives then uncooked food. They eat.

One grandson discovers the cooked *kitu* yam on the earth beneath the house. He shares it with his four brothers and they eat.

Next day they go hunting pig with nets ; five men go forth, but four hunt pig. One watches his grandmother from the fringe of the bush. She takes the fire from her pubes and proceeds to cook the food. The grandson rushes out and seizes the fire. She says : " Give

me the fire back or to-day I shall die." He says : " Die then, for
you cooked food you ate, and I with my brothers uncooked food
you gave us and we ate." Deprived of her womb's fire she died.
The fire ignited the bush. Rain came down and put it out everywhere. The five brothers go searching for it. At last they find a
tawatawa tree and a *dadabwa* snake coiled about it, his body protecting a piece of the fire. They threw the snake off and took the
fire. The fire burnt the snake's belly, hence its markings. If rain
comes the *dadabwa* snake he wails, " My fire ! My fire ! " Long
ago he coiled about the fire protecting it.

It is believed that fire still issues from the pubes of old women.
The fire is called *kaia* or *kaiana*, and it may sometimes be seen at
night going to all points of the compass. It is greatly feared.

Fire is made by rubbing a blunt rounded ended stick in a groove
worn to fit it in the threshold. The groove is termed *kemwani*, the
stick rubbed in it is called *kekusi* ,and the act of rubbing it is *'usi*, *'usi*.
Kusi or *'usi* is the term for the male member, and in bad language
the sex act is sometimes spoken of as " *ta 'usi 'usi be i sabelulu*, we
copulate and it flames up ", *sabelulu* being the term for fire catching
and flaming. There is thus a parallelism in terminology between
fire-making and the sex act.

We thus find an association between :—

(1) A principle of heat that has to be stimulated to an extraordinary pitch for the practice of sorcery, that is evidently deficient
in states of bad health or in running amuck when ginger is chewed
with believed restorative properties, that also is necessary in the
practice of wind ritual in squall warding off (not otherwise, I believe),
in canoe lashing, and in incantation to make the canoe speedy, in the
incantation over the *seuseula*, or sea-mat to ward off breakers ; generally
in creating or in warding off evil.

(2) The *kaiana* fire associated with witchcraft, as a hot body
is with sorcery.

(3) Ordinary fire, in the belief of its origin from the *kaiana* fire.

(4) Sex.

There is no one term that covers this association unless it is *yaiyai*,
heat. But *yaiyai* is not so expressively used as a rule. The association
remains loose as one comes on it in native thought, and the assembling
of it is partly my own. A native connects *kaiana* fire and the origin
of ordinary fire and a sex terminology for the *kaiana* fire and for the
making of fire ; but I never heard all this linked up with the sorcerer's
ginger and hot body apart from the ordinary term for heat, *yaiyai*,
used for the sorcerer's body. The sorcerer, while engaged in sorcery,
abstains from connection with his wife or with anyone else. " He
does not diffuse his heat."

The complex of ideas concerning heat, found in the idea that
the sorcerer's body must be hot with ginger chewing, no eating,
no sex indulgence, and parched with drinking salt water is a widespread one. I am indebted to A. R. Brown [1] for a collection of its
distribution, in part.

[1] A. R. Brown, *The Andaman Islanders*, pp. 266–309.

Heat of the body is connected with spiritual danger, stormy seas, the condition at initiation and in the dance, and with fire in the Andamans. In the Achehnese of Malaysia heat is used to typify all evil spiritual influences. *Mana* in Malaita of the Solomons is connected with heat in the baleful aspects of black magic.

So in Dobu also heat is connected with sorcery, with the pubes of witch women (which also void the volcanic crystals used in one form of sorcery), which void *kaiana* fire in the night, with sex, and with fire in its everyday aspect.

I may add one further belief concerning the *kaiana* fire. It is sometimes conceived in the following fashion. If one sleeps touching the legs of a witch a gigantic testicle within her body will pass over, mount the leg, and lodge in the scrotum—hence elephantiasis. This gigantic testicle emerges at night and is seen, a ball of fire, as the witch flies in mid-air. This belief is the Dobuan parallel of Dr. Seligman's finding from Bartle Bay, the *labuni* which the witches send forth at night. " *Labuni* exists within women and can be commanded by any woman who had children. . . . It was said that the *labuni* existed in, or was derived from, an organ called *ipona* situated in the flank and literally meaning egg or eggs " (p. 640, *Melanesians*).

Dr. Malinowski gives a belief from the Trobriands, commenting on the Bartle Bay equivalent. " There is also a belief that a *yoyova* [1] develops within her a something, shaped like an egg, or like a young, ripe coco-nut. This something is called as a matter of fact *kapuwana*, which is the word for a small coco-nut." (p. 238, *Argonauts*).

Labuni and *kapuwana* have the same night-flying properties as the Dobuan gigantic testicle. They are the variant euphuisms or variations of the same belief.

[1] A witch.

APPENDIX V

FURTHER NOTES ON THE BLACK ART

In discussing the black art every belief cannot be easily organized under systematic heads, nor easily interpolated in an examination of the main functioning points. I assemble here a collection of olla podrida.

I was once introduced to a professional diviner with the recommendation that he had the comparatively rare power of shrivelling the male member of his victim up to nothing and of rejuvenating it at his pleasure.

Volcanic crystals, called *sinasina* in Dobu, are possessed by nearly everyone. They are believed to fly of their own power if left about. Actually they are only taken out when a man or a woman uses them with a spell to project into the body of a victim. They can be removed from a sick body that contains one or more by one of them who knows the spell to project and eject them. This removal is like a trick in appearance, but actually the sorcerer does not think of it as a trick. The presence of the crystal in his hand after he has projected it magically at a victim, or before he has ejected it from a patient is immaterial. The immaterial on the contrary is material in effecting his purpose. That is all there is to it. There is no esoteric teaching about the practice that might reconcile it with our manner of thinking that the whereabouts of the material object is the important fact.

These crystals are also sometimes used by the diviner. He gazes into one.

Plants of many kinds are used in sorcery. One man I knew had a plant which did not hurt him when he held it, but he had only to brush another man with it for the other to sicken and die. I asked him : " Why then does it not hurt you when you grasp it ? " Back came his answer " It is like a dog. It does not attack its owner—only other individuals."

The sensitive plant has been introduced into parts of Dobu since white contact. The Dobuans fear it greatly, handle it only with wooden tongs, and believe that a little of it planted under a man's path will kill the path user.

There are many plants believed to be poisons. *Cerbera odollam* (*budobudo*) and *Excoecaria Agallocha* were the only two of these, besides the sensitive plant, that I was shown. The knowledge of these is supposed to be secret, but *Excoecaria* is widely known as is also the sensitive plant. I judge that *Cebera odollam* is a much closer secret than the other two named. The fish poison, *derris*, used also in attempted suicides, is no secret whatever.

It is believed that food or tobacco accepted from any person not closely related or else a very old and tried friend is liable to contain poison.

It is interesting to note that fish poison is used without magic spells and is effective ; that *Excoecaria agallocha* is used as an abortifacient without magic spells and almost certainly effective ; that *Cerbera odollam* sap is used as a poison in feuds without magic spells, and although it is ineffective, the seeds would be actually very effective. Assuming that in this last case an oral tradition has come to allow a lapse of correct tradition we have a case of magic not being used except when the herb is useless, as with the herbs of garden magic. Since this is a reasonable assumption it strengthens the case for a mistake in the traditional lore concerning the *Cerbera*. Certainly the Dobuan spurns vigorously the bare idea of using spells with the *Excoecaria* or with the *Cerbera*, or with the *derris*. His attitude is no whit different from a European scorning the idea of praying for relief from stomach-ache at the same time that he takes salts. Yet herbs such as *Cerbera* and *Excoecaria* (not *derris*, which is more public) are classed as *igu kaiwe* " my vegetable product " (and secret) as it is most directly translated, but which also means " my vegetable product and magic spell going with it ", by extension. One term covers all magic, and all magic herbs, and all secret herbs used without magic. There are other differentiating terms that are more specific, of course. *Kaiwe* in non-magical use means tree merely, or wood.

A BATCH OF DANCE SONGS

I

Yawara sinasinage	I wander without a mother
anua i boi ya keno	the village darkens I sleep
kau yawara sinage	wandering alone motherless
yawara sinasinage	I wander without a mother
musa ma nuanuada be	would I were with our sister
duae i siwa be ya numa	soup she'd pour for my drinking
kau yawara sinage	wandering alone motherless
anua i boi ya keno	the village darkens I sleep
yawara sinasinage	I wander without a mother

II

ku yamwaliegu	you await me
orai galagalala	the sea coast is booming
tau ku yamwagu	my man, you await me
eiagu ku ona	my brother-in-law speak
guregure keona	a gureguri keona bird
nuagu i kuku	my mind is wavering
tau ku yamwagu	my man you await me
ku yamwaliegu	you await me.

This song requires some explanatory notes. The first part represents a woman talking to her lover. The first three lines of the second part, preceding two lines that are the coda, represent the lover talking to his brother-in-law. He and his brother-in-law have gone together to his secret assignation. He has been disturbed by a noise ; is it only a bird, he asks of his brother-in-law, who is standing sentinel over his love-making.

This situation of two men joining in an assignation is common enough. One stands sentinel while the other is engaged with the woman. Then they reverse rôles. They call each other *igu esua* thereafter, i.e. my partner in the seduction of a woman.

III

iyano masaliguia	you had me awake night long
budia wainena	budia woman
lololi iyanoguia	flute playing arousing me
iyano masaliguia	you had me awake night long
ida tana u naba be	our basket you carry and
ta sulu dimwadimwaro	we shall dip up sand
oraia numa toli	sea water we'll drink
lololi iyanoguia	flute playing arousing me.

The reference to drinking sea water means a way of refreshing the body after a night devoted to love-making.

IV

ima keda dumaduma	our path is different from thine
garoi maleogana	the abode of ghosts is far
masinagu ima keda	with my mother alone our path
ima keda dumaduma	our path is different from thine.

wa kobukobuluyegu	thou hast hated me from jealousy
kaulia ya gogoi	my bundle of spears I fashion
mwanegu kena ya ila	to thee, my wife I return.
ma sinagu ima keda	with my mother alone our path.

The husband sings of his intention of murdering his wife and of remaining alone with his mother. " Our " is used in the exclusive form.

V

moraba imisikwabuia	moraba under your sleeping mat
wa da keno gikelegu	lie on your back
keno gike gikelegu	lie on your back, your back.

manutai kabueguia	white cockatoo's cry deceived me
ya pili kunu boi maia	I fled away by night.
wa da keno gikelegu	lie on your back
keno gike gikelegu	lie on your back, your back.

The youth addresses the woman, Moraba. He is not married to her so he has to flee at first-bird song to escape detection. A false bird song deceived him. He returns and tells her to prepare for him.

VI

waga niuniuwani	a canoe at midnight
sinege leionai	the widow Leionai
kamwadoge niuwane	mourns softly at midnight
waga niuniuwani	a canoe at midnight

wa keno lagae	you lie with your head inland
buyeta nedodauna	through the tree blossoms
yalowai delideli	the clouds appear racing
kamwadoge niuwane	mourns softly at midnight.

A fisherman's canoe comes to where the widow, Leionai, is mourning for her dead husband at midnight. The widow is next depicted as watching the clouds pass overhead from beneath a *buyeta* tree.

VII

Kuyoni gwama kuyoni	Kuyoni child kuyoni
Ku lolo ya gebe	undress that I may see
ku lolo ya geagebe	undress that I see, see.

Kuyoni mudumuduna	Kuyoni her mons of Venus
saliwa tupwauuna	white as the white pandanus flower
ku lolo ya gebe	undress that I may see.

VIII

tobuio geigeoi	vulvas of evil
kulena maudoian	a cooking pot full around
maudoi maudoian	full, full around.

maudoi maudoian	full, full around
kami buio ta kai	your vulvas we eat
ma wagwao sukweyare	with a crowd of my mother's brothers
kama kelamgogon	our assembly feast
kulena maudoian	a cooking pot full around.

This is a cannibal song.   The vulva was a most highly prized cut.

IX

i dogu idoguragura	he mourns and he mourns
manucodia ! mwawasaia	black bird of Paradise is dead
dinegwa ! doguragura	dinegwa he mourns

bwebweso manucodi nina	black bird of Paradise from Bwebweso
kaena lomena ta nono	low falling your lament we hear
manucodia i mwawasaia	black bird of Paradise is dead
dinegwa i doguragura	dinegwa he mourns.

The bird of paradise is here given a place in the Dobuan spirit home, Bwebweso ; *dinegwa*, a small bird mourns for him and is answered.

X

guniye i kenigu	a wasp has stung me
iyoi ! sinagu nimagu	ow ! my mother, my hand
nima, nimagu nimagu	hand, my hand, my hand !

nimagu wada koba be	my hand you use magic on
gaburaia y da keno	and under the house let me lie
iyoi ! sinagu nimagu	ow ! my mother, my hand
nima, nimagu nimagu	hand, my hand, my hand !

XI

ya ma koiwagana	Would I were with my magic one.
mainamo ya keno	now unscented I sleep
wabua me koiwagana	dark skinned, my magic one.

wa bwauwane, wa da ila	you call in vain, you may return homeward.
mane gaiobura si latu	where in Gaiobura do they anchor
kada keno mulo mulolawa	our lying sweet odoured
wabua me koiwagana	dark skinned my magic one.

The woman refers to her lover in terms of his love magic, sweet-scented Koiwaga.   He is on the sea or anchored at Gaiobura.   She repulses other wooers.

XII

mwaneio ya ileilenawa	your wife I send back there to you
Seduna be u dedoi	Seduna for your wailing
dune be u de udedoi	you see and wail, wail

u gelu yau u dorodoro	embark and come to sea
Samaroa sinadiao	Sanaroa mothers.
sabi ai si dedoi	wishing to marry they wail
Seduna be u dedoi	and you Seduna wail

A man is going to Bwaioa, from Sanaroa Island.   He embarks his sister's daughter intending to take her away from her husband, Seduna, and marry her off more satisfactorily in Bwaioa.   Seduna wails so piteously on the shore that his wife is returned to him. The song taunts him by saying that the mothers of this place wailed because they couldn't go off to marry as the traveller's sister's daughter was to go off and marry elsewhere ; and Seduna wailed with the mothers (i.e. older women). Of course these older women did no such thing—the song is merely a way of calling Seduna an old woman.

XIII

wa do ila wa do ila	you may return you may return
waga i lopupunaia	the canoe is broken in pieces
Suyalai wado ila	you may return to Suyolai
sinia lasai i laia	the reef broke it in pieces
wabuwa lumadiega	from its dark breast
ya tauia besomaiu	I go aimlessly
Suyalai wa do ila	You may return to Suyalai.

XIV

tana ku ilenama	my pouch you return to me
tutuna lasa malele	the waves break pounding
igu etabu	my etabu
tana ku ilenama	my pouch you return to me
diwana loweboda	he closed the pouch with magic within it
yalebe sinebwaina	Yalebe, most beautiful woman
ku yamawagu	you await me
ta da taona	we shall come round to you
igu etabu	my etabu
tana ku ilenama	my pouch you return to me.

Etabu is the relationship between two men, who interchange their sweethearts temporarily. As the song says they will also share such a thing as a pouch containing love magic.

XV

to waga bwaina sana	a fine canoe it was
Basima lobuninaia	capsized by Basima
i lobulobuninaia	blown over, blown over.
koianiya kenokeno	the hill lay there
Waibudo kaniyana	rain fell for Waibudo
Yaloa si delideli	the clouds rushed over it
Basima Lobuninaia	capsized by Basima.

Waibudo is the name of the canoe owner.

XVI

wauliulita-lie	the wind blows fitfully between calms
Yawaula bwogabwogaia	on the sea deep Yawaula.
wauliulita-lie	the wind blows fitfully
manueda ta yaliliwa	gently gently paddling
MeKenaia patalidi	fleet of Kenaia.
kadi nea gwarumumuna	*their* paddles hurl back the swishing water
Gogom ulitalie	Gogom, the wind fitful.

Dobuan war canoes meet at sea. The fleet of Kenaia village is returning exhausted and quietly after ravaging the coast of Duau.

The other war canoe, Gogom of Nekumara village, is going out fresh
with strong paddling.

XVII

to sinebwaina sana	since she was a beauty
u gimi aluenaia	you first abducted her
u alualuenaia	you abducted her.
ya tanatana gogwaia	So your basket is shut
tana i yomumuraia	your basket stays with you
u gimi aluenaia	you first abducted her
to sinebwaina sana	since she was a beauty.

The song refers to a runaway marriage. The groom and his
people have " kept their baskets shut ", i.e. not made any exchanges
of arm-shells or spondylus shell necklaces to validate the marriage.
This song was presumably originally a way of scoring off people
so mean.

XVIII

tau da gwaie sinana	a man must tell the mother.
Yawaula goyuyua	Yawaula is cold
ora goyuyua	a deep sea and cold.
tai kewa yasilai	the slain man is brought back
Kaburigu i da mia be	O that Kaburigu might remain
i da kamwadoiyegu	and mourn me, dying before him.
Yawaula goyuyua	Yawaula is cold
tau da gwaie sinana	a man must tell the mother.

Over the cold sea, Yawaula, a man, Kaburigu, is brought home
slain to his mother.

XIX

Dobu i doedoe	the Dobu floats
Ted i bwau masalaia	Ted crys out all night
Dobu i doedoe	the Dobu floats.
" Netiane " bwaulaga	" Netiane " he called shorewards.
Dinda tai butu	Ginger a fine fellow.
kabi libulibuye	caught by some rubbish.
Dobu i doedoe	the Dobu floats.

Ted was the white owner of a schooner named the Dobu;
Netiane, otherwise called Ginger (Dinda) was the native skipper in
charge of the native crew, but under Ted's orders. The song records
Ted's calling out all night for his skipper, who was on shore caught
by rubbish, i.e. strange women.

This collection of songs, together with those discussed in the
body of the book, will give a fair idea of the range of subject matter
and of style in the dance songs of Dobu. There are numberless
songs composed by individuals announcing that they feel sick, unroll
a mat, let them lie down, and so on ; or remarking that they were
stung by nettles in the Trobriands—an announcement that is cryptic
in the absence of further gossip, since it may be literally intended,
or a figurative reference to the Trobrianders. Even in such songs
there is usually a line referring to some less personal fact of the-wind-

is-rustling-in-the-trees type. Very many songs die a quick death. Those I have given are not of the rapidly evanescent variety. They have been approved, used in dancing, and sung about the villages and the seas. But evanescence in Dobuan songs is only a matter of degree. Old songs die out of favour and remembrance, except a few, of which " I go inland to Bwebweso ", etc., and " Woman of the North-East Wind, " etc. are types—songs embodied in the traditions concerning the spirits of the dead. The ethnologist cannot garner the best songs of Dobu derived from centuries of song-making history, but only the best contemporary songs, for the value of a song is felt as greatest if it is good and new. The dance itself is probably as old as anything in Dobu ; the form of the dance song is probably equally old. But through that form there flows in a continual current of contemporary comment. Cannibal songs and war songs alone cannot be composed anew now, and some of these will probably be retained over many generations.

Appendix VII

CONCLUSION

In this volume I have with intent not dealt with language and legends or with material culture. Without intent I have not said all that might have been said. As instances of omission that occur to me there is the old custom by which the recovered corpse of a fellow slain in war is erected on a platform in a coco-nut palm top right in the village. There the corpse decays, and cannot be taken down until the corpse of an enemy, of one of the enemy responsible for the death, is brought into the village for eating.

There is again the initiation of the boy as a warrior. He is taken out alone and told to climb a tree to a height of about 12 feet. A bristling fence of vertical 7 feet spears, too wide to jump out over, is erected beneath him, butts on the ground, points beneath him. He is told to jump on to the spear-points. He does not know the point of the ceremony, unless it is that he must jump to his death. Many boys refused to jump, it is said. Some did as they were so imperatively and solemnly urged to do. As the boy jumped on to the spear-points, the entire fence of spears was jerked down from the vertical to the horizontal by a concealed device so that the boy had no more than a bad fall and a shaking. He was then admonished to tell none of the uninitiated youngsters.

Of these customs I know the bare outline only. I know that there must be other points that I have not made, but they are of such slight character as may be dealt with in an occasional article or two at a later date. I have given the great body of the culture, with the exceptions noted. I have omitted also reference to my knowledge of surrounding cultures, with the exception of Basima, which I have treated briefly. Some Dobuan custom extends far. The paranoid-like fear of sorcery from the ownership of greater wealth than ones' fellows extends along the south coast of New Guinea, it would appear, from a reference to it in the Annual Reports.[1] It occurs amongst the Motu, 400 miles to the west. It would appear to have a range comparable in extent to that of *vada*.

It has not been my aim to open hypotheses or theoretical points, but to add to our knowledge of an area from which we have already a stout body of studies; on the Trobriands from B. Malinowski, on Goodenough Island from D. Jenness, on Rossel Island from W. Armstrong, on the Orokaiva of the adjoining north-east coast of the mainland from F. E. Williams, and on the different peoples of the adjoining south and south-east coast of the mainland from C. G. Seligman and from B. Malinowski.

[1] *Report on British New Guinea for year ending 30th June*, 1912, pp. 99–100.

REVISION OF CHAPTER VI, SECTION III
Dominant Sex Attitudes

Malinowski wrote that amongst natives where the position of women in society was high they were unchaste, but to this rule the Dobuan islanders were an exception. It may be noticed about this point that amongst some travellers' stories there are reports that entire nations or tribes of women are red-haired and chaste, or long-nosed and unchaste. They all went to the same schools and learned the same lessons and they all made the same statements. The child was mother to the woman. The positions of children, adolescents, and women in society were identical. Mothers who allowed their sons of eight, nine, or ten years of age to sleep in the homes of other mothers with daughters of the same tender age flung themselves and their elder daughters into the arms of sailors whenever an outrigger canoe, a merchant ship, or a naval vessel came into land.

Amongst Papuans there were tribes in which parents allowed children to go to sleep in the homes of other children's parents at an age when they were naturally unreproductive. There were also some tribes in which amorous parties for adolescents were arranged once a yam crop season, a time which might sometimes approximate to a year. There are some missionaries' stories that Pacific islanders were free from all restraints in the enjoyment of the sexual passions, and Bougainville and his ship's doctor once brought a passionate story to France that the only god or goddess worshipped in Tahiti was Venus. In his introduction to this book, Malinowski writes that he is corrected in it on an important point, as it is shown in it that Dobuan women are unchaste. He explains that Dobuan Island youths who worked for him as his domestic servants in the Trobriand Islands told him in reply to his enquiries on the topic that Dobuan women were chaste. He explains again that Trobriand islanders, having never obtained any favours from Dobuan women, had accused them of "that unpleasant characteristic, chastity, in a wholesale manner."

On considering Malinowski's view we may note that such a

one as those who accused Dobuan women of unpleasant chastity was probably one of the schooner's crew who landed up in Tewara Island in 1928 on a day when the men were away fishing on the reef for the palolo annelid. As we have said, we were never told the story, but we think that such a one probably seduced Kadibweara, whose marriage to Kinosi was arranged, and that our discussion of their divorce lacked the story. There is some mention of some antagonism shown towards us in our first month in Tewara Island in this book, which was written without as good a surmise of the reason for it as that which we make now, thirty years later, for a second edition. Our purpose in landing in Tewara Island was not to investigate a question whether the island women were chaste or not. The largest Dobuan Island is Normanby Island, but we did not go there. Our purpose was not to investigate a question of how many persons spoke the same language. We went from Tewara Island to the adjoining coast of north-east Fergusson Island, an island where we found that five to six languages were spoken. The topic of purpose has some importance and it is highly relevant to the interpretation of conclusions reached.

Some of the previous section of this chapter was written with reference to some of Malinowski's notions of fact at a date before his theory of the reduction of sociology to terms of psychological behaviourism was written, and before Roheim's discussion of Egg Laying Day in the Dobuan islands ("Tauhau and the Mwadare," *International Journal of Psychoanalysis,* 1932) was published. Amorous parties for adolescents in the Trobriand Islands were once arranged on an evening of a feast day in Milamala, the palolo worm or All Souls Moon in which the marine worm, *Leodice viridis,* class *Polychaetae,* phylum *Annelida,* swarmed to reproduce on the surface of the sea, and in which the Trobriand islanders believed that the ghosts of ancestors of their matrilineages returned to their villages. In the Dobuan Islands similar parties were once arranged on a similar feast day called Egg Laying Day. The Dobuan name for the feast day referred to yams, called eggs in this context by metaphor, grown in clones by asexual plant reproduction and given as gifts to relatives by marriage in exchange for gifts of shell currency from them. It was on such days in the moon of the reproduction of the palolo worm in the Trobriand Islands that yams were also given as gifts to relatives by marriage in exchange for gifts of shell currency. From Malinowski's and Roheim's works it is clear that it was on such days that it was considered that behaviourism in social psychology and in social anthropology in the Trobriand Islands and psychoanalysis in the same subjects in the Dobuan Islands had come into their own. Adolescents did not bear many love children following Egg Laying Day, either because, unlike the palolo in this respect, they were not all ovulating, or because many of them were married not long afterwards. Malinowski, however, made a mystery of this point. Roheim suggested that the yam storage house symbolized the womb and that the yams stored in it symbolised sperm. The yams were called eggs by the Dobuans in metaphor, and the yam storage house was called the skin of mouth, but the former discrepancy was overlooked, and the latter was met with a mistranslation, as the opening to the body, not clearly definitive of the womb.

Leodice viridis lives with its head end in clefts in coral reefs and with its hinder end out of the clefts. The hinder ends break off and swarm at the surface of the sea on the first day of the last quarter of an October or a November moon. The date by solar reckoning is variable within a range of thirty-five days in a cycle of nineteen years. If All Souls Moon in the Trobriand Islands were kept with precision, as Easter and Passover are in other ecclesiastical calendars that combine lunar and solar reckoning, it might coincide with the date of the swarming of the palolo, which is determined by the effect of moonlight and sunlight on the creature. According to a chart of time reckoning published by Malinowski, different Trobriand Island districts are now keeping All Souls Moon at different solar dates, and it may incidentally be remarked about the dates that all of them are in advance of the earliest date at which the palolo swarms. Again it may incidentally be remarked that in his chart of time reckoning Malinowski equates thirteen synodic months or lunations, 383 days 21 hours, 32 minutes, 36.14 seconds, with a solar year minus 6 hours, 9 minutes, 9.5 seconds. His view that tribes or nations all went to the same schools, learned the same lessons, made the same statements, spoke the same languages, and were chaste or unchaste, united or disunited in policy and the like is not one in which there is much sense discernible. Malinowski, however, is said to have studied the natural sciences in the University of Cracow under the Austrians. It is obvious from his calculations that something was not what it should have been.

Darwin assumed that men and other mammals possessed naturally given, highly generalized, but partly unlearned predispositions or tendencies to parental care, to mutual aid and sympathy, and to interest as well as pleasure in the society of others. It was an assumption about their nature, not that Darwin was a traveller whose histories of points which he studied were called into question on account of reliability. Darwin's assumption about mammalian predispositions differs from behaviourists' views in social anthropology and in social psychology that physiological needs for food, water, a sexual mate, security, health, and shelter motivate animal and human learning and behaviour. In general, animal behaviour is not accounted for in terms of physiological needs and learning to satisfy them. *Leodice viridis,* for example, does not need to learn to calculate the dates in a calendar. Granted that the position of the mammals differs from that of the *Annelida* in particulars, it need not be concluded that one story is as good as another.

Amongst the Dobuan islanders the term *loiawe* was used sometimes to mean a custom by which parents allowed their young sons of eight, nine, or ten years of age to go to sleep in the houses of others with young daughters of the same age. The custom was probably one of permitted pleasure and interest in the society of others. The term *loiawe* was used sometimes to mean the conjugation of mature organisms, other than human beings, in the animal kingdom. There may, perhaps, be tribes or nations whose members all went to the same schools and spoke the one language and who are not remarkable for the chastity of their spoken languages. The Poles, Austrians, Germans, British, French, Russians, Italians, Americans, and Dobuans have not been cited by anyone as being remarkable in that respect. The fact that they have not been cited as remarkable for chastity in speech is one of the few facts of restraint in views of them for which national and tribal characterologists might be commended, if it were known what they discussed.

Malinowski's discussion of his question whether women were chaste or not referred as much to children and to adolescents as it did to women. We noted that in his books he applied his question to the Dobuan islanders, and we made a few enquires whether the *loiawe* in its meaning of a custom was associated with conjugation or not. At that date and when we wrote this book we had not then heard the term *loiawe* used in its meaning of the conjugation of mature dogs, pigs, birds, and insects. We received no replies about children that need be recorded in Latin; but we understand that some of the missionaries assumed from an absence of chastity in the language of the people that a discussion of the conduct of children, to be complete, should protect the written chastity of their mother tongue by being written in Latin. However that may be, if the Dobuans were amused at the natural inconsequence of their young offspring as far as reproduction was concerned, they were not amused if they had a daughter of thirteen or fourteen or so years of age and if a strange youth of the same age was found in their house at dawn. In such a case they arranged a shot-gun marriage on the spot. Most marriages were arranged without such a provoking incident, and parents and senior kindred who arranged them and the youth who were married were not amused in cases in which their marriages did not last long.

With reference to tall stories and denominational differences in them the Tewara islanders advised us not to introduce the topic of the Trobriand Island legend that human conception was caused by the reincarnation of ancestral ghosts in the Trobriands. The occasion for this advice was one in which we were preparing to go with them by outrigger canoe on a *Kune* or *Kula* trading voyage to south Boyowa Island in the Trobriand group. They did not say that it was a taboo, but then they usually did not when it was. We concluded hastily that they had disagreed on the topic in the past. We thought no more of it, and in the Trobriands we disregarded their advice, and asked their Trobriand trade friends to narrate the legends, which they did with pleasure. There had been a question whether Malinowski had been relating a tall story of his own invention about the entire topic, and we aimed to check some points about it. In his introduction Malinowski has it, apropos of that incident, that we taunted the Trobriand islanders once again with ignoring physiological paternity, and that our Tewara Island canoe mates objected to our rudeness to their trade friends. That was not the case, as we did not taunt the Trobriand islanders or offer them a discourtesy. We asked to hear the legend, as Malinowski understoood, since there was a question whether he had told a misleading story about it or not. It transpires that the Trobriand islanders ignored the human ova as well as the sperm, physiological maternity as well as physiological paternity, if ova and sperm must be called a special class of mothers and fathers. We do not take a view that they must be. The reference in Malinowski's story about a taunting of the Trobriand islanders in the first place is to an incident in which he relates that a Greek trader taunted a Kitava islander with ignoring whether the genitor of an infant by his wife was its pater, or another man, or an ancestral ghost of a former member of his wife's lineage. In that story a wife's unchastity was assumed. It transpires that there was something else to the objection our Tewara Island canoe mates took to our having asked to hear a Trobriand Island legend about human conception; for, in reconsidering a question of what it was, we have noticed that they probably observed a taboo against relating any legends on any topic whatsoever and against asking to hear any related on voyages outward bound or in ports of call. The Trobriand islanders may also have observed the same taboo and assisted one of their trading visitors to infringe it with pleasure, for all we know to the contrary.

The story of depopulation in Dobu Island since 1891 may perhaps be due to gonococcus, *Neisseria gonorrheae,* as that of depopulation in New Ireland is. Problems of overpopulation, underpopulation, and depopulation, and of denominational differences of opinion about them may possibly be headaches. If the New Ireland population had taken vows of poverty, obedience, and chastity in their reception into Buddhist or Roman Catholic orders they might have stopped the spread of *Neisseria gonorrheae,* but not prevented depopulation. There is a story by Sir William MacGregor in his *Annual Report on British New Guinea for 1895–6* that a Trobriand Island chief had a wide influence and that the Trobriand islanders used thumping and not chemical means if they aimed to secure an abortion. There is controversy in Seligman, Leo Austen, Malinowski, Gluckman, Cunnison, and Uberoi about Sir William MacGregor's assumption concerning the extent of the area of influence of a Trobriand Island chief before 1883. Malinowski repeated Sir William MacGregor on the topic of abortion without acknowledgment of the source. His story was that plants were waved as wands in magic and not taken internally as drugs, and that they were ineffective if they were taken internally. The point we wish to make here is that the story of depopulation in Dobu Island since 1891 may have nothing to do with discussions of Sir William MacGregor's *Annual Report on British New Guinea for 1895–6* in its references to the Trobriand Islands. It may have nothing to do with the use of plants, taken internally, as abortifacients. They may or may not be ineffective. One plant may perhaps be effective, and perhaps damaging, and one may perhaps be variable in its action and possibly harmless in its biological action. Whether this is so or not is not a question in the social sciences.

Although the story of the plant drugs once used in these islands is still incomplete, it may be added to it that the bites of shell-fish are sometimes fatal in the area. The species of shell-fish which is dangerous is not yet identified and the mechanism of fatality from its bite is not identified. It may conceivably be one of anaphylactic shock to which some persons, previously bitten without fatal results, may be subject. In any event, the Dobuans treat shell-fish bites by external treatment with a few drops of the sap of *Excoecaria Agallocha,* carefully dropped into the wound from a snapped-off twig. As it is a powerful vesicant it is not allowed to touch intact skin. In his work *Malay Poisons and Charm Cures,* Dr. J. M. Gimlette confirms that if this sap is taken internally it is fatal. He does not, however, agree with Dr. M. Greshoff, quoted above, that the sap from the branches of *Cerbera odollam* is not poisonous. His view is that there is a cardiac poison, a glucoside, thevetine, in the sap of *Cerbera odollam.* The plant drug mentioned above as not identified has been identified since the first edition was written. It is *Aristolochia tagala, Cham,* with which *Aristolochia megalophylla, K. Schum,* is probably a synonym. It contains aristolochic acid, an aromatic hydrocarbon, which when decarboxylated, is 1-methyoxy-5, 6-methylenedioxy-9 nitro-phenanthrene. Some species of *Aristolochia* also contain aristolactone. The structure of the acid is

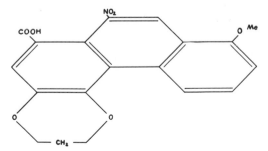

and that of the lactone is

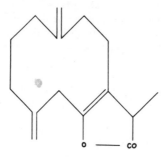

Neither the acid nor the lactone is an analogue of a compound in the path for the building up of cholesterol from acetic acid in the mammalian body.

We shall not discuss the topic of the motives of behaviour any further at this point, but revert to the text of the first edition, not rewriting Chapter IX, but rewriting Appendix I, Dobu and Basima, instead.

INDEX

Aberrancy, 248
Ability, distrust of, 176
Abortion, 239 f., 246, 273, 299
Accidents, due to witchcraft, 150
Acting, 11
Adanatu (place), 34, 35
Address, rules for, 14
Administration, effects of, 30, 62, 157, 241, 287; and witchcraft, 166, 167, 288 ff.; *see also* Government
Admiralty Islands, 39, 40; economic exchanges, 165, 206; healing magic, 114; sex life, 248, 278; witchcraft, 157
Adolescence, of youths, 275 f.; of girls, 276
Adoption, 17, 20, 86; supernatural, 187
Adultery, 7, 49, 50–2, 61, 62, 77, 79, 90, 92, 135, 192, 247, 277; co-operative, 67, 153, 247, 300; sentiments regarding, 78, 91, 242, 249
Adze, inheritance of, 18; use of, 207
Affinal relationship terms, 37
Age, death never attributed to, 81
Aged, respect for the, 84
agu (prefix), 67
ai epwepwopwo, 29
ai lobukuna, 29
Akasaoleole (charm), 168
Albinism, 248
Alliance, principle of, 35
Alo, bewitching of, 156; illegal marriage of, 85
Amphlett Islands, 182, 218, 225; dancing, 250; Dobuans in, 151; and the *kula* ring, 202 f., 208
Amuck, running, 54, 163, 248, 295
Anabuyueta (legendary character), 119
Ancestors, 98, 99, 163; as birds, 95; graves of, 1, 2; spirits of, 178
Ancestress, mythological, 31
Ancestry, traced through females, 3; legendary, 31, 35
ane (plant), 123, 186, 226
Anointing of body, 128, 230, 254, 276
Ante-natal magic, 115
Antiaris toxicaria (poisonous plant), 172
'Anuabada (place), 265
Arctic madness, 287
Arm-shells, as marriage gift, 189; as sexton's fee, 194; trade in, 202 f., 214

asa kopuana, 194
Ascendant relatives, terms for, 37, 39, 40, 41
Assonance, 252 f., 256

" Bad " significance of, 136, 177
bagi (shell necklace), 214, 224, 230
bagura (garden), 139
bake (obscene invective), 79, 244 f.
Bananas, cultivation of, 105; as gifts, 156, 190
Banks Islands, burial custom in, 115
barau (sorcerer), 151
Barrenness : *see* Sterility
Barter, 208 : *see also* Kula
basi, 234
Basima (on Normanby Island), 116, 123, 141, 218, 250; dialect, 260; organization and magic, 280 ff.
Bastards, 67, 238, 239
Bathing, ceremonial, 228 f.
Bats, fear of, 153
Beach-combers, native, 70, 74, 79, 83
Beauty, charming for, 218 f.
Beggary, due to improvidence, 70
Betel-nut, as betrothal gift, 26, 189; buried with the dead, 186, 193; charm for, 142, 218; magic acquisition of, 181
Betrothal, 24, 63, 102 f.; of children, 29, 60, 74
bilubilu (plant), 122
binama (hornbill), 139
Bird of Paradise, 302
Birds, as embodied spirits, 111, 113; legendary origin, 220; meta-morphosis, 94 f.; as totem, 31, 32, 72
Birth control, 240 f.; *see also* Abortion
Black art, 133–177, 254, 280 f.; in dissolution of marriage, 192; official attitude towards, 288 ff.; *see also* Magic ; Sorcery ; Witchcraft
Black satin bird, 255
Blasphemy, 161; in use of names, 100
Bleeding, 63
Blood relationship, terms of, 37
Blood transfusion, magical, 16
bobo'ana (desirable), 176
Boils, 144
Bolapas (mythological character), 31
bomagu, 233 n.
bomama, 108, 222, 233 n.

315

bomana, 233 n.
bonu (ulcers), 144
Boundary Catchers, 110, 113
Boundary Man, 14, 16, 17, 38, 53, 57, 58, 72, 196, 279 ; marriage, 28 ; as spell-teacher, 148
Boyowans : *see* Trobrianders
Boys, forbidden to sleep at home, 10, 21 ; training of, 275 ff. ; initiation as soldiers, 306 : *see also* Youths
Bread-fruit tree, 197
Bride-price, 98, 189
Brothers, and magic, 16, 17, 97, 232 ; terms for, 37
Brother-sister relationship, 8, 10, 35, 38, 62, 72, 278
Brown Eagle, spirit double of, 126 ; totemic ancestor, 31
Budibudi, Bay of, 124
budobudo (poisonous plant), 170 f., 174, 240, 298
Buleima (variety of yam), 116
Bulela (first planter of yams), 111, 113, 115, 117, 119, 125, 126
Bunelala (legendary character), 99, 118, 282
Burial alive, 179
Burial customs, 11, 68, 115, 193, 257, 277 ; in Basima, 281
Burning of leaves spell, 109, 121, 122, 125, 128
Bush clearing, 104, 105, 109, 127, 223
Bush creeper, charmed, 81, 142, 147, 150, 154, 168 f. ; personality of, 102
butubutu, 146
Bwai, to diviner, 156, 164
Bwaidogu (place), 265
bwaima (house platform), 227
Bwaioa (neighbouring island), 86, 136, 156, 159, 185, 198, 207, 218, 302
Bwakela (place), 142
bwalogo (rock limpet), 143
bwanakupwa, 190
bwanawe, 31
Bwarakwaiyoyo (wind goddess), 212 f.
Bwaruada (neighbouring place), 259
Bwebweso (abode of the dead, on Normanby Island), 12, 143, 180 f., 186 f., 237 f., 256, 263, 277, 302 ; meaning of word, 187
bwebwesala (sea-bird), 261
bwobwore (sexton's perquisite), 194 ff.
bwokumatana (divination term), 155, 156, 158
bworabwora (variety of banana), 190

Calophyllum inophyllum, 122 n.
Cannibalism, 61, 77, 80, 90, 302, 306
Canoe, 213 ; charming of, 97, 216 ; its impersonality, 133 ; inheritance of, 18
Cerbera odollam (poisonous plant), 171 f., 175, 240, 287, 298

Ceremony, 76
Charms, antithesis in, 142 ; involved, 227 ; teaching to children, 274. *See also* Incantations ; Spells
Child-birth, 246, 273
Children, betrothal, 29, 60, 74 ; burial, 257 ; inheritance, 3, 13, 57 ; influence on *kula*, 228 ; and magic, 15, 71 ; and mourning, 11 ; punishment, 64 ; relationship with parents, 3, 18, 20, 57, 71, 82 ; terms for, 37 ff. ; truant, 73
Cockatoo, as totem, 32, 34
Coco-nut, in abode of spirits, 187 ; in *kula* ritual, 225 ; milk compared with semen, 238 ; oil, 128, 230 ; private ownership of, 79
Coco-nut frond, spell of the, 138, 142, 145
Coco-nut palm, charm for, 142
Collaterals, terms for, 37
Communal labour, 103 f., 120
Community : *see* Village, organization of
Competition, 176
Complexion, 248
Cook, male, 190, 192
Cook Islands, fire walking in, 115
Cooking, ceremonial, 190
" Copyright," in songs, 251, 261
Cosmetics, 215, 276
Cordyline terminalis, 114, 115
Coriphilus fringillaceus, as totem, 32 ff.
Corporal punishment, dread of, 65
Corpse, disposal of, 11, 68, 193 f., 257, 277, 306 ; inheritance of, 8 ff. ; and lice, 181 ; of murdered person, 180 ; twitching, 155
Corpulence, 248
Coughing, superstition concerning, 27
Counter-magic, 100, 102, 128 f., 143 ff.
Courtesy, 151 ; terms, 35
Cousins, terms for, 37
Crab, in spell-binding, 169
Creation, theories of, 94 f., 98
Crime, punishment of, 78, 288 f.
Cripples, 177
Crops, 94, 118, 129, 131 ; inheritance of, 18
Cross-cousins, 14, 37, 38 ; and boundary man, 16, 17, 73 ; and magic, 86 ; marriage between, 27, 28, 59, 60, 73, 79
Croton, in graveyards, 1, 115, 250
Crow, as totem, 33, 34
Crystal gazing, 154, 298

dadabwa (snake), 296
Daloyos (mythological character), 31
Dance songs, 250 f., 300 f.
Dancing, 92, 250 f., 283, 305 ; in Basima, 283 ; and divination, 165 ;

exchanges at, 193 f.; and *kula*, 221, 230; mourning, 11, 187
Darubia (place), 139, 141
Daughter-in-law, pre-nuptial duties, 102
Dead, spirits of the, 114, 178 f.; legend of the, 182 f.
Death, 4, 10, 133, 147, 155, 277; gifts following, 18; legendary origin, 186; resulting name changes, 37; never natural, 81, 97, 128, 135, 150; restoration from, 89, 90, 162, 284 f.; sudden, 286
Dede (place), 267; hot-springs legend, 136
Deformed persons, 136, 176 f.
Delirium, 154
Delousing, 50, 90, 219
Derris (a poison), 50, 174, 298
Descendant relatives, terms for, 37, 39, 42
Dialects, 258
didila (charm), 138, 142, 145 f.
didina (charm), 142, 145
Digging stick, 116, 120
Digitaria sanguinalis, 89
Dilia (place), 142, 143, 218
Dilikaiai (place), 268
dinegwa (bird), 302
Disease, 76, 128, 133, 135; charms and exorcisms, 80, 82, 93, 97, 126, 137 f., 145 f., 149; demons of, 144; introduced, 136, 138
Disembowelment, magical, 162, 175
Diu (place), 142
Divination, 8, 30, 45, 150 f., 154–66, 175, 177 f., 275, 289, 298; in Basima, 282 f.
Divorce, 3, 15, 45, 49, 82, 91, 191, 277; for inefficient gardening, 119; in neighbouring communities, 9
diwai belong tamberan (shrub), 115
Dobu Island, size and character, 18; canoes, 213; in *kula* ring, 202 f.; unwritten literature, 92; population, 30, 240; poverty, 60, 103; Trobrianders in, 74
Dobuans, character, 15, 56, 136; legendary origin, 31; and sea-faring, 211
Dog, as companion, 267; legendary, 99, 227, 270 f.
Dokanikani (ogre), 181
Domdom Island, magic origin, 265
Doubles, in magic, 126 f., 144, 146 f.
Doweta (place), 142
Dreams, 181
Driftwood, 123
Drought, 131, 192
Drum, 221, 250; legend of, 222
Duau : *see* Normanby Island
Duels, between women, 44, 248
dugumalala (funerary feast), 187
Duntna Moligogona (charm), 168

Dutuna (place), 146
Dysentery, 136

Eagle, as disease demon, 144; *see also* Brown Eagle
Ear-piercing, 274
Earth-Back : *see* Magic Peg
Earth-Belly : *see* Pouring, Place of
Eating, 74, 226 f.; *see also* Food; Meals
'Ebadidi (Fergusson Isl.), 142
ebwainina (part of incantation), 227
Economic system, 189–234; its importance, 191
Education, to combat sorcery, 293
Edugaura (locality), 32, 34, 35
egoyainina (part of incantation), 227
egurewa (metamorphosis), 94
ekekwaro (gifts), 190
eketosika (garden boundary), 110
ekwasi (food), 190
Elephantiasis, supposed cause of, 297; charms and *tabus*, 80, 138; demon, 144
Elopement, 78
elowaila, 109
emanua (metamorphosis), 94
Emetics, 50
Enai'a (locality), 33, 35
Endogamy, 30
Enemies, and marriage, 36
Engagement : *see* Betrothal
Entrances (in garden-magic), 122–5
enunulatui (contracting a disease), 143
Epidemics, 138
esaesa (rich man), 214
Escort, as witchcraft protection, 77
etabu, 303
Eugenia malaccensis, 197 n.
Exchanges, economic, 25, 26, 28, 43, 60, 69, 77, 102, 165, 205 f., 232; at death and mourning, 193 f.; harvesting, 106; marital, 25 f., 193 f.; overseas, *see* Kula; of water, 206
Exoecaria Agallocha (tree), 239, 298
Excreta, 150
Exogamous marriage, 91
Exorcism, 80, 144 f.; teaching of, 148; *see also* Charms; Incantations; Spells

Face-paint, 276; in trade, 207, 214
Familiars, 178
Family, 4, 75, 277 f., 280
Fasting, 295
Father, relationship with offspring, 3, 5, 15, 277 f.; at burial, 193; excluded from deceased wife's village, 13; inheritance and, 2; name changing on death, 38 f.
Father-daughter love, 278
Father-in-law, and marital exchanges, 192
Father-right, 20

Father-sister-right, 20
Fear, 23, 74, 99, 113, 137, 141, 149, 151 f., 163, 170, 208
Fergusson Isl., 114, 141 f., 151, 186, 207 f.; dancing, 250; yam houses, 283
Feuds, spells in, 147, 157, 175, 299; see also Vendetta
Fidelity, marital, 6, 76, 79; means of ensuring, 244; rareness of, 249, 277
Fiji, fire walking in, 115
Fire, origin of, 95, 99, 263, 295; method of producing, 296; see also Kaiana
Fire walking, 115
First fruits, 31, 115, 123; month of, 124
Fish, 70, 97, 104; legendary origin, 266; marriage gift, 190; at mourning feast, 196; poisonous, 170, 174; as totem, 36
Fishers, a despised class, 70
Fishing net, inheritance of, 18
Food, customs and rules concerning, 58, 64, 66 f., 74, 137, 170, 189 f., 196, 228; ceremonial eating at marriage, 26, 74, 192; gift for garden work, 120; see also Eating; Meals
Footprints, 150
Foster parents, 17
Free love, 29
Friendships, 67, 137; a cause of suspicion, 155
Funeral ceremonies, 10, 38; see also Burial; Corpse

Gabuwana (coral reef), 219, 222, 226, 229, 262
Gadimotu (strait), 268
Gaiobura (place), 302
Gangosa, supposed cause of, 126, 142; charms and exorcisms for, 80, 113, 138 f., 141, 145 f.
Garden magic, 70 f., 82 f., 104, 111 f., 133 f., 282, 295, 299; passed from father to child, 118
Gardening, co-operative, 103, 120; time for, 108, 127; jealousy in, 135
Gardens, 94–132; customs concerning, 75; inheritance of, 18, 69 f.; lay-out, 110; privacy, 104 ff.; protection, 83, 201; ritual, 94 ff., 106 ff., 129, 222; in Basima, 282
Garea (place), 143
gau, in magic, 162
geboboi (hold of canoe), 124, 216, 224 f., 228
gelaboi (sea witch), 153 ff., 165, 178; (variety of yam), 112
Genealogy, 3, 9, 31
Gifts, betrothal, 26, 63; funerary, 18; wedding: see Exchanges

ginebwabwaba (female homosexuality), 244
Ginger, in magic, 142, 162, 170, 213, 224, 295
Girls, chastisement of, 64; and prenuptial intercourse, 10, 21, 25, 29, 239, 241 f., 248, 276
Giuri (place), 142
Globe fish, poisonous, 170, 174
God, reputed equivalent of, 113
gomakara (monitor lizard), 221 f.
Gomakarakedakeda (necklace of legend), 218 ff.
Gomanumusa yam, 124
Gomayawa (the Pleiades), 219
"Good," significance of, 136, 177
Goodenough Isl., dancing in, 250, 283 n.
Goose-flesh, demon of, 144
gorto (magic "medicine"), 284
gosiagu, 35
Government, native, 83 f.; white, 3, 104, 160, 274; see also Administration
Grandmother yams, 122, 126
Grass skirt, 68, 78; as personal term, 64, 245
Grave-digger, 194
Graveyard, 1, 4, 68, 115
Green Parrot, totemic ancestress, 31; garden magic of clan, 118
Greenstone, trade in, 202, 207; in kula ritual, 225
gu (suffix), 67
Guiaboga (place), 268
Gumasila (island), 150, 221
Gumawana (in the Amphletts), 218, 221, 267
Gums, inflammation of, 144
gurewa, 94
Gurewaiya (islet), 219

Hair-cutting, 50
Harvest, 75, 105 f., 129; and dancing, 250, 283; a festival of death, 18; time of, 127, 223; in Basima, 283
Heat, in magic, 295 f.
Herbs, in garden ritual, 129; in magic, 298 f.
Hernandia peltata, 122 n.
Hibiscus, in divination, 154
Hill Man, sorcery of, 158 f., 174, 287
Hill of the Rocks charm, 112, 115
Homosexuality, 243 f.
Hookworm, 161; demon of, 144; tabus for, 138
Hornbill, spirit double of, 126, 139, 141
Hospitality, 215
House, privacy of, 4, 278; disposal after death, 4, 11, 195; for marriage or storage only, 21
House Platform, Place of the, 110, 116, 119, 122; see also Bwaima

Husband, not wife's co-villager, 2 ; garden work of, 105 f. ; jealousy, 7, 104, 247 f. ; terms for, 37
Hypnotism, in magic and sorcery, 162 f., 284 f. ; see also Vada

Iagaina Isl., legendary origin of, 265
igu (prefix), 67
igu esoi, 67, 141, 300
igu kaiwe, 299
i guguia, 84
Illness, 77 ; see also Disease ; Sick Persons
Immortality, 99, 178, 187
Improvidence, 69, 74, 83
Incantations, 74, 77 f., 83, 95, 99, 122, 138 f., 168 f., 181 ; for disease and healing, 143, 150, 295 ; fear of, 113, 140 f. ; on kula, 224 ff. ; secrecy of, 107, 124 ; teaching of, 147 f. ; theft of, 107 ; trade in, 96, 100, 229, 231 ; for winds, 211, 213, 295
Incest, 57, 61, 243, 278 ; of co-villagers, 7, 27, 49, 69, 90, 269 ; in folklore, 90 ; in marriage, 29, 44
Incompatibility, superstition concerning, 16
Incontinence, charms and tabus for, 80, 138, 144
Indentured labour, 51, 62, 71, 96, 103, 240, 277
Infancy, 274
Infants, unwanted, 60 ; training of, 274
Influenza, 136
Inheritance, laws of, 2, 8, 13 ff., 18, 28, 38, 40, 60, 62, 73, 82 ; of magic, 17, 40, 82 ; of names, 13 f., 38, 40 ; of seeds and crops, 18, 69, 72
" In-laws," 278 ; see also " Those-resulting-from-marriage "
Insane persons, treatment of, 53
Insults, 79, 201, 234, 244, 249, 283
Intestinal disease, charm for, 80 ; demons of, 144
Invalids : see Sick Persons
Invisibility, charm for, 78, 162, 167 f.
Islands, legendary origin of, 265

Jambos malaccensis, 197 n.
Jealousy, connubial 6 f., 77, 91, 104, 134, 247 f. ; between brothers, 16 ; of possession, 135, 210
Jests, obscene, 238
Joking relationships, 245
Justice, in divination, 164 ; native ideas of, 167

kaiana (miraculous fire), 99, 152, 223, 231, 295 ff.
kaiawana (tree), 219
kaikai (garden boundary), 110, 131 n.

kaiwe (tree), 299
kalena (part of song), 251
Kalena Sigasiga (gangosa incantation), 139
kalitabu (shellfish), 220, 268
kamweai (perspiration), 32
kaniagu (rain-term), 132
kamiana (rain-term), 108, 131 n.
kapali (spider), 121, 125 f.
Kapoka (place), 143, 146
karumoi (spondylus shell), 224 ff.
kasa sona, 99 f., 213, 237
Kasbwaibwaileta (legendary character), 99 f., 216 f., 223, 229 f., 262
Kasiara palm, spell of the, 125 f., 128, 130, 134
kasitana (perspiration), 32
katuesiki (gift), 189
Kawaganutu (love-charm), 236 f.
kawagosiana, 155
kawawerebana (witchcraft term), 45
keaweawasina (food), 185
Kebadidi (place), 140
kebana (mat), 31
kebudi (garden stick), 109
keda (path), 221
Kedagwaba (place), 227
Kedatete (Tewaran village), 220
keginae (plant), 123
Kekewage (supernatural being), 186 f.
kekusi (in fire production), 296
kelamoa, 83
kemwami (in fire production), 296
kemwata (shrub), 186
Kenaia (village), 303
keno (to lie), 256
kenoduma (cohabitation without intercourse), 244
kenokinoki (a game), 220
kenolua (cohabitation), 244
ketomatasekera (tree), 239
Kibi (constellation), 219, 223
Kidneys, 140
Kilakila, as totem, 34
Kinship : see Relationship
Kitava Isl., 211, 213
Koiakutu, the Hill of Lice, 181
Koita (tribe), 284
Koiwaga (in love-magic), 237
Koiyawabu (place), 140, 142
kokwa gote, 32
kokoko (fish), 266
Kokua (place), 227, 228
Kotukotu Isl., legendary origin of, 265
Koyatabu, Mt., 117, 140 f., 143, 282
Kubwagai (Tewaran village), 46, 268
Kubwana (Venus), 223 n., 228
Kula (overseas exchange), 131 n., 152, 169, 189, 198, 237, 277 ; magic ritual of, 209, 215, 221 f., 262, 295 ; non-economic character, 205 ; compared with potlatch, 234 ;

sharp practice in, *see* Wabuwabu ; time of, 201, 223
Kulada (place), 142
Kulia (variety of yam), 125, 128
Kuloia (bird), 224
kune (= *kula*), 224, 226
kunukunuwana (garden boundary), 110, 131 n.
kunututu (sexton's perquisite), 194
kusikusinetara (snake), 183
Kuyagas (variety of yam), 216
Kwaluia Isl., legendary origin of, 265
kwatea (plant), 282
Kwato (place), 265
Kwatobwa (place), 268
kwesi (marriage gift), 98, 189, 270

lakua (crab), 169
Lalaiya (Tewaran village), 220
lamalama (plant), 215, 229, 237
lamoa, 83, 93
Lamona (place), 140, 142
lamusi (sail), 211
Land, inheritance of, 8 f. ; legendary origin, 266
Leaves, charmed, 237
Legends, 92, 95, 98, 119, 136, 262 ff. ; totemic, 31
legiagia (a shore-bird), 147
Legumatabu Isl., legendary origin of, 265
lelebuyo, 226
Lesopi Isl., legendary origin of, 265
Liana, poison from, 174
Lice : *see* Corpse, Delousing ; Koiakutu
Limpets, spirit doubles of, 126 ; use in magic, 143
lo (prefix), 138
lobinama (hornbill), 139, 141, 146
lobonu (ulcers), 144
lobutobuto (leg " asleep "), 144
lobwaloga (tertiary yaws), 143
lobwebwai (disease), 144
Local units, 30
Locality, 72 ; arrangement of, 32 ; disunion in, 34 ; endogamy of, 30, 35
logaga (disease), 144
logau (spell of invisibility), 162, 168
logumo (disease), 144
loiaio (disease), 144
loiawe (pre-nuptial intercourse), 242, 248
lokwalawa (disease), 144
lolas (exorcising spells), 144 f.
lolawa (boils), 144
lomagawau (disease), 144
lomague (swelling), 143
lomolo (incontinence of semen), 144
lomwata (flying snake), 147
losakasakalulu (goose-flesh), 144
losakwara (hookworm), 144
losilai (paralysis), 146
Lousing : *see* Delousing

Love, 30 ; incantations for, 97, 100, 102, 235 f., 276
Love song, 260
lowana (tree), 139 f.
Lusançay Islands, 124, 132, 212
luugu (an Entrance), 122

Madalabuna Isl., legendary origin of, 265
Magibweli (cave in 'Tewara), 146
Magic, antinomy in, 125 ; bestowal of, 16 ; for disease, 80, 113, 126, 137 ff., 149 ; enticement of yams, *see* Yams ; faith in, 149 ; fear of, 113, 149 ; fees for, 17, 129, 135, 155, 171 ; hypnotic, 162 f., 284 ff. ; inheritance of, 17, 40, 85 f., 135, 171 ; in the *kula*, 210 f. ; validated by legend, 262 ; materiality, 15 ; public, 123 ; secrecy of, 100 ; and sexual intercourse, 134 ; its social value, 171 ; sympathetic, 287 ; teaching of, 15, 71, 147 f. ; in theft, 136 ; " trying out," 134 ; for winds, 97, 100, 124, 213
Magic Peg, Place of the, 110, 112 f.
magilode (betel palm), 220
Magisewa (Tewaran village), 220
Magnas Bravas (poisonous plant), 172
mague (shellfish), 143
Mailu (tribe), 285
Maiwortu, the dramatized widower, 11, 13, 256
Maize : *see* Tabuwara
makamakaiau (spirit double), 147
Malaria, demon of, 144 ; spell for, 80
mana, 233 n.
Mango tree, legend concerning, 263 ff.
manua (bird), 94
Manus, of the Admiralties, 39 f., 165
Marital grouping ; *see* Susu
Marriage, 21–30, 103, 222, 248, 278 ; survey of system, 51 f. ; between (1) Boundary Man and Owner, 59 f., (2) co-villagers, 7, 17, 58, 60, 69, 79, (3) enemies, 36, (4) relations, 6, 28, (5) strangers, 20 f., 86, 153, 193, and (6) in the same totem, 35 ; disagreements in, 6, 43–52, 119 ; dissolution, 49 (*see also* Divorce) ; economic exchanges, 43, 74, 102, 189 ff. ; enforced, 22 ; impermanence of, 6, 51 f., 278 ; jealousy in, *see* Jealousy ; prohibited degrees, 27, 249 ; not a private matter, 191 ; parental rights over, 102 ; repeated, 9 ; safeguards in, 76, 77, 79 ; should be self-supporting, 60 ; *wabuwabu*, 193
Marshall Bennet Islands, 201 f.
Massim, burial custom among, 115
matabora (mourning prohibition), 185
Maternal ancestors, graves of, 1

Matrilineal marriage, discouraged, 28
Meals, customs concerning, 25, 74, 228 ; see also Eating ; Food
Measles, 136
Medicine men, 77, 100, 138
Megarewa (the sky-people), 220
Memory, charm for, 148
memwai (shellfish), 220
Meningitis, demon of, 144 ; spell for, 80
Metamorphosis, 94 f., 98
miaewaewara (mourning feast), 196
Micturation, 247
Missions, effect of, 30, 104, 106, 113, 159 f., 241 f., 274, 287
moata (snake), 139
Mokukasi (charm), 168 f.
Monitor lizard, 217, 221 ff.
monolawa (variety of yam), 112
Monsoon, 132, 259
Moon, salutation of, 228
Mother-child affection, 15, 277
Mother-in-law, and daughter's betrothed, 22 ; and marital exchanges, 192 ; privileges of, 63, 74 ; suspected of witchcraft, 92, 153 ; tribute from widower, 156
Mother-right, 3, 17, 19 f., 68
Mothers, unmarried, 239
Mother's brother's right, 20, 64
Mourning, 4, 10, 78, 155, 194, 254 f. ; badge of, 12 ; exchanges, 23, 193 f. ; song of, 255
Mumugwa (village), 238
Murdered person, disposal of corpse, 180
Murderer, magical punishment of, 179
murimuri, 197
Murua (Woodlark Island), 119, 220, 229 ; canoes of, 213 ; in the kula ring, 201 f. ; occupations, 213
Murua octopus charm, 117, 119, 126
muyoi yam, 124
mwadi (ginger), 170
Mwagoru (tree), 197
mwagura (mourning badge), 12, 194
mwali (armshells), 139, 214, 224
mwamwasipa (variety of yam), 112
mwanina (spouse), 63
Mwaniwara (East Point, Tewara), 12, 146, 220, 229, 256
Mwatiua (place), 268
mwedole (fish), 124
mweia (first fruits), 31 f.

Nabana (place), 146
Nabelit (supernatural being), 282
Nakedness, 274
Names, in charms, 227 ; disuse of deceased's, 31 f. ; inheritance of, 13, 38, 40 n. ; multiplicity of, 32 ; use of personal, 62–8, 5, 13 f., 24, 31 f., 100, 113 f., 129, 141 ; protective of trees, 82, 93 ; of supernatural beings, 99, 113, 129

nana (garden boundary), 110, 131 n.
nanoa (launching logs), 226 f.
Navel, as relationship term, 64, 73
Nebagieta (supernatural being), 140, 142
Nebubunebuero (supernatural being), 114, 123, 125 f., 130
Necklaces, trade in, 202 f.
Nedaonara Isl., legendary origin of, 265
Negigimoia (supernatural being), 31
Nekumara (village), 304
Nemwadole (supernatural being), 99 f., 114, 123 ff., 130
New Guinea, sorcery in, 153
New Hebrides, burial custom in, 115
niaura (food gift for garden work), 120
Night, fear of, 23, 74, 153, 257
Nightmare, 24, 178, 181
Nipuna creeper, 111, 114 ff.
Niue, first-fruits ceremony in, 115
niueta (marriage gift), 189
niu lamoa (protected palm), 83
Niwaroa (Tewaran village), 220
nokonoko (tree), 121, 125
Normanby Island (Duau), 46, 141, 181, 202, 207, 263, 303
Nose, eaten-away, 141 f.
Nose-boring, 268, 274
Nothopanax (plant), 123
Nuakekepaki, legend of, 98, 267

Obscenity, 79, 238, 242, 244 f.
Octopus, 117, 119, 126
Offenders, punishment of, 53, 56, 84, 93
Omnipotence, possessors of, 101
Omuri (locality), 33 f.
Opossum, as marriage gift, 189
Orion, 127, 223
Ornaments, inheritance of, 18 ; in trade, 204 f.
Ordeals, 155
Osprey, as disease demon, 144
Overseas expeditions, 85 : see also Kula
" Owners of the Village," 5, 14, 72, 279 ; forbidden to intermarry, 27 ; quarrels between, 84 ; relationship terms among, 40
Ownership, private, 79, 81, 93 ; of spells, 80

Palms, inheritance of, 8 f. ; private ownership, 79
Palolo worm, 104, 123, 259
Panamoti Isl., in the kula ring, 202
Panamoti, Star of (Venus), 259
Pantheon, the Dobuan, 101
Paralysis, charm for, 80, 138, 142, 146
Partnerships, in overseas exchange, 214 f.
Passion, crimes of, 91

Paternal ancestors, graves of, 1 f.
Patrilocal marriage, 9
Peacemaking, and exchange, 209
Peg, in garden magic, 110, 114 f., 120
Penis, diviner's power over, 298 ; native term for, 296
Perjury, opinion of, 289
Personal appearance, its importance, 215
Personal property, inheritance, 18
Personality, of impersonal objects, 132 ; see also Winds ; Yams
Perversions, 244, 248
Petticoat government, 74
pies (shrub), 112, 114 f., 118, 126
Pig, as marriage exchange, 28, 189 ; at mourning feast, 198 ; wild, 291
Pig-hunting, 70, 85, 197, 295
Piracy, 270 ; in legend, 268 f.
Planting, 105, 109 f., 118 ff., 127, 132, 223
Plants, use in magic, 298 ; poisonous, 50, 172, 239
Pleiades, the, associated with gardening, 127, 130, 223, and with magic, 118, 220 : see also Gomayawa
Poetry, 252
Poets, 251
Poisoning, 9, 137, 150, 155, 169 f.
Poisonous plants : see Plants
pokala (offer of gift), 218, 224 f., 228
Polygamy, 248 ; in Basima, 281, 283
ponake (variety of banana), 190
Population, decrease of, 6, 87
Porcupine fish, as disease demon, 144
Port Moresby, Papua, 202
Possession, by spirits of animals, etc., 126
Possessive affixes, 67
Pottery, trade in, 202 ff., 207 f.
Pouring, Place of, 110, 112, 1·15 ff., 119, 121
Poverty, 60, 103 ; disgraceful if acknowledged, 83 ; jealousy and, 135
Prayer, analogy with magic, 101
Pregnancy, imitation of, 246 ; incantations and charms for, 96, 241 ; hurtful spell for, 168 ; theories concerning, 238 ff.
Pride, a crime, 171 ; in kula exchange, 234
Primogeniture, and magic, 16
Private parts, modesty concerning, 246 f.
Procrastination, in legend, 183
Procreation, native theory of, 238 f. ; Trobriand theory, 239, 241
Prohibited degrees, 27, 249
Prohibitions, ritual, 222 f.
Property, inheritance of, 18 ; protection of, 81 ff., 93, 138, 143 ff.

Prudery, 77, 242, 246 f.
Puberty, 276 f.
Pubic leaf, 68, 230, 246, 274
Pumice, 124
puri-puri (sorcery), 290
putautaona (term in tabu), 145 f.
pwatukwara (exchange), 192
pwopwosa (shellfish), 219
Pwosipwosimo (Tewaran village), 220

Quarrels, between co-villagers, 84 f. ; and spouses, 6, 119 ; and magic, 166

Rain-maker, 138, 214, 263, 266 ; cleanliness of, 132
Rain-making, 84, 99 f., 131 n., 132, 289, 292
Rains, 131
Rank, non-existent, 128
Rape, 77, 243, 247
Raputat (village), 216
Reduplication, in song and speech, 256
Reflection, as the ghostly self, 180
Reincarnation, 127 n.
Relationship terms, 36–43, 53, 62 ff., 72 f. ; use of, 5, 13, 45 ; changes on death of father, 37 f. ; bwosiana, 37 ; eiana, 37 ; elaba, 73 ; eyena, 63, 66 ; gosiana, 63 ; ina elaba, 72 ; kedana, 37 ; kedeana, 37 f., 41 f., 105 ; labalaba, 73 ; lamusiana, 63 ; lawana, 37 ; manena, 37 ; mono, 37 ; natuna, 37, 42 ; Navel, 64, 73 ; neno, 37 ; nibagu, 14 ; nibana, 37 ff., 41 f. ; nuuna, 37 f., 41 f., 44, 72, 92 ; nuu-yaiebara-na, -yaiyumne, -yaiobara-na, 72 ; sina, 39 ; sinana, 37, 39, 41 f., 72 ; sina-yaeyumne, -yaiabara-na, 72 ; tama, 39 ; tamana, 37 ff., 41 f., 73 ; tasina, 37 f., 40 f., 44, 72, 105 ; tasi-yaiobara-na, 72, 158 ; toni-kasa, 269 ; tubu, tubudi, 39 ; tubuna, 37 ff., 41 f., 73 ; wana, 37, 41 f., 73 ; yae-yumne, yaiabara, yaiebara, 72 ; yaiana, yaiyana, 37 f., 41 f.
Reputations, built on magic, 134
Residence of spouses, alternate, 2, 4 f., 9 f., 58, 60, 64, 75 f. ; exceptions, 20, 76, 86
Resultants from marriage : see "Those-resulting"
Resuscitation, magical, 89, 90, 162, 284 f.
Rhyme, absent in Dobuan poetry, 253
Rhythm, 252 f.
Ridicule, as deterrent of sorcery, 290 ; as punishment, 53, 56, 58, 93
Ringworm, 30, 52, 215, 248
Ritual, of gardens, 94 ff., 106 ff.; value of, 97 ; secrecy important, 101

Rivalry, 176
Rock, legendary, 98 ; magic making of, 219
Rossel Island, 202

sabelulu (flaming fire), 296
sagali (mourning feast), 199, 250, 257
Sago, 48, 156 ; as marriage gift, 190 ; at mourning feast, 196 ; trade in, 207 f.
sagusagu (palm), 219, 223
Saido tree, legend of the, 87 f.
Sailors, Dobuans as, 211, 213, 269
sakwara (tree), 167 ; as disease demon, 144
Samarai (place), 265, 292
Samuela, legendary yam ancestress, 117, 120, 125, 127
Sanaroa (island), 194, 207, 211, 216, 221, 225, 302 ; legendary origin of, 265
sapisapi (shell), 234, 268
Sawaiowas (place), 143
Sawatupa (place), 121, 125, 139, 141, 263, 266
Scaevola fructuscens, 215 n., 229 n., 237
Scansion, of poetry, 252 f.
Scorn, as punishment, 53, 56
Sea, legendary origin of, 95, 98, 266 ; fear of, 201 ; its bitterness, 266
Sea-water, drinking of, 300 ; in garden magic, 117, 119 ; in sorcery, 161, 295
Sea-witch : *see* Gelaboi
Seafaring, 201, 210 ff.
sebuwana (gift), 189
Secrecy, of incantations, 95 f., 100, 128, 174 ; of ritual, 101
Seduction, 66 f., 135, 176, 238, 247, 300
Seed, inheritance of, 69 f., 102, 108, 118, 120 ; importance of in marriage, 74 ; planting, 110 f., 118 ; separate for the sexes, 118
Segata Isl., legendary origin of, 265
Sekaikaiawana (charm), 168
Selewegia (place), 142
Semen, native theory concerning, 238 ; *tabus* for incontinence of, 138, 144
Sensitive plant, 298
Separation, temporary, of spouses, 75
Serenading, 251
seuseula (canoe mat), 224, 296
Sex, native theory of, 235 ff.
Sexes, obscurity of terminology, 41 f.
Sexual intercourse, excessive, 76, 244 ; analogy with fire-making, 296 ; pre-nuptial, 10, 21, 25, 29, 239, 241 f., 248, 276 ; secrecy concerning, 22 ; *tabu* between birth and weaning, 246, 273 ; theories concerning, 134, 238 ff.
Shadow, in magic, 142, 180 f.

Shame, 242, 246 f.
Shark, as disease demon, 144 ; legendary origin of, 266
Shellfish, as disease demon, 144 ; spirit doubles of, 126, 143 ; stinging, 143.
Shields, not used by Dobuans, 275
sibukaka (plant), 224
Sick persons, 136, 176 f. ; removed to own village, 4 ; treatment of, 144, 147
Sigasiga (place), 139, 141
sigata (garden boundary), 110
Silana (place), 226
Silasila (place), 185
silasila lawa, 192
Similagaga Isl., legendary origin of, 265
Sinaketa (Trobriand village), 221
sinasinate (sea-urchin), 220
Sineboganbaura (charm), 168
Sinebomatu, wind-goddess, 186 f.
Singing, at close of mourning, 11
sipwana (part of song), 252, 256 f.
Sisiyana (place), 139, 141
Sister, native terms for, 37 ; use of term, 7, 69
Sister-brother relationship : *see* Brother-sister
sita (mat), 31
siudana (yam gift), 195
siwabu (*tabu* term), 82, 116, 122
Siwabudoi (an Entrance), 122
Siyawawa (village), 216
Skull, disposal of, 13, 40, 180, 187, 277 ; dance with, 12, 250
Sky people, 220, 223
Slang, 244
Sleep, spirits and, 178, 181
Smell, divination by, 154
Snake, emblematic of paralysis, 139, 142, 147
Social organization, 1–21, 48, 61, 66, 74, 90–3, 280
Social success, 135
Society Islands, fire walking in, 115
soki (poisonous fish), 170, 174
Solamanake (place), 139
Solicitary gifts, 218, 224 ff.
Solitude, fear of, 77, 153
Solomon Islands, burial custom in, 115
Solomanaki, Mt., 265, 266
Son, inheritance of, 2, 17 ; excluded from deceased father's village, 2 ; and father, 3, 5, 15, 277 f.
Son-in-law, pre-nuptial duties of, 22, 102
sone charms, 124, 128, 131
Song, 250 ff. ; " copyright " in, 251, 261 ; emblematic of social code, 82
Sorcerers, 167 ff. ; other villagers regarded as, 7, 76, 91 ; work and methods of, 150 ff.

Sorcery, 30, 36, 56, 150 ff., 167 ff.,
171 ; official attitude towards,
288 ff. ; not used mutually by
brothers, 16 ; a criminal offence,
166, 288 ff. ; denial of, 152 ;
fear of, 47, 78, 145, 151, 155 ;
hypnotic, 163, 284 f. ; and *kula*
exchange, 209, 217 f. ; averted by
payment, 175 ; reprisals in, 156 f.,
163 ; suppression of, 290 ;
suspicion of, 9, 23 ; teaching of,
147 f. ; *see also* Magic ; Witchcraft
sosomwakumwakupwa (incontinence
of urine), 144
Space, Dobuan conception of, 131 n.
Spatula, use in magic, 162
Speech, courtesy in, 151
Spells, use in feuds, 147 ; in the
kula, 210 ; mobility of, 124 ; for
sickness and death, 150 ; teaching
of, 80 f., 137, 147 f. ; placed on
trees, 79 ; " trying out," 149 ;
see also Charms ; Incantations
Spider, in garden magic, 126 ; *see also*
Kapali
Spirit, infection by, 180 ; laying of a,
179 ; of the dead, *see* Dead ; of
warriors, 182 ; trap for, 179 f.
Spirit doubles, of animals, 126 :
see also Doubles
Spirit yams, 123
Spitting, 180
Spondylus shell, as marriage gift, 189 ;
trade in, 202 ff.
Stealing, actual and magical, 81, 83,
93, 136, 145 ; charm for, 168 ;
co-operative, 153 ; due to improvidence, 70 ; of incantations,
107 ; sentiment regarding, 107 ;
see also Thief
Step-children, 15, 17, 82
Sterility, objection to, 65, 273 ; herbs
for producing, 129
Stomach, and magic, 148 ; swelling
of, 179 f.
Strangers, debarred from villages, 1 ;
distrust of, 215 ; marriage with,
20 f., 86, 153, 193
Success, criteria of, 176, 238 ; in
kula exchange, 215, 232
Suckling, 273
Sud-est (island), 220 f.
Suggestion, and disease, 171 ; and
magic, *see* Hypnotism
Suicide, in self-pity, 3, 6, 7, 48 ff.,
91 f. ; after *bake*, 79, 245 f.
Sulphur-crested cockatoo, as totem,
32, 34
sulua (fish), 226, 228
sumwana (personal leavings), 154, 167
Sun, legend concerning, 228
Supernatural beings, 98 f., 101, 111,
113, 122 f., 125, 127, 130, 133, 136,
140, 178 f., 223, 262, 271 f., 282
Suspicion, 9, 23, 43, 137, 155, 207, 209

Susu, the system, 2, 5, 71 ; favoured
by law, 18 ; and marital grouping,
7, 15, 17 ff., 43, 61, 69, 72, 90 f.,
119 f., 135, 195 ff., 241, 274, 277 f. ;
responsible for marriage exchanges,
43, 191 ; use of names within, 66 ;
names and legends, 31 f. ; ownership of seed, 108
Swallowing of boy, magical, 24
Sweeping, on marriage, 25, 77
Sword-fish, in legend, 265
Sympathetic magic, 127, 287

Tabu, special Dobuan significance,
254 ; teaching of, 148 ; brother-
sister, 9 f. ; inheritance, 28, 82 ;
disease-spells, 82, 93, 138, 143,
171, 295 ; in feuds, 157 ; on food
and property, 58, 138, 141, 143,
197 f. ; in love affairs, 143 ;
women's, 152
tabuwara (maize), in magic, 127
tai sinabwadi (local magnates), 84
Tanubweala (Tewaran village), 220
tapui (Samoan hieroglyphic), 138
Taro, marriage gifts of, 190
tatapeno (shellfish), 122, 125 f., 130
tauhau, Tauwau, 136 and n., 152,
230
tawatawa (tree), 296
Teeth, blackening of, 276
Tewara, 30, 46, 86, 146, 193 f., 207 ;
adultery in, 61 ; and *kula* ritual,
225 ; legendary origin of, 265 ;
tabus, 138 ; women, 250, 267
Theft : *see* Stealing
Thief, 136, 145 ; dread of spells,
80 ; treatment of, 55 f., 79, 83
" Those - resulting - from - marriage,"
5, 9, 15, 22, 41, 84, 189 ff. ; eviction
of, 7 ; at mourning and funerals,
10 ff. ; absent from weddings, 26 ;
use of personal names, 14, 63, 66 ;
and Owners of the Village, 6, 64,
77, 87
Thunder, magic production of, 230 f.
ti (*Cordyline terminalis*), 114 f., 118,
126
Tobacco, 170
Tobebeso and Tobwaliton (sea-
monsters), 98 ff., 132, 263, 266
Tokedokeket (ogre), 270
tokenobeku (magicians), 181
Tokuku (place), 140, 142
tokumali (indicative of disease), 176 f.,
245
tolu (memory charm), 148
tomot (persons), 109
tonewa (fish), 142
toni-waga (canoe owner), 224 f.
Toothache, demon of, 144
Totem, 187 ; distribution, 32 ff. ;
inter-marriage discouraged, 29, 53 ;
linked, 36, 228
Totemism, 30 ff., 72 ; and garden

magic, 118 ; and *kula* exchange, 209

Trading, effect of, 30 ; native, 207 f. ; *see also* Kula

Trap, for spirits, 179 f.

Treachery, 56, 137

Trees, and metamorphosis, 95 ; magical protection of, 82, 93, 138, 144 f. ; spells for, 79 f. ; spirit doubles of, 126 ; *tabu* on after a death, 197 f. ; as totem, 36

Trespass, 80

Trobriand Islands, 40, 124 ; dancing, 250 ; Dobuans in, 74 ; garden magic, 114 ; incantation, 107 ; village incest, 90 ; in the *kula* ring, 201 f. ; in legend, 212 ; mother-right in, 21 ; witchcraft, 74, 151 ; yam houses, 283

Trobrianders, albinos among, 248 ; compared with Dobuans, 136 ; and the *gelaboi*, 165 ; *gwara tabu* of, 198 ; and legends, 186 ; poisoning method, 170 ; theory of procreation, 239, 241 ; women of, 265

Trocus shell, 132, 202

Tribut (Tewaran village), 220

" Trying out," 134, 145, 149, 170, 233, 238

Tuberculosis, 136

Tubetube (island group), in the *kula* ring, 202 f., 208

Tuesia (place), 146

Tulia (variety of yam), 116

Tuma (islet), 212

tunaseana (sea-charm), 216, 226 f., 231, 271

Turtle, supernatural, 113, 123, 126

tuva (a poison), 174

Udaudana (village), 216

Ulcers, 144

Uloga (place), 146

Ulogu (place), 143

Upas-tree, 172

Urine, incontinence of, 138, 144, 159 f.

uvalaku (*kula* fleet), 210

Uwamo (island), 216, 225

Vada (hypnotic sorcery), 284 ff., 289, 291 n., 294

Vakuta (island), 218, 221 f., 228

Vendetta, 282 ; and divination, 166 ; against adulterer, 61, descendants, 24, wives, 3, 6 ; *see also* Feud

Venus : *see* Kubwana ; Panamoti, Star of

Vigna marina, 121

Village, organization of, 1 ff., 30, 35, 43, 60, 72, 92 ; privacy of, 76

Villagers, distrust among, 9, 23, 43 ; and marriages, 43 ; strangers' opinion of, 76, 91 ; use of term,

2 ; *see also* " Owners of the Village "

Visitors, not allowed within doors, 4, 75, or at a meal, 74

Vocabulary, 258

Volcanic crystals, in magic, 154, 298

Vulva, eating of, 302

wadai (non-conforming widower), 57, 59, 78 f.

Wadana Isl., legendary origin of, 265

Wabuna (locality), 33 ff.

wabuwabu (sharp practice in *kula*), 193, 216 f., 232, 234

Walada pool, 262

Walibua (neighbouring district), 117

Wamea (in the Amphletts), 218

Wanoge (legendary being), 99, 236 f.

War, and marriage, 36

War-songs, 261

Warrior, initiation of, 306

Waruma (place), 267

Wasp, as disease demon, 144

Wata (island), 182, 225

Water, charming of, 216, 295 ; in charms and exorcism, 144, 147 f. ; exchange of, 206 ; *see also* Sea-water

Water-gazing, 154, 156, 165

Wattle tree, in magic, 143

watuatuke (fish), 265

wawari (hypnotic sorcery), 285

Weaning, 246, 273

Weeding, 105, 120

wekani (love invocation), 236

Wenio, Weniogwegwe (legendary dog), 99, 226 f., 270 f.

werebana (witches), 150, 153

Whites, 30, 164 ; influence of, 30, 164 ; native evaluation, 109, 136 ; *see also* Administration ; Government ; Missions

White Pigeon, totemic ancestor, 31

Widow, 65 ; mourning of, 13, 57, 78, 194 ; work of, 106, 195

Widower, and marital exchanges, 192 ; mourning of, 11 ff., 57, 78, 177, 194, 256 ; song of the, 11, 91, 255 ; work of, 106 ; *see also* Maiwortu

Wife, garden work of, 105 ; and jealousy, 6, 7, 77, 91, 104, 134, 247 f. ; a form of property, 133 ; terms for, 37 ; suspected for witch, 92, 153 ; *see also* Divorce ; Marriage

Wife-beating, 3

Winds, invocations to, 211 ; and *kula* ritual, 225 ; magic for, 97, 102, 124, 213, 295 ; personality of, 212 ; public legends of, 263 ; spirits of the, 263

Witchcraft, 30, 36, 45, 74, 99, 150 f., 178, 181 ; criminal officially, 288, but not to natives, 78 ; denial of, 152 ; examples of, 24, 44 ; and heat, 295 f.; legal background, 157; official attitude towards, 288 ff.; protection against, 77; its universality, 81

Witches, other villagers regarded as, 7; work and methods of, 150 f.; flying, 150, 152, 261, 295, 297

Women, responsible for death, 151; and inheritance, 2; respect for in public, 54, 64; and spells, 152; strike of, 78; supernatural powers, 40; and white men, 74; and witchcraft, 150 f.

Woodlark Island : see Murua

Words, power of, 130

Wreckers, in legend, 268

Yabowaine (supernatural being), 111, 113, 115, 118, 125 f., 282

yadiyadi (condemned trees), 197

yaiyai (heat), 296

Yams, eaten by the dead, 181; eyes, 117, 130, 282; first fruits, 123; grandmothers, 222; harvesting, 105 f., 122; incantations for, 97, 106 f., 109, 123 ff., 127 f.; in kula ritual, 225; as marriage gift,

189, 192; importance of in marriage, 74; mobility of, 108, 118, 124, 128, 282; in mourning exchange, 195; legendary origin, 95, 111, 117, 282; magic enticement, 83, 101, 134, 283; ownership of, 69, 108; personality, 101, 107 f., 120, 122, 127, 130, 133, 135, 222; sea-legend concerning, 119 f.; as sexton's fee, 194; slicing of, 116, 127, 130; spirits, 123; storage, 118, 122, 283; training of, 121; womb of, 123

yamsu (variety of yam), 128

Yarata (N.W. wind), 212, 263

yatala (divination term), 155, 156

Yauboda (charm), 168

Yauyana (straits), 268

Yawaigili (atoll), 212

Yaws, charm for, 80, 138, 143; exorcism for, 147

yodudu (a shore-bird), 147

Youths, duties and position when betrothed, 25

Yowana (islet), 212

Yuyuwe (tail of Orion), 127

Yuyuna (tail of Orion), 223